Stillbirth and the Law

Stillbirth and the Law

JILL WIEBER LENS

UNIVERSITY OF CALIFORNIA PRESS

University of California Press
Oakland, California

© 2025 by Jill Wieber Lens

Library of Congress Cataloging-in-Publication Data

Names: Lens, Jill Wieber, author.
Title: Stillbirth and the law / Jill Wieber Lens.
Description: Oakland : University of California
    Press, 2025. | Includes bibliographical references
    and index.
Identifiers: LCCN 2024039549 | ISBN 9780520393578
    (hardback) | ISBN 9780520393585 (paperback) |
    ISBN 9780520393592 (ebook)
Subjects: LCSH: Unborn children (Law)—United
    States. | Stillbirth—Law and legislation—United
    States. | Stillbirth—Proof and certification—
    United States. | Fetus—Legal status, laws,
    etc.—United States. | Fetal death—United States. |
    Abortion—Law and legislation—United States. |
    Parent and child (Law)—United States. |
    Pregnancy—Complications—Prevention.
Classification: LCC KF481 .L46 2025 | DDC
    344.7303/2198392—dc23/eng/20240828
LC record available at https://lccn.loc
    .gov/2024039549

34 33 32 31 30 29 28 27 26 25
10 9 8 7 6 5 4 3 2 1

For Caleb

CONTENTS

ACKNOWLEDGMENTS

I owe thanks and gratitude to so many people who have helped me along the way with this project. First, I want to thank my husband for his constant support. He is my rock and I am grateful for his patience, understanding, and encouragement. I also want to thank my children Hannah, Gretchen, Caleb, and Brandon. I love you all more than you could ever know.

Thank you also to my therapist, Rebecca Fox. You reassured me that it was mentally healthy to focus my legal research on stillbirth. I am forever grateful.

Thank you to the many in the legal academy who have encouraged and supported me in my research. This includes Greer Donley, David S. Cohen, Rachel Rebouché, Maya Manian, Yvette Lindgren, Dov Fox, Jamie Abrams, Nadia Sawicki, Meghan Boone, Mary Ziegler, Aziza Ahmed, Naomi Cahn, Jordan Woods, Alex Nunn, and Todd Pettys. Thank you also to Mary Ziegler, Bridget Crawford, and Chris Odinet for teaching me about the process of writing a book. Thank you to Bridget Crawford, Dr. Karen Gibbins, Mike Green, Lynn Paltrow, Dana Sussman, and Adam Thimmesch for reading draft chapters. And thank you to Maura Roessner for believing in this combination personal and academic project.

Thank you also to those in the stillbirth community. I am grateful for this community and to those parents who have shared their children with me and allowed me to share their stories in my work.

Thank you to the administrations at the University of Arkansas School of Law and the University of Iowa College of Law for the support during the writing process. And thank you to Mollie Angel for her invaluable research and editing assistance.

Introduction

Caleb

My husband and I were both surprised when I got pregnant this third time. We already had two daughters. It took eleven months and fertility drugs to get pregnant with my second daughter. We didn't expect it to work so easily with this third child. But it did. I warned my husband that I had been burping a lot, a fun early pregnancy sign for me. And on a Sunday morning, I took a pregnancy test and saw a faint positive. Blood tests on Halloween 2016 shortly after confirmed my pregnancy.

I was tired a lot in early pregnancy, and my gag reflex was on fire. We were delighted to learn that the baby was a boy. So delighted. We hadn't found out the sex in either of my earlier pregnancies. I wanted to this time; my husband much less so. The nurse pretty much gave it away when she said, "I think you'll want to know!" We were so excited, although my oldest daughter bawled when we told her. I have a picture of the tantrum.

Everything was fine until I failed my gestational diabetes test. I was shocked. I'm in shape and had no issues with my girls. But I had gestational diabetes, which now meant a low-carb diet. I controlled it fine, but I did complain a lot because I really like carbs.

I had gestational diabetes and I always measured big. At each doctor's appointment, I would be measuring a few centimeters more than the weeks I was at. My doctor said it was no big deal, that I just had a little more amniotic fluid. But she did want to do an ultrasound at 36 weeks to check the baby's size. That whole 36th week, I felt extra anxious. I was randomly convinced that the baby was breech and I would need a C-section. I remember emailing a friend and saying, "you'd think I'd be more chill the third time around." But he wasn't breech. And even though my belly measured at 39 cm, he was measuring at 6 pounds on the ultrasound. I was relieved and the doctor sent us home. I started strongly planting the idea of inducing at 39 weeks in my husband's head. I felt very large.

Two days later, on Father's Day 2017, I put Caleb's car seat in the car. That is still hard to think about.

That night, I did Caleb's kick count and felt him move around 9:00 p.m. I remember thinking it was slightly different. He still easily got to the 10 kicks, but it was different somehow. I chalked it up to the fact that I was sitting in a chair instead of laying down like usual. (And this memory may very much be colored by what I know happened later that night.)

I woke up at 11:00 feeling uncomfortable. Not in pain, just uncomfortable. I walked around a bit and tried to go the bathroom. I went back to bed.

I woke up again about an hour later, still uncomfortable. We called the on-call doctor. She said I was likely having muscle pain and to take a bath. I told her that I hadn't felt Caleb moving. She wasn't alarmed and just told me to monitor him. I asked for how long, and she said a few hours. I took a bath, and it did help. I don't really remember specifics, but I think I had moments of lightheadedness. Eventually we just decided to go to the hospital because my brother was visiting, so we had childcare. I wasn't alarmed really. I knew something was off, but I wasn't alarmed. I had a bladder infection while pregnant with my second daughter and that hurt way more than this. Still, on the way to the hospital, I blasted the air conditioning on myself, which is very odd for me because I'm always cold.

We got to the hospital, and I felt relatively fine while checking in, but I was annoyed that it was taking as long as it did. We got to the triage room, and they put the fetal heart and contractions monitors on me. I remember various nurses unsuccessfully trying to find his heartbeat. I remember one nurse asking me if my belly was always so hard. The answer was no, but it was very hard at that moment. Looking back, it felt like when Caleb liked to push his butt up into my ribs, which I usually massaged to get him down. But it was constant now.

No one really said out loud the obvious—that Caleb had died. They still did the normal triage questions with me. A nurse asked if I was going to breastfeed or bottle feed. The nurses left us alone at one point and I remember just screaming. They all rushed back in, trying to help.

We waited for an ultrasound. I don't remember specifics, but it wasn't quick. The tech did the ultrasound and, of course, still didn't confirm Caleb's death. I remember that they put a monitor back on me after the ultrasound and I asked, "Is everything okay now?" They told me it was a monitor for my contractions. They didn't say so, but there was no need for a monitor for his heartbeat.

I texted my regular doctor around 4:00 a.m. to tell her that they couldn't find Caleb's heartbeat. She arrived around 5:00 a.m., the same time that the on-call doctor finally arrived and said out loud that Caleb had died. The on-call doctor told me that I had had a placental abruption, that my placenta had detached from my uterus. They told me that my baby had died, and that I needed to deliver him immediately because I was bleeding internally. My water broke, the only time that happened naturally for me. I assumed it was blood, but it was my water.

I looked at my doctor and asked how I was supposed to do this—how was I supposed to give birth to my dead baby. She offered to do a C-section, but I didn't want surgery on top of everything else. My memory is a little blurry on the next steps. I know that the anesthesiologist said I couldn't have an epidural because of my physical state, which also meant natural childbirth for the first time. Eventually, my doctor and I agreed that she would give me something to knock me out.

I gave birth to Caleb. Some of the contractions would wake me up. I remember being so confused as to what hurt. I remember reaching down, trying to figure out why my vagina hurt so much. I think I remember feeling his head, but I might be making that up. Caleb Marcus Lens was born at 6:09 am. He was 19 inches long and just shy of 6 pounds (5 pounds, 15.8 ounces). My husband Josh witnessed all of it. He said one of the nurses cried the whole time.

I woke up later to see my husband holding our baby. My first words were "is that him?"

Then, we spent time with Caleb. It's so strange that his birthday was, of course, the saddest day of my life, but it was also one of my happiest days. It was the only day I got to hold Caleb in my arms. I held him as much as I could. I was still very groggy from whatever drugs I was on, so Caleb and I napped together. Numerous times I had to tell myself to wake up and stay awake because this was the only time with him that I was going to get.

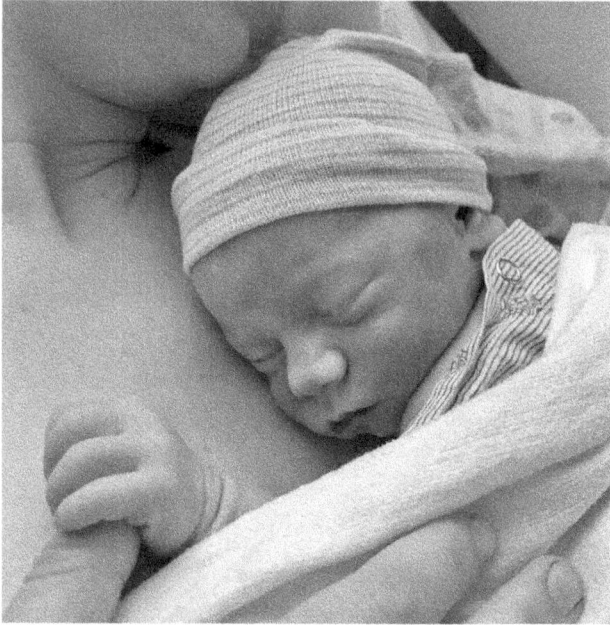

Figure 1. Author's stillborn son, Caleb Marcus Lens.

Our medical care was amazing. They encouraged us to spend time with and hold Caleb. They did not rush us in any way. They took pictures for us. They reassured me over and over that his death wasn't my fault. I eventually asked if I could hold him skin to skin, and I got to. This was such a maternal thing for me, to hold him skin to skin like I did his sisters. I held him on my chest and held his sweet little fingers. He looked just like a sleeping newborn (see figure 1). He looked like he could wake up at any minute. But I knew that his body wasn't as warm as it should have been. The nurses also warned us that his skin might start falling off. That was hard to hear.

Eventually, it was time to say goodbye. Again, no one rushed us. They insisted we could have more time. I said that more time wouldn't make it any easier to say goodbye.

The next day, we went home without our baby. I don't think it's at all possible to explain what that's like. It's impossible to understand unless you've gone through it. Our hospital gives you a big water bottle when you have a baby to encourage water drinking for breastfeeding. I still have the bottles from the girls. I didn't take Caleb's home; I didn't want the water bottle if I couldn't have him. We went home to our two daughters to grapple with the fact that our son and their baby brother had died only two weeks before I had planned to have labor induced.

All in all, I think we had the best possible experience of stillbirth. The medical staff, especially the labor and delivery nurses with us before and after Caleb was born, were wonderful. Our daughters' day-care teachers were amazing. One was also a child life specialist who came over, explained cremation to the girls, and made memory boxes with them. The leader of a local support group also had a kid in my youngest daughter's day-care class; she came over to our house numerous times to help. We had a beautiful funeral. My dearest friends flew in for it. I think the entirety of the Baylor University Law School, where I worked, and the Baylor University Athletics Department, where my husband worked, attended. I didn't want the funeral to end. We got a random letter from Baylor Libraries a few weeks later that they were dedicating a children's book to Caleb. Someone sent me in the mail a necklace charm that said "hope." People brought us food for over a month. We attended a support group. We went to therapy. No one rushed us back to work; I'm pretty sure that my employer would have still let me have my full maternity leave. I often couldn't figure out if I was over-whelmed with emotion about Caleb's death or about the kindness of people.

I also want to accentuate how our immediate focus after Caleb's death were our daughters. Hannah was five and Gretchen was two. Josh told them when I was still in the hospital. We were and continue to be very open and honest with them. There was no way to hide our grief, nor do I believe it would have been healthy to do so. I'm not sure Gretchen understood much of it. That first night I was home, when I was rocking Gretchen before bed, she said, "baby brother" and pointed to my belly. It was heartbreaking and dif-ficult to keep telling her that Caleb died. Josh slept on Gretchen's floor for at least two weeks. I'd wake up, realize I was alone, and go climb in bed with Hannah. The fact that those sweet girls needed to eat was really the only rea-son I got out of bed. I'll forever be grateful to them. And I'll also forever be angry that they learned about death so early in their lives, and that they were deprived of their little brother Caleb.

I went back to work in August. A large part of my job as a law professor is to research and write. Before Caleb's death, my research mostly focused on damages in lawsuits. Once I went back to work after Caleb's death, that research just seemed so trivial. I also couldn't stop googling about stillbirth and being horrified with what I learned.

In the United States, pregnancy losses before 20 weeks are called miscarriages and after 20 weeks are called stillbirths. Miscarriages are relatively commonly, affecting 20-25% of pregnancies. Stillbirths are much rarer. Currently in the United States, about one in 175 births is a stillbirth.[1] More specifically, in 2021, out of 1,000 births (live and stillborn), 5.73 babies were stillborn. In 2020, the rate was 5.74 out of 1000 births, and in 2019, the rate was 6.02.[2]

The risk and rate are very small, but they still translate to a significant number of babies born stillborn every year in the United States. In 2021, 21,105 stillbirths were reported, following about 21,500 in 2019, and 22,500 in 2018.[3]

Put more concretely, about 60 to 65 babies are stillborn each day in the United States. That's about three kindergarten classes. Stillbirth occurs ten times as often as infant deaths due to Sudden Infant Death Syndrome.[4] The number of stillbirths exceeds the number of all infant deaths combined.[5]

The stillbirth rate in the United States is bad. It is higher "than in many other high-income countries."[6] More specifically, in 2015, the US stillbirth rate (after 28 weeks to enable international comparison) was 23rd out of 49 high-income countries.[7]

Our general stillbirth rate is bad, but the rate is much worse for marginalized persons. For as long as we've gathered data on stillbirths, Black women have always had a higher rate than white women. Today that disparity is at least double[8]—thus about 1 in 85 births by Black woman is a stillborn baby. Studies also show that poor women similarly face double the risk of stillbirth compared to women with economic means.[9]

These disparities are not going to go away on their own. In 2019, the stillbirth rate for Black women was 2.08 times greater than for white women. It went up to 2.18 times greater in 2020, a 5% increase.[10] In 2021, the stillbirth rate for Black women was 9.89 out of 1000 births. It was 4.85 out of 1000 for white women.[11]

It doesn't have to be like this. Certainly, some stillbirths are unpreventable. Caleb's probably was unpreventable as we learned later it was likely due to some sort of abnormality. But only about 10% of stillbirths are due to unpreventable fetal abnormalities[12]—although the number of stillbirths due to fetal abnormalities will likely increase in the United States now that abortion is illegal in many states (more on that later).

Other stillbirths are preventable. I'm not implying that 90% of stillbirths are preventable. That's not true. But some stillbirths *are* preventable. And we must reframe our approach; start from the premise of possible preventability instead of assuming unpreventability.

That possibility of preventability is evidenced by the fact that, as discussed, other high-income countries have much better stillbirth rates than the United States. Not only are their rates already lower, but some of those same countries have adopted initiatives to specifically lower their stillbirth rates.[13] And the initiatives have worked. The Netherlands started a program in 2001 that led to a 55% decrease in the stillbirth rate over the next fourteen years. Scotland implemented a program that decreased its rate by 22% in just four years. England decreased its stillbirth rate by almost 20% in a decade.[14] Admittedly, some of those decreases have slowed, likely due to the Covid-19 pandemic. But the decreases still happened, demonstrating that preventability of some stillbirths is more than possible.

We are not seeing any similar decreases. The US stillbirth rate declined dramatically over the twentieth century, but it's been relatively stagnant for most of this twenty-first century. In a 2016 study published in *The Lancet* medical journal, of the listed 49 high-income countries, the US annual percentage for stillbirth-rate reduction from 2000 to 2015 was lower than all but one other country.[15] A 2020 report by UNICEF listed stillbirth and stillbirth rate data from 2000 to 2019 for 195 countries. The annual rate of reduction in the United States for that time frame ranked 185th out of 195.[16]

Studies specific to the United States show that the country could have similar success if it attempted to reduce its stillbirth rate. A study published in 2018 suggested that at least 25% of stillbirths in the United States are preventable.[17] The study also concluded that over 46% of stillbirths at term (after 37 weeks) were preventable. And the authors of the study were clear that they considered their estimates conservative.

As I learned more about stillbirth generally, I started wondering how laws affect stillbirth in the United States and elsewhere—connecting my professional and personal lives. I was afraid that this wasn't necessarily healthy. It seemed obsessive. I asked my therapist. She chuckled a bit and said that it definitely seemed healthy for someone like me. I'm so grateful to her.

Inspired by Caleb and really as the best way I can figure out how to still parent him, I now devote my research to how laws affect stillbirth. I hope Caleb is proud of me. I also hope he knows how proud I am to be his mama.

＊　＊　＊　＊

This book is loosely organized in three parts: how laws affect (1) stillbirth prevention; (2) the lived experience of stillbirth; and (3) conceptions of stillbirth.

The first four chapters address how laws affect stillbirth prevention. The chapters explore some legal reasons why our rate is so bad and is remaining that way. Data, data collection, and incentives created by medical malpractice law all affect stillbirth prevention efforts. Chapter 1 focuses on data we have about stillbirths and their causes. It's not a pretty picture. The best tool we have for determining causes is a fetal autopsy. But only about 20% of stillborn babies are autopsied in the United States. The chapter explores the reasons why we don't have more fetal autopsies and compares fetal autopsies after stillbirth to state routinization of autopsies after suspected deaths due to Sudden Infant Death Syndrome. Laws routinizing and paying for autopsies help reduce SIDS death rates and could do the same for stillbirths.

But even if we have better data, we also need to have a good system of collecting that data to enable epidemiological studies, medical studies, and to increase public awareness. Chapter 2 describes the system we currently have, which is the issuance of fetal death certificates (FDCs). The system is decentralized as the federal government has no authority to issue vital statistics. State control means nonuniformity even concerning when FDCs must be issued—not all states use the 20-week definition of stillbirth for issuance. FDCs also have numerous data quality issues, including incomplete data (the "fetal weight" blank is just blank) and accuracy issues (the cause of death is listed as "stillbirth"). Everyone who knows anything about stillbirth knows that FDCs are hindering our knowledge of stillbirth. We need something more; we need surveillance registries.

Chapters 3 and 4 then turn to the incentives doctors have to prevent stillbirth. I would hope there's a huge moral incentive to preventing stillbirth, but there isn't much of a legal one. Chapter 3 describes how other countries, mainly the UK and Australia, have incorporated and emphasized stillbirth prevention measures within medical standards of care. The chapter compares those prevention measures to US medical guidelines. Many would likely think that a US doctor's failure to perform any prevention measures would be malpractice. It's not. The United States hasn't adopted these prevention measures and tort law is extremely deferential to the medically set (by US doctors) standard of care. As long as doctors act consistent with that accepted practice (and don't take these extra measures to prevent stillbirth), they won't be liable. That's an incentive to *not* do anything extra to prevent stillbirth. US tort law appears unequipped to force changes to standards of care, but the chapter does describe possible changes to tort law that could aid prevention efforts.

Chapter 4 further explains how the damages for medical malpractice causing stillbirth aren't that significant. How tort law values damages for tortiously caused stillbirth is unnecessarily confusing. Sometimes the damages are just for an emotional injury, sometimes for injury to a body part, and sometimes for the lost parent-child relationship. None of those will add up to a huge amount of damages. This isn't just a stillbirth thing; really, the damages for the wrongful death of a living child will almost always be substantially less than the damages for the wrongful death of an adult. States also often limit the amount of "noneconomic" damages that a plaintiff can recover, which will affect damage valuations of stillbirth. Put simply, it's much cheaper, tort damage-wise, to kill an unborn baby than to injure him—also disincentivizing stillbirth prevention.

The next part of the book changes from a focus on prevention to a focus on how laws do and can affect the lived experience of stillbirth. Chapter 5 focuses on people's lack of awareness about the possibility of stillbirth until it happens to them. While grappling with your child's death, you also must grapple with the confusion that stillbirth still happens in the twenty-first century in one of the richest nations in the world. This chapter explores the reasons why doctors don't talk about stillbirth with pregnant patients. Those reasons—its rarity, the possibility of it overwhelming the overly emotional pregnant woman, and its supposed unpreventability—don't justify the nondisclosure. Informed consent law exists to ensure that patients are educated; it is also an ethical principle requiring doctors to educate patients about material risks of procedures and conditions. Doctors should be talking about the risk of stillbirth with pregnant patients before it happens. It is easily material. This disclosure would also reduce shock and stigma when stillbirth does occur, and improve doctor-patient relationship communication, reducing the urge to blame.

Chapter 6 is aspirational. It uses the reproductive justice framework to detail certain basic human rights that should exist for pregnant people and stillbirth parents. The reproductive justice framework recognizes that the right to have a child is equally important to the right to not have a child (*i.e.*, abortion). Reproductive justice rights are positive rights, meaning the government is obligated to provide them for its citizens. I apply the framework to stillbirth and detail rights to (1) prenatal care including stillbirth prevention; (2) perinatal hospice and palliative care in cases of fatal fetal abnormalities; (3) control regarding the method of giving birth (or not) to your stillborn baby; (4) mental and emotional health care after your child's stillbirth; and (5) tailored medical care in any subsequent pregnancy.

The last three chapters focus on how laws affect societal understandings of stillbirth. Chapter 7 looks at two legal contexts that depend on live birth—wrongful death claims and tax benefits. Historically and still in some states today, parents lack a wrongful death claim for their tortiously killed stillborn child, even though they would have a claim if their child was killed tortiously just after birth. Similarly, parents are not entitled to any tax benefits if their child dies just before birth but are entitled to federal tax credit if their child dies right after birth. This live birth distinction depicts stillbirth as materially different from newborn death. But, at least in these contexts, it's not. This chapter explores why the live birth distinction makes little sense in these two contexts and suggests alternative dividing lines.

Chapter 8 describes how the abortion debate and abortion laws affect understandings of stillbirth. It describes how the abortion debate essentially erases pregnancy loss by implying that all pregnancies end in either abortion or live childbirth, and how "choice" rhetoric contributes to blame after still-birth. The chapter also describes the antiabortion movement's weaponization of stillbirth and pregnancy loss generally and its hypocrisy in caring so much about a fertilized egg, yet little about a term stillborn baby. The abortion-rights movement has avoided the topic of pregnancy loss as much as possible, but it doesn't have to. Fetal value within pregnancy loss is subjective, an idea fundamentally inconsistent with the antiabortion idea that every fertilized egg is a person. Much of the supposed tension between abortion rights and pregnancy loss has been manufactured by the antiabortion movement. And the realities of the tenuousness of fetal life and the many antiabortion fetal life hypocrisies should be part of abortion-rights narratives going forward.

Chapter 9 describes how stillbirth has sometimes also become a crime. It describes how (marginalized) women have already been arrested and prosecuted for supposedly causing their child's stillbirth, and how this will only get worse now that abortion is illegal in many states. It comments on the surprising confidence in the conclusion that drug use causes stillbirth and explains the many cultural and legal forces contributing to that confidence. It also comments on ideas of the wrong and right ways to lose a pregnancy, questioning whether there is any right way. It describes how criminalization is unlikely to prevent stillbirth, but very likely to compound the traumas of stillbirth for stillbirth parents. Last, it suggests campaigns to undermine the reasons many are quick to conclude drug use causes stillbirth, including increasing awareness and research regarding its causes.

The last chapter concludes with a bit of genuine optimism. Laws can be changed. It just takes initiative, education, and advocacy. Stillbirth parents have been pushing for change for years, and they've been successful. I'm optimistic that now is the time when we can achieve even broader successes.

ONE

Missing Out on Cause-of-Death Data

No medical professional brought up the possibility of autopsy for Caleb. I vaguely remember bringing it up the next morning. The discussion, though, was about how it was unnecessary because the problem was that my placenta detached, not Caleb. Honestly, I was relieved to not have to make that decision. The thought of Caleb getting cut up was a little too much for me at that moment. They did do a placental pathology, which revealed no abnormalities.

A few years later, I met Dr. Harvey J. Kliman, MD, PhD, a research scientist in Obstetrics, Gynecology, and Reproductive Sciences and the director of the Reproductive and Placental Research Unit at Yale's School of Medicine. I asked him to look over my records, including the slides of my placentas from both Caleb and my subsequent pregnancy (emergency C-section due to abruption during labor). After three years identifying as an abruption mom, Dr. Kliman told me I wasn't one. I had never had an abruption, neither with Caleb nor Brandon. Dr. Kliman found something on Caleb's placenta called "trophoblast inclusions," leading him to conclude that Caleb died due to an unknown genetic abnormality.

My initial reaction was anger to not learn this until three years later. I also felt immediate relief that Caleb's death wasn't due to my body failing. It felt very strange to go from an explanation to basically a lack of one. But I'm privileged to even have found out this much.

*　*　*　*

We need data. We can't try to prevent something unless we know why it happens. Data is necessary for medical studies, epidemiological studies, and for public education and awareness. Data is also needed on an individual level. Parents should be able to find out why their children were stillborn, and data could potentially prevent birthing parents from blaming themselves. Data is also needed to rebut the powerful inevitability myth surrounding stillbirth; the lack of data and investigation simply fuels the myth, which then discourages investigation and the pursuit of data.

Fetal autopsies can greatly improve our available data. We know this. So why aren't we doing more fetal autopsies? Doctors either intentionally or unintentionally discourage stillbirth parents from getting one. And even if stillbirth parents want one, they're expensive. The hospital may pay for it, or not. Private insurance may cover it, or not. Medicaid does not cover the cost of fetal autopsy. Stillbirth is surprisingly expensive and an autopsy that may not reveal the cause(s) of death doesn't seem worth the cost.

Still, we know that fetal autopsies would greatly improve our available data, especially of cause(s) of death. Not too long ago, states realized that infant deaths due to Sudden Infant Death Syndrome (SIDS) were a public health crisis. To reduce their rates, they started paying for autopsies. Autopsies meant more data, and state-paid autopsies expressed the importance of SIDS as a public health crisis.

There's no need to reinvent the wheel. We can do the same thing with fetal autopsies after stillbirth that we did with autopsies after SIDS deaths. Importantly, however, especially in post-*Roe* America, we must also legislatively protect any data gathered in fetal autopsies after stillbirth. The purpose of data is to prevent, not to blame.

DETERMINING THE CAUSE OF DEATH

I will discuss fetal death certificates much more extensively in the next chapter, but a brief introduction is needed here. The FDC is the legal document issued after stillbirth. State laws mandate that a FDC be filed within days of the baby's stillbirth. The standard FDC is produced by the National Center for Health Statistics (NCHS), which is within the Centers for Disease Control (CDC).

The standard FDC has a section asking about the cause(s) of death.[1] Question 18 (see figure 2) asks "Cause/Conditions Contributing to Fetal Death." Question 18a then more specifically asks for the "Initiating Cause/

18. CAUSE/CONDITIONS CONTRIBUTING TO FETAL DEATH

CAUSE OF FETAL DEATH

18a. INITIATING CAUSE/CONDITION

(AMONG THE CHOICES BELOW, PLEASE SELECT THE ONE WHICH MOST LIKELY BEGAN THE SEQUENCE OF EVENTS RESULTING IN THE DEATH OF THE FETUS)

Maternal Conditions/Diseases (Specify) _____

Complications of Placenta, Cord, or Membranes

- ☐ Rupture of membranes prior to onset of labor
- ☐ Abruptio placenta
- ☐ Placental insufficiency
- ☐ Prolapsed cord
- ☐ Chorioamnionitis
- ☐ Other Specify)

Other Obstetrical or Pregnancy Complications (Specify) _____

Fetal Anomaly (Specify) _____

Fetal Injury (Specify) _____

Fetal Infection (Specify) _____

Other Fetal Conditions/Disorders (Specify) _____

☐ Unknown

18b. OTHER SIGNIFICANT CAUSES OR CONDITIONS

(SELECT OR SPECIFY ALL OTHER CONDITIONS CONTRIBUTING TO DEATH IN ITEM 18b)

Maternal Conditions/Diseases (Specify) _____

Complications of Placenta, Cord, or Membranes

- ☐ Rupture of membranes prior to onset of labor
- ☐ Abruptio placenta
- ☐ Placental insufficiency
- ☐ Prolapsed cord
- ☐ Chorioamnionitis
- ☐ Other Specify)

Other Obstetrical or Pregnancy Complications (Specify) _____

Fetal Anomaly (Specify) _____

Fetal Injury (Specify) _____

Fetal Infection (Specify) _____

Other Fetal Conditions/Disorders (Specify) _____

☐ Unknown

Mother's Medical Record No. _____

Mother's Name _____

Figure 2. Question 18 of CDC–created standard fetal death certificate, last revised in 2003.

Condition" and Question 18b asks for "Other Significant Causes or Conditions." Both questions then have listed possible causes/conditions. Question 18a further instructs to "select the *one*" cause/condition that "most likely began the sequence of events resulting in the death of the fetus."

State laws mandate that the medical professional attending the stillbirth complete this cause of death information. The medical professional attending the stillbirth is likely an obstetrician whose daily job is to deliver living babies.

To assist that obstetrician in completing the FDC, the NCHS also produces a "Facility Worksheet for the Report of Fetal Death."[2] It pretty much repeats the information on the FDC and adds information on where to obtain the required information (e.g., pregnant woman's medical records). The Worksheet also explains that the purpose of the cause of death questions are to "get a description of those conditions that, in your opinion, contributed to the fetal death."[3] And it directs the clinician to "report any condition judged to be a cause of death even if it has been reported elsewhere on the worksheet."[4] (The second page of the FDC has a place to list whether risk factors like diabetes, hypertension, or use of artificial reproductive technology were present in the pregnancy, and whether infections like syphilis were present).

The NCHS also produces a "Guide to Completing the Facility Worksheets of Live Birth and Report of Fetal Death" to assist those completing the FDC.[5] This one guide for both live birth certificates and FDCs makes sense because many of the same questions are on both. The inclusion of both in one guide also helps to accentuate that they are equally important. The Guide has seemingly extensive information, including needed definitions, more specific instructions, and sources of the information needed to be completed. As an example, the Guide clarifies for Question 24 that the medical attendant at birth is the medical professional physically present regardless of title.[6] It also clarifies that for the question on Neonatal Intensive Care Unit admission, defining that such units are those that provide continuous mechanical ventilation as opposed to special care nurseries.[7]

But there's nothing in this Guide about how to answer the FDC cause-of-death in question 18. No instructions, no definitions. There's no mention of question 18 at all. The only question that is on the FDC but not on the live birth certificate mentioned in the Guide is the method of disposition (FDC question 13), asking about burial, cremation, and the like.

The NCHS also has video training for completing FDCs and the cause of death question. In a training entitled "Applying Best Certificates for Reporting Medical and Health Information on Birth Certificates," the NCHS explains that clinicians should "provide [their] best medical opinion" on the cause of fetal death.[8]

None of this—the FDC itself, the Facility Worksheet, the Guide, and the video training—is much help for an obstetrician to determine the cause of fetal death. Really, the extent of the instructions is to select the one more likely cause, select other significant causes, and to provide the best medical opinion. Again, this is an obstetrician whose usual job is delivering babies. Obstetricians certainly see miscarriages often, but they are not legally required to determine the cause(s) of the miscarriage. Obstetricians are not likely to see stillbirths often given their rarity. My doctor had been practicing for ten years and I was the first term (after 37 weeks) stillbirth she ever saw. I suspect the average obstetrician doesn't even know where to start reporting on the cause(s) of death. And these NCHS materials are not very helpful.

Most often, a medical professional completes the cause of death information on the FDC. But not always. State laws usually mandate that a coroner or medical examiner complete and file the FDC if the stillborn baby is born outside of a hospital or if an inquiry is legally required.[9] Both coroners and medical examiners investigate certain deaths. Generally speaking, a medical examiner is someone with medical training, whereas a coroner is an elected position. States have different systems, some with state centralized medical examiner offices and others with county-based coroner systems.[10] State laws can require coroner/medical examiner inquiries or investigations if the death is suspected due to certain crimes or other circumstances. For instance, Rhode Island law mandates medical examiner involvement if there's a reasonable belief that the death was due to "homicide, suicide, or casualty," "criminal abortion," or "an accident involving lack of due care on the part of a person other than the deceased.[11] Missouri law, as another example, mandates that the coroner investigate if there's a reasonable belief that the death was due to "violence by homicide, suicide, or accident," "criminal abortions, including those self-induced," or the death occurred "in any unusual or suspicious manner."[12]

Please set aside, for the moment, the idea of stillbirth being a crime and the possible arrest and prosecution of the birthing person. That is covered in chapter 9. The discussion here will focus on the resources provided to medical examiners or coroners in determining cause(s) of fetal death.

Specifically, the NCHS produces the "Medical Examiners' and Coroners' Handbook on Death Registration and Fetal Death Reporting."[13] And it actually has some helpful instructions for completing the cause of fetal death. It repeats the instruction about best medical opinion, but explains that conditions "can be listed as 'probable' if not definitively diagnosed."[14] The Handbook also instructs that any "conditions in the fetus or mother, or of the placenta, cord, or membranes should be reported if they are believed to have adversely affected the fetus."[15]

The Medical Examiners' and Coroners' Handbook also instructs that "if an organ system failure is listed as a cause of death, always report its etiology. Always report the fatal injury (e.g., stab wound of mother's abdomen), the trauma, and impairment of function."[16] The Handbook is also clear that if any testing is pending when the FDC is completed, like a fetal autopsy or microscopic exams, the medical examiner or coroner should file a supplemental report as soon as that information is available.[17]

When the examiner is uncertain, the Handbook advises as follows:

> In this case, the certifier should think through the causes about which he/she is confident and what possible etiologies could have resulted in these conditions. The certifier should select the causes that are suspected to have been involved and use words such as "probable" or "presumed" to indicate that the description provided is not completely certain. Causes of death on the fetal death report should not include terms such as "prematurity" without explaining the etiology because they have little value for public health or medical research.[18]

Ultimately, this Handbook instructs that "reporting a cause of fetal death as unknown should be a last resort."[19]

Notably, the Handbook also explains the importance of the information regarding the cause(s) of death. In addition to the mention of explaining etiology because of the value for public health and medical research, the Handbook explains that the data needs to be as specific and precise as possible because "cause of death is used for medical and epidemiological research on disease etiology and to evaluate the effectiveness of diagnostic and therapeutic techniques.[20] Specificity and particularity is also important because this data "is a measure of health status at local, State, national, and international levels."[21]

There's a *lot* of information in the Medical Examiners and Coroners' Handbook on how to complete the cause of fetal death information on the FDC. But the average obstetrician wouldn't ever have any reason to consult this handbook. And the Facility Worksheet and Guide, the documents that the obstetrician would possibly consult, say *nothing* about probable/presumed causes, the need to update if new tests are completed, and the importance of this data for public health and medical research.

One last note on cause of death data. Iowa has an additional and separate system to attempt to gather data on stillbirths and their causes. More on this later (in chapter 2), but Iowa had for a time what's called a surveillance registry. As part of this attempt to gather more data, Iowa's Department of Health and Human Services created its own evaluation protocol and evaluation form.[22] The form was and is voluntary for hospitals to complete. It asks for data on obstetrical history, data from an interview with the birthing parent and family about baby's movement and sleeping position, prenatal care information, testing at stillbirth diagnosis, and information from gross exams of the fetus, the placenta, and the umbilical cord. The only question directly addressing the cause of death requests the listing of "probable factors contributing to [the] fetal death." The phrasing of the request is likely less intimidating for health-care providers.

We could do more to determine the cause(s) of stillbirth. Fortunately, we already know what we need to do.

THE GOLD STANDARD

Experts agree that the best way to determine the cause(s) of stillbirth is with two examinations—a fetal autopsy and a placental pathology. Studies show that the combination of these two procedures will identify possible or probable cause(s) of death in 75% of stillbirths.[23] The American College of Obstetricians and Gynecologists (ACOG) and the Society for Maternal-Fetal Medicine specifically recommend both procedures after stillbirth.[24] The fetal autopsy is often labeled the "gold standard for determining the cause of death."[25] Every epidemiologist who studies stillbirth who I have ever spoken to has insisted we need fetal autopsies.

Placental pathologies are now relatively common. It's estimated that placental exams occur in about 65% of stillbirths.[26] A 2022 ProPublica investigation determined this using 2020 data. What that also means, as the article describes, is that "in thousands of stillbirths" in 2020, "the placenta was thrown out without ever being tested." Note also that the data shows placental exams were "performed or planned"; less than 65% may have actually been performed.

Sixty-five percent isn't great. But it's much, much better than the rate of fetal autopsies. Again, per ProPublica, fetal autopsies were planned or performed in less than 20% of stillbirths in 2020.[27] A 2020 study similarly found that a fetal autopsy was performed in only 21% of stillbirths in 2014–2016.[28]

That 2020 study also described characteristics in which fetal autopsy was more likely to occur. The chances of fetal autopsy increased with later gestational age but decreased with increased maternal age. The fetal autopsy rates were higher for the stillbirths of Black and white women and the lowest for Hispanic women. The study also found that the rate of fetal autopsy increased with maternal education; women with a doctorate degree had double the rate of fetal autopsy compared to those with an eighth grade level of education. And women who already had at least one living child were less likely to have a fetal autopsy performed than those without living children.

This study tells us that the autopsy data that we do have is not representative. We have less data on babies born stillborn to less-educated women. There are racial and class disparities in who gets a fetal autopsy—who knows enough to want one, who knows enough to insist on one despite a system that doesn't necessarily encourage fetal autopsies, and who can access one.

Autopsies are also more than just a medical diagnostic. I've previously described a fetal autopsy as a method of parenting—that autopsies "enable parents to parent their stillborn child by determining how he died."[29] Studies point to this effect. In one study in Ireland, parents explained that they got an autopsy for the baby's sake, to do everything possible to determine the reason(s) for his death.[30] Another study explained that fetal autopsies ensure parents that they've "explored every potential cause."[31] And another study described that parental responsibility drove many parents to consent to fetal autopsy—their "obligation as parents to find out what had gone wrong and to obtain factual information for themselves, [and] for their baby."[32] Other studies show that "the autopsy seems to allay guilt and anxiety in parents of stillborns. Even when no definite cause of death is found, emphasis on the baby's normality seems to alleviate a great deal of parental concern."[33]

Studies also confirm that parents rarely regret getting a fetal autopsy, but they often regret not getting one. More specifically, in one study, "no parent who consented to autopsy expressed regret about their decision," but "some form or regret or uncertainty about the choice was common among those parents who did not have an autopsy, including realization of a missed opportunity to find a possible explanation for the baby's death."[34]

Fetal autopsies are also helpful to parents because they can reveal information relevant for subsequent pregnancies. This is consistent with the parental responsibility motive for fetal autopsy. Parents "desire to avoid a similar fate for future children," and to obtain "factual information . . . for future children."[35] These benefits of autopsies to parents also make it important to remember the class and race disparities in who is currently getting fetal autopsies in the United States.

So we know what to do—both to get more answers and to benefit stillbirth parents. Then why aren't we doing it; why don't we have more fetal autopsies?

REASON 1: THE DISCOURAGEMENT

It's important to remember that the decision whether to have a fetal autopsy occurs within the initial shock of stillbirth. The birthing parent first learns that the baby died in the womb, something that they likely didn't know was even possible. Then, the birthing parent learns that they still need to give birth. And then, the birthing parent is supposed to decide whether to have a fetal autopsy performed—whether they want their child cut open to attempt to figure out why the child died. Needless to say, that's a lot. And the difficult conversation and decision about fetal autopsy all occur within those shocks.

The way that the possibility of fetal autopsy is brought up can also easily affect the parents' decision.[36] Sometimes doctors don't bring up the possibility at all. If it's never brought up, the autopsy isn't going to happen. But even when doctors do bring it up, the way they do so can easily discourage parents—intentionally or unintentionally—from having one done. Unfortunately, parents report in studies that they felt actively discouraged from considering a fetal autopsy.[37]

Why would doctors intentionally discourage? It could be benevolent-ish (really paternalistic) thinking that it's just best for the parents to move on. It was only thirty years ago that the standard of care was to take the baby away right after birth.

Another explanation for the discouragement could be that the doctor is worried about liability.[38] Maybe the doctor is worried that something in the autopsy will point to doctor fault and causation. Studies confirm that doctors worry about being blamed for stillbirth when it happens. In studies, parents have even reported having their baby autopsied through a separate institution because of the potential conflict of interest. Or maybe, doctors are aware that if they were to get sued, the case would be more difficult for the birthing parent if there's no autopsy. The lack of an autopsy is thus helpful to the doctor in case of potential lawsuit.

I am going to assume that most doctor discouragement, however, is unintentional. Doctors who deliver babies just don't have much practice discussing autopsies.[39] They're used to being with patients on their happiest days, not their saddest. Their training is not in bereavement care, and stillbirth is rare enough that they don't have to have discussions about autopsy too often. Plus, doctors are not educated about the process of fetal autopsy and its benefits. Their lack of education obviously means they can't educate parents either.

For instance, it's important for parents to be informed that an autopsy may not reveal the cause of the stillbirth. And parents need to know obviously that their stillborn child will be cut into. But these two ideas can easily be discouraging, especially when combined.[40] Another unintentional reason for discouragement could be the doctors' overconfident diagnosis.[41] If the doctor is convinced that the placenta was the reason for the stillbirth, there's no reason for fetal autopsy.

I also think the usual medical response to stillbirth—the "this happens" shrug—unintentionally discourages autopsies. This presents stillbirth as a freak thing, which implies there isn't much point to an autopsy. If it's just a freak and unpreventable thing, there doesn't seem to be any valid reason to allow them to cut your baby open. The "this happens" shrug also implies that we have studied stillbirth and we can't do anything to prevent it. That's not true, especially the thorough study implication.

Imagine how parents would respond if instead doctors presented the topic of autopsy with (1) stillbirth is rare, but it does happen; (2) around 22,000 stillbirths a year in this country, and our rate is much higher than other high-income countries (and we're not making the progress they are); (3) fetal autopsy may not reveal a cause(s) but it is the best test we have to determine the cause(s); and (4) your child's autopsy could help mean that other parents don't have to go through this. This approach is both honest yet not discouraging.

REASON 2: THE COST

The cost is another reason why we don't have more fetal autopsies in this country. Fetal autopsies cost money. I've seen that they cost at least $1000, but that seems too low.

Some hospitals automatically cover the costs of fetal autopsy if the autopsy is performed there (although some parents likely don't want the same institution where their child died also investigating why he died). Unfortunately, I can't find any statistics or information on how many hospitals do this.

Otherwise, private insurance may cover the costs of fetal autopsy. It also might not. Sometimes we have federal or state laws mandating insurance coverage of things like birth control or IVF, but there's no legal mandate anywhere that private insurance cover the costs of fetal autopsy. I have no idea whether my insurance would have covered a fetal autopsy. The thought of having to call the insurance company the day of Caleb's death to figure that out just adds insult to injury.

We do know that Medicaid—mostly state-run insurance for people below a certain income level—does not cover the costs of fetal autopsy. Medicaid pays for just under half of the births in this country. That doesn't mean that half of stillbirths occur in pregnancies covered by Medicaid, but an overlap likely exists given that poor women face double the risk of stillbirth. We're also likely to have an increased number of pregnancies covered by Medicaid now that abortion is illegal in many states and most of those abortion-illegal states have higher poverty rates.

An important sidenote here is that if a state were to mandate insurance coverage of fetal autopsies, that's just private insurance. It wouldn't apply to Medicaid. Mandating private insurance to cover fetal autopsy wouldn't apply to about half of births. And Medicaid covering fetal autopsies means federal or state governments would be paying, which might be a nonstarter.

If there's no insurance coverage for fetal autopsy, the parents have to pay for autopsy out of their own pockets if they want one. Stillbirth is surprisingly expensive, from medical expenses to burial and funeral costs.[42] It's not surprising that, if forced to pay out of pocket, people with lesser financial means would decline an autopsy that may not reveal a cause(s) of death.

Cost issues exist for any specialist review, whether it be a fetal autopsy or review from another specialist. The placenta expert who reviewed my information is not free. Only parents with economic means can afford fetal autopsies and specialist reviews. It shouldn't be that parents are able to figure out why their child died only if they have money. That's morally wrong. Parents shouldn't be denied the benefits of a fetal autopsy because of their income. The lack of an explanation in those cases also feeds bad mom stereotypes that poorer pregnant people are at fault for their child's stillbirth.

It's also economically inefficient. As mentioned, the fetal autopsy could easily reveal a problem that could reoccur in future pregnancies. If discovered in the autopsy, things could be done to prevent that problem in future pregnancies.

QUALITY CONCERNS

It's not enough to just have more fetal autopsies performed, however. We also need to make sure that the autopsies are performed by pathologists who know what they are doing. ACOG has explicit guidance about who performs fetal autopsies: "It is preferable to use a pathologist who is experienced in perinatal autopsy and to have a physician who is experienced in genetics and dysmorphology examine the fetus."[43] In short, a perinatal pathologist is needed.

We already have a shortage of pathologists in this country,[44] a shortage that the Covid-19 pandemic exacerbated. The nationwide shortage of pathologists was on display for all to see as bodies sat in refrigerated trucks outside medical examiner offices. It wasn't just that there were so many more deaths. It was also that there weren't enough pathologists to perform autopsies as quickly as usual.

Pathology isn't really that attractive of a field. It requires nine years of education post college (medical school, a fellowship, and then more training). And usually, aspiring doctors don't go to medical school to spend their careers with deceased patients. The hours might be better than other specialties, but the pay is likely worse.

Even if there were enough pathologists, fetal autopsy requires a special kind of pathologist—a perinatal pathologist. Apparently, however, perinatal pathology is one of the least attractive pathologist specialties.

If there were more fetal autopsies, maybe the specialty would become more attractive. The Stillbirth Health Improvement and Education for Autumn Act of 2021 ("Shine for Autumn Act"), which passed the House of Representatives but never got out of legislative committee in the Senate, contained measures aimed at attracting more pathologists. Specifically, it mandated that the Secretary of Health and Human Services create a Perinatal Pathology Fellowship Program.[45] More perinatal pathologists are needed; inaccurate data won't help.

Coroner or medical examiner investigation of fetal deaths, again of deaths where state law mandates referral because of suspected crimes, may include fetal autopsy. State laws mandate that the fetal autopsy be performed by a pathologist.[46] But not a perinatal pathologist obviously (as these laws apply to all deaths). Notably, Missouri law recognizes the need sometimes for a more qualified pathologist. It mandates the involvement of a "certified child death pathologist" for deaths of children, but only the deaths of a child "who is eligible to receive a certificate of live birth."[47] Presumably, a child death pathologist is a certified pediatric pathologist, which would include some training on perinatal pathology. Regardless, the Missouri statutory requirement of a child death pathologist does not apply to stillborn children, meaning it has no specialization legal requirement for fetal autopsy.

SIDS AUTOPSIES AS A BLUEPRINT

More fetal autopsies are needed to help figure out why stillbirths are still happening at such an alarming rate in this century. The same need existed for autopsies after infant deaths suspected to be due to Sudden Infant Death Syndrome. If you're a parent, you've likely heard of SIDS. Many new parents are terrified at the possibility of their babies dying in their sleep. (I was.)

Numerous state legislatures long ago declared SIDS a public health emergency. To borrow from California statute: "The Legislature finds and declares that sudden infant death syndrome is a serious problem within the State of California and that the public interest is served by research and study of sudden infant death syndrome and its potential causes and indicators."[48] A necessary part of research is autopsies. That's why many, many states mandate and provide *free* autopsies for suspected SIDS deaths.[49] The common language in statutes is that autopsy is necessary when an infant "dies suddenly and unexpectedly."

Notably, if the purpose is to gather research to help prevent SIDS death, state law should also mandate fetal autopsies after at least term stillbirths. There's research suggesting a connection between term stillbirths (after 37 weeks) and SIDS deaths, suggesting that term stillbirths may just be earlier SIDS deaths.[50] So any emphasis on SIDS research shouldn't be limited to traditional SIDS deaths.

Regardless, some states mandate autopsies for more than just suspected SIDS deaths, instead mandating autopsies for all unexpected infant and child deaths. Louisiana law, for example, more broadly states that "the unexpected death of infants and children is an important health concern" and that "collecting data on the causes of unexpected deaths will better enable the state to protect some infants and children from preventable deaths and will help reduce the incidence of such deaths."[51] Louisiana recognizes that research from autopsies is needed to help prevent all unexpected infant and child deaths.

Autopsies are one part of a greater system of formalized state review of infant and child deaths as part of infant and child fatality review teams. Most states have a formalized system, usually created through legislation or executive order.[52] The review is described as "a multidisciplinary, multi-agency process designed to examine the causes and circumstances of child deaths."[53] The review team usually includes representatives from "public health, law enforcement, social services, and clinical medicine (usually a medical examiner, pediatrician, or general practitioners)."[54] Formal review was originally created for just suspicious-looking deaths, but reviews are now public-health focused. The purposes of review teams are (1) "identifying and collecting data pertaining to the cause and manner of child deaths," and (2) "providing prevention recommendations to state or local agencies based on this data."[55] The American Academy of Pediatrics describes that "the process of fatality review has identified effective local and state prevention strategies for reducing child deaths" and "can be a powerful tool in understanding the epidemiology and preventability of child death locally, regionally, and nationally; improving accuracy of vital statistics data; and identifying public health and legislative strategies for reducing preventable child fatalities."[56]

There's really nothing similar for stillbirths. Some localized "Fetal & Infant Mortality Review" teams exist.[57] But it's limited. For instance, there's three teams in the entirety of Texas, and two in Missouri.[58] Plus, grouping fetal mortality with infant mortality also likely means less priority for stillbirths.

Just as state laws mandate autopsies after suspected SIDS deaths, state laws could also mandate autopsies after stillbirths. This would increase opportunities for research. Possibly equally important, however, is the expressive value of such state mandates. Babies shouldn't be dying in their sleep. Infants and children shouldn't be dying unexpectedly. The state is communicating that these deaths are tragic and so important that the state is providing funds for autopsies. It's a clear expression that the state thinks these autopsies are needed. A state's similar endorsement of the importance of fetal autopsies after stillbirth would also powerfully express to parents that stillbirth is a public health problem and that fetal autopsies are needed to help prevent preventable stillbirths. This state expression helps persuade parents to want fetal autopsies.

Any state mandate, however, needs to also take into account the quality of data. State law must mandate that the autopsy be performed by a qualified pathologist, which means a perinatal pathologist. This type of mandate could also increase interest in the specialty given the increased demand.

THE DANGERS OF FETAL AUTOPSIES

The lack of fetal autopsies and answers contributes to the blame felt by many stillbirth parents. If we can't explain why the baby is stillborn, we also can't negate the possibility that the pregnant person is to blame. You can tell a birthing parent over and over that it's not her fault. But that's not that powerful if you can't also tell her why her child was stillborn.

Ironically, more fetal autopsies could also lead to more blame. I can't advocate for fetal autopsies after stillbirth without also acknowledging the danger of those fetal autopsies—especially in post-*Roe v. Wade* America. If the results of the fetal autopsy indicate the pregnant person's contribution, do those results have to be provided to the police? Could the results of fetal autopsy then be used to arrest and prosecute the birthing parent? Many of the state infant and child death review systems mentioned earlier originated from a criminal law lens although they are today focused on public health.

The danger of criminal consequences from increased fetal autopsies is very real. A January 2023 StatNews article reported that perinatal pathologists are very cognizant of how law enforcement may be interested in their work.[59] They're already cognizant of pressure to determine why the baby was stillborn and if it was the birthing parent's fault.

As will be discussed thoroughly in chapter 9, these criminal prosecutions are already happening, mostly to poor women and women of color. Health-care providers are snitching to the police about their patients' possible drug use. State-paid fetal autopsies are magically available when the police suspect the pregnant person caused the baby's stillbirth.

The StatNews article also noted that potential criminal consequences may deter stillbirth parents from pursuing additional testing. What if it turns up incriminating evidence? And what if the pathologist reports it to the police, either voluntarily or because of legal obligation? It may just be safer to not do any additional testing. This is a deterrent that deprives us of data on stillbirths, deprives stillbirth parents of the opportunity to parent their child, and deprives parents of the opportunity to learn about medical conditions that could be treated ahead of time in future pregnancies.

The dangers of more fetal autopsies after stillbirth are real and disproportionately distributed on marginalized persons. At the same time, it's not a zero-sum game. We can improve data without subjecting stillbirth parents to potential criminal consequences. The state could provide fetal autopsies and also prevent law enforcement from obtaining the data. A bill in New Jersey dictated that the work product and any reports created by the Fetal

Infant Death Review committee "shall not be subject to public inspection, discovery, subpoena, or introduction into evidence in any civil, criminal, legislative, or other proceeding."[60] Specific language like this is necessary. Generic reference to protections via existing privacy laws is likely insufficient to protect stillbirth parents from the very real threat of prosecution (more on that in chapter 9).

The need for legal data protection is something the stillbirth community must always recognize within advocacy. This must be a high priority, but it is not always recognized so, as advocates tend to be white and upper middle class and not likely to be investigated for their child's stillbirth.

It's a double bind. The lack of further investigation feeds into the internal and external blame of the birthing parent—the lack of an explanation implies fault on the stillbirth parent's part. But we're also scared to further investigate because of the possible determination of fault on the stillbirth parent's part. But we can overcome the double bind; we can and must legislatively protect the data.

COMMUNICATING CAUSE OF DEATH INFORMATION

A last important component of improved cause of death data is ensuring this information is communicated in the best way possible. To get personal again, on Caleb's FDC, for "Initiating Cause/Condition," my doctor checked the box for placental abruption and also listed "gestational diabetes—diet controlled." She also listed gestational diabetes as an "Other Significant Causes or Conditions" contributing to Caleb's death. I was irate when I first saw my gestational diabetes listed as a cause. It made me feel at fault. Plus, no one mentioned the risk of stillbirth due to gestational diabetes when I was diagnosed; to the contrary, I was told it was no big deal if I managed my diet well. It can't both be no big deal yet listed as a contributing cause of my son's death. I have chosen to assume that my doctor was trying her best to be comprehensive and mistakenly listed the gestational diabetes as a cause rather than just checking it as a risk factor on the second page of the FDC. But even that—if gestational diabetes is a risk factor for stillbirth, I should have been informed so.

Studies of parents after stillbirth confirm that many problems exist with how doctors communicate information regarding the cause of fetal death.

Far too many parents report that their doctors and nurses were "cold or indifferent" and express dissatisfaction "with the information offered them about the stillbirth, and with the manner in which the information was communicated."[61]

Plus, often causes and risk factors are based on maternal health conditions. If the stillbirth is due to the mother's syphilis, the mother can easily feel at fault. It's the same as how I felt with the mention of my gestational diabetes on Caleb's FDC.

It's important to always consider how stillbirth parents may interpret information on their child's FDC. At the very least, pregnant patients should be informed that their maternal health condition could increase the risk of their baby's stillbirth. The FDC cannot be the first time stillbirth parents learn of the potential link between the health condition and stillbirth.

TWO

Primitive Data Collection

While walking out of the hospital without my son, I remember being told that we would get Caleb's death certificate in the mail in a few weeks. My immediate, unspoken thought was "what about his birth certificate?" I pushed him out of my vagina no different than I had his older sisters.

I later learned that I would only get a "fetal death" certificate for Caleb. I would not get any legal record of his birth, but only of his "fetal death." That legal reality can be jarring for stillbirth moms. But it is the reality. Fetal death certificates are how we count the number of stillbirths in this country and gather data on them.

* * * *

Just as we can't prevent something if we don't know why it's happening, we also can't know that something is a problem unless we know it's a problem. We need the data and we need to collect it to know there's a problem. Collected data enables education of the public and increased awareness. Collected data enables education of our lawmakers and explanation of the need for prevention efforts. Collected data enables studies of the causes and risk factors for something. Collected data is the needed starting point.

For over a century, we've recognized the importance of tracking stillbirths. For over a century, we've required some form of legal registration, always via a state–federal partnership with states registering stillbirths legally and then sharing that information with the federal government.

Fetal death certificates (FDCs) are the only source of state and national data—data about the parents, about the birthing parent's medical conditions, and so on—that we have on stillbirths. But it's a primitive system, increasingly unhelpful to those studying stillbirth. That unhelpfulness is

23. Premature?_____ Weeks of		24. Cause of this stillbirth	{ Before labor
Stillborn? gestation 40			{ During labor

Figure 3. Questions 23 and 24 on a 1946 Minnesota-issued (live) birth certificate.

because, as studies demonstrate, FDCs are undercounting stillbirths, missing data, and full of inaccurate data.

Effective data collection is an initial hurdle hindering any stillbirth prevention efforts. We can't make something "count" unless we actually take the care to count it accurately. But there is hope for the future in the form of data surveillance registries.

FROM BIRTH AND DEATH CERTIFICATES TO FETAL DEATH CERTIFICATES

As mentioned, we have been keeping track of the number of stillbirths in the United States for over a century. From the early 1900s to about midcentury, states legally registered stillbirths as both births and deaths—issuing both birth certificates and death certificates. For example, 1905 Pennsylvania law dictated that "[s]tillborn children, or those dead at birth, shall be registered as births and also deaths, and a certificate of both the birth and death shall be filed with the local registrar in the usual form and manner."[1] The birth certificate merely had a place to note if the baby was stillborn, a normalization of stillbirth very foreign to modern day. Note also the "stillborn child" language in the statute, language that differs from today. States continued to issue both birth and death certificates for stillborn babies long into the twentieth century.[2] For instance, even my mom's 1946 birth certificate was applicable to both live births and stillbirths. Her 1946 Minnesota Certificate of Birth had a place to note if the baby was stillborn and, if so, the cause of the stillbirth, and whether it was before or during labor (see figure 3).

Note that it was and is state laws that require registrations of stillbirths (and births and deaths). The federal government doesn't have any power to require the issuance of vital statistics. This is because it was the colonies that first saw the need to issue vital statistics and did so.[3] When the Constitution was adopted and ratified, the power to issue vital statistics remained with the states. Long after, Congress passed laws requiring the federal government to collect data on vital statistics. But that's different than a law requiring the issuance of vital statistics. That federal law assumes that states will continue to produce the data, which the federal government is then obligated to collect.

A state-by-state system, however, can easily pose problems for data quality, which the federal government realized. Thus, the federal government created the Model Vital Statistics Act for states to hopefully use (again, the federal government lacks the power to mandate use of the Act). The first Model Vital Statistics Act was released in 1907.[4] The Model Act provision on registration of stillbirths was the same as Pennsylvania's, that stillbirths be registered with birth and death certificates. The federal government also created model birth and death certificates for states to hopefully use as early as 1905.[5] Again, the birth certificate had a box to check if the baby was stillborn.

The federal government later suggested changes for the legal registration of stillbirths. In 1939, the federal government announced that birth and death certificates should no longer be used for stillbirth. Instead stillbirths should be registered with "stillbirth certificates."[6] Eventually most states made this change. In 1955, the federal government again changed the language, from a stillbirth certificate to a "fetal death" certificate.[7] And then in the late 1970s, the federal government changed the word certificate to record, to reflect that stillbirth is not a legal event as it does not change any legal status and thus should only be maintained as a record (although everyone still calls them certificates).[8] Note again though that the federal government's changed suggestions did not necessarily mean that all states changed to registration of stillbirths. At least one state was still using both birth and death certificates for stillbirths until the 1960s.[9]

This shift from birth certificate to stillbirth certificate and ultimately to fetal death record also reflects the shift of childbirth moving from the home to the hospital and the medicalization of pregnancy and childbirth.[10] In the early 1900s, we recognized that stillbirth involved childbirth—that a woman would give birth at home to a baby who happened to be already dead. But by midcentury, stillbirth, like childbirth, was a medical event with clinical language. Consistently, the medical practice for stillbirth was to take the baby away and never let the mother see the baby.[11] The paternalistic thought behind this practice is that the pregnant person would be better off focusing not on the stillborn baby they just birthed, but instead on pursuing a subsequent pregnancy. It wasn't until the 1980s that parents successfully convinced doctors to allow them to see and hold their stillborn babies—a practice that research almost unanimously confirms is beneficial for parents.[12] Legal registration of stillbirths, however, remains the same—the clinical and cold "fetal death record."

Legal registration of stillbirths remains a state-federal partnership today. The power to issue vital statistics remains with the states and a few registration areas like Washington, DC and New York City. The registration areas collect the vital statistics and then pass them on to the federal government. The federal government is then legally obligated to collect that data, and publish it.[13] This is now done through the National Vital Statistics System, which is currently located with the National Cooperative Health Statistics System at the Centers for Disease Control. There aren't any time requirements for publication. The CDC is very quick about posting live birth data. For instance, 2020 provisional live birth data was available just five months later, in May 2021.[14] The usual time lag for stillbirth data is much longer. I couldn't find the 2020 stillbirth data on the CDC's website until September 2022, so closer to eighteen months. I first located the 2021 stillbirth data on CDC's website in August 2023.

FDCs are the only source of data for stillbirths in the United States. The *only* data source. And their many problems are well documented. Because of nonuniformity, FDCs are undercounting stillbirths. And numerous data quality issues exist—both data incompleteness and data inaccuracies.

FDC PROBLEM NO. 1: UNDERREPORTING

The Model Vital Statistics Act includes a suggested law for when fetal death certificates should be issued. But states don't have to follow it. They can do whatever they want. State control of issuance of fetal death certificates immediately means the possibility of nonuniformity. Any nonuniformity means that we are undercounting stillbirths. And we have nonuniform standards for issuance of FDCs.

States currently use one of three different standards. One popular standard is to mandate issuance of an FDC if fetal weight exceeds 350 grams, or, if weight is unknown, if the pregnancy was 20-weeks gestation or later.[15] Only if fetal weight is unknown does gestational age matter—even though any pregnancy loss after 20 weeks is a stillbirth regardless of fetal weight. A weight of 350 grams is likely to correlate to 20 weeks, but not necessarily. Any stillborn babies weighing under 350 grams won't be counted. And many stillborn babies suffer from fetal growth restriction, presumably increasing the chances that a stillborn baby will not be counted because he does not weigh 350 grams at birth. Strangely, this "weight first, medical definition of stillbirth second" standard is the one suggested in the current Model Vital Statistics Act, which is from 1992.[16] The 1992 Revised Act does not explain why it switched to this suggested standard.

Fortunately, most states still use the 1977 Revised Act standard of (1) 20 weeks, and, if gestational weeks are unknown, 350 grams; or use just a (2) 20-weeks standard. Both of these standards reflect the 20-week definition of stillbirth. To get accurate numbers though, it's not enough for just the majority of reporting areas to use the correct standard. We need them all to.

Some states use an even earlier standard for issuance of a FDC, including Pennsylvania (16 weeks) and Arkansas (12 weeks).[17] These earlier standards for issuance increase the quality of data collected. A 16-week standard is much more likely to capture the early stillbirths than a 20-week standard.

The current nonuniformity is much better than it used to be. Historically, many states used a definition exclusively based on fetal weight—500 grams. That weight is not likely to correlate to 20 weeks, but instead be closer to 24 weeks.[18] The use of this standard blatantly undercounts stillbirths. Tennessee used a 500 gram threshold for issuance of a fetal death record until 2012, and New Mexico did the same until 2014.[19] According to the 2020 CDC report on stillbirths, South Dakota still uses the 500 gram standard for issuance.[20] That's not true. South Dakota changed its law from 500 grams to 20 weeks in 2007.[21] The CDC, however, did not learn about South Dakota's change until I mentioned it when presenting to the National Institute of Child Health and Human Development Stillbirth Working Group of Council in November 2022. Every CDC national report on stillbirths from 2007 to 2020 has inaccurately stated that South Dakota only tracks stillbirths over 500 grams. It was a mistake. But it also communicates stillbirth's priority level.

Although the extent has decreased, nonuniformity still exists as some states still use a weight-first standard for issuance. It may not seem like a big deal, but, again, any nonuniformity means systematic undercounting of stillbirths. Experts agree: "the number of fetal deaths in the United States is undoubtedly under-reported."[22]

It's an unnecessary misstep. This is not a controversial subject. If a new bill was introduced in the state legislature to change from the 350-gram standard to a 20-week standard, there's no rational reason to oppose it. Simply change to the 20-week standard. Similarly, there's no valid reason for the Model Vital Statistics Act to use the weight-first standard for issuance. Simply change to the 20-week standard and model to the states the right way to define and register stillbirths.

At the same time that we're undercounting stillbirths, we're also counting some non-stillbirths as stillbirths. Studies confirm that some abortions are registered as fetal deaths.[23] Most states require legal registration of abortions as "induced terminations of pregnancy" (ITOP). But sometimes FDCs are issued. This issuance is especially likely if the abortion was due to a fetal anomaly—maybe an anomaly that was likely to cause either stillbirth or infant death. In that case, the abortion caused that inevitable death to occur sooner rather than later. And maybe, classifying those abortions as fetal deaths may ultimately make sense. If stillbirth was likely anyway, maybe that fetal death should be included with stillbirth data instead of with abortion data. But under current definitions, no abortion, even if related to fetal anomaly, should be issued an FDC.

Notably, the current definitions do leave room for the possibility of an abortion being issued with birth and death certificates instead of as an ITOP.[24] The 1988 Handbook on the Reporting of Induced Terminations specifically states that in the unlikely event that an "induced abortion procedure . . . result[s] in a live birth," then "a certificate of live birth is to be prepared for the infant."[25] And a death certificate would also be prepared for the later death. The 1992 Revision of the Model State Vital Statistics Act and Regulations defines an "'induced termination of pregnancy' as "the purposeful interruption of an intrauterine pregnancy with the intention other than to produce a live-born infant and which does not result in a live birth." In a pre-viability labor induction abortion, the intent is not to produce a live born infant, but it can result in a live birth—presumably not meeting this definition of ITOP. If the ITOP definition does not apply, a birth certificate and then a death certificate would be issued for the induction abortion.

Returning to stillbirths, state-issued FDCs are not the ideal system for gathering data on stillbirths (or really any vital statistics). Nonuniformity has decreased, but even seemingly minor variations in state laws will lead to undercounting. There are many reasons to question the accuracy of our state and national stillbirth numbers, especially historically but even still today.

FDC PROBLEM NO. 2: DATA INCOMPLETENESS

FDCs aren't catching all stillbirths, but there are also problems with the data on the FDCs that are issued—or actually with the data *not* completed. As briefly mentioned in chapter 1, FDCs ask for medical information regarding the causes and conditions contributing to fetal death, information on prenatal care, pregnancy history and outcomes of other pregnancies, history of cigarette smoking before and during pregnancy, the presence of defined risk factors (diabetes, hypertension, use of infertility treatment, specified infections), the method of delivery, and fetal congenital anomalies.[26] It also asks for information on the mother's education, ethnicity, race, and marital status. Notably, the FDC does not ask for any of this information regarding the father.

Very often, however, the data is simply not completed on FDCs. The field for fetal weight will just be blank, or the field for a history of cigarette smoking will be blank. Over 9% of FDCs issued in 2013 were missing the stillborn child's birth weight; only 0.1% of 2013 live birth certificates were missing the birthweight.[27] A 2008 study found other important information missing from FDCs: pregnancy weight gain (70% of records with missing values), number of prior pregnancies (11%), alcohol and tobacco use during pregnancy (18%), paternal age (74%), and cause(s) of death (69%).[28] Another study found data regarding birth weight and prenatal care visits were more likely to be missing for earlier stillbirths than for later stillbirths.[29] Again, Black women face almost triple the risk of early stillbirth compared to white women, and thus may also face a higher risk of an incomplete FDC for their child's stillbirth.

One suggested reason for the commonality of "data incompleteness" is simply a lack of care. I don't mean anything nefarious. FDCs just don't matter as much as live birth certificates. FDCs' role as the only source for data on stillbirths is underappreciated. Medical professionals may just not use the same care completing an FDC that they do for a live birth certificate. Plus, the fatalism surrounding stillbirth makes data seem less important.

Studies have also showed a disparity in which FDCs are more likely to be incomplete. One study compared the FDCs issued in Salt Lake City (Salt Lake County) and Atlanta (DeKalb County).[30] Of the two, the DeKalb County FDCs were much more likely to be missing data like maternal education, ethnicity, receipt of prenatal care, number of prenatal care visits, information on smoking during pregnancy, whether it was the first pregnancy, and birth weight.[31] The study did not find any difference in the rate of incomplete data based on the pregnant patient's race or class; there was no indication that FDCs were more likely to be incomplete for Black stillborn babies compared to white stillborn babies.[32] But the study did find a geographic disparity—that the FDCs completed in Salt Lake County were more likely to be complete than the FDCs completed in DeKalb County.[33] And geographic disparities can easily translate to racial disparities. More Black people live in Atlanta than in Salt Lake City. If medical personnel in Atlanta are taking less care in filling out FDCs, that means that the incomplete and inaccurate fetal death certificates are more likely to be for Black babies. On the other hand, the more complete and accurate FDCs complete in Salt Lake City are more likely to be for white babies.

FDC PROBLEM NO. 3: DATA INACCURACIES

Data is missing, and the data that is included in FDCs is often inaccurate. The same study of FDCs from DeKalb County and Salt Lake County found that the data on the DeKalb County FDCs were more likely to be misreported. The frequent inaccurate data was the number of prenatal care visits, gestational age, birth weight, and maternal race.[34] A study of Wisconsin FDCs found that information about congenital abnormalities and about the cause of death were often inaccurate.[35] Another study focused on Georgia FDCs with implausible gestational ages and fetal weights. It concluded that at least one-quarter of the FDCs had inaccurate data.[36]

The inaccuracy could be due to a lack of care. Again, I don't think anyone completing a FDC is intentionally careless. But FDCs are just not as important for individuals compared to birth certificates. The average health-care worker is likely unaware of the importance of FDCs in the context of gathering data on stillbirth.

Many inaccuracies are simply due to a lack of knowledge. It's not at all surprising that the "cause of death" information on the FDC would be inac-curate. As discussed in chapter 1, we expect an obstetrician who rarely ever sees stillbirth to determine the cause of death without much direction. Plus, legally, FDCs are required to be completed within days of the stillbirth.[37] That's not enough time for any testing or investigation to be completed. A placental pathology may not be able to be finished in that time, and a fetal autopsy almost certainly won't be completed within that time.

The FDC has a spot to check whether an autopsy was performed, and whether the FDC was completed before the autopsy. The FDC thus contem-plates that further (more accurate) testing would be completed *after* the FDC is filed. Yet the FDC nowhere indicates the importance of updating the FDC if the autopsy produces new information. The Standard Death Certificate, which is also often legally required to be prepared shortly after the death, contains strong language emphasizing the need to amend: "Should addi-tional medical information or autopsy findings become available that would change the cause of death originally reported, the original death certificate should be amended by the certifying physician by *immediately* reporting the revised cause of death to the State Vital Records Office."[38] No similar lan-guage appears on the standard FDC. As discussed in chapter 1, the Coroners' Handbook includes language about the importance of amendment, but the Facility Guide does not.

Even if this language were present, it's not easy to correct (or fill in miss-ing) data on an FDC, especially not medical data. Each state has a process for amendment of FDCs. And in many states, the same attendant physician who attested to the original fetal death certificate is the only person who can request amendment of medical information.[39] That means the original doc-tor, determining that their initial diagnosed cause of death was incorrect, has to be the one completing the paperwork to amend the FDC.

Ana Vick's son Owen Nathaniel was stillborn in 2015. The doctors gave her no explanation for this death, instead offering that sometimes healthy babies just die. After she became more involved in more stillbirth advocacy,

Ana asked Dr. Kliman to review her medical information for his opinion on Owen's cause of death. Dr. Kliman concluded that Owen's death was due to a "cord accident." (I'll separately note that many stillbirth parents believe that the word "accident" connotes unpreventability and dissuades research about potential preventability.) Dr. Kliman's office sent his report to the Vicks and to the doctors who treated Ana during her pregnancy and Owen's birth.

Wanting Owen's FDC to be accurate to help enable research of the causes of stillbirth, Ana decided to get Owen's FDC amended. The process has been, to say the least, extremely frustrating. The obstetrician at Owen's birth was uninterested and ultimately declined to help as hospital lawyers advised against any sort of amendment. The NICU doctor who tried to resuscitate Owen initially said she wanted to help, but that it was an unusual request. About a year later, that doctor also declined to seek an amendment, again saying that hospital lawyers advised against it. A birth attendant at the hospital suggested that Ana contact the California Department of Health, which she already had done numerous times. Ana is not a physician and thus cannot initiate a physician amendment of medical information on an FDC. In the meantime, Owen's FDC is wrong.

All Ana wants is for Owen's FDC to be as accurate as possible in the hope that research will improve. And there's really nothing she can do.

Ana's difficulty raises broader questions about whether FDCs ever get amended. Theoretically, there's less awkwardness when a doctor learns medical information from an autopsy rather than from a report from a specialist years later. Hopefully that lesser awkwardness means that doctors do more routinely amend FDCs due to information learned in an autopsy. But maybe not. The paperwork is still a hassle. And there doesn't seem to be a point unless the doctor understands the importance of the FDC in enabling research on stillbirth. Consistently, a ProPublica investigation found that only 18 of nearly 2,000 FDCs issued in Georgia between 2019 to 2021 with a missing cause of death had been updated.[40]

FDCS AND COVID-19 INFECTIONS

The limitations of FDCs became even clearer during the Covid-19 pandemic. Anecdotes and studies suggested an increased risk of stillbirth from unvaccinated Covid-19 infection during pregnancy, especially during the Delta variant. Due to data collection limitations, however, we'll likely never know the extent of any connection between Covid-19 infection and stillbirth.

The anecdotal reports of increased risk of stillbirth due to Covid-19 infection gained steam in the second year of the pandemic. In April 2021, clinicians in Ireland noted that six stillbirths had occurred a few weeks after the pregnant person had Covid-19. In each of the stillbirths, the placenta had been extremely damaged.[41] In September 2021, Mississippi health department officials reported that their number of stillbirths during the pandemic was twice what would have been expected pre-pandemic.[42] Doctors in Alabama also reported seeing more stillbirths during the pandemic than before.[43]

The suspected reason for increased stillbirths is due to what Covid-19 infection in pregnancy can do to the placenta.[44] The placenta is a shield against most viruses, but it's not able to hold up as well against Covid-19. The blood vessels in the placenta can collapse, diminishing the oxygen it normally provides to the baby, and it ends up inflamed and scarred. A ProPublica story describes a doctor in Ohio who studies placentas after stillbirths explaining that one she looked at in October 2021 was the most withered and scarred placenta that she had ever seen. The pregnant person had had Covid-19 absent vaccination.

The CDC officially noted the increased risk of stillbirth from Covid in a study published on its website in November 2021.[45] The study relied on data from the Premier Healthcare Database Special Covid-Release, a large hospital-based administrative database. According to the study, the database includes more than 900 geographically diverse medical providers and represents 20% of inpatient admissions in the United States. The study looked at outcomes when Covid-19 infection was present at time of deliveries between March 2020 to September 2021. The study found increased risk of stillbirth if the mother was unvaccinated and Covid positive at time of delivery. The risk increased even more during the period when the Delta variant was predominant:

> The rates of stillbirth in women without COVID-19 at delivery in this analysis (0.64% overall) were similar to the known prepandemic stillbirth rate of 0.59% (6). However, 0.98% of COVID-19–affected deliveries pre-Delta and 2.70% during the Delta period resulted in stillbirth.

The risk of stillbirth increased from 0.59% pre-pandemic to 2.7% if unvaccinated and infected with Covid at delivery during the Delta variant.

This CDC study is limited because it looked only at Covid infection at the time of delivery. The theory about why Covid might be causing stillbirths, however, is that it deteriorates the placenta.[46] If an unvaccinated pregnant person gets Covid at 20 weeks, the placenta could start deteriorating then, but the stillbirth may not occur until term. That stillbirth would not have been captured in the data though because the pregnant person did not have Covid at the time of the delivery.

The CDC has also collected data on Covid in pregnant patients through its Surveillance for Emerging Threats to Mothers and Babies Network ("SET-NET"). Health departments in thirty-four reporting areas have reported data, some just 2020 data (7 areas) and some 2020–2021 data (27 areas). The CDC published this data on one of its Covid Tracker pages, and ceased doing so in November 2022.[47] In a report dated October 11, 2022, this tracker lists 114,219 people with Covid-19 who completed pregnancy, 115,832 birth outcomes among pregnant people with Covid-19 (which covers multiple gestation pregnancies), 114,781 live born infants, and 1051 pregnancy losses. The report doesn't define pregnancy losses, but I'd be surprised if the reporting areas had access to much data on miscarriages (plus, the percentage of pregnancy losses from the birth outcomes is way too low to include miscarriages). Generally speaking, data for SET-NET comes from "public health investigations, vital records (e.g., birth certificates or administrative data), laboratory reports, and medical records."[48]

Note these data sources. The study about Covid infection at delivery was the Premier Healthcare Database—not FDCs. SET-NET presumably uses FDCs, but numerous other sources of information also.

These studies are not relying (solely) on FDCs to study Covid-19 infection and stillbirth because FDCs wouldn't be very helpful. FDCs likely have little to no information about Covid-19 infection. The model FDC hasn't been amended to specifically request data regarding Covid infection during pregnancy.

The lack of CDC action on FDCs was not because the CDC was unconcerned about the possible effect of Covid-19 infection in pregnancy. To the contrary, as early as April 2020, the CDC realized the need for data about

Covid-19 infection and pregnancy. The NCHS began working with certain states to develop additional approaches to collect data on Covid during pregnancy outside of the standard birth data reporting process.[49] Specifically, the NCHS and ultimately the CDC recommended changes to live birth certificates: (1) adding Covid-19 to the already-existing list of infections present and/or treated during pregnancy and at what time in the pregnancy, or (2) adding a completely new question regarding Covid infection.[50]

But it was only live birth certificates. And live birth certificates are only issued for pregnancies ending in live births. The measures specifically will not capture any data about Covid infections in pregnancies ending in stillbirth.

The NCHS did not make these same recommendations for FDCs. It seems like such an obvious thing to do, to recommend adding a question about Covid infection during pregnancy to the FDC. But it didn't. So instead, FDCs—our *only* source for national data on the causes of stillbirth—likely won't tell us much about Covid and stillbirth.

I should note that I've heard rumors that the CDC wanted to do this for FDCs also, but that states couldn't and/or wouldn't do it. But state resistance shouldn't preclude the CDC from making best practice recommendations. Not all states made changes to their live birth certificates either, but the CDC still made the best practice recommendations. The CDC could and should have done the same with FDCs—recommending the best practice and accentuating that stillbirths were also a concern.

Even though FDCs do not have any Covid-specific questions, there is a spot on the FDC for "Other (Specify) Infections present and/or treated during this pregnancy." This is the most obvious place to write "Covid-19" on the FDC. But even if it is listed, the NCHS is not gathering that data nationally anymore. In 2014, the NCHS dropped 36 items of data from the national fetal death data file.[51] This included data like the total number of prenatal doctor visits, the date of the last prenatal care visit, information of infections during the pregnancy (like listeria, Group B Strep, and "Other" infections), and information regarding certain fetal anomalies. There hasn't yet been an official revision of the standard FDC, but, in 2019, the "Facility Worksheet for the Report of Fetal Death" was revised.[52] And the "Other (Specify) Infections present and/or treated during this pregnancy" question is gone.

Presumably, the intent of these changes in data collection was to simplify the FDC. The NCHS is very familiar with all the problems with FDCs. Maybe a simpler FDC is more likely to be completely filled out with accurate data. I can quibble with the wisdom of this decision and weigh the benefits of simplification versus the loss of data when stillbirth rates are not decreasing. But it doesn't really matter. The reality is that we don't have national data on other infections present during pregnancies that end in stillbirth.

That said, maybe Covid-19 infections didn't end up as harmful as indicated by the anecdotes and studies. Stillbirth rates did increase in other countries. In England and Wales between 2020 and 2021, 2,597 babies were stillborn in 2021.[53] That's a 9.5% increase disrupting an otherwise consistent decline in the stillbirth rate. The UK-based pregnancy-loss charity, Tommy's, responded to the released data that Covid-19 was likely directly affecting stillbirth rates—because it can cause problems to the placenta.[54] Tommy's also took the opportunity to accentuate the need for vaccination for pregnant people. In 2022, there were 4.0 stillbirths per 1,000 births, essentially unchanged from 2021, but still higher than the 2020 rate.[55]

But no such similar increase occurred in the United States. There was not a significant change in the stillbirth rate between 2019 to 2020, from 5.70 stillbirths per 1000 births to 5.74 births. And the rate did not really change between 2020 (5.74 stillbirths per 1000 births), and the 2021 (5.73 stillbirths per 1000 births).[56] The 2021 data would have covered pregnancies during the Delta variant, which was thought especially dangerous for pregnancy. And thus the 2021 data suggests that Covid-19 infection does not significantly increase the risk of stillbirth. Which is a relief.

Still, the better approach would have been to specifically gather Covid-19 data and stillbirth data. Then, we could know the lack of a significant increased risk instead of inferring it from the 2021 data. We would also be better informed if there's any increased risk. Because if there's any increased risk at all, pregnant people should know so and evaluate that increased risk when determining whether to get vaccinated.

STILLBIRTH SURVEILLANCE REGISTRIES
Better data collection alternatives exist. Instead of passive reliance on incomplete and inaccurate FDCs, epidemiologists studying stillbirth wish

that we had what are known as surveillance registries. Surveillance registries exist for all types of public health concerns—cancer, birth defects, and so on. Registries enable access to medical records, immediately increasing the chances of complete and accurate data. Studies have shown it would be very easy to create stillbirth registries based on already-existing birth defect registries.[57]

A few states have or have had stillbirth registries. Arkansas created a "reproductive outcome monitoring system" in 1985.[58] With funding from the CDC, Iowa gathered stillbirth data through its already existing birth defect registry from 2005-2015. But then the funding ran out. The New Jersey legislature created a stillbirth registry in 2015, but never funded it.[59] The Metropolitan Atlanta Congenital Defects Program has also been expanded to gather data on stillbirths.[60]

Registries would collect much better data. Better data does not mean better outcomes, of course, but we have to start somewhere. Registries actively surveil stillbirths—trained abstractors visit hospitals, review medical records, and record relevant information. Clinicians then review and record the information. If an FDC is missing information, nothing can be done. A registry, on the other hand, has access to medical records and can fill in any missing pieces. Access to medical records also means an easy ability to obtain accurate information. And if data does need to be corrected, that can happen easily (without the need to legally amend an FDC).

In 2021, the SHINE for Autumn Act was introduced in the United States Congress.[61] The bill would provide money to states to create stillbirth registries. The bill passed the House of Representatives with wide bipartisan support. It was introduced in the Senate, had bipartisan co-sponsors, but never got out of committee. The bill was reintroduced in the next Congress in the summer 2023.

State registries would be a huge step forward in improving stillbirth data and data collection. A huge step forward, but also one that depends on states choosing to take the money and set up a registry. And registries don't mean prevention measures. But prevention measures aren't possible without initial data showing the need for prevention.

The idea of a *surveillance* registry can be frightening, especially in states where abortion is illegal, when the line between pregnancy loss and abortion will be even blurrier (a subject I discuss much more in chapter 8). But, as discussed in chapter 1, we can have accurate data and also protect it—we can, in legislation, specifically preclude the use of data by law enforcement or prosecutors. A 2022 California law clarifies the coroner's role in preparing FDCs for stillbirths and specifically mandates that any coroner-created FDCs "shall not be used to establish, bring, or support a criminal prosecution."[62] As already emphasized, protections like this are doable; stillbirth data does not need to lead to criminal prosecutions. I refuse to give up on better stillbirth data when legislative protections of data are possible.

MEMORIAL BIRTH CERTIFICATES

I want to conclude this chapter with a newer legal development. As noted at the beginning of the chapter, historically states issued birth certificates for stillborn babies. There was simply a box to check on the birth certificate for whether the baby was stillborn or born alive. And some states continued this system even as late as the 1960s. But no longer. Now, stillbirth parents only get records of "fetal death." This can be jarring for many stillbirth parents. Stillbirth mom Sari Edber described the illogic in receiving only an FDC: "I was in labor. I pushed, I had stitches, my breast milk came in, just like any other mother. And we deserved more than a death certificate."[63] Similarly, stillbirth mom Heidi Kauffman described finding out that would only get FDC as "a slap in the face."[64]

After Joanne Cacciatore gave birth to her stillborn daughter Cheyenne, she called the county to ask about Cheyenne's birth certificate.[65] Cacciatore was told that there was no birth certificate. She was told that she didn't give birth to a baby, but to a "fetus." That phone call sparked a movement pushing for some state recognition of their child's birth in addition to his death.[66]

Despite initial resistance from reproductive rights groups (more on that in chapter 8), over 40 states now issue memorial birth certificates for stillbirth. Today's stillbirth birth certificates are specifically *not* vital statistics; they are memorial. The only legal record of a stillborn baby remains an FDC.

News coverage of these state laws explained that "to thousands of parents who have experienced stillbirth, getting a birthing certificate is passionately important, albeit symbolic."[67] These certificates can provide dignity and validation, no different than the dignity and validation some feel about their marriage licenses or baptismal certificates. Perhaps this validation can help some stillbirth parents with their grief.

On a personal level, I do not feel any dignity or validation. I obtained Caleb's Texas-issued "Certificate of Birth Resulting in Stillbirth," which is such an awkward title. For me, the only thing Caleb's birth certificate symbolizes is the supposed tension between stillbirth and abortion rights, but that's a whole other story (covered in chapter 8).

THREE

Standards of Care and Malpractice

Both my husband and I are lawyers. It didn't take us long after Caleb's death to wonder if different medical care would have saved him. What if the on-call doctor had told me to come to labor and delivery right away (instead of telling me to take a bath)? Why was the on-call doctor so unconcerned about Caleb's lack of movement?

I don't believe that Caleb's stillbirth could have been prevented with different care. Obviously not if he died due to an abnormality. If Caleb had died due to abruption, he theoretically wouldn't have died had he not been in my womb. But no sane doctor would have delivered Caleb before 37 weeks. It's not the standard of care; in fact, it would have violated the standard of care. But some stillbirths are due to doctor conduct. Whether that conduct violates the standard of care and is thus medical malpractice, however, is a whole other question.

* * * *

Many stillbirth parents believe, or at least wonder if, different medical care would have saved their child. And other countries do think different medical care can prevent some stillbirths. Other countries have recently implemented "safer baby bundles" with such changed medical practices specifically aimed at reducing their (already lower) stillbirth rates. This chapter begins by introducing England's and Australia's safer baby bundles.

The chapter then turns to the United States and reviews whether the measures within these safer baby bundles are also part of US standard medical care. In the United States, standard medical practices are set not by the government, but by medical professionals, essentially the American College of Obstetricians and Gynecologists (ACOG) and the Society for Maternal-Fetal Medicine (SMFM). In short, US medical guidelines have some overlaps with the safer baby bundles, but there's also a lot of distinctions. A lot. The intent of this discussion is not to judge the substance of any of these medical guidelines nor to accredit or discredit any studies cited in the guidelines. The intent is to simply compare.

The chapter then turns back to a discussion of the law, specifically the law of medical malpractice. Assuming the practices in the safer baby bundles would prevent (some) stillbirths, a layperson would likely think that a doctor's failure to use those practices constitutes malpractice. But likely not. US medical malpractice liability defers heavily to the standard of care set by medical professionals (ACOG and SMFM), even if other practices would prevent stillbirth. And the heavy deference only encourages doctors to keep doing what they are doing.

Tort lawsuits in the United States thus are not likely equipped to motivate adoption of measures in the safer baby bundles. But some tort law reforms could help with stillbirth prevention. Those changes include adopting a less deferential reasonable doctor standard of care and recognizing an assumption-of-risk defense if stillbirth prevention measures do injure the baby.

THE SAFER BABY CARE BUNDLES—AND US ACOG GUIDELINES

In 2009, Sands, a stillbirth and neonatal death charity in England, published a report called "Saving Babies' Lives."[1] The report got the Scottish government's attention. A group chaired by the Government Senior Medical Officer was formed and got to work. In 2013, Scotland's Minister for Public Health announced the creation of the Maternity and Children Quality Improvement Collaborative (MCQIC) and its ambitious goal of reducing the number of stillbirths and neonatal deaths in Scotland by 15% by 2015.[2] Scotland's initiative included focuses on risk assessment, prevention, and surveillance of pregnancies at risk of fetal growth restriction; raising awareness of reduced fetal movement; effective fetal monitoring during labor; and reducing smoking in pregnancy. Scotland met its 2015 reduction goal of 15% and actually reduced stillbirth rates by 23% in the five years after the creation of the MCQIC.[3]

In 2015, England's Secretary of State for Health announced a national goal to reduce the country's stillbirth rate (and maternal deaths and neonatal deaths) by 50% by 2030, including a 20% reduction by 2020. To reach those goals, in 2016, England announced its Saving Babies' Lives Care Bundle.[4] The first version of the Care Bundle focused on four elements of care: 1) reducing smoking in pregnancy, 2) risk assessment and surveillance for fetal growth restriction, 3) raising awareness of the importance of fetal movement, and 4) effective fetal monitoring during labor.

A 2018 report evaluated the Saving Babies' Lives Care Bundle and found great success—stillbirths had already declined by 20% in the areas implementing the Bundle. Based on the report, in 2019, England's National Health Services announced the Saving Babies Lives Care Bundle Version Two.[5] Some changes were made in the four already existing elements, including additional carbon monoxide testing for pregnant persons and a mandatory referral to a trained stop smoking advisor. Version Two also highlighted new principles to be applied as part of implementation: offering choice to pregnant patients and respecting autonomy; promoting continuity of carer, essentially ensuring that each pregnant person sees the same midwife throughout the pregnancy; and increased education for pregnant people on healthy pregnancies.

Then, in 2023, England's NHS announced the Saving Babies Lives Care Bundle Version Three.[6] Updates were made throughout, even citing studies that were published just months earlier. The updates throughout also were due to reviewing how to "improve equity, including for babies from Black, Asian, and mixed ethnic groups and for those born to mothers living in the most deprived areas."[7] Version three also added a new element concerned with managing pregnancy with pre-existing diabetes. A version three means that England's NHS introduced the safer baby bundle to reduce stillbirths and has updated and revised it twice in less than ten years.

Based on research from Scotland and England, Australia also recently implemented its own Safer Baby Bundle to aid in its goal of "reducing stillbirth rates at least 20% by 2023."[8] It focused on five elements: (1) supporting women to stop smoking in pregnancy; (2) improved surveillance of fetal growth restriction; (3) raising awareness of and improving care for reduced fetal movement; (4) raising awareness on the importance of sleeping on one's side later in pregnancy; and (5) improving decision-making about the timing of birth for those with risk factors for stillbirth. Unfortunately, the Covid-19 pandemic interrupted the implementation of the bundle, also hampering meeting the 20% goal.

The United States does not have any government-issued guidelines to prevent stillbirth. Governments in the United States don't usually issue medical guidelines, although many state governments are eager to ban abortion, and gender-affirming care for transgender children. Here, medical practices are dictated by doctors and medical professional organizations themselves. ACOG and/or SMFM create practices bulletins and guidelines defining the standards of pregnancy care.

ACOG does have two guidelines specifically aimed at stillbirth prevention—for pregnancies where stillbirth is a higher risk. They are "Indications for Outpatient Antenatal Fetal Surveillance" and "Antepartum Fetal Surveillance." The Indications Committee Opinion 828 recommends additional surveillance for pregnancies with "conditions for which stillbirth is reported to occur more frequently than 0.8 per 1,000 . . . and which are associated with a relative risk or odds ratios for stillbirth of more than 2.0 compared to pregnancies without the specific conditions."[9]

The Opinion then lists specific conditions. They include fetal growth restriction (discussed more in what follows); maternal conditions including hypertension, preexisting and gestational diabetes, systemic lupus erythematosus, sickle cell disease, renal disease, thyroid disorders, use of IVF, substance use; heightened BMI or maternal age over 35; history of previous stillbirth or other adverse pregnancy outcomes; and placental conditions like chronic abruption, placenta previa, oligohydramnios (decreased amniotic fluid), and polyhydramnios (increased amniotic fluid).[10]

Note the listing of the use of IVF for pregnancy as a condition for which additional surveillance is recommended. Additional information in a SMFM guideline explains that "pregnancies achieved with IVF have a 2- to 3-fold increased risk for stillbirth even after controlling for maternal age, parity, and multifetal gestations."[11] SMFM recommends surveillance starting at 36 weeks because the use of IVF creates a risk "for stillbirth of >2.0 when compared with pregnant people without the condition," thus consistent with ACOG's Indications Opinion.

IVF is extremely expensive in the United States and inaccessible for many; overwhelming, it is white, wealthier couples using IVF. These women will also receive additional surveillance aimed at preventing stillbirth. Note that a Black woman's chance of stillbirth in the United States is also double that of a white woman (not because of race, but because of structural racism). Practice Bulletin 828, the one listing when additional surveillance is needed due to increased risk of stillbirth, admits this. But it does *not* recommend additional surveillance because of the heightened risk: "until further data are available on the effects of specific factors resulting from racism, recommendations regarding fetal surveillance cannot be made." The guideline instead suggests that doctors examine their "prejudices and biases." To summarize, the doubled chance of stillbirth due to IVF (used overwhelmingly by wealthy white women) necessitates additional surveillance, but not the doubled chance of stillbirth due to underlying racism.

The Indications Opinion also lists maternal age over 35 as a possible basis for additional surveillance, surveillance to be "individualized" "based on cumulative risk with other factors."[12] A separate Obstetric Care Consensus produced by ACOG and SMFM provides more information.[13] It clarifies that additional antenatal fetal surveillance to help prevent stillbirth is appropriate for maternal age over 40. Like with IVF, that separate Care Consensus explains that age over 40 has that double risk of stillbirth and thus should involve additional surveillance. But for maternal age of 35–59, "there is insufficient evidence to recommend routine antenatal fetal surveillance in the absence of other risk factors for stillbirth, and whether to offer surveillance to these individuals should be individualized."

Committee Opinion 828 details the indications for surveillance and Practice Bulletin 229 explains the surveillance techniques that could be used.[14] They include a maternal assessment of fetal movement (although doubting its usefulness, more on that follows), a contraction stress test (CST), which examines how the fetal heart rate responds to contractions; a nonstress test (NST), which tests whether the fetal heart rate accelerates with fetal movement; a biophysical profile (BPP), which is an NST and an ultrasound to examine fetal breathing, fetal movement, fetal tone, and amniotic fluid volume; a modified biophysical profile, which is an NST and an ultrasound to determine amniotic fluid volume; and an umbilical artery doppler velocimetry, which is an ultrasound that studies the blood flow in the umbilical artery.

Surveillance is recommended, but there are "no large clinical trials to guide the recommended frequency of antenatal fetal surveillance and, thus, the optimal frequency remains unknown." Weekly is suggested for most conditions, with more frequent testing reserved for the highest risk circumstances.

Both Guidelines 229 (indications for surveillance) and 828 (types of surveillance) are clear that best practices are unknown. Most recommendations are based on circumstantial and observational evidence. Randomized controlled trials for stillbirth are very difficult due to the low risk; ACOG explains that any test "would require randomizing tens of thousands of pregnant individuals," and likely closer to hundreds of thousands. Again, the risk of stillbirth is about 1 in 170. Randomized controlled trials would need to be extremely large to both capture the risk and demonstrate any reduction of that risk due to a prevention measure. Trials are much easier for specific higher-risk populations. But much less practical for the 1 in 170 lower-risk populations.

Still, ACOG suggests surveillance and explains it is widely used even though not "definitively demonstrated to improve perinatal outcome." ACOG is also clear that decisions need to be individualized and that its guidance "should not be construed as mandates or as all encompassing."

But again, this is for high-risk pregnancies. ACOG calls for increased surveillance when the risk of stillbirth is known (except for when the increased risk is due to racism). The safer baby bundles, on the other hand, are for *all* pregnancies.

The United States lacks any guidelines for stillbirth prevention in all pregnancies, but some of what's in the safer baby bundles can be found in ACOG guidelines. The following discussion compares the recommendations in the safer baby bundles versus ACOG guidelines. Again, the discussion is not comprehensive and instead focuses on specific measures with the greatest distinctions and overlaps: (1) maternal fetal movement monitoring, (2) going-to-sleep position, (3) smoking cessation, (4) fetal growth restriction detection, and 5) timing of birth considerations.

MATERNAL FETAL MOVEMENT MONITORING

Both England and Australia's safer baby bundles include a changed medical practice to teach pregnant people to monitor their baby's movement for any changes and to report any such changes to the care provider immediately. England's bundle explains that "enquiries into stillbirth have consistently described a relationship between episodes of RFM [reduced fetal movement] and stillbirth."[15] It cites numerous reports/studies that highlight "unrecognised or poorly managed episodes of RFM . . . as contributory factors to avoidable stillbirths" and studies that "have confirmed a correlation between episodes of RFM and stillbirth." The bundle also explains that "the relationship between RFM and stillbirth appears to be mediated by placental insufficiency." Australia's bundle similarly explains that "maternal perception of fetal movement has long been used as an indicator of fetal wellbeing and vitality."[16] Over two pages in the bundle are devoted to discussion of studies and literature about the benefits of raising awareness of both fetal movement and the dangers of reduced movement—and how that increased awareness led to decreases in stillbirths. Both bundles mandate education and discussion of the importance of monitoring fetal movement with pregnant people after 28 weeks. This includes providing prepared materials for women to take home.

ACOG agrees in its practice bulletins that "maternal perception of fetal movements is the oldest and most commonly used method to assess fetal well-being" and that decreased fetal movement (DFM) is associated with an increased risk of stillbirth.[17] But that is the extent of the agreement. In a different publication, ACOG notes that movement monitoring is inexpensive, but focuses on the uncertainty of the effectiveness noting that no consistent evidence shows it will reduce stillbirth in low-risk pregnancies. ACOG concludes that there "are insufficient data to make specific recommendations regarding fetal kick counts."[18]

In Practice Guideline 229, ACOG addresses some of the existing data—but not any of the studies that England and Australia's bundles cite in favor of education about fetal movement monitoring. Instead, ACOG cites two studies that found no difference in perinatal outcome depending on whether women were educated on monitoring fetal movement. ACOG also notes that most of the data for one of the studies came from a trial in England called the AFFIRM trial. The practice guideline explains that the AFFIRM trial showed an increase "by a small degree" of negative consequences: increased prenatal appointments and fetal evaluations and possible "increased risk of iatrogenic preterm birth, induction of labor, and cesarean birth." Also negating the use of monitoring according to ACOG is that "neither the optimal number of movements nor the ideal duration for counting movements has been defined."[19]

ACOG relies on the AFFIRM trial to doubt the effectiveness of movement monitoring, but both England and Australia specifically do not. They admit that the AFFIRM trial showed no significant reduction in stillbirths. But they also emphasize that the trial did show a decrease in babies with fetal growth restriction born after 40 weeks, which suggests that emphasis on movement "identified a population of high-risk babies with placental insufficiency who had a timely birth, thus preventing stillbirths that would have otherwise occurred."[20] Australia's bundle also notes that the AFFIRM trial "did not assess maternal awareness of DFM or clinical uptake of the intervention," leaving room for possible wide variety in clinician conduct and reasons to not rely on the trial.[21]

Both Australia and England also responded to the AFFIRM trial's suggestion of the increase in labor inductions and C-sections (but not increased prenatal visits like ACOG does). Again, Australia noted the lack of evaluation of the clinical uptake of the interventions and concluded that "data do not clearly indicate that raising awareness of DFM causes harm." Australia chooses to continue emphasis on movement and will monitor and collect data to evaluate.[22] England's baby bundle version three (2023 update) similarly acknowledges that same suggestion from the AFFIRM trial, but also notes other studies that showed initiatives increasing awareness of fetal movement that "were not associated with increases in caesarean births or induction of labour."[23]

In short, Australia and England both think the benefits of emphasizing maternal fetal movement monitoring outweighs any potential consequences (more on those interventions, especially induction, in the timing of birth discussion).

Despite ACOG's relative dismissal of the potential of monitoring fetal movement, one group in Iowa has been working on increasing awareness of the importance of monitoring fetal movement since 2008. Five stillbirth moms discovered research from Norway that teaching pregnant people to monitor fetal movement during the third trimester of pregnancy led to a 30% reduction in stillbirths. They formed Healthy Birth Day, Inc., a group dedicated to raising awareness, and developed a program called Count the Kicks. They've even now developed an app to help pregnant people keep track of movement—and more easily discover any changes in baby's movement. According to Count the Kicks, Iowa's stillbirth rate went down 32 percent in the first decade of its programming.[24] More recently, Iowa consistently maintains one of the lowest stillbirth rates in the nation.[25]

A study published in February 2023 looked specifically at Iowa's stillbirth rate versus the rates in neighboring states of Illinois, Minnesota, and Missouri.[26] The study found that "only Iowa demonstrated a clear decrease in stillbirths, which was statistically significant"—a decrease of its stillbirth rate by 1% every 3 months between 2005 and 2018. Except for smoking, risk factors for stillbirth like obesity, maternal age, and hypertension increased over the period that Iowa's stillbirth rate declined.[27] Ultimately, the study concluded "the stillbirth rate in Iowa is decreasing, where this is not true for the three states and for the USA as a whole"—and thus "lessons could be learned from Iowa."[28]

But ACOG seems uninterested in those lessons. I've previously suggested that resistance to maternal fetal movement monitoring may be based on medical paternalism—a worry that fetal movement monitoring would cause women unnecessary anxiety. This paternalism relies on stereotypes of pregnant women as hysterical and overly emotional, which I discuss more in chapter 5. That anxiety could turn into additional doctor's appointments, which could annoy doctors, especially if they are uncompensated for them as maternity care is generally one global payment that would not increase for additional visits. A study in Norway, however, showed no significant uptake in doctor's appointments due to anxiety about fetal movement; the increase was 0.2%.[29]

Any concerns about anxiety must also be balanced with concerns about self-blame after stillbirth. What about the woman who learns later that other countries believe monitoring fetal movement can help prevent stillbirth? She will find out—it only takes a few minutes on Google. What about this woman who now forever wonders if she could have saved her child had she paid better attention to his movement? It's unlikely any reassurances will be able to quell those haunting thoughts.

Some would counter that emphasis on monitoring fetal movement would cause self-blame. But this naively underestimates the extent of self-blame that already exists (discussed more in chapter 9). And England and Australia's baby bundles work to counter this possible self-blame consequence— with very clear language that monitoring fetal movement will *not* prevent all stillbirths. Pamphlets in both England and Australia explain that around half of women who experienced stillbirth did not notice any reduced fetal movement ahead of time. This language is reassuring post-stillbirth, messaging to women that it's not their fault. Plus, assuming the pregnant person does monitor fetal movement, education beforehand reassures a woman she did all she could, helping to alleviate self-blame. Education about the importance of fetal movement is more likely to alleviate self-blame rather than increase it.

It's also possible that the emphasis on medicalization of prenatal care and childbirth in the United States contributes to the resistance of fetal movement monitoring. A pregnant person's monitoring their baby's movement is not an impressive scientific or technological advance. It's done by the pregnant person; it returns power to the pregnant person as only the pregnant person can monitor fetal movement. That's inconsistent with the general medicalization of pregnancy care in the United States. Note also that pushes for medicalization in this country coincided with physicians replacing (ousting) midwives as the primary care providers during pregnancy and childbirth. In England and Australia, on the other hand, midwives remain the primary care providers for pregnancy and childbirth.

Monitoring fetal movement may not seem consistent with medicalization, but part of it is—medical assessments or interventions are needed if a pregnant person experiences decreased fetal movement. The first step is empowering the pregnant person to express concerns about reduced movement to her doctor.

Australia's baby bundle materials tell the pregnant person that changes in the baby's movement "may be a sign that they [the baby] are unwell."[30] The handout instructs pregnant people to not eat or drink something to attempt to stimulate movement as that "does not work." Instead, "contact your midwife or doctor immediately" if concerned and the materials emphasize "you are not wasting their time." England's leaflet similarly explains that a change in movement can indicate the baby is unwell and instructs women to call their health-care provider immediately as "midwives are available 24 hours a day 7 days a week."[31] It instructs "do not put off getting in touch with a midwife or your maternity unit" and to "not worry about phoning" as it is important to talk to a medical provider "even if you are uncertain" as the provider will "very likely" "want to see you straight away." The pamphlet also urges women to contact their medical provider again in case the decreased movement occurs again. It says plainly, "never hesitate to contact your midwife or the maternity unit for advice, no matter how many times this happens."[32]

ACOG obviously lacks any patient materials about fetal movement monitoring. But there is scattered language suggesting that women report any concerns. Practice Bulletin 229 states "although not all women need to perform a daily fetal movement assessment, if a woman notices a decrease in fetal activity, she should be encouraged to contact her health care provider, and further assessment should be performed."[33] There is also a question about fetal movement on ACOG's "Special Tests for Monitoring Fetal Well-Being Frequently Asked Questions" website. The answer to the question "what are fetal movement counts?" states "if you have felt fetal movement less often than what you think is normal, your health care professional may ask you to keep track of the fetus's movements. . . . There are different ways kick counts can be done. Your health care professional will tell you how often to do it and when to notify him or her."[34] This language essentially communicates that the obstetrician will tell the patient if and when she should express concerns about reduced movement (although it remains unclear how the woman would know to monitor in the first place).

Some women do report concerns. In the stillbirth community, stories abound of women having concerns but not wanting to bother their doctor, or of women being dismissed if they do express those concerns. Stories about dismissal abound in pregnancy care generally, especially for women of color. Numerous high-profile Black women have shared their experiences. Tennis star Serena Williams almost died after childbirth when doctors dismissed her concerns about blood clots.[35] Representative Cori Bush also shared her experiences when testifying before a Congressional committee.[36] When Bush was five months pregnant, she was sitting in her doctor's office that had a sign stating: "If you feel like something is wrong, something is wrong. Tell your doctor." Bush did. She told her doctor about her severe abdominal pain. He told her she was fine and sent her home. A week later, Bush went into labor and her son was born at 23 weeks gestation. Fortunately, he survived. Bush's doctor later apologized and promised to do better. In her next pregnancy, she went into preterm labor at 16 weeks. The doctor she saw told her that she would lose the baby—that she should go home, let her child "abort," and just get pregnant again "because that's what you people do."[37] Bush's regular doctor was called, the same one who had promised to do better, and he placed a cervical cerclage on Bush's uterus. Bush went on to have a successful pregnancy.

Studies confirm these anecdotes, including a 2022 study that examined the reproductive health experiences of Black women in the South.[38] The study found that "experiences of racism were evident across . . . a range of reproductive health services," including "prenatal care."[39] Numerous participants reported that medical professionals dismissed their concerns. One participant in the study explained that she had sought care for childbirth because she was overdue and felt something was wrong. She was told to go home, but her mother insisted that she be hooked up to a baby monitor. When the monitor showed a reduced fetal heartbeat, the medical providers finally agreed to provide her care. The participants in the study commonly used these phrases to describe their experiences: "lack of empathy, lack of rapport, hard-to-understand terminology, insufficient health information, loss of autonomy, and feeling undervalued or unwelcomed within the facilities."[40]

Dismissal of women based on obstetrical racism could help explain the continued racial disparity in Iowa's stillbirth rates. As mentioned, the Count the Kicks program has dramatically increased awareness of fetal movements in the state. And Iowa's stillbirth rate has gone down, but the racial disparity in Iowa remains dramatic. In 2018, the stillbirth rate for white women was 3.303 out of 1000 births; it was 10.32 out of 1000 births for Black women.[41]

ACOG's guidelines do, perhaps surprisingly, say how clinicians are to respond to concerns about decreased fetal movement. Practice Bulletin 229 states that "regardless of the fetal movement approach used, in the absence of a reassuring count, further fetal assessment is recommended." More specifically, "maternal reports of decreased fetal movement should be evaluated by an NST, CST, BPP, or modified BPP."[42] But then Committee Opinion 828 makes that surveillance permissible: "one-time antenatal fetal surveillance at the time the decreased movement is reported *may* be considered."[43] "Should" versus "may" just adds on to the other mixed messages about fetal movement monitoring—it doesn't work, may increase interventions, some women should do it, and maybe we want women expressing their concerns.

No mixed messages can be found in Australia's and England's bundles given the clear endorsement of maternal monitoring of fetal movement. Australia's baby bundle instructs clinicians of exactly how to evaluate reduced fetal movement.[44] The baby bundle includes steps of what test to do first (listen to fetal heart, obtain detailed fetal movement history, assess for any coexisting conditions and symptoms, and evaluate whether risk factors for stillbirth are present), and then next (an NST), and then, if needed, next (ultrasound). England's safer baby bundle similarly details how a clinician should respond to concerns regarding decreased fetal movement (listen to fetal heartbeat, assess fetal growth, NST, ultrasound).[45] Checklists like these can help alleviate the influences of conscious and unconscious biases. England's third version of its baby bundle also notes that care providers "should ensure whether inequalities (particularly relating to ethnicity and deprivation) are being adequately addressed when there are incidents relating to presentation with or management of RFM."[46]

In summary, both England and Australia conclude that the evidence shows that education about the importance of fetal movement monitoring will help reduce stillbirths. They also conclude that the benefits of movement monitoring outweigh possible consequences. ACOG, on the other hand, doubts the effectiveness and relies on the possible consequences to conclude otherwise.

GOING-TO-SLEEP POSITION

Australia's safer baby bundle also includes education of pregnant people on the importance of going to sleep on their side to reduce the risk of stillbirth.

It cites studies showing the association and determines that the going-to-sleep position is an "identified and modifiable risk factor for stillbirth."[47] Australia believes that these studies "indicate that 1 in 10 late pregnancy stillbirths could be prevented if all women in the last three months of pregnancy avoided going-to-sleep in the supine position." The bundle also explains the biological reason for the connection between the going-to-sleep position and stillbirth: lesser blood flow to uterus when falling asleep on the back. And thus, after 28 weeks of pregnancy, women should be told to "settle to sleep on either side for any episode of sleep" and the bundle recommends public health awareness campaigns on this prevention mechanism.

England's baby bundle also mentions the settling-to-sleep position within advice points for pregnancy. But it is not a distinct element of their bundle.[48]

ACOG's guidelines lack any information about settling-to-sleep position. There is an "Ask ACOG" entry on ACOG's website that says "as your belly grows, sleeping on your back may not be good for you. It puts the weight of your uterus on your spine and back muscles. In the second and third trimesters, lying on your back may compress a major blood vessel that takes blood to your uterus, making you feel dizzy and possibly reducing blood flow to your fetus." The entry concludes: "Sleeping on your side during the second and third trimesters may be best."[49]

If ACOG agrees to the possibility of reduced blood flow, why not recommend settling to sleep on one's side? One possible negative consequence is that women may become anxious if they wake up no longer on their side. But Australia's bundle tells clinicians to explain this is not something to worry about. "As the going-to-sleep position is the one held longest during the night, women should not worry if they wake up on their back, but should just roll back to sleeping on their side."[50] Refusing the prevention measure is not the only way to prevent anxiety; other solutions exist to help alleviate it.

And again, any concerns about increased anxiety must be balanced with likely self-blame after stillbirth. Think of the woman who learns later that going to sleep on her side may have saved her child's life. She will learn that. And then she'll live the rest of her life wondering whether she could have saved her child's life had she gone to sleep on her side.

SMOKING CESSATION

Both Australia and England's baby bundles are very clear about the association between smoking and increased risk of stillbirth. England's baby bundle states that "smoking increases the risk of pregnancy complications, such as stillbirth" (and preterm birth, miscarriage, low birthweight, and SIDS deaths).[51] Australia's baby bundle similarly declares that smoking during pregnancy is "one of the single most important avoidable causes of stillbirth and other serious adverse pregnancy and child outcomes."[52] It also notes that "disadvantaged women" are more likely to smoke during pregnancy. The bundle element also explains that smoking affects placental development by reducing blood flow, and that, conservatively, smoking during pregnancy increases the chances of stillbirth by 40%.

In England, clinicians are to offer carbon monoxide testing to pregnant women and to offer help, including immediate referral to a specialist and an appointment within 24 hours.[53] Clinicians are also to arrange in-house treatment from a trained tobacco dependence adviser and nicotine replacement therapy.[54] In Australia, the bundle explains that smoking is an addiction and that a combination of strategies is needed to help people stop, including carbon monoxide monitoring, behavior change counseling, and nicotine replacement therapy.[55] Specifically, the bundle cites studies showing that use of nicotine replacement therapy (gums, lozenges, mouth sprays, and patches) can help women quit and is safer for pregnancy than continuing smoking.

ACOG does have a practice bulletin for clinicians about the dangers of smoking in pregnancy. Stillbirth is (sort of) listed among the many increased risks: "orofacial clefts, fetal growth restriction, placenta previa, placental abruption, preterm labor, low birth weight, increased perinatal mortality, ectopic pregnancy, and decreased maternal thyroid function."[56] Perinatal mortality would include stillbirths after 28 weeks (and infant deaths up to 7 days).

ACOG Committee Opinion 828, one of the high-risk for stillbirth pregnancy guidelines, is more blatant about the connection between smoking and stillbirth.[57] It explains that smoking 1 to 9 cigarettes a day increases risk of stillbirth 9% above nonsmokers, and that smoking 10+ cigarettes per day increases the risk of stillbirth by 52%.

As for clinical recommendations, ACOG tells providers to "inquire about all types of tobacco or nicotine use," counseling techniques, and referral to a tobacco quit line if beneficial.[58] Unlike England and Australia, ACOG does not endorse the use of nicotine replacement products, noting that the evidence is insufficient whether the benefits outweigh the harms. It acknowledges that reviews have suggested these therapies increase the rates of smoking cessation during pregnancy, but that trials in the United States have been "stopped by data and safety monitoring committees because of either adverse pregnancy effects or failure to demonstrate effectiveness."

Australia's baby bundle also recommends risk-based additional monitoring near the end of pregnancy if the pregnant person smokes, specifically mentioning it as a factor to be considered in discussions regarding appropriate timing of birth.[59] ACOG does not. Despite the heightened risk of stillbirth, "there is insufficient evidence to recommend routine antenatal fetal surveillance" later in pregnancy "for pregnant patients who smoke cigarettes and e-cigarettes.[60] ACOG does, however, suggest such surveillance for fetal growth restriction, and smoking increases the risk of fetal growth restriction.

In short, ACOG guidelines, of course, also advise that clinicians inform women of the risks of smoking during pregnancy and help women with ideas on how to stop smoking. Stillbirth prevention is not the emphasis, but it could be the effect.

DETECTION OF FETAL GROWTH RESTRICTION

Both England and Australia clearly express the need to detect fetal growth restriction (FGR) during pregnancy to prevent stillbirth. England's baby bundle is very clear that "strong evidence links undiagnosed FGR to stillbirth," which is why "antenatal detection of growth restricted babies is vital" and can "reduce stillbirth risk significantly because it gives the option to consider timely delivery of the baby."[61] Both the second and third version of England's baby bundle emphasize the "vital" importance of detecting FGR such that the doctor and patient can consider "timely delivery of the baby at risk."

England's safer baby bundle has always included a "risk assessment and surveillance pathway" for detecting FGR and a management pathway when diagnosed (updated and revised twice after the initial bundle).[62] Doctors are to use the tool to determine if the patient is low or high risk and then surveil. If low risk, clinicians are to measure fundal height (which is a tape measure measuring the pregnant belly vertically) and plot those measurements on a chart. For increased risk, ultrasounds to assess growth are recommended starting at the third trimester (28 weeks). The bundle version two admits this will lead to more ultrasound scans, but "more frequent ultrasound scans and extending scans to term is associated with improved antenatal detection of FGR." Ultrasounds are suggested for every 3 weeks, and suggests the use of umbilical artery doppler between 18 and 23 weeks. In order to improve practices for the future, the element also requires the auditing of cases where FGR is not detected pre-birth.[63] Version three of the bundle also includes instructions for management of FGR diagnosed before 34 weeks of pregnancy and after 34 weeks.[64] Version three of England's baby bundle states that these tools have made a "measurable difference to antenatal detection of FGR across England."[65] A focus in version two of the bundle was to reduce interventions for those only marginally at risk, and version three maintains that focus on "introducing more nuanced risk assessment" to seek to "reduce intervention whilst maintaining the focus on delivering babies at risk"[66] (more on interventions in the timing of birth section).

Australia's bundle defines FGR as "a fetus that has not reached its growth potential" (to distinguish from a fetus that is small for gestational age, because not all fetuses that are small for gestational age are necessarily FGR).[67] Just like England's bundle, Australia's bundle notes that FGR is "an important risk factor," citing studies showing one in three term stillbirths "were related to abnormalities in fetal growth." And then the bundle explains that "reductions in adverse outcome associated with FGR have been shown with improved risk assessment and antenatal detection combined with careful management and timely birth."

As far as detection and surveillance, Australia's bundle has an extensive assessment tool called the FGR "care pathway."[68] The first level says to assess risk factors at each appointment, and cautions that more than 50% of FGR cases occur despite no risk factors. If lower risk, doctors should use fundal height and plot those measurements on a chart starting at 24–28 weeks visits. If higher risk or FGR is suspected based on fundal height measurements, clinicians should use ultrasound to monitor fetal growth. Uterine artery doppler should be used if available, and the frequency of ultrasounds should depend on the extent of risk factors. Ultrasounds should also be the surveillance mechanism if the patient is unsuitable for SFH measurements. For high risk, ultrasounds should be performed "2–4 weekly from 24 weeks until birth." Notably, Australia's baby bundle also states that one evaluation of decreased fetal movement should be an ultrasound for possible "undetected FGR."[69]

Australia's bundle also includes education, explaining it is "good practice to inform women about FGR at each antenatal visit (including their booking visit) and, where there is a diagnosis of FGR, ongoing communication throughout" is needed. Clinicians are to provide advice and support if any risk factors are modifiable.

ACOG Practice Bulletin 227 defines FGR as estimated fetal weight or stomach circumference at less than 10th percentile and agrees that FGR "is associated with a significantly increased risk of stillbirth, with the most severely affected fetuses being at greater risk."[70] The Bulletin also lists the risk factors—certain maternal disorders, substance use and abuse, maternal nutrition issues, multiple gestation, teratogen exposure, infectious diseases, and certain genetic and structural disorders. "All pregnant patients should be screened for risk factors for fetal growth restriction through a review of medical and obstetrical history."[71] And clinicians should do "fundal height measurements" at every visit after 24 weeks. The Bulletin also cautions that such measurements don't work as well in cases of maternal obesity, multiple pregnancy, or history of uterine fibroids.

As for surveillance after diagnosis, ACOG's FGR Practice Bulletin states that optimal levels of surveillance are unestablished. "Most growth-restricted fetuses can be adequately evaluated with serial ultrasonography every 3–4 weeks" and no more frequently than every 2 weeks because of inherent errors within measurements precluding interval growth.[72] ACOG also recommends use of an umbilical artery doppler in addition to the non-stress tests and/or biophysical profiles, but states to not start antenatal surveillance, meaning nonstress tests or biophysical profiles, until gestational age is late enough that "delivery would be considered for perinatal benefit." The high-risk surveillance guidelines, 828 and 229, also state additional surveillance is appropriate for fetal growth restriction.

FGR, like smoking cessation, seems to be an area with many overlaps between the safer baby bundles and ACOG/SMFM guidelines. But it does appear that the safer baby bundles have more detailed tools for detection of growth restriction (detection versus surveillance post diagnosis). And a study in the United States suggests that more could be done. That study was possible because of the differences in standard US prenatal care based on the pregnant person's age.

Remember that ACOG states that maternal age over 40 at time of delivery triggers the need for additional fetal surveillance, including additional ultrasounds, to help prevent stillbirth; the guidance is not about fetal growth restriction, but the surveillance techniques are the same. Over 40 should include additional surveillance, but decisions about additional surveillance for maternal ages 35–39 should be individualized. Many doctors do provide that additional surveillance if maternal age is 35–39. A study published in 2021 looked at that differing care for those who would turn 35 just before delivery and those who were just under 35 at delivery based on a national sample of 50,000 commercially insured pregnancies between 2008 and 2019. For those just under 35 versus those just over 35, there was little difference in the number of prenatal care visits and basic ultrasounds. But there were significant increases in "antepartum surveillance and detailed ultrasound scans, as well as increases in visits with MFM [maternal-fetal medicine] specialists and total ultrasound scans performed."[73]

The study also looked at whether those changes in prenatal care improved perinatal outcomes. And it did. Patients who were just over 35 at the time of delivery "were substantially less likely to experience a perinatal death" (fetal death after 28 weeks through infant death within 7 days of birth) than those just under 35 at the time of delivery. The results "suggest that changes in clinical behavior stemming from the [advanced maternal age] designation were associated with substantial improvements in perinatal survival." The study could not, however, point to the precise increases in medical care that made this difference. It did note, however, that the "prenatal services to monitor fetal growth and improve perinatal survival, including detailed ultrasound scans and antepartum surveillance, were the prenatal services with the largest increases at the AMA cutoff."[74]

Another element of Australia's safer baby bundle is "improving decision-making about the timing of birth for women with risk factors for stillbirth."[75] The element explains that the risk of stillbirth increases at term, from 0.11 per 1000 births at 37 weeks to 3.18 stillbirths per 1000 births at 42 weeks. There are obviously "no reliable screening tests to identify all babies at risk of stillbirth" and thus prenatal "care of women based on the presence of risk factors, followed by appropriate timing of birth, is the mainstay of management to reduce preventable stillbirths." The bundle element then lists the increased risks of stillbirth: over 35 years old, smoking late in pregnancy, overweight/obese, use of artificial reproductive technology, alcohol/drug use, prior stillbirth, social disadvantage, and certain races and/or ethnicities. The bundle tells clinicians to reassess the patient's stillbirth risk at 34 weeks and to document that assessment. If risk exists, clinicians are to perform additional surveillance. And the risk factors and results of surveillance can inform educated decisions on the timing of birth.

Australia's bundle is very clear, however, that any benefits of earlier induction need to be weighed against the risks, as "there are significant associated morbidities for the baby born too early," including "increased short- and longer-term mortality and morbidity and worse developmental outcomes" for babies born at 34–36 weeks and those born at 37–38 weeks.[76] Thus, the approach must be individualized. Clinicians are to provide women "with individualised information based on risk assessment to support informed, shared decision-making on timing of birth." An individualized approach based on risk factors is the best way of "increasing early birth only when there are appropriate indications." The bundle also mandates the collection of data on how many inductions or elective C-sections happen before 39 weeks and the number of babies admitted to NICU if born after 36 weeks.[77]

England's bundle doesn't have an element devoted to timing of birth. But it does discuss timing of birth within both the fetal growth restriction and reduced fetal movement elements. In the fetal growth restriction element, England's baby bundle is very clear at the possible benefits of delivery at 37 weeks: "as antepartum stillbirth is the major single cause of perinatal death at term, earlier delivery will prevent perinatal death."[78] The "dilemma" with early delivery though is that it "reduces the risk of a very rare but serious adverse event (stillbirth or neonatal death) while increasing the risk of much more common but less severe adverse events." The bundle explains the difficulty of balancing "the risks of causing mild harm to relatively large number of infants in order to prevent serious harm to a relatively small number." To make this more explicit, the bundle explains that "at 37 weeks, 10 inductions will lead to one additional baby being admitted for neonatal care but it will require more than 700 inductions to prevent each perinatal death." And thus, early induction should be used only when the risk of still-birth is increased. The bundle element notes "there is a range of expert opinions on some interventions" and it provides "some flexibility in the choice of pathways."

In the reduced fetal movement element, England's bundle discourages, but leaves open, the possibility of early induction. If the pregnancy is after 38 weeks and 6 days, the doctor should "discuss induction of labor with all women and offer delivery to women with *recurrent* RFM after 38+6 weeks [38 weeks and 6 days]."[79] In cases of recurrent RFM, the doctor is to also advise the woman of the increased risk of stillbirth and given the option of induction. But "prior to 39 weeks' gestation, induction of labour or operative delivery is associated with small increases in perinatal morbidity and neurodevelopmental delay. Thus a recommendation for delivery needs to be individualised and based upon evidence of fetal compromise . . . or other concerns."

There's a long history of debate regarding timing of birth in the US. ACOG has advised against (not medically indicated) induction of labor before 39 weeks since at least 1982 because induced labor before 39 weeks increases the risks of respiratory and digestive problems, hypoglycemia, and other disabilities.[80] It also increases the chances the baby will need to spend time in the Neonatal Intensive Care Unit.

Despite ACOG guidance, the rate of inductions before 39 weeks rose between the 1980s and 2005 and did not start to go back down again until 2009.[81] It was often suggested that the reason for the increase was (selfish) women requesting early induction for convenience, trying to schedule birth like they do a hair appointment. But doctors obviously also went along with it. Some doctors also benefit from inductions—creating more stability in their schedules (although that can be negated by increased length of labor)

Standards of Care and Malpractice

and possible financial benefit if the doctor's practice is arranged such that the doctor must deliver their own patients to receive full reimbursement of fees.[82]

There's also some suggestion that doctors may also have been more open to early inductions after ACOG declared in 1989 that women should be induced by 42 weeks because of the risk of stillbirth due to decreased placental function and reduced amniotic fluid.[83] In her important work on the C-section epidemic in the United States, Theresa Morris suggested that the fear of medical malpractice liability for stillbirth "drives the practice of inducing women earlier and earlier."[84] Yet her discussion assumes induction after 40 weeks, meaning past the due date—not inductions before 39 weeks. But there could be a connection.

The increase in early inductions gained the attention of ACOG and others, including the March of Dimes, which started its own campaign against early inductions around 2011 consistent with its focus on preventing premature birth.[85] A *New York Times* article about the March of Dimes campaign explained that "well-educated women" were more inclined to schedule birth based on convenience, that doctors may do the same, and that "sometimes doctors, fearing a malpractice suit if something should go wrong if a pregnancy proceeds to term, choose to deliver babies when they are alive and well."[86] The campaign was called "Healthy babies are worth the wait"—emphasizing that the best place for the baby to develop is in the womb. Sidenote that this idea can be painful for stillbirth parents to hear. Caleb was in that supposed safest place. Under the theory that I had an abruption, had my fully developed baby boy been *anywhere* else than inside of me, he wouldn't have died. My supposedly safest place for Caleb, my body, was also the scene of his death.

In 2009, ACOG issued another practice bulletin to reaffirm the 39-week rule.[87] In 2013, ACOG redefined "term" to differentiate early term (37–38 weeks), full term (39–40 weeks), and late term (41 weeks).[88] These new definitions reinforced that 37 and 38 weeks isn't "term" in the same way as 39 weeks, further dissuading induction of labor before 39 weeks.

In a 2013 committee opinion, ACOG again expressed concern at the increase in "nonmedically indicated" deliveries at 37 and 38 weeks. It explained the possible health consequences of early-term delivery, including respiratory issues and admission to NICUs. But it was very clear that

Standards of Care and Malpractice

these consequences of early-term delivery "need to be balanced against the ongoing risk of stillbirth from week to week in early-term pregnancy."[89] It's not as if ACOG had previously recommended early delivery if stillbirth risk was increased for whatever reason, but still there was some concern that reducing the ability to induce before 39 weeks could affect term stillbirths. ACOG thus expressed the need for more research regarding pregnancies at increased risk for "in utero morbidity and mortality." ACOG mentioned specific concern that one state's Medicaid program had stopped reimbursement for not medically needed deliveries before 39 weeks and how this could limit provider's options.

In 2019, ACOG released another committee opinion discussing the 39-week rule and stillbirths. It concluded that efforts to reduce early-term births "have not adversely affected stillbirth rates nationally or even in states with the greater reductions in early elective delivery."[90] The Opinion noted that two studies reported an increase in stillbirth rates at 37 and 38 weeks "although the overall risk was small." And then it counters that "other studies with considerably larger sample sizes and population-based data have shown either a decrease in stillbirth or no statistically significant change, and no association with increasing gestational age at term and stillbirth." The opinion then specifically discussed looking at birth and fetal death data and the fact that when early-term deliveries went down, the early-term and later stillbirth rates did not increase.

Except there was an increase. The 2015 study by Sarah Little and others,[91] which ACOG cites, states that the 2005 rate of stillbirth at term was 123/1000 births and the 2011 rate was 130/1000 births. It's not a statistically significant increase, and other factors could explain it like increases in diabetes, but it is an increase. The Little study also looked at state data and found no statistically significant increase in the states with the highest decrease in early-term births, which is encouraging that the 39-week rule is not affecting all term stillbirths. It did find a significant increase in stillbirths for women with diabetes but determined it unrelated to the decrease in early-term births. The Little study looked only at overall stillbirth rates as opposed to week-specific stillbirth rates.

The other study ACOG cites, a 2015 study by Marian MacDorman and others, looked at week-specific stillbirth statistics.[92] In the Committee Opinion,

ACOG describes that this study found that "the stillbirth rate across preterm and term gestational ages remained unchanged" despite the decreases in early-term births. But the MacDorman 2015 study was a little more complicated. Comparing 2006 and 2012 data, the study found a 15–16% increase in stillbirth rates at 34–36, 37, and 38 weeks. But the study determined the increases were due to the decrease in births in those weeks, which made the denominator in calculated stillbirth risk lower—thus increasing the rate. Instead of the math used to determine the traditional stillbirth rate (the number of stillbirths in a gestational week divided by the number of live births and stillbirths during that week, which is then multiplied by 1000), it used a different calculation for the "prospective stillbirth rate." That calculation is the number of stillbirths in a gestational week divided by the number of live births and stillbirths during that week or later. The study found no "statistically significant differences" in the prospective rate at any gestational age. The study describes the prospective rate as a better predictor of actual stillbirth risk in a week because it compares the number of stillbirths to the number of pregnancies. That may be true. It's also concerning, however, that the study that looked at stillbirths specific to gestational weeks used a different methodology to conclude the 39-week rule did not affect term stillbirths.

But even assuming no increase in the stillbirth risk, it's not as if all of the deliveries before 39 weeks that the 39-week rule now prevents were about stillbirth risks. It's not as if all the babies induced before 39 weeks would have been stillborn had they not been induced early. But that's not the same as showing that a stillborn baby would have been stillborn anyway even if early delivery had been available.

The 39-week rule has developed much more force than that of an ACOG guideline. Formal quality measures exist for hospitals, usually used for accreditation purposes or as part of legal requirements to obtain Medicare reimbursement. One accreditation standard set by the Joint Commission in 2009 is the number of "elective" deliveries before 39 weeks that occur at the hospital (elective meaning not ACOG-defined medically indicated).[93] The Joint Commission believes that the number of elective deliveries before 39 weeks indicates poorer quality of care at the hospital. Hospitals, thus, commonly now prohibit any "elective" labor inductions before 39 weeks because of the risk of losing Medicare reimbursement. (Also, the number of stillbirths occurring at the hospital is not a Joint Commission formal quality measure. One would think the number of stillbirths occurring at a hospital, especially those during labor, would be relevant to the quality of care at the hospital. But no.)

Hospital prohibitions reinforce the 39-week rule, as do insurance payment policies—or really nonpayment policies. A 2011 Texas law prohibited Medicaid coverage for not medically necessary deliveries before 39 weeks. Other states did the same shortly after.[94] In South Carolina, both Medicaid and Blue Cross Blue Shield implemented a nonpayment policy for not medically necessary deliveries before 39 weeks.[95] Not surprisingly, the resulting decrease in "elective" early deliveries in the Medicaid population was more dramatic than in the privately insured population.

The 39-week rule is for not medically indicated deliveries—leaving the question then, when is induction before 39 weeks medically necessary? In 2021, ACOG released Committee Opinion 831 clarifying these medically necessary instances.[96] The Opinion includes a page and a half of listed medical conditions and the proper timing of birth (one as early as 30 weeks and some as late as 39 weeks). For instance, delivery is allowed at 38 weeks for FGR if estimated fetal weight is between the 3rd and 10th percentile, and at 37 weeks if under 3%. Delivery is also allowed before 39 weeks for hypertensive disorders and prepregnancy diabetes with complications. Other conditions include uncomplicated multiple gestations (ranging from 32 to 38 weeks and 6 days); complicated multiple gestations (ranging from 32 to 36 weeks and 7 days); diabetes, pregestational and gestational (39 weeks); HIV (38 and 39 weeks depending on viral load). ACOG also notes that its timing recommendations are based on "expert consensus and relevant observational studies" and that "decisions regarding timing of delivery always should be individualized to the needs of the patient."[97]

Separately, the high-risk additional surveillance practice bulletins note that, if past 37 weeks, consideration of delivery may be appropriate if results of fetal assessment tests are not reassuring. More specifically, ACOG Practice Bulletin 229 notes that a BPP score of 6 out of 10 "should prompt further evaluation" and/or "consideration of delivery" even if before 39 weeks (but after 37 weeks).[98] But those tests would only be performed if surveillance is medically indicated in the first place.

This Committee Opinion 831 regarding medical indications for induction before 39 weeks does not mention stillbirth. Some of the indications are conditions that increase the risk of stillbirth. But the word doesn't appear; there's no mention that the risk of stillbirth is the risk that makes pre-39-week induction medically appropriate. There's no explanation that early-term delivery for fetal growth restriction is due to the increased risk of stillbirth. There is only vague language that the doctor should "balance the maternal and newborn risks of late-preterm and early-term delivery with the risks of further continuation of the pregnancy."[99] ACOG is quick to explicitly spell out the risks of inducing early, but not the risks of continuing the pregnancy in these situations.

Note that ACOG's list of conditions allowing delivery before 39 weeks is very different than the Australia evaluation of risk factors. Those listed risk factors were not medical conditions necessarily. Some were, but others were social and demographic factors like age, social disadvantage, and race/ethnicity. ACOG's pre-39-week guidelines do not contemplate the possibility of induction due to social demographic factors even though it does admit that those factors increase the risk of stillbirth.

ACOG's maternal age Care Consensus does recognize the propriety of early childbirth due to increased risk of stillbirth due to age.[100] But early is 39 weeks pregnant and the age is over 40. "The rate of stillbirth at 39 weeks of gestation in women aged 40 years and older is nearly the same as the rate of stillbirth for women aged 25–29 years who are beyond 41 weeks of gestation." And thus, if maternal age is over 40, delivery at 39 weeks or later "should be considered in the absence of additional maternal or fetal co-morbidities." ACOG does not make the same recommendation for those with maternal ages 35–39 because the chances of stillbirth at 39 weeks are not as high as for those over 40. Yet ACOG does note that induction at 39 weeks generally has not been shown to increase "adverse neonatal outcomes" in low risk pregnancies.

None of England, Australia, or the United States want any more babies born before 39 weeks than medically necessary. But England and Australia do expressly acknowledge that earlier delivery could prevent some still-births. ACOG does not. ACOG instead explains that since stillbirth rates remained steady when early deliveries decreased, early deliveries are not needed to help prevent stillbirth.

Moreover, doctors in England and Australia also have more wiggle room for early induction because of broader recognition and awareness of various increased risks of stillbirth due to demographics. Even if US doctors had more flexibility, they would be limited by the effect of accreditation standards and payment prohibitions. The doctor may want to induce early, but the hospital won't allow it. The doctor may want to induce early, but then the delivery will not be paid for by Medicaid (and the patient likely lacks the means to pay). There are other coercive forces affecting the doctor's plan of action.

England and Australia's bundles specifically recognize that "early" delivery can sometimes be appropriate. The widespread and very successful campaign against "early" deliveries in the United States has created a disapproving connotation, no different than the connotations for "elective" and "on demand" in C-section and abortion discussions. These negative connotations make it difficult for the medical procedure to ever be appropriate— even when the doctor thinks so and the patient agrees.

SMALL PLACENTAS

One stillbirth prevention strategy that is perhaps slowly gaining steam, but is not standard of care in the United States or anywhere else, focuses on the placenta. The placenta rarely gets any attention, but it is the baby's source for everything in the womb—oxygen, nutrients, everything. A placenta that can't keep up or is deteriorating can't support the baby; a crude analogy is a gas tank that's running out of gas. This is the same reason ACOG recommends induction of labor at 42 weeks—because the placenta can no longer support the baby.

A 2023 study looked at about 1,250 previously explained pregnancy losses, ranging from 6-week miscarriages to stillbirths at 43 weeks.[101] Miscarriage losses were 70% of that total and the other 30% were stillbirths. The study determined that one-third of the previously unexplained stillbirths were associated with a small placenta, meaning placentas weighing below the 10th percentile for gestational age. In fact, the study found a "significant proportion of extremely small placentas weighing less than the 1st percentile for their gestational age."

Ann O'Neill's son could have been in that study. He was stillborn on his due date in 2018. Elijah was 3,997 grams (8.8 pounds), over the 81st percentile.[102] But his placenta was only 397 grams, about the 3rd percentile. Elijah's autopsy report noted that the placenta was small "despite" Elijah's large size. The pathologist noted the "possibility" that there was a mix-up and that the 397-gram placenta wasn't actually Elijah's. It was; O'Neill had genetic testing done to confirm so. It makes a lot of sense that Elijah died because his placenta couldn't support him any longer.

Dr. Harvey J. Kliman, MD, PhD—a research scientist in Obstetrics, Gynecology, and Reproductive Sciences and the director of the Reproductive and Placental Research Unit at Yale's School of Medicine—is one of the authors of the 2023 study. He believes that many stillbirths are due to small placentas.[103] The study explained that the finding of one-third of the pregnancy losses being associated with a small placenta was "of clinical utility, as prenatal identification of a small placenta may reveal important growth discordance between the fetus and its primary supporting organ."

But then the question remains—how do we detect small placentas *before* the baby dies? Fortunately, researchers are working on this. Possibilities might include ultrasound or magnetic resonance imaging.[104]

Dr. Kliman invented something called the estimated placental volume (EPV) to estimate the size of the placenta in utero.[105] The doctor takes certain measurements of the placenta during an ultrasound. The doctor can then put those measurements into an app that calculates the volume of the placenta. The test is simple, taking less than a minute, costing nothing and easily done within an already routine ultrasound. Some doctors have started doing EPV routinely. A group of stillbirth parents have formed a group called "Measure the Placenta" to raise awareness of measurement via EPV.[106]

A case study involving EPV was also published in late 2023.[107] The patient was a 28-year-old woman with her first pregnancy. Her pregnancy was normal except for failing the initial one-hour gestational diabetes test, but passing the more intensive three-hour test. The patient reported decreased fetal movement at 32 weeks. Nonstress test and ultrasound were performed. All was normal, but the EPV showed a very small placenta—less than 0.1 percentile for gestational age. Dr. Heather Florescue ordered another growth scan in two weeks due to the EPV. The next ultrasound and EPV showed a placenta at the 0.7 percentile. The ultrasound at 37 weeks showed a decrease in fetal weight from the 65th percentile to the 38th percentile in just two weeks, and EPV was again down to less than 0.1 percentile. At 38 weeks, oli-gohydramnios (decreased amniotic fluid) was diagnosed but the NST was still normal as it had been throughout. The patient was admitted for induction due to the amniotic fluid. Labor did not progress and the doctor eventually did a C-section. The baby was 5 pounds, 14 ounces, in the 12th percentile; the placenta weight was in the 0.14th percentile. Mom and baby were fine.

The case study criticizes the utility of nonstress tests, "the most widely used assessment of fetal wellbeing." To quote the authors: "NST fails as a screening test. When NST is normal, there is no trigger for further testing and stillbirths occur; in our clinical experience, many women who experience stillbirth had a normal NST within a day or two prior to their loss. The false-negative rate of NST ranges from 0.2% to 0.8%, almost perfectly overlapping with the national fetal death rate of 0.2–0.3%." In this case study, NSTs were "normal throughout the pregnancy" and "low EPV was the only factor that prompted more frequent follow-up. Without these EPV measurements, the inadequate fetal growth and oligohydramnios might have gone undetected, potentially leading to stillbirth." More plainly, "EPV was crucial to preventing stillbirth in this scenario."

But no method of placental measurement is clinically validated, and obviously not accepted practice. Another hurdle is that adoption of any measurement requires more openness to "early" delivery and thus revisions to the 39-week rule. The 2023 study of unexplained pregnancy losses suggested that EPV could "provide clinicians with additional data and tools to . . . help determine when to deliver." Similarly, the study explained that "although not currently clinically validated, the identification of a fetus with a small placenta, when balanced with other clinical risk factors, may support an earlier delivery to potentially prevent antenatal stillbirth." Without a revision, the doctor would be stuck: what if the placenta measures consistently low from 32 weeks to 37 weeks, what does the doctor do? Violate the 39-week rule and risk malpractice if the baby is injured due to the early delivery?

Again, no one wants any more inductions before 39 weeks than are necessary to prevent stillbirths. But we should be open to, if not want, inductions before 39 weeks that are necessary. Placental measurement is yet another potential tool that doctors could have at their disposal, but don't. Hopefully studies to clinically validate methods of placental measurement are on the horizon.

MEDICAL MALPRACTICE?

This chapter thus far has described many medical practices that other countries have implemented to attempt to reduce stillbirth—practices that are not part of prenatal care in the United States. Many may react to these descriptions and immediately think "malpractice!" If US doctors aren't doing everything possible, including measures adopted in other countries, that must be malpractice.

Fears about tort liability, in fact, were one of the motivations for England's Safer Baby Bundle. An investigation at Furness General Hospital revealed avoidable maternal deaths, stillbirths, and neonatal deaths.[108] Just five months later, the government announced its intent to cut those rates in half by 2030. Of course, health care in England is government-run, which also means that it's the government paying damages if doctors commit malpractice.[109] In that way, possible malpractice liability directly regulates medical practices. In short though, England's National Health Service was worried about liability for stillbirth so it adopted its safer baby bundle specifically to better help prevent stillbirth.

But back to the United States—it's incorrect to assume that failing to perform stillbirth measures is malpractice. It's likely not. This is because the elements of the safer baby bundle are not part of the standard of care in the United States.

To back up, a medical malpractice claim is part of the tort law system in the United States, through which an injured person can sue the person who injured them. A medical malpractice claim is one against a doctor for inadequate care that injured the plaintiff. It could be a surgeon who leaves a sponge in the patient causing infection. Or it could be a doctor who misdiagnoses a patient's condition and does a total knee replacement, eventually necessitating amputation. The patient can sue the doctor for damages based on the plaintiff's injury.

Theoretically, potential malpractice liability should motivate a doctor to provide the best possible care. The possibility of a malpractice lawsuit should motivate doctors to act as carefully as possible. And, in the United States, "a fear of liability is deeply rooted in the culture of the medical profession," especially for obstetricians/gynecologists, who are sued more than other doctors.[110]

But there's a big but. Medical malpractice (medmal) law in the United States is heavily deferential to the set standard of care. Liability is only possible if the plaintiff shows that the doctor breached (violated) the standard of care. The standard of care is what a reasonable doctor, exercising the level of skill and knowledge common to the profession, would have done under similar circumstances. So if a patient presents with symptoms X, Y, and Z, what do doctors typically do (consistent with the level of skill and knowledge common to the profession)? That is the accepted practice. If the doctor did the accepted practice, the doctor didn't breach the standard of care and can't be liable.

Doctors set the accepted practice; doctors decide what to do with patient symptoms X, Y, and Z. It makes sense; doctors, nor juries, are best equipped to determine the appropriate medical treatment. More specific to the stillbirth context, ACOG and SMFM set the accepted practices. And tort law defers to that doctor-set accepted practice. A plaintiff cannot show that the doctor breached the standard of care if the doctor complied with the doctor-set accepted practice. Legal scholars have criticized this deference (more on that follows), but it's how tort law works.

This deference has stark effects for stillbirth prevention efforts. As discussed, the current US accepted practice doesn't include educating pregnant patients about the concerns surrounding reduced fetal movement. By not doing these prevention measures, a doctor in the United States is complying with the accepted practice. And complying with the accepted practice means the doctor won't be liable for malpractice even though the baby was stillborn. Moreover, if the doctor deviates from accepted practice—say, by inducing labor at 37 weeks due to concerns about stillbirth—and the baby is born alive but injured, the doctor *will* be liable for malpractice for the deviation if sued.

Add those two together and you see that tort law *disincentivizes* additional stillbirth prevention. Plainly, the doctor won't be liable if the baby is stillborn if the doctor followed current accepted practice. And the doctor will be liable if she deviates from the accepted practice in an attempt to prevent stillbirth and the baby is born alive but injured.

Do note that tort law's deference to doctor-set standards would also apply if ACOG were to change the accepted practice and integrate stillbirth prevention measures. If ACOG guidance stated to educate pregnant people on the need to monitor fetal movement, a doctor wouldn't be liable for medmal if he did so. The doctor wouldn't be liable for medmal for complying with the new standard of care, even if the baby was injured.

Doctors are hopefully morally incentivized to better assess for fetal growth restriction or advise women to sleep on their side, consistent with the safer baby bundles. But they aren't tort-law legally incentivized. Doctors need not worry about legal liability for stillbirth as long as they follow the US standard of care. And the US standard of care is not aimed at stillbirth prevention, at least when compared to the existing safer baby bundles.

GOING FORWARD AND POTENTIAL TORT REFORMS

Tort law, despite its mystical power, is not currently equipped to force changes to the standard of care. And, we don't have government-provided health care that could mandate the implementation of a saving babies lives bundle. There's nothing in the United States that can (or will) force ACOG to adopt a safer baby bundle.

But some reforms are possible even without changes to ACOG guidelines. For instance, the 39-week rule need not be a part of hospital accreditation standards nor a part of Medicaid reimbursement rules. Removal of these outside forces and hurdles would better enable a doctor to work within the limited discretion provided by ACOG guidelines.

There are also two potential reforms to tort law that may not motivate a change to the standard of care but could still aid stillbirth prevention efforts. Those changes are (1) shifting to the reasonable doctor standard of care instead of the accepted practice, and (2) allowing the doctor a defense based on the pregnant person's consent.

This first change, shifting to a reasonable doctor standard not determined by the accepted practice, is already underway, although moving very slowly. As described, tort law is extremely deferential to the doctor-set accepted practice. It's important to know, though, that tort law does not do this in other areas. Most law students learn the *T.J. Hooper* case, in which a barge on a tugboat was damaged because the operators of the tugboat did not have a radio on board to be alerted of impending bad weather.[111] The custom among tugboat operators at the time was to not have a radio on board. Judge Learned Hand was quick to explain that custom does not dictate reasonable conduct—just because it was customary to not have a radio on board does not mean it is reasonable to not do so. He then ultimately found the lack of a radio on board to be unreasonable because radios are inexpensive and would help prevent extensive property damage. Note how the finding disregards what was customary in the industry.

A distinction exists between deferring to the tugboat industry versus doctors. Jurors can do the cost-benefit analysis of keeping radios on tugboats; they can't really do the same with medical procedures (nor do we necessarily want them to).

But arguments similar to *T.J. Hooper* have worked in some medical malpractice cases. *Helling v. Carey* is a relatively famous tort case in which the eye doctor didn't do a simple test on the patient because she was younger than 40 and the accepted practice was to do this test on patients over age 40.[112] The jury found the doctor not liable, consistent with his compliance with the "universal" accepted practice. The Washington Supreme Court reversed, finding the doctor liable because the test was simple and inexpensive, and it would have saved the plaintiff from permanent visual damage.

Helling is one example of jurisdictional movement "to a *reasonable practice standard* that allows the jury to consider evidence that a custom is no longer reasonable or acceptable."[113] In 2001, the Wisconsin Supreme Court similarly explained "if what passes for customary or usual care lags behind developments in medical science, such care might be negligent, despite its customary nature."[114] Deference is very much still the more common rule, but some jurisdictions are moving to a less deferential standard.

Helling reminds me of EPV, the test to measure the volume of the placenta. EPV is similarly simple, inexpensive, and easy to do (although admittedly not currently clinically validated). Despite the required deference to the accepted practice (which doesn't include any kind of placental measurement), I can see a jury determining that the doctor should have done an EPV because it's so simple, especially if the stillbirth occurred close to 39 weeks

Standards of Care and Malpractice

to minimize issues with the 39-week rule. Juries would be even more inclined to find liability in an EPV case later in pregnancy if the standard for breach was the more flexible "reasonable doctor" or "reasonable practice" standards.

A reasonable doctor standard enables continued deference but also wiggle room for juries. Doctors wouldn't be able to avoid liability for stillbirth just by saying, "I did the accepted practice." A reasonable doctor standard would better motivate interest in stillbirth prevention.

A second change to tort law that could help save babies from stillbirth is empowering the patient's informed consent. Suppose the pregnant person expressed numerous concerns about reduced fetal movement and the doctor recommended inducing at 37 weeks to prevent stillbirth. And suppose that the pregnant person understands the risks of inducing at 37 weeks, risks like increased chance of respiratory illness, accepts those risks, and believes that the chances of avoiding stillbirth outweigh the risks. Suppose the baby is born alive but has a chronic lung condition due to the early induction.

As already discussed, if the parent sues the doctor for the early induction, the doctor will almost certainly be liable. Even if the doctor performed the labor induction perfectly, the doctor violated ACOG's guidelines as ACOG does not recognize reduced fetal movement as a reason to induce before 39 weeks.

The pregnant patient's informed consent—understanding the risks of respiratory illness and agreement to assume them, technically known as assumption of the risk—is *not* a defense to medical malpractice.[115] As the DC Court of Appeals explained, "the superior knowledge of the doctor with his expertise in medical matters and the generally limited ability of the patient to ascertain the existence of certain risks and dangers that inhere in certain medical treatments, negates the crucial elements of the defense, *i.e.* knowledge and appreciation of the risk."[116] This law—that a patient cannot assume the risks of medical malpractice—reeks of paternalism, suggesting that a patient needs protection from medical malpractice even when they make an informed decision consenting to the procedure. But it is the law.

Scholars have written that the law precluding a knowledge-based defense to malpractice isn't nearly as broad as it seems.[117] While courts are very unlikely to enforce broad language like the patient "waives all claims for medical malpractice," courts have allowed the defense in more narrow circumstances. Two prominent examples are patients' consent to experimental or alternative therapies, and patients' consent to surgery without use of blood products due to religious concerns.[118] Professor Nadia Sawicki suggests that one reason courts have been inclined to recognize the defense in these two factual circumstances is that these patients in these circumstances are more informed.

ACOG did something similar in 2020. In 2020, ACOG and SMFM released an updated "Management of Stillbirth" Obstetric Care Consensus allowing labor induction before 39 weeks in cases involving prior stillbirth.[119] But it depends on informed consent. The guideline explains that despite the increased infant health risks of delivery before 39 weeks, "maternal anxiety with a history of stillbirth should be considered and may warrant an early-term delivery" after 37 weeks "in women who are educated regarding, and accept, the associated neonatal risks." In short, induction after 37 weeks is okay if the pregnant person gives informed consent.

This is tricky legally, however. Is ACOG changing the accepted practice— allowing induction at 37 weeks with informed consent? The law typically sees informed consent as separate from the accepted practice. The more likely interpretation is that the accepted practice is still inducing at 39 weeks, but allowing informed consent to override the deviation from the accepted practice. If so, that may not hold up legally; informed assumption of the risk is generally not a defense to medical malpractice.

And courts tend to get a little confused about "informed consent" when we're talking about pregnant people. For instance, a (selfish and/or emotional) pregnant woman may want a vaginal birth, but the doctor wants to do a C-section (supposedly) to protect the fetus.[120] This is especially common in cases where the pregnant person has previously had a C-section and wants vaginal birth after C-section (known as a VBAC) in the next pregnancy. The woman understands the risks of a VBAC and still wants it. Yet, the doctor goes to court to get a court order enabling the doctor to do a C-section, overriding the pregnant person's informed consent to a VBAC.

Said more plainly, tort law almost presumes that a patient can never know and understand the risks of a procedure to the same extent as the doctor. And this differential of knowledge is even stronger within pregnancy and childbirth as doctors have painted themselves as the experts for decades. I would expect courts to evaluate closely whether the pregnant person really understood the risk. Conscious and unconscious biases could affect both whether a doctor believes a pregnant person is even capable of this understanding and whether a court determines a pregnant person had the understanding.[121] This may discourage a doctor from pursuing this type of informed consent from marginalized pregnant persons. Informed consent can't be available only for privileged patients. Informed consent is not a solution, but it is a good step forward in the context of stillbirth prevention.

* * * *

Although I'm optimistic that these changes could help, I also need to be honest about my cynicism.

Doctors seem to benefit most from the fatalism and inevitability surrounding stillbirth. The less we know about stillbirth, the less doctors and medical practices (or lack thereof) seem to be a possible cause. Even though changing medical practices wouldn't create more liability for doctors, changing the accepted practice to include stillbirth prevention starts a potential conversation of how medical practices can affect stillbirth. Maybe some doctors would just rather not have that conversation at all.

At the same time, medicalization has made doctors the experts on pregnancy and childbirth. That's frustrating. You shouldn't be able to both claim expertise and then shrug when a baby is stillborn. In my next pregnancy, I complained to my high-risk doctor that term stillbirth still happens in 2017 in the United States, the most developed nation in the world. He looked at me and said, "we still don't even know why childbirth starts." It was honest and refreshing.

We know so much, but we also know so little. It's time to rethink the things we think we know, things like whether changing medical practices can help prevent stillbirths.

FOUR

Valuing Stillborn Babies

While my husband and I were thinking about whether our on-call doctor acted negligently, I knew that under Texas law the most we (actually just me) would be able to recover in damages in a lawsuit against that doctor was $250,000. That is a lot of money, but it also isn't. Really, at that limit, it would have been incredibly difficult to find an attorney willing to take our case. A plaintiff's attorney gets paid around one-third of the damages recovered. Stillbirth cases just really aren't worth it monetarily for plaintiffs' attorneys, when they know they'll be paid $83,000 at most.

I've talked to so many stillbirth parents who do possibly have valid medical malpractice lawsuits but can't find an attorney willing to take their case. Tort law has the power to raise awareness and spark change. (I don't necessarily think it's the most efficient way to do so, but the way our systems are set up in the United States, it's one of the only ways). But stillbirth just isn't worth enough money in tort to even provoke lawsuits.

* * * *

The last chapter described how tort law's deference to the accepted practice disincentives doctors from acting to prevent stillbirth. Another part of tort law also disincentivizes stillbirth prevention—the damage measurements. In a 1977 California Supreme Court case, Justice Tobriner described stillbirth as a "wholly intangible injury . . . for which any monetary recovery can provide no real compensation."[1] Well yes, but the same could be said for many injuries, including the death of a living child. And just because compensation is difficult doesn't mean we shouldn't try. Curiously, just nine years earlier, Justice Tobriner authored a famous opinion allowing a mother to recover damages for her emotional distress at observing her child killed by a negligent driver, another seemingly wholly intangible injury that can never be compensated. More on that case later.

Fortunately, no court agrees with Justice Tobriner about stillbirth being not fit for compensation. But that doesn't mean we necessarily award significant damages. The types of damages available for stillbirth differ according to the legal claim available. Currently, two types of claims exist.[2] Each state recognizes one of these types of claims.

The first is the birthing parent's traditional tort claim, like a negligence claim against a speeding driver or a medical malpractice against a doctor. This is the traditional claim, but only a few states still use it now. The damages for this negligence claim are limited to the emotional distress accompanying the stillbirth.

The second claim is a wrongful death claim. The vast majority of states allow (both) parents a wrongful death claim to tortiously caused stillbirth. The damages for this wrongful death claim are limited to compensation for the lost parent-child relationship.

And damages can be further limited for either claim if the state has a law limiting the recovery of damages, called a damage cap. Damage caps were very popular with state legislatures in the 1980s and 1990s. They usually cap only the "noneconomic" damages and thus have the harshest effect in cases like for stillbirth where the significant damages are for emotional trauma.

Put bluntly, the damages for stillbirth aren't that expensive, especially when compared to the damages for a long-term injury to a baby born alive. And the relative inexpensiveness of stillbirth hurts the ability to use tort law to motivate changes in medical practices.

NEGLIGENCE AND EMOTIONAL INJURY

The birthing parent's traditional tort claim originates from English courts and is called a common law claim. This claim allows the birthing parent to sue and recover damages for any injuries they suffer. But what injury does the pregnant/birthing person suffer?

The stereotypical first cases involving stillbirth were claims brought by women alleging that tortious conduct caused them to lose their pregnancies. The pregnancy loss was their only injury. Obviously, something physical happens with that pregnancy loss, ranging from bleeding in early pregnancy to childbirth in later pregnancy, childbirth including labor with contractions and the delivery of the baby, the size of which will depend on the length of the pregnancy.[3] But the judges decided that that these women had not suffered a physical injury. Instead, their only injury was emotional distress; the stillbirth was merely a manifestation of that emotional distress.

It's hard to know why judges chose the "emotional" injury classification. Maybe it was (male) judges' views of "hysterical" women wanting damages for a seeming noninjury. Maybe judges dismissed stillbirth as just a women's issue, not a real injury.[4] Maybe judges viewed pregnancy loss as just something that women have to go through, no different than how we commonly dismiss complaints about pain in childbirth even still today. Or, maybe judges dismissed possible causal links, reverting to the idea that pregnancy losses were a natural thing and inevitable regardless of the tortious conduct. Stillbirths were much more common in the early 1900s than they are today, and public knowledge of the frequency of pregnancy loss was also much higher. They were also automatically lesser experiences compared to the then still relatively high infant and child mortality rates.[5]

Regardless of why, courts' classification of pregnancy loss as an emotional injury is hugely consequential. Tort law treats injuries differently depending on their type—physical injury and property damage are well-accepted, but emotional injuries are more suspect.

The hesitation means that courts allowed claims for pure emotional distress in only limited circumstances. The first circumstance and test was the impact rule, requiring the plaintiff to have been physically impacted in some way, although not physically harmed.[6] The second test was the zone of danger test, requiring that the plaintiff had been within the immediate area of physical danger from the tortious conduct.[7] The third test is from a California Supreme Court opinion authored by Justice Matthew Tobriner called *Dillon v. Legg*.[8] It allows recovery for emotional distress caused by observing a family member being injured by a tortfeasor if the plaintiff contemporaneously observes that injury, is near the scene of the accident and injury, and a close family relationship exists between the plaintiff and that family member. The *Dillon* case itself involved a mother who saw her daughter killed by a negligent tortfeasor.

These tests make it difficult to recover damages if tortious conduct caused your child's stillbirth. One dramatic example of this is a 1977 California Supreme Court case *Justus v. Atchison*.[9] The baby's stillbirth happened in labor with both the mother and father present. The father wanted to also sue for damages for his child's death. The Court said no because of the restrictive emotional-distress case rules. Although he was present for his child's stillbirth, he did not actually witness the death given that it occurred in the womb.[10] Also, the father voluntarily stayed during labor, apparently negating his right to recover damages.[11] The California Supreme Court has walked back this holding a bit, lightening the analysis about voluntary presence.[12] But it's otherwise still applicable law. It is very difficult for a non-birthing parent to bring a claim for tortiously caused stillbirth in California.

New York courts made it difficult for even the birthing parent to bring a claim until this century. Until 2004, New York required a birthing parent to show a physical injury "distinct from that suffered by the fetus and not a normal incident to childbirth" before they could recover any damages for emotional distress.[13] The rule was intended to limit recovery for damages in cases of emotional distress, instead requiring some physical injury before the plaintiff could recover damages. The extra requirement was an affirmation that "tort liability is not a panacea capable of redressing every substantial wrong." It took until the twenty-first century for New York courts to finally stop requiring this extra hurdle to allow birthing parents to recover damages for tortiously-caused stillbirth.

If the parent can surpass these obstacles and establish negligence, they can recover damages for their emotional distress due to their child's stillbirth.[14] But even this is complicated. The birthing parent can recover damages for the "mental anguish . . . resulting from . . . the loss of a fetus as part of the woman's body." But they cannot recover damages for "the loss of a fetus as an individual."[15] That's a quote from a Texas court explaining Texas law.

This idea of damages appropriately recognizes that stillbirth happens in the pregnant person's body, and it includes emotional distress damages due to the trauma of birthing your stillborn baby. But it treats the fetus as a body part. No different than the emotional distress one would suffer if they lost an arm or a leg. (Again yes, this is Texas law.) Notably, this limitation on damages means no damages are recoverable for the death of a child or the lost parent-child relationship. Those would be damages based on the loss of the fetus as an individual and those are not allowed under this common law standard.

This limitation does not necessarily mean that juries would award only low damage awards for traditional negligence claims. But the limitation does craft how juries would think about what amount to award—not as a death of a child, but instead as bodily injury.

WRONGFUL DEATH AND LOSS OF RELATIONSHIP

Different damages are available if the state recognizes a wrongful death claim for tortiously caused stillbirth, which the overwhelming majority of states do. Most of these states limit the wrongful death claim to stillbirths after viability, so after 24 weeks (more on that in chapter 7). Regardless, the recoverable damages include damages for the lost parent-child relationship. But to understand the damages, a history lesson is needed.

The previously described negligence or medical malpractice claims are court-created common law claims. Under the common law, there was no tort claim for death. A person who died obviously couldn't bring a lawsuit (because they're dead). And no one else, family members or whoever, could sue over that person's death either.[16] This created a twisted incentive. If you wanted to commit a tort, it was best to kill the person instead of injure them.

That obviously makes no sense. Starting in the mid 1850s, state legislatures stepped in to alter the common law through statute. State legislatures created a claim for the dead person, known as "survivorship" causes of action. These claims allow the estate of the dead person to sue the tortfeasor for damages the dead person suffered *before* death, like medical expenses incurred for the injury before the eventual death. State legislatures also passed "wrongful death" statutes.[17] These laws allow a family member to sue the tortfeasor for killing the dead family member. The lawsuit is technically under the statute, but still requires the plaintiff to show that the tortfeasor committed a tort (still defined by the common law). A wrongful death claim against a defendant for tortiously causing a child's death still requires the parent to show the defendant committed a tort.

Originally, the only recoverable damages for wrongful death were "pecuniary."[18] Pecuniary means economic damages—the economic contributions that the deceased family member would have contributed to the home. The main idea behind wrongful death law in the 1850s was to enable a family member to sue the tortfeasor for the economic contributions that the deceased family member would have continued to contribute to the household had he lived.[19] The stereotypical (and sexist) idea of a wrongful death claim is for a stay-at-home mom to be able to sue if her husband is tortiously killed. She has no income and is certainly in a rough spot economically if her husband dies. This is the situation that the wrongful death claim is ideally situated to help.

But child death also fit well within the pecuniary damage limitation. As mentioned, state legislatures started passing these laws in the mid-1800s. This was very much the time of child labor, which remained prevalent until the early 1900s. When a child was killed, the parents suffered a loss of expected economic contributions.[20] Child labor was prevalent as was infant and child death. Childhood, especially infancy, was simply a time of death.[21] Parents expected at least one of their children to not survive. Some historians have suggested that parents were even indifferent to their child's death because of the expectation.[22] Indifferent or not, parents expected at least one of their children to die.

Finally, in the early 1900s, child labor started to decline. Also at this time, society started to realize that child and infant death was not inevitable—that it could be prevented.[23] (Cough, cough, stillbirth.) Sociologist Vivian Zelizer points to these two changes as evidence of the changing valuation of children—from economic to sentimental.[24]

Those societal changes prompted changes to wrongful death damages also. Eventually, legislatures and courts recognized the value of the familial relationship and started to also allow damages for the relationship lost when the family member was tortiously killed. These are called loss of consortium damages.[25] Some state courts added these damages by creatively interpreting "pecuniary" in wrongful death statutes to include loss of consortium damages. Other state legislatures specifically amended their wrongful death statutes to allow recovery of loss of consortium damages.[26]

Loss of consortium damages are available for wrongful death, but damages for general emotional distress—damages unrelated to the death of the fetus as an individual—usually are not. Note that the mother in *Dillon*, the famous California case in which a mother observed her daughter's tortiously caused death, had a wrongful death claim for her damages due to the lost parent-child relationship. But the mother also filed a common law negligence claim because she could not recover damages for her emotional distress due to observing her daughter's death under the wrongful death claim.[27] And the California Supreme Court agreed with her that this common law negligence claim should exist.

It wasn't long after the creation of wrongful death statutes that courts started wondering aloud whether wrongful death law should also apply to stillbirths. In 1916, the Wisconsin Supreme Court did so. But widespread application of wrongful death law to viable stillbirths didn't start until the 1950s (more on that in chapter 7). The viability limitation meant wrongful death law could apply to stillbirths after 24 weeks, but not to those that occur between 20 and 23 weeks. Generally, no survivorship claim exists for stillbirth though. The dead fetus has no legal rights. The parents do have a right, however, a right in the form of a tort claim for the wrongful death of their unborn child and will be able to recover damages for the lost parent-child relationship.

Some may think that no relationship is lost in stillbirth—that any real parent-child relationship doesn't exist until after birth. Decades of research on prenatal attachment disputes this. Regardless, with any infant or young child death, most of the lost relationship is expected—what would have been. In the context of child death, Professor Joellen Lind elegantly explains that lost relationship—the parent never getting to "read books to her, or teach her how to ride a bicycle."[28] "These activities would have generated ongoing, occurrent emotions, ideas, perceptions, and other experiences for both parties."[29] She also describes that being a parent is "one of the most important roles we play in life" that "can define in large part who we are."[30] It's hard to differentiate how this lost relationship is any different depending on whether the baby dies shortly before or after birth.

Even though lost relationship damages are available, the damages for the wrongful deaths of children (stillborn or living) are lower than one would think. Specifically, wrongful death damages for the death of a child are almost always much lower than wrongful death damages for the death of an adult.[31] That is because of the existence of pecuniary economic damages. A case involving the wrongful death of an adult with financial dependents, a spouse or children, will involve damages for both loss of consortium *and* lost economic contributions.

But both types of damages are not available for the wrongful death of a child (again, stillborn or living). Pecuniary damages are legally available, but practically nonexistent as children no longer contribute financially to parents like they did in the mid-1800s. And thus, the only damages that can be recovered for the wrongful death of a child will be for lost relationship. The practical lack of any economic damages immediately reduces the overall size of damage awards for wrongful death of children claims—and makes them smaller than damage awards for the wrongful deaths of adults.

JURIES, DAMAGE AMOUNTS, AND BIAS

To summarize this unnecessarily complicated legal setup for damages for stillbirth, states recognize either (1) the birthing parent's negligence claims for emotional distress damages (not including the loss of the fetus as an individual), or (2) the parents' wrongful death claims for loss of consortium damages (not including general emotional distress damages).

Courts will instruct juries on these damage limitations. It's unclear whether the average juror could appreciate these distinctions. Even if the juror wanted to follow the court's instructions to award damages for the plaintiff's emotional distress, but not for the loss of the fetus as an individual, how does one do that? Judges in Texas have specifically made this criticism.[32] The ever-present abortion debate in our country should also make it more difficult for the jury to specifically not think of the fetus as an individual and not award damages for emotional distress due to the loss of the fetus. But ultimately, the jury will choose a damages amount and we'll never know why it chose the number it did (because we never know anything about jury deliberations). We'll never know if the jury did consider the fetus as an individual when it awarded damages for emotional distress. Instead, we presume that the jury followed the court's instructions. And courts are very unlikely to change whatever damages amount that the jury awarded.

What will the jury look to as they decide the damage number? A Louisiana judge suggested these factors for considering the amount of damages the parents suffered for the wrongful death of their stillborn child:

> 1. the stage of pregnancy at which the stillbirth occurs; 2. the medical history of the mother with respect to previous childbirths; 3. the number of children the couple presently has; 4. whether the mother used artificial means to induce pregnancy, i.e., fertility drugs; 5. the probability of pregnancy going to full term; 6. any prior history of miscarriage; 7. prenatal care of the stillborn child; 8. parental preparation for the forthcoming child, i.e., house additions, baby crib and any other indicia of the degree of expectation exuded by the parents.[33]

These factors seem intuitive, but, as Dov Fox and I have argued, their effect can be confusing and invite considerations of racial and class biases.

The first factor, the stage of the pregnancy and the timing of the stillbirth does seem like it should matter. This factor also relates to factor five as the probability of the pregnancy ending in live childbirth increases as the pregnancy progresses; note however that factor five erroneously assumes that the pregnancy progressing to term means live childbirth. Regardless, pregnancy-loss research confirms that timing can matter for grief and that grief is likely greater the later in the pregnancy that the stillbirth occurs.[34] At the same time, that research always cautions that people experience pregnancy loss differently and thus the gestational age of the stillborn baby is not determinative.[35]

The second and sixth factors—the medical history with respect to previous childbirths and any prior history of miscarriage (assumedly the judge meant prior history of any pregnancy loss)—also seem logically relevant. But again, we must be careful how we evaluate them. If the plaintiff has had prior miscarriages or stillbirths, does that increase or decrease the damages? In reality, prior losses can mean less grief for the most recent one. Pregnancy-loss research shows that women are likely to seek to protect themselves emotionally by not getting too attached in a next pregnancy.[36] So practically, a subsequent loss may mean less emotional distress and damages should be lower, but that is because the loss for this stillbirth is subjectively lower, not because of some sort of objective "this is her second stillbirth so we should lower the damages." Moreover, realize that Black women and poor women are statistically more likely to have that history of miscarriage and/or stillbirth. So if the effect of prior pregnancy loss is to decrease damages, this will disproportionately affect Black women and poor women.[37]

What about the third factor—number of (assumedly living) children the couple already has? The fact of other living children does not magically erase the pain of stillbirth. Parents may become more grateful for their living children, so maybe it makes stillbirth easier. Or, maybe those other living children also mean having to explain death to those children at a very early age, so perhaps it makes things more difficult. More broadly, this factor could again encourage bias based on race and class. That bias is on full display in a Maryland case, *Robinson v. Cutchin*.[38] Robinson is a Black woman whose doctor sterilized her within the C-section delivery of her sixth child. The court explained that her inability "to have a seventh child after previously giving birth to six children is hardly something which would offend her reasonable sense of personal dignity," including three children who had been born out of wedlock. It's highly unlikely the judge would have said the same of an upper-class white wife and husband who had been planning to have a seventh child.

The same problems exist with the possibility of additional children born after the stillbirth. Historically, this was seen as the best way to get over stillbirth—just focus on getting pregnant again. As mentioned, medical care involved taking the baby away such that the mother could better focus on that next pregnancy. Fortunately, I only once was told the dreaded "you can have another" after Caleb's death, but many others hear that sentiment much more.[39] A new pregnancy persists as the solution for pregnancy loss generally with the "rainbow baby" phenomenon, meaning the next baby is the rainbow after the prior storm of pregnancy loss.[40] It is a divisive phenomenon, however, and I personally resent the sentiment. Brandon is a blessing, but Caleb was not a storm. He was and is my son.

This sentiment of replaceability is especially strong with marginalized women due to racist breeder and Welfare Queen stereotypes. As mentioned in chapter 3, Representative Cori Bush shared her story that a doctor told her to go home, let her child "abort," and just get pregnant again "because that's what you people do."

Assumedly, the replaceability sentiment would persuade juries to reduce the damages for stillbirth. The New Jersey Supreme Court specifically mentioned a subsequent pregnancy within its decision to reduce a damage award for stillbirth.[41] A defendant argued before the Virginia Supreme Court that a mother was not really injured by her son's stillbirth because she later gave birth to twin girls.[42]

Legal rules prohibiting ideas of replaceability exist in claims for the death of a spouse. In those claims, the jury is not allowed to hear that the spouse remarried.[43] A marriage to a new spouse does not magically erase the experience of a spouse dying; there is no replacement spouse. And it's not enough to tell the jury to not consider the remarriage. Because of the possibility that the jury will consider it improperly, courts exclude evidence of the remarriage, meaning the jury will never learn that the plaintiff remarried.

But no such rule exists for deceased children—even though jury misuse of a subsequent child is possibly more likely than misuse of a new spouse. Some courts, however, have seen the parallel between "replacement" children and a "replacement" spouse. Specifically, a Louisiana court discussed the possible prejudicial effect of evidence of subsequent children and specifically held that later children are "not mitigating factors."[44] This should be well-accepted by all courts. And the evidence should be excluded, meaning the jury will not even know about a later pregnancy, to preclude its prejudicial effect.

None of this is to say that the inability to have another child is not some sort of distinct injury (although it really shouldn't be within the lost relationship damages). But the flip side can't be that having a subsequent child magically fixes everything.[45]

The fourth factor the Louisiana judge mentioned was whether the mother used fertility drugs or other reproductive technology to get pregnant. Relatedly, studies have shown "a significantly increased risk of stillbirth" when IVF is used to get pregnant.[46] Regardless, what is the effect on damages if the plaintiff had used fertility treatment? The safe assumption is that the judge thinks it should increase the damages—that the use of something like IVF shows how badly the plaintiff wanted to have a baby, which must mean even greater damages for emotional distress or lost relationship.

But does it? It shows a greater economic investment for sure, but that's just because the person who got pregnant easily didn't need to use something like IVF. Plus, it's important to consider who is using IVF. IVF is really expensive. Reproductive-justice advocates have already identified the cost of reproductive technologies as a barrier to poor women's right to have a child.[47] Anyone getting additional damages for stillbirth in a pregnancy started with IVF is likely to be wealthy and white.[48] This also sets up a contrast then between the white wealthy woman using IVF and desperate to have a child versus the "breeder" and "Welfare Queen" marginalized women who can easily get pregnant—tapping into stereotypes about wealthy and likely white "good" parents versus hyper-fertile "bad" poor mothers and "bad" mothers of color.

The Louisiana judge's last factor about "parental preparation" also possibly invites similar biases, specifically "classist ideas about deserving parents."[49] The good parents "prepare for the arrival of their baby by buying organic clothes, fancy strollers, and building extravagant nurseries." The good parents are the wealthy parents who have the money to buy the organic clothes and fancy strollers. The amount parents spend on raising (living) children is based not on love, but on how much money the parents have.[50] The extent of parental preparation could easily be much more about parental income than it is about expectations or emotional investment.

Focusing on parental preparation could also invite cultural biases. In some cultures, not preparing is required. In a 2022 essay, Rae Hoffman Jager described her difficulty combining Jewish customs with her son Fox's stillbirth at 32 weeks.[51] She explained that they had done everything "right" from a Jewish perspective—including making no announcement, no baby shower, no preparing of the nursery. She explained that "in Jewish culture, one does not celebrate something *before* it happens in the event that something bad—the evil eye—might cause it to not manifest." Did she and her husband expect Fox to be born alive any less than any other person at 32 weeks? No.

The prenatal care of the stillborn child factor—the seventh factor—can also too easily tap into class biases. Does extensive prenatal care show more emotional investment in the pregnancy? Or does it just reflect income and access?[52] Not everyone has equal access to prenatal care as access depends on health insurance. People with lower socioeconomic status can obtain health insurance through Medicaid. And, in fact, Medicaid covers about half of all births in the United States.[53] Prior to passage of the Affordable Care Act, poor women could only access Medicaid after becoming pregnant, which often resulted in delayed prenatal care.[54] The Affordable Care Act included Medicaid expansion, but the Supreme Court made that expansion not mandatory.[55] Some states have expanded Medicaid, enabling more people to be eligible before they get pregnant. But not all states have, meaning delays in accessing prenatal care continue if pregnant people are unable to sign up until pregnancy.

Texas is one of those states refusing to expand Medicaid coverage under the ACA, meaning pregnant people cannot sign up for Medicaid until pregnant. A 2019 ProPublica investigation found that about 21% of all women who give birth in Texas don't get prenatal care until the second trimester, and another 10% don't start until the third trimester or never do so.[56] The reasons for this? One often does not even realize pregnancy until around six weeks (or later), and that's already the middle of the first trimester since the weeks of pregnancy start at the last period, before actual pregnancy. Then, the application is long and any even small error can delay things. And if the delay is too long, many doctors refuse to see a patient beyond a certain week of pregnancy, maybe as early as 20 weeks. Plus, not all doctors treat Medicaid-insured pregnant people because Medicaid does not reimburse as much as private insurance. Some doctors cap the total number of Medicaid patients they will see. And there's not always an option of another provider. A lack of prenatal care very well may reflect poverty and a lack of access more so than a lack of emotional investment in the pregnancy.[57]

One last thing. The Louisiana judge describes that the extent of preparation indicates the "degree of expectations" the parents had. The same is true for other factors like the timing of the stillbirth, the medical history (as a prior stillbirth increases the chances of another), and the probability of the pregnancy progressing to full term (which, again, inaccurately assumes progression to term means live childbirth). Many legal rules are based on expectations, but there's two types—the subjective expectation, meaning the parent's actual expectation, and the reasonable expectation. And the parent's subjective expectations aren't always reasonable. It's possible that a

Valuing Stillborn Babies

pregnant person has a nursery ready at only eight weeks pregnant, expecting their child will be born alive at the end of pregnancy. Eight weeks, however, is very much still within the window of possible miscarriage before 12 weeks. There's a wide chasm between parents' expectations and medical probabilities. Parental expectations are fueled by the extensive misinformation in our country regarding the unlikelihood of pregnancy loss, by the silence surrounding pregnancy loss, the medicalization of pregnancy and childbirth, and the abortion debate's single-path narrative that all pregnancies end in abortion or with the birth of a living child.[58] All those factors make the parent's expectation of live birth even early in pregnancy seem more reasonable even though inaccurate. It's unclear how to reconcile subjective versus reasonable expectations within damage awards.

This Louisiana judge's attempt to clarify factors that should be relevant to determining the amount of damages for stillbirth is admirable. And many of the factors seem intuitive. But we need to be aware of the possible infiltration of racial and class biases, and to think about how to mitigate those biases. Solutions might include jury instructions specific to these biases, or just a focus on more diversity in juries. But we need something. And that something must also mitigate the effects of assumptions that the white, wealthy parents are more deserving.

DAMAGE CAPS

Courts are likely to be very deferential to whatever damage amount the jury determines, but one thing can and will affect that jury-chosen amount—noneconomic damage caps. Damage caps and the division of economic versus noneconomic damages is newer to tort law; both are products of the tort reform movement that started in the 1970s and 1980s. According to the newer distinction, economic damages are the economically verifiable and "objective" damages like medical expenses and lost wages. These damages are verifiable because a bill or wages verify the amount. Amounts of noneconomic damages, on the other hand, are not verifiable. They are damages like pain and suffering, emotional distress, and lost relationship. Noneconomic damages are supposedly less predictable and objective, and more arbitrary and subject to jury whims.[59] The damages for stillbirth, whether it be for a negligence or wrongful death claim, are (likely) all noneconomic.

This tort reform movement claimed that damage verdicts were out of control and especially hurting doctors. Republicans don't tend to like tort lawsuits, especially not against doctors. (Unless it's to authorize anyone, anywhere, to sue a doctor for performing an abortion or providing gender-affirming care to trans kids.) Numerous state legislatures were convinced that tort verdicts were driving up the price of medical malpractice insurance premiums, causing doctors to either stop practicing medicine or move to a different state where premiums would be lower. To prevent this, many state legislatures passed caps on the recovery of noneconomic damages. Recovery of economic damages, on the other hand, remained unlimited. Over 20 states currently have a noneconomic damage cap in medmal claims.[60]

Numerous feminist legal scholars have criticized caps on noneconomic damages, arguing that they disproportionately affect women's damage recoveries in tort. Injuries likely to cause extensive noneconomic damages and minimal economic damages occur disproportionately to women. They include hostile-work-environment sexual harassment, sexual assault, and reproductive harms.[61] Moreover, women are less likely to recover as much as men in economic damages because of the use of gender-based earning tables—statistical tables of what women have historically earned, which is less than what men have historically earned.[62]

Caps on noneconomic damages have dramatic effects in stillbirth cases, and really in any case involving the death of children. The reason is obvious—any economic damages are likely minimal, and the main damage is noneconomic. But the recovery of noneconomic damages is capped, often at $250,000, and that amount is usually not tied to inflation.[63]

As discussed earlier, wrongful adult-deaths cause both economic and noneconomic damages, whereas wrongful child-deaths cause only noneconomic damages. Adding a cap on those noneconomic damages makes the damages recoverable for wrongful child-death even lower. A few states inexplicably have higher caps for wrongful-death-of-adult damages than for wrongful-death-of-children damages. New Hampshire law limits noneconomic damages to $150,000 for the death of a spouse and $50,000 for the death of a child.[64] Tennessee's noneconomic damage cap for wrongful-death claims is $750,000, but increases to $1 million in wrongful-death-of-a-parent cases.[65] These caps makes little sense. Noneconomic damage caps should be higher for wrongful-death-of-children cases because there's no economic damages to recover. Economic damages will be available for the wrongful death of an adult, and they won't be capped.

Also remember that most noneconomic damage caps apply only to medical malpractice claims and not to other legal claims. This sets up a strange situation where recovery for stillbirth due to medical malpractice has damages limited to $250,000, but damages are unlimited if the stillbirth is due to negligent driving. So the doctor whose job it is to safely deliver the baby will pay only capped noneconomic damages. But the texting driver who didn't even know that the person was pregnant will pay unlimited noneconomic damages.

Texas, where Caleb was born, has a unique combination of laws on tort-caused stillbirth and tort reform damage caps. The "pro-life" Texas legislature amended its wrongful death statute in order to specifically apply that law to stillbirths. The law provides a wrongful death cause of action for the death of an individual and defines "individual" as including "an unborn child at every stage of gestation from fertilization until birth."[66] But there's an exception. Texas's wrongful death law does not apply to the death of an "unborn child" if the death is due to "a lawful medical or health care practice or procedure of the physician or the health care provider."[67] So Texas's wrongful death law applies to stillbirths due to tortious conduct by anyone other than a doctor. Said another way, in Texas, a stillbirth is a death of a person and addressed under wrongful death law. But *not* if the stillbirth is due to medical malpractice. If due to medmal, then stillbirth is just an injury to the pregnant person, no different than an injury to their arm.

More concretely, had Caleb died due to a car accident, my husband and I could have sued the tortfeasor for wrongful death and recovered our full noneconomic damages for the lost relationship with our son. But if Caleb died due to medical malpractice, I (and only me) would be limited to a medmal claim specifically not allowing me to recover damages for my emotional distress based on Caleb as an individual. And my damages could be capped at $250,000.

The lack of a wrongful death claim against a doctor for stillbirth also matters for another reason regarding noneconomic damages. Texas has a $250,000 noneconomic damage cap for medmal causing nonfatal injury, but it has a different damage cap if the medmal causes death. Texas law imposes a $500,000 damage cap on damages (all noneconomic and some economic) for wrongful death due to medmal.[68] That amount is also tied to inflation. As of January 2023, the number of damages recoverable would exceed $2 million. If Texas law applied wrongful death law to medmal-caused stillbirths, parents would be able to recover over $2 million dollars. But it doesn't. Medmal-caused stillbirth in Texas is only a medmal/negligence claim, which is subject to the $250,000 cap.

These aren't just coincidences. Both sets of laws were passed in 2002. The same legislature (1) amended Texas's wrongful death law to apply it to stillbirths, (2) denied the wrongful death claim for stillbirths if due to medmal, and (3) passed the $250,000 caps on noneconomic damages in medmal claims.

Ultimately, the tort reform push overwhelmed the antiabortion push in these Texas laws. Stillbirth is the death of a person if due to a car accident, but not if due to medmal. The (supposed) need to protect doctors was more important than protecting fetal life. Texas legislators were perfectly okay with a higher cap on noneconomic damages for wrongful death (of living people) claims based on medmal; apparently that would not hurt doctors too much. But they denied the wrongful death claim for doctor-caused stillbirth, meaning the $250,000 cap applies.

Importantly, noneconomic damage caps do much more than reduce damages. They also make it difficult, if not impossible, to find an attorney willing to take the case and file the lawsuit in the first place. The lawyer knows that at most $250,000 in damages will be recovered, and the lawyer knows that there will be expert witness expenses. Even if the case is solid, an attorney would be wary to file a lawsuit because it is not economically worth it.[69] It's important to remember that damage caps don't just mean lesser damages, they also mean fewer lawsuits filed.

Tort law is one of the very few methods of redress available after injury in this country. It's also one of the few methods that exist to incentivize certain doctor conduct. But tort law can't do anything if no attorney will take the case.

DEAD BABIES VERSUS DAMAGED BABIES

In her fantastic review of the malpractice system in the United States, Louise Marie Roth interviewed numerous doctors about medical malpractice insurance. One of those doctors told her, "A dead baby doesn't pay as much as a damaged baby, so they [medmal insurers] don't want a damaged baby because that pays out the most."[70]

That doctor is right. Damages for stillbirth (and infant death) are for emotional distress or damages for lost relationship—noneconomic damages, which might be capped. Damages for an injured baby, on the other hand, include economic damages, and possibly a lot of them. Damages could include the cost of medical care for the rest of the child's life, the child's lost economic capacity (for work when they'd be old enough), in addition to the parent's emotional distress and possibly even still lost relationship damages. Damages for a "damaged" baby could be very, very significant.

This disparity in damages also relates to incentives related to the 39-week rule discussed in chapter 3. Compliance with that rule and refusal to induce labor before 39 weeks protects a doctor from liability for medmal. Violating that rule and inducing labor at 37 weeks, on the other hand, is a huge liability risk. The measure of damages in each possible situation creates the same incentives. Refusal to induce labor before 39 weeks may result in stillbirth, but the damages are likely not that significant. Inducing labor at 37 weeks may save the child from stillbirth but could easily cause a respiratory illness and possibly a long-term one, which could create significant economic damages in tort. Any doctor should be much more afraid of damages for respiratory illness than for stillbirth, which is the same perverse incentive wrongful death law was originally created to correct.

I refuse to believe that any doctor evaluates what treatment to do because of possible tort damages—that a doctor would choose treatment allowing the baby to be stillborn because it would be (much) cheaper than if the baby were injured and born alive. I refuse to be that cynical. But if a doctor were to make that cost-benefit calculation, the doctor would be much better off letting the baby be stillborn.

Insurers, on the other hand, do make cost-benefit calculations. And they'd vote for stillbirth over birth injury every time.

REFORM POSSIBILITIES

Few of the problems with damages explored in this chapter are unique to stillbirth. What can be done?

One relatively easy first step is to pass laws repealing noneconomic damage caps. This is relatively easy in the mechanism, but less so practically. Still, tort reform measures and noneconomic damage caps are far less popular than they used to be, at least for the time being. A 2018 Arkansas state constitutional amendment to cap noneconomic damages in all lawsuits to $500,000 was opposed most vehemently by antiabortion groups, because the cap put a dollar limit on the value of human life.[71] The amendment was eventually removed from the ballot due to wording, and there have been no efforts since to revive the issue. More recently, California revised its 1975-set $250,000 cap on noneconomic damages in medmal claims. After intense public pressure and a successful-looking ballot initiative campaign, the California legislature and Governor Newsom passed a law increasing the cap to $350,000 for injury cases and to $500,000 for wrongful death cases immediately and mandating yearly incremental increases (but not tied to inflation).

But much more is needed than eliminating damage caps. Dov Fox and I recently proposed a more-principled formula for measuring damages for reproductive loss.[72] The formula covers all reproductive losses, ranging from negligently destroyed frozen embryos to negligently caused stillbirths at term.

The first step of the formula starts fresh without tethering the injury in pregnancy loss to emotional distress or lost relationship. People should be free to define their injury as they experienced it and recover appropriate damages. Maybe they did not experience stillbirth as the death of their child. If so, they should be allowed to seek damages for their emotional injury only. Maybe someone else very much experienced their child's stillbirth as the death of their child. They should be able to seek damages both for their emotional distress and the lost parent–child relationship. Given that juries are always asked to tailor the amount of the damages to the particular plaintiff's injury, juries should similarly also be capable to tailor the amount of damages to however the plaintiff defines her injury.

Moreover, this flexibility and subjectivity is needed because everything about pregnancy loss has changed. Laws about stillbirth date back to the early and mid-twentieth century. Home pregnancy tests, ultrasounds, pressure on prenatal bonding, and weekly emails about the size of your "baby" have changed everything about pregnancy and pregnancy loss. Women have been told for fifty years that "life begins at conception"; regardless of whether they agree, that narrative affects the experience. "Not much about pregnancy today would make any sense to anyone in the 1970s. And none of it would make any sense to someone in the early 1900s." No plaintiff should be forced to fit herself into laws that don't reflect today's experience.

Importantly, Fox and I also advocate for measures to attempt to alleviate the effects of race and class stereotypes within the jury's determination of damages in step 1. Other than the powerful work on the problems of using race and gender-based tables to predict future lost wages, legal scholarship on the effect of such stereotypes in civil damage awards is sparse. Measures we propose are jury instructions specifically identifying "biases about women of color and/or poor women that may lead jurors to misbelieve that they didn't really want, need, or deserve a child." Similarly, plaintiff's attorneys need to preempt certain biases, like explaining the plaintiff didn't get prenatal care because she lacked access as opposed to being irresponsible, or that the plaintiff went back to work shortly after her child's stillbirth because she needed to economically. We propose measures that would more specifically identify these biases in hopes of alleviating them.

The damage measure that Fox and I introduced has two more steps. The second step is to reduce the damages from step 1 proportionately according to the chances the plaintiff would have given birth to a living baby. This step affirms whether the plaintiff's expectation of live childbirth was reasonable. This step would have little effect in cases of stillbirth, however, given that the chance of live childbirth was extremely high. Again, only about 1 in 175 births each year in the United States are of stillborn babies. Yet the chance of stillbirth for a Black woman is much higher, closer to 1 in 90. The second step Fox and I propose specifically prohibits the application of a reduced chance of live childbirth because of the use of race or class. There's little doubt that obstetrical racism and classism contribute to those higher chances of stillbirth, and tort damages should not replicate that racism and classism.

The third step was then to leave room for the jury to increase damages based on traumas if the jury deems it appropriate. For instance, the trauma of birthing your dead child may be a reason the jury would want to increase the amount of damages.

Eliminating a noneconomic damage cap is something state legislatures could do tomorrow if they wanted to. Our proposal for damages for reproductive loss would take much more reform. But proposals like these are important first steps in provoking broader conversations. Current rules on evaluating damages for stillbirth problematically (1) attempt to separate emotional distress and lost parent–child relationship, (2) invite application of race and class biases, (3) arbitrarily cap damages, and (4) incentivize death over injury.

FIVE

Blindsiding Parents

The morning after Caleb's birth, my doctor came again to check on me. I'll never forget one part of the conversation. We were talking about placental abruptions. She mentioned that it was something she worried about in her pregnancies. She knew about the possibility of abruption and stillbirth due to her medical training, and it was thus something she was concerned about in her pregnancies.

Obviously, I didn't know much of anything about stillbirth and even less about stillbirths due to placental abruptions. I wasn't mad that she hadn't told me of this possibility. But I was struck by our knowledge disparity. She knew of this severe and grave possibility in her pregnancies, but I had no idea. (At the same time, she later told me that Caleb was the first term stillbirth she had seen in her 10+ years of practice. So really her knowledge of this possibility was more hypothetical, but still much more tangible than anything I knew.)

Regardless, why didn't I know of the possibility of stillbirth before Caleb died? I mean, I knew that the word existed. But I didn't know what it was really; I emailed my assistant at school that I had miscarried. And whatever comprehension I had of stillbirth, I certainly didn't think it happened anymore. I mean, it was 2017. Doctors are able to save babies born severely premature around 22 weeks and are transplanting uteruses. Certainly, babies don't randomly die at 37 weeks of pregnancy anymore.

Except they do.

. . . .

Nobody knows anything about stillbirth until after their baby dies. This affects the experience. It's a lot to process—your baby died and you need to give birth to your dead baby—while also trying to grapple with the fact that stillbirth is apparently still a thing that happens. The lack of knowledge adds shock, disbelief, and confusion to the likely overwhelming grief.

For decades, we've tried to empower patients in their health care consistent with the rights to bodily autonomy and self-determination. We've tried to alleviate the knowledge disparity between doctors and patients—emphasizing that it's the patient who makes the decision and thus needs to be educated to make that decision. Both laws and medical ethics have driven this change.

But doctors aren't telling pregnant people about stillbirth. You won't hear the word "stillbirth" until after your baby has died. Why not? Numerous reasons exist for a doctor's nondisclosure. They include that stillbirth is rare, that the emotional pregnant woman can't handle that sort of bad news, doctors don't want to be bothered with unnecessary reassurance visits, and the inevitability myth. None of these reasons justify nondisclosure.

Both doctors and pregnant people, and the public generally, would benefit from honest discussions about risks that exist in pregnancy, including risks that can and can't be mitigated or prevented. No one is benefiting from the silence surrounding stillbirth (except maybe doctors).

WHAT DO YOU MEAN THERE'S NO HEARTBEAT?

I'm far from the only parent who didn't know about stillbirth until it happened to their child. Studies confirm parents' lack of knowledge. Studies show that parents thought stillbirth was extremely rare,[1] that it didn't happen modern-day, or that it only happened modern-day in low-income countries with lesser quality prenatal care.[2] Studies show that women assumed medical advancements meant stillbirths didn't happen anymore. Even women in high-risk pregnancies report being aware of and concerned about premature birth, yet unaware of the possibility of stillbirth.[3] The overreporting of huge successes in neonatology, combined with the continued taboo of stillbirth and pregnancy loss more generally, means we are in a situation "in which expectations concerning reproductive outcomes are higher than the level of medical competence."[4]

Alan Goldenbach wrote a beautiful essay after his child's stillbirth, explaining that weeks after Shalom's death, he went to a bookstore to search for any mention of stillbirth in the pregnancy books. He found nothing. He found nothing even though these books are supposed to prepare couples "for every possible twist or turn" in pregnancy.[5] Goldenbach was shocked by his son's death, which is common after stillbirth as "most mothers experience at least some degree of disbelief" and insistence that the diagnosis of stillbirth must be mistaken.[6]

Not only do pregnant people have to deal with the shock that their baby died in the womb, they will soon learn that they also have to give birth to their dead baby—that stillbirth involves childbirth.[7] Ultrasounds are usually thought of as a tool to help with prenatal bonding. But they are also tools to confirm stillbirth. After learning of their child's death in the womb through ultrasound, many women have described themselves as human coffins.[8]

This lack of knowledge beforehand only worsens the trauma. You must not only grapple with the fact that stillbirth is still a thing that happens but also that it happened to your child. It's very different from miscarriage in that respect. We know about miscarriage. Studies show that we overwhelmingly underestimate its commonality, but we know about it more than just as an abstract concept. After a miscarriage, a person can think "I know that this happens sometimes; it's awful that it happened to me, but I do realize that it's something that happens." None of that is possible after stillbirth. To the contrary, "the parents of a stillborn child probably have one of the hardest times of any bereaved adult dealing with the reality of the death and the permanence of the changed expectations that it entails."[9]

After you give birth to your stillborn child you can then learn that you are one of many, many people who have done so. We learn that in the United States of America, in 2017 and today, fetuses sometimes die in the womb even at term. Only then does one learn that, as ACOG advises, "stillbirth is one of the most common adverse pregnancy outcomes."[10]

INFORMED CONSENT AND THE RISK OF STILLBIRTH

Informed consent law is a tort medical malpractice lawsuit based on a doctor's failure to disclose a potential risk of a medical procedure when obtaining the patient's consent, and then the risk occurs after the procedure. The failure to disclose the risk means that the patient's consent was not informed and a potential lawsuit exists.

Originally, informed consent law relied on the same accepted practice standard discussed in chapter 3. Whether a doctor should have disclosed risk X when obtaining consent for a surgery depended on whether doctors customarily disclose risk X. Doctors thus very much controlled what information patients would be eligible to know when consenting to a procedure. It was a paternalistic standard, with doctors deciding what patients needed to know regarding their health care.

Courts moved away from this paternalistic standard because of its inconsistency with a patient's right of self-determination—the patient has the right to determine what should happen to their body.[11] Courts instead created the materiality standard. It requires doctors to disclose all material risks, material meaning a risk that a reasonable person would want to know. Whether a risk is material depends on the chance of it happening and on its severity. Maybe the chance of a paper cut is low, and it's obviously just a paper cut. That's not material. Maybe the risk, however, is death. It's a very low risk, but still, it's death. That risk then might be material. And doctors could be liable in tort for failing to disclose all the material risks.

Informed consent is not just a legal mandate; it is also an ethical one. Four foundational bioethics principles exist: autonomy, nonmaleficence, beneficence, and justice.[12] Autonomy respects and supports autonomous decisions, nonmaleficence aims to prevent harm, beneficence aims to relieve harm, and justice concerns the distribution of benefits, risks, and costs.[13] The go-to treatise on the Principles of Bioethics describes three parts of autonomy: a patient acting "intentionally," "with understanding," and "without controlling influences."[14] Similar to the legal shift, bioethics literature describes that the shift in emphasis from doctor-focused to patient-focused disclosure was "autonomy driven."[15] The bioethics principle of informed consent, however, is more demanding than the legal version—it requires both disclosure and ensuring that the patient understands the disclosed risks.[16] Understanding depends on the language used and the complexity of the information.[17] Studies show that patients especially have trouble understanding the benefits of a procedure, and can have difficulty processing information even just based on the difference between explaining the chances of survival or of death.[18]

Blindsiding Parents

ACOG has specifically adopted informed consent as an ethical mandate. In an ethics opinion published in 2009 and reaffirmed in 2015, ACOG explains that "informed consent is an ethical concept that has become integral to contemporary medical ethics and medical practice."[19] The Committee's opinion also adopts informed consent's materiality standard as a guiding ethical principle, emphasizing the importance of the rights to bodily integrity and self-determination. It also explains that the ethical concept of informed consent includes two parts—enabling a patient's comprehension and their free consent. Comprehension means a patient must be aware of and understand her "situation and possibilities."[20] This ethics principle ensures "external freedom and freedom from inner compulsion, but also freedom from ignorance."[21] To repeat, informed consent as an ethics principle means a patient's *freedom from ignorance*.

ACOG's 2021 ethics opinion on informed consent further emphasizes its basis within the bioethics principles of patient autonomy and self-determination—and that autonomy is considered the "first among equals" of the four bioethics principles (autonomy, beneficence, nonmaleficence, and justice).[22] The opinion also describes that informed consent is a "means to responsible participation by patients in their own medical care and to a stronger relationship with their obstetrician-gynecologist."[23] The 2021 ethics opinion, which replaces the earlier one, does not contain the same freedom from ignorance language.

What does this all mean for the risk of stillbirth? I would argue it means doctors are obligated—legally and ethically—to disclose the risk of stillbirth to pregnant patients. The risk of stillbirth is easily material. Admittedly, the risk is low (although it can be higher in certain circumstances). But it is a risk that your child will die. The risk of stillbirth seems to be the exact type of risk envisioned within the transition from the customary standard to materiality standard—one that isn't traditionally disclosed because of its low risk, but quite possibly should be under the materiality standard because the gravity is so severe. Both informed consent law and ethics principles recognize the importance of the shift to the materiality standard to fulfill self-determination and bodily autonomy.

But there's no informed consent legal cases in the United States based on the failure to disclose the risk of stillbirth. The only cases involving stillbirth and informed consent are abortion cases. North Dakota and Missouri once had abortion "informed consent" statutes mandating that a woman be told of an increased risk for stillbirth after an abortion.[24] That's not medically accurate, but also not the point. The point is that the only context in which we've been concerned about disclosing the risk of stillbirth is as a prerequisite (really a scare tactic) to abortion.

One reason there's no informed consent cases based on the failure to disclose the risk of stillbirth though is that the law doesn't apply as well as I wish it would. Informed consent is traditionally tied to a procedure—that the doctor needs to disclose all medical risks of a procedure so that the patient can make an informed decision whether to have the procedure. There is no procedure associated with the risk of stillbirth. There's plenty of procedures associated with pregnancy, but I'm talking about disclosure of the general risk of stillbirth in pregnancy.

Even without the connection to a procedure, though, it's not that much of a stretch to apply informed consent to the disclosure of the risk of stillbirth.[25] Courts already have expanded informed consent law outside the confines of a specific procedure, especially in pregnancy cases. Wrongful birth claims are based on the failure to diagnose or disclose a fetal anomaly. That disclosure would be related to a procedure, an abortion, but also not because the pregnant person never considers the possibility of an abortion due to the nondisclosure. Still, it's a stretch. Others have suggested that perhaps the failure to disclose could just be a basic medical malpractice claim.[26] Unfortunately, that medmal claim would not use the materiality standard and instead rely on the traditional standard of care, whether doctors customarily disclose the risk of stillbirth. And they don't.

But nothing about legal liability alters ethical obligations. Again, in ACOG's words, doctors have an ethical obligation to ensure patients' freedom from ignorance. Plainly, pregnant patients are currently ignorant of the risk of stillbirth. So I ask again, why aren't doctors talking to pregnant patients about the risk of stillbirth? A few reasons exist—its rarity (often combined with underestimating the harm), an unfounded presumption that disclosure will cause pregnant patients anxiety (which also has some economic implications), and the assumed inevitability of stillbirth.

REASON FOR NONDISCLOSURE NO. 1: THE RARITY

ACOG states that "stillbirth is one of the most common adverse pregnancy outcomes," but it is much less common than miscarriage. That relative rarity is at least part of the reason doctors don't feel the need to disclose the risk. In a UK case, *Pearce v. United Bristol Healthcare NHS Trust*, the plaintiff was two weeks past her due date and begged her doctor to induce labor or deliver via C-section.[27] The doctor said no and the baby was stillborn about a week later. The plaintiff brought an informed consent claim against the doctor. The Court applied (or at least used language consistent with) the materiality standard, yet still concluded that the doctor didn't need to disclose the risk of stillbirth because it was "very, very small," insignificant, and "something like 0.1 to 0.2 percent."

But under the materiality standard, the rarity of the risk doesn't dictate whether a risk needs to be disclosed. The materiality standard depends on both the extent of the risk and the gravity of the risk. The risk of stillbirth is rare (although definitely increased at 42 weeks), but the severity is *very* high. The rarity does not negate the severity. Again, the risk of stillbirth seems like the exact type of risk that wouldn't be disclosed under the traditional standard, but maybe should be under the materiality standard. Legally and, perhaps more importantly, ethically, doctors should be discussing stillbirth with pregnant patients.

This rarity idea is implicitly related to an underestimation of the harm of stillbirth. For instance, in *Pearce*, the court mentioned that the risk was very rare and also undervalued the harm. It acknowledged that her child's stillbirth was "obviously extremely distressing," but also mentioned that the plaintiff had already had a(nother) sixth child. The new baby minimized the harm. Cultural platitudes like "you can have another" mask these harms. This type of undervaluation is especially possible for marginalized populations. I've already shared Representative Cori Bush's story—being told to go home and let her child "abort" as she "could get pregnant again because that's what you people do."[28]

It's a very odd idea—that the doctor could be the one thinking that stillbirth is not a big deal. Especially in legal disputes, doctors are often painted as the only ones thinking of and trying to save the fetus—the only ones advocating for the fetus in so-called maternal-fetal conflicts.[29] Michelle

Oberman explained that these are not maternal-fetal conflicts, but maternal-doctor conflicts.[30] I've never understood that depiction of the doctor as the only one concerned about the baby. And it definitely doesn't make any sense in the context of stillbirth. After stillbirth, the birthing parent is the one who goes home without their baby. There's no doubt that stillbirth could affect a doctor and all the medical practitioners in the delivery room, but the long-lasting consequences of stillbirth—the physical, the psychological, the social, the economic consequences, and more—stay with the family, not the doctor. So yes, it is possible that the doctor's calculus of not bothering to mention stillbirth includes underestimating its harm.

Plus, rarity can't explain nondisclosure of stillbirth given that doctors customarily warn pregnant patients of even rarer outcomes. Doctors warn pregnant people to not eat soft cheese or deli meat because of the risk of listeriosis. Listeriosis can cause miscarriage, premature birth, stillbirth, or neonatal death. But the actual risk is very low, much lower than the general risk of stillbirth.[31] Only about one in seven cases of the approximately 1,600 cases of listeriosis in the United States each year is in a pregnant person. That's 200 cases in 4 million pregnancies each year. And even getting listeriosis does not guarantee a negative pregnancy outcome. It may not transmit to the baby and is treatable with antibiotics. Yet doctors advise patients to avoid soft cheese and deli meat.

Similarly, testing for Down Syndrome and the other trisomies is now routine in pregnancy even though the stillbirth rate is four times greater than the rate of Down Syndrome. The risk of Down Syndrome when the pregnant person is 35 years old is only 1 in 350, yet testing will be recommended.[32]

And every parent is told of the possibility of death by Sudden Infant Death Syndrome. Parents are warned over and over to put their baby to sleep on the baby's back, but aren't warned about stillbirth. Yet stillbirth is *ten* times more common than SIDS deaths.[33] To quote a parent in a 2011 article in *The Lancet*: "If stillbirth really is ten times as common as cot death, we cannot be the only ones who had bought three sleep positioners but had never once considered the possibility of stillbirth."[34]

The risk of stillbirth is higher than all of these risks, yet they are disclosed and stillbirth is not. Plus the risk of stillbirth is specifically elevated in some circumstances. The risk for Black women is closer to 1 in 86ish pregnancies. That's a lot higher than the average 1 in 175. Rarity doesn't hold up as well as a reason for nondisclosure when the risk isn't all that rare.

Another circumstance where the risk of stillbirth could be elevated is due to (unvaccinated) Covid-19 infection during pregnancy. As I already discussed in chapter 2, one CDC-released study of unvaccinated Covid-19 infection at birth showed a quadrupled risk of stillbirth during the time the Delta variant was prevalent.[35] At the same time, the 2021 stillbirth numbers were consistent with the 2020 numbers, so maybe unvaccinated Covid-19 infection does not increase the risk of stillbirth.

But if there is any possibility of increased risk, that increased risk specifically invokes another informed consent issue: Covid-19 vaccination. Fortunately, Covid-19 vaccination negates the possibly increased risk. Yet the vaccination rate for pregnant people in the United States is shockingly low. Part of the reason for that low vaccination rate is that we are not telling pregnant people all the material risks of unvaccinated Covid-19 infection and stillbirth. The messaging about vaccination and pregnant people has been poor from the beginning. Pregnant people were not included in the vaccine trials, so we didn't know if it was safe for pregnant or lactating people. Then we figured out it was safe, and messaging accentuated its safety. But accentuating the safety of the vaccine is not the same as disclosing the material risks of not getting vaccinated. Informed consent law and ethical principles mandate disclosure of both the risks of getting vaccinated (essentially nonexistent) versus the risks of not getting vaccinated (a possibly higher risk of stillbirth).

Rarity alone cannot justify nondisclosure of the risk of stillbirth; rarity does not equal immaterial. And the risk also isn't always low.

REASON FOR NONDISCLOSURE NO. 2: UNNECESSARY ANXIETY

Related closely to rarity is the second reason that doctors do not disclose the risk of stillbirth to pregnant women—doctors don't want to unnecessarily scare them.

This is medical paternalism. This is a doctor decision that pregnant people will melt or go hysterical if they learn that their baby could die in the womb even after 20 weeks of pregnancy.

This also reflects a stereotype of pregnant women as overly emotional and possibly hysterical—that they can't handle the idea of this very low risk of their unborn child dying.[36] One would think that the fact of the low risk would be reassuring. The risk of losing the pregnancy was much greater before 20 weeks, and especially before 12 weeks. The pregnant person already has gotten past the highest risk of pregnancy loss. Yet, the emotional pregnant woman might collapse if she's told that a chance of stillbirth still exists.

The idea of the pregnant woman as overly emotional and possibly hysterical is common in legal cases. Many of these cases involve pregnant women desiring vaginal births after prior cesarean deliveries and doctors insisting that C-section delivery is proper.[37] Many abortion cases also include these sexist categorizations, of stupid and irrational women making poor decisions. A prominent example is that a woman would just collapse upon learning how a D&X (dilation and extraction) abortion works—that the doctor pulls the fetus out feet first and then punctures and compresses the skull so that it can also fit through the cervix. Justice Kennedy's opinion in *Carhart v. Gonzalez* described that a doctor may choose to not disclose the specific details because of a woman's reaction to it, which, in his mind, supported a ban on such procedures instead of mandatory disclosure.[38] (His opinion also ignored that some women terminating due to fetal anomaly preferred the D&X because the baby would be in one piece, which is discussed more in chapter 6.)

This depiction of the overly emotional pregnant woman was also present in the *Pearce* UK case. The Court specifically mentioned that the plaintiff was "distressed" when she asked her doctor to induce labor at 42 weeks. The doctor told her to "not behave like a child." In affirming the doctor's nondisclosure of the possibility of stillbirth, the Court stated: "Particularly when one bears in mind Mrs. Pearce's distressed condition, one cannot criticise [the doctor's] decision not to inform Mrs. Pearce of that very, very small additional risk."[39]

Stillbirth researchers in Australia have done actual research on the anxiety myth surrounding disclosure of stillbirth. A 2020 study asked women who had received prenatal care and had a live birth "how would you feel if your health care providers discussed with you about stillbirth alongside with some tools (fetal movement monitoring) to possibly detect that your baby was unwell."[40]

44.5%	They would feel "very calm" or "slightly calmer"
23.9%	They would feel "neither anxious nor calmer"
27.1%	They would feel "slightly anxious"
4.6%	They would feel "very anxious"

Some of these same researchers did a more recent study of people generally (not just those who had recently given birth) to learn more about public awareness of stillbirth. In that study, only 20% agreed with the statement that "talking about stillbirth with pregnant women would cause them to worry unnecessarily." Another 30% of participants were neutral on this statement, and 50% specifically disagreed.[41] Fears about anxiety due to disclosure of the risk of stillbirth are likely exaggerated.

This idea that disclosing the risk of stillbirth would harm pregnant people then triggers informed consent law's therapeutic exception. The *Canterbury* court explained that even the materiality standard does not require disclosure of a risk that would cause a patient to "become so . . . emotionally distraught . . . as to foreclose a rational decision, or complicate or hinder the treatment, or perhaps even pose psychological damage to the patient."[42] The exception exists, but the *Canterbury* court limited its application: it must be applied narrowly. A broad application would be a return to the paternalistic "doctor knows best" standard. Plus, a doctor is not allowed to simply presume instability. By definition, the therapeutic exception cannot justify not disclosing the risk of stillbirth to *all* pregnant people.

Moreover, ethical principles reject the therapeutic exception. ACOG's 2021 Committee opinion on ethics states it is "ethically unacceptable because it suggests that physicians always know what is best for their patients," and that it's "never ethically acceptable to withhold information without the patient's knowledge and consent."[43] It explains that autonomy is the first among equals of ethical principles, and that autonomy trumps benevolence, especially when benevolence is presuming a lack of autonomy. Again, it is unethical to not disclose stillbirth because it would (supposedly) make pregnant people scared or anxious.

True, discussions about stillbirth can be scary. Studies show that doctors often avoid this scary word, instead vaguely instructing women to monitor the baby's movement because it's "safer" for the baby or to call the doctor if the baby seems to be moving less. Neither of these vague instructions convey the true risk of stillbirth and the connection between it and reduced fetal movement.

To truly educate patients, scary words are needed. Analogous products liability law already mandates that the language in warnings must sufficiently convey the nature and extent of the danger; a warning may be inadequate if it warns only that the product is "flammable" instead of "explosive."[44] Similarly, to effectively warn about the risk of stillbirth, we need to say the word "stillbirth."[45] I'm not sure any other words specifically convey the nature and extent of the danger. And honestly, I'm not even sure that the word "stillbirth" is enough. Do people know what that means? Do people know that doctors can't necessarily prevent it? Especially if you see it listed as a possible complication with preterm birth, I think many people assume the baby wouldn't actually die from "stillbirth," just like the doctors can now help babies survive after premature birth. Similarly, vague language like "complications" doesn't convey the possibility of the baby dying in the womb; it also implies something that doctors can fix.

That's why disclosure of the risk of stillbirth must also include an explanation that stillbirths very much still happen. This is needed to overwhelm the assumption that medicalization of pregnancy has ended stillbirths. Pregnant people must realize that stillbirth is still a real risk—that doctors can't necessarily prevent stillbirth (although certainly more stillbirths are preventable than doctors are currently preventing). Disclosure of the risk of stillbirth must also include the harsh, specific details of the baby dying in the womb and then the necessary childbirth.

There is no euphemism for stillbirth that will still convey the fact that babies can die even shortly before birth and that stillbirth also means childbirth of that dead baby. There are no words other than stillbirth and death that similarly convey the risk. This is scary, but it's appropriate. It is scary in a similar way to learning about the possibility of SIDS, which is also terrifying for a new parent. But we still warn parents of SIDS.

This also relates back to the ensuring understanding part of the bioethi-cal principle of autonomy. The emphasis should be on language that helps understanding. It's not possible to teach people about stillbirth and to ensure that they understand stillbirth without scaring them a bit. If you're not scared, I don't think you really understand stillbirth.

It's not any fun to talk about stillbirth. But temporary discomfort can't compare to the likely long-term devastation. Self-blame after stillbirth is widespread. I shudder at the thought of the stillbirth parent who later learns they could have reduced the chance of their child's death had they realized that reduced fetal movement indicated that their baby was in trouble or had they just gotten a simple vaccine. And parents will figure that out eventually.

REASON FOR NONDISCLOSURE NO. 3: ECONOMIC DISINCENTIVES

Regardless, doctors supposedly not wanting to scare pregnant people may not be as benevolent as it seems. Maybe it's not that doctors don't want to scare pregnant people about stillbirth because it likely won't happen. Maybe it's that doctors don't want to deal with pregnant people coming in for extra appointments worried about stillbirth. That's not benevolence—that's annoyance.

It's also economic. Doctors frequently use "global billing" for prenatal care. Global billing is a one-time charge that covers all prenatal care, includ-ing childbirth. If pregnant people come in for extra appointments because they're worried about stillbirth, there's no extra compensation for those extra visits. And thus we have an economic disincentive to disclosing the risk of stillbirth.[46] Many have already suggested that economic incentives are behind the alarming increase in C-sections in the United States as C-sections have higher reimbursement rates for doctors. This influence may not be intentional; "considerations of financial benefit and convenience may occur subconsciously, shifting behavior without health care providers being aware of the impact of economic concerns on their decision making."[47] Cost and convenience, mainly avoiding annoyance, may also be lurking behind the disclosure of stillbirth.

Regardless, fears about extra doctor visits are likely exaggerated. After Norway started emphasizing the importance of reduced fetal movement and its connection to stillbirth, the number of women presenting with reduced fetal movement "remained unchanged during intervention" and the rate of "unplanned repeat visits" for such reduced fetal movement "was consistently very low," but did increase 0.2 percent.[48]

That said, I went in for unplanned visits in my next pregnancy after Caleb's stillbirth. I had more planned visits too with the maternal fetal medicine specialist. But I also had more unplanned visits. I needed a few simple reassuring "let's listen to the fetal heartbeat" checkups, and at least one early visit to labor and delivery just because the baby's kicks felt more subdued. At the same time, I think my fear of *another* stillborn baby is a bit different than any supposed fear resulting from mere disclosure of the risk.

REASON FOR NONDISCLOSURE NO. 4: THE INEVITABILITY MYTH

Another reason doctors may not disclose stillbirth is because of assumed inevitability. Fatalism surrounds stillbirth even though not all stillbirths are unpreventable. Other countries' better rates, other countries' successful decreases, dramatic differences in state rates, and studies showing preventability all show some extent of preventability.

But even if stillbirth was inevitable, why would that be a reason to not disclose its possibility? Stillbirth is something that could happen within pregnancy. The chance is low (and its rarity should be part of the disclosure), but it can happen. Why would the inability to prevent alter bodily autonomy principles? Not disclosing because of inevitability is tantamount to not telling a patient of an unchangeable prognosis. If death is likely from procedure X, we don't not tell the patient about that likelihood because of its unpreventability.[49]

And like the underestimation of harm, the fatalism myth may be stronger when applied to marginalized populations. There's no doubt that the stillbirth rate is much higher for Black women. But racism, not race, is the risk factor. Similarly, poor women face a much higher risk. Structural obstacles to health care in this country help explain that discrepancy, although it is also present in countries with universal access to care.

As Brie Clark has pointed out, stereotypes of Black pregnant women are less about them being emotional women who will worry too much about stillbirth and more about seeing them as "unfit, inherently dangerous to their children, and untrustworthy."[50] Do these racist stereotypes make Black women's stillbirths seem even more inevitable? Is there then less incentive to try, a sort of "why bother" attitude, to prevent stillbirths of Black babies? But, as Clark explains, these stereotypes usually lead to more surveillance of Black pregnant women—questioning their conduct, suspecting that they are endangering their baby. Except, Black women are currently getting less surveillance medically in that they're receiving inadequate prenatal care; there's little doubt that Black women and poor women have a higher rate of stillbirth at least in part because they are not receiving quality care. Again, even if stillbirth were inevitable, that does not change ideas of bodily autonomy and the need to inform. But Black women have long been subject to medical care that undermines their autonomy, especially in pregnancy.

This undermined autonomy also makes me think of some language in the ACOG informed consent opinions. While the opinions are clear that doctors can't ethically withhold information, there is language that the "amount and complexity of information be tailored to the desires of the individual patient and to the patient's ability to understand this information."[51] Similarly, "it is acceptable to communicate information over time based on the patient's stated preferences and ability to understand the information."[52] I don't think that the fact that a risk of stillbirth exists is complex, nor do I think it is difficult to understand. But I could see doctors claiming that it could be complex for some patients—especially those who fit "bad mother" stereotypes. Even ACOG admits that doctor assessment of patient capacity is subject to bias.[53]

BENEFITS OF DISCLOSURE—AND THE "DEAD BABY" CARD

The lack of a reason not to disclose, however, is not the same as a reason to disclose. Would disclosing the risk of stillbirth actually do any good?

Disclosure of the risk can help stillbirth parents by both reducing the shock when their baby is stillborn and reducing the stigma that surrounds stillbirth. Studies of cancer patients show that they want all the information, good and bad. Knowing potential outcomes, good and bad, better prepares patients for the unknown future. And with stillbirth, the future isn't that unknown; it's highly likely the baby will not be stillborn. But knowing ahead of time of the possibility of stillbirth can reduce the shock that comes with it. The same is true for stigma. Studies have specifically shown that parents feel that the nondisclosure of the risk of stillbirth within prenatal care "exacerbate[s]" their feelings of having to stay silent and their self-blame.[54] Reducing the shock and stigma, even if only to a small extent, are tangible benefits of disclosure.

Another benefit of disclosure is improving the doctor–patient relationship. Studies show that doctors worry about being blamed for stillbirth. Blame is especially likely when communication is poor and trust in the doctor is lacking. Disclosure of the risk of stillbirth ahead of time improves communication and trust. And "a patient who is not blindsided may feel less urge to blame the doctor."[55] Notably, one of the reasons courts moved to the materiality standard is because additional doctor disclosures and communication is more likely to discourage "recriminations and litigation, in the event of an adverse outcome."[56] More information and more communication likely leads to less blame.

Related to communication, there are sometimes emergency (actual or supposed) situations where the doctor says "stillbirth" before it happens. Obstetric violence is the term used to describe mistreatment during childbirth, including pressuring child-birthing women into C-sections. As Professor Elizabeth Kukura describes in her important work on obstetric violence, "doctors and nurses present stories of disfigurement, brain damage, and fetal death to scare women into consenting to unwanted medical intervention."[57] In journalist Jennifer Block's words, doctors pull the "dead baby card" to try to coerce a C-section.[58] Kukura describes that doctors "choose language intended to shock and frighten, rather than to inform and assist in effective decision making."[59]

This is difficult. Many, many women have been pressured into medical procedures they didn't want. These women—and advocates fighting against the overmedicalization of pregnancy and childbirth—think that the doctor is lying about the risk of stillbirth to get the woman to consent to a C-section. The language "dead baby card" implies the doctor is at a minimum exaggerating the risk of stillbirth. Misconceptions that stillbirth doesn't happen anymore further imply that the doctor is at best exaggerating and at worst lying.

But what if the doctor is neither exaggerating nor lying? What if the doctor truly believes that the baby will be stillborn without an emergency C-section? Then the doctor isn't trying to coerce. Then, the doctor is trying to save the baby's life. Kukura is right that the doctor should use language to educate and inform the patient. But again, there's no euphemisms for stillbirth, death, or fetal death that also sufficiently convey the harm of stillbirth. And frankly, if stillbirth is a real possibility, the pregnant person should be scared. Remember that self-blame is rampant after stillbirth. I can't imagine the distress I would feel if I refused a C-section that my doctor recommended, and my baby was stillborn.

Something that would dramatically help in these situations though is if the (supposed) emergency wasn't the first time the doctor said the word stillbirth to the pregnant person. If the doctor had previously had discussions with the patient about the risk, this language is scary, but not shocking necessarily. Plus, the doctor should be up front that the risk of stillbirth exists despite medicalization and that doctors don't necessarily know everything about stillbirth. The doctor can quantify the belief that the baby may die such that the pregnant person can better understand the risks and make decisions about their care.

More communication means less of a power and knowledge imbalance and more trust.[60] And more trust means that the patient is more likely to believe the doctors and understand the stakes of the decision whether to consent. That informed consent could end up saving more babies and birthing persons from stillbirth.

SIX

Reproductive Justice and Stillbirth

I really have nothing to complain about with respect to the medical care I received during my pregnancy and childbirth with Caleb. My doctor never dismissed me when I had concerns (which I really didn't). The care we received when he died and was born was fantastic. My doctor gave me the choice of a C-section, which I declined. The medical team supported us in every way possible. After, we attended a helpful local support group. Our insurance covered and continues to cover therapy. My doctor was also there for my mental health needs. I still remember sitting in the parking lot outside of the law school just bawling at the thought of Caleb being in pain when he died. I texted with my doctor and she reassured me that he likely wasn't in pain (which she can't know, but I appreciate the reassurance). I received wonderful care in my next pregnancy. My new doctors never turned down my requests for additional reassurance visits or testing, and insurance paid for everything.

But that's just my experience. Not everyone receives the same quality of medical care that I received—care in pregnancy, childbirth, postpartum and beyond, and in subsequent pregnancy. Consistent with reproductive justice, however, we all have a right to quality medical care.

*　*　*　*

You're likely familiar with the reproductive-rights movement. In the United States, the reproductive-rights movement is most often focused on the right to not have a child, which translates to rights to contraception and to abortion. The movement was quite successful in court, although it's sometimes hard to remember all those successes more recently.

Despite its success, many were concerned about the reproductive-rights movement, including many women of color. A responsive movement, which women of color later named the reproductive-justice movement, emerged. Both historically and today, women of color have faced reproductive oppressions much broader than issues surrounding contraception and abortion. For instance, marginalized women, especially enslaved Black women and Native American women, have had their children taken away from them. These oppressions continue today in the forms of higher rates of investigation, removal of their children, and termination of parental rights within what's known as the child welfare system. Marginalized women also faced and continue to face oppressions limiting their right to get pregnant, like involuntarily sterilization and practical inabilities to obtain fertility treatment given the expense. The reproductive justice movement thus recognizes not only the right to not have a child, but also the equally important rights to have a child and to parent him with dignity. This emphasis on the right to have a child reflects the types of reproductive oppressions women of color faced and continue to face—oppressions depriving them of the right to have a child.[1]

The reproductive-justice movement also recognizes the important differences between rights and access, and more broadly integrates negative and positive rights. Even if a right to abortion existed, the "right" did not mean people could access and obtain abortion care, especially not marginalized persons. The reproductive-justice movement is more broadly based within a human rights approach, meaning "what governments owe to the people they govern."[2] The reproductive justice approach thus recognizes both negative rights and positive rights. Applied to abortion, for example, this would mean a negative right that the state cannot criminalize abortion care, and a positive right requiring the government to ensure access to abortion care. Similarly, a positive right related to artificial reproductive technology would be ensuring access to such care.

The reproductive-justice framework is very broad. Literature emphasizes rights and access to "contraception, comprehensive sex education, STI prevention and care, alternative birth options, adequate prenatal and pregnancy care, domestic violence assistance, adequate wages to support our families, [to] safe homes"; "to reproductive technology, parental leave from work after childbirth"; and to "affordable, high-quality child care."[3]

But there's minimal mentions of pregnancy loss. Assumedly that is due to concerns about fetal personhood (a supposed tension I will discuss in depth in chapter 8), the same reason the reproductive-rights movement has avoided pregnancy loss for years. My scholarship seeks to cure that omission, including this chapter. One cannot have a child and parent him with dignity unless one can get pregnant and *stay* pregnant. Stillbirth and pregnancy-loss prevention generally is an inescapable part of the right to have a child. Lack of interest in such prevention is an oppression that falls hardest on marginalized persons, just like the other reproductive oppressions the reproductive-justice movement highlights. Black women face double the risk of stillbirth (and late miscarriage, meaning 10–20 weeks), and poor women face double the risk of stillbirth.

Integration of stillbirth prevention into the reproductive-justice framework emphasizes the need for more research. It also emphasizes the need to investigate systemic and institutional reasons why stillbirths occur—a needed shift from a focus on the individual and her "choice."[4]

Many reproductive-justice-based rights can and should exist with respect to stillbirth. Some are discussed in other chapters, like the right to fetal autopsy after stillbirth (chapter 1) or to financial assistance via something like a tax credit (chapter 7). This chapter focuses on health-related reproductive-justice-based rights: the right to prenatal care that will help prevent stillbirth, birth justice rights, the right to culturally appropriate mental and emotional health care after stillbirth, and the right to what's known as rainbow clinic care in a subsequent pregnancy.

THE RIGHT TO PREVENTATIVE PRENATAL CARE

The reproductive-justice movement already recognizes the right and *access* to health care as a high priority issue. And it already recognizes prenatal care as especially important.[5] But reproductive-justice literature is not explicit about why prenatal care is needed, and how prenatal care can help reduce the risk of stillbirth—as needed to protect one's right to have a child.

Studies confirm the connection between prenatal care and the risk of stillbirth. Numerous researchers attribute the decrease in the stillbirth rate in high-income countries in the twentieth century to improvements in prenatal care.[6] But those decreases stalled at the start of the twenty-first century. A 2012 study affirmed that quality prenatal care improves the chances of good maternal and infant outcomes and attempted to specify how few prenatal care appointments is too few. It found that those who attended less than 50% of the recommended care visits had an "almost threefold increased risk of late stillbirth," defined as after 28 weeks.[7] The study concluded that "it is the substantial underutilization of care (rather than a relative reduction in the number of visits) that is associated with increased mortality." The study suggested that one reason that underutilization increased the risk of stillbirth was the decreased opportunity to identify if the baby is small for their gestational age, or what is normally called fetal growth restriction in the United States.

Further revealing the importance of prenatal care is an empirical study of stillbirths in Tennessee completed by Meghan Boone and Ben J. McMichael.[8] From 2014–2016, Tennessee had a law criminalizing drug use while pregnant. Public health and medical organizations have warned that these laws would deter women from seeking prenatal care. Boone and McMichael's study confirmed that consequence. The laws "reduced the probability of a mother receiving prenatal care by approximately 6.2 percentage points." Less prenatal care translated to more stillbirths. Specifically, Boone and McMichael concluded that the law "increased fetal deaths by 0.225 for every 1,000 births," translating to an additional 20 stillborn babies in 2015.

Reproductive justice demands more than the right and access to prenatal care, however. It must be access to *quality* care. Unfortunately, even when women have access to prenatal care, like in countries with government-run health care, studies show a disparity in stillbirth rates for poor women and Black women. One study in Sweden expressed dismay at the class disparity found because of equal access to *free* prenatal care.[9] Studies have specifically suggested that better quality health care for poor women and Black women would help alleviate the class and race disparities in stillbirth rates.[10] Reproductive justice mandates that the state do whatever it can to ensure that marginalized women have access to and receive quality care.

This requires two steps in the United States, neither of which is easy. The first is to improve access to health care, which means both expanding health insurance and working to solve maternal care deserts. The second step is to ensure that the prenatal care provided includes initiatives to reduce still-birth. Fortunately, we can and should borrow from the initiatives other countries have already implemented; details of other countries' safer baby bundles were discussed in chapter 3.

Again, stillbirth is interfering with the reproductive-justice right to have a child, especially for Black women and poor women. The failure to investigate and incorporate stillbirth prevention measures is yet another reproductive oppression (that should be) included in the reproductive-justice framework. One reproductive-justice right needed to combat that oppression is the right to quality prenatal care that will help decrease the risk of stillbirth.

THE RIGHT TO PERINATAL HOSPICE AND PALLIATIVE CARE

Sometimes, however, stillbirth is unpreventable. Sometimes the pregnant person learns during pregnancy that her baby will die in the womb or shortly after. The baby is diagnosed with a fatal condition or abnormality. The pregnant person really has (or did have) two options: abortion or continue the pregnancy until it ends.

Fortunately, specialized medical care has emerged to care for these pregnant people and their families if they choose to continue the pregnancy. It's called *perinatal hospice and palliative care* (PHPC). It is the "confluence of pediatric palliative care, perinatal hospice, and perinatal bereavement."[11] The hospice part of care is medical care focused on comforting the baby if it survives birth for longer than hours. The palliative care part of the model starts earlier, at the time of diagnosis, providing "support for families" and "focus[ing] on the reduction of suffering, whether physical, psychological, spiritual, or existential."[12] Others have described the palliative care as "emotional, social, and spiritual support."[13] Many questions about it remain, including its cost, availability, and still-being-defined standards of care. But many who, willfully or not, continue pregnancies after certain fetal diagnoses could benefit greatly from this care.

PHPC originally had nothing to do with abortion. But as the field expanded, antiabortion leaders started using it as "a political tool."[14] Pre-*Dobbs*, a prominent anti-abortion group, the Americans United for Life

(UAL), created the Perinatal Hospice Information Act Model Legislation and Policy Guide.[15] The model laws framed PHPC as the better alternative to abortion. One model law required that women be told of this care before she can receive an abortion.[16] (Note that the required disclosure was at the time of sought abortion, not at the time of diagnosis of the fetal condition, suggesting a main intent to dissuade abortion.) The laws paternalistically described that continuing the pregnancy with PHPC would be more psychologically beneficial than abortion.[17] Arkansas's "Women's Right to Know" law expressly states that termination "can pose severe long-term psychological risks for a woman, including the risk of post-traumatic stress, depression, and anxiety," whereas continuing the pregnancy with PHPC allows families to be "emotionally and spiritually prepared for the death of their child."[18] (As if there wouldn't be any trauma, stress, depression, and anxiety simply based on the fact that your child died regardless of how he died.)

PHPC came up in the discussions surrounding Kate Cox's late 2023 legal battle against Texas when she sought an abortion. Cox's unborn child was diagnosed with Trisomy 18, a condition that is almost always fatal before birth or shortly after. Cox and her husband wanted to terminate the pregnancy for many reasons. She could not obtain an abortion in Texas legally, however. Although a lower Texas court granted an injunction allowing her to obtain an abortion, state Attorney General Ken Paxton appealed it and the injunction was stayed (put on pause). The Texas Supreme Court later reversed the injunction, finding that Cox's desired abortion was illegal, after Cox had already left the state to obtain medical care. Reacting to the initial injunction, antiabortion group Texas Right to Life explained that the best option for Cox was PHPC: "Every child is uniquely precious and should continue to be protected in law no matter how long or short the baby's life may be," and that "the compassionate approach to these heartbreaking diagnoses is perinatal palliative care, which honors, rather than ends, the child's life."[19]

PHPC for women like Cox is especially important post-*Dobbs* in states where abortion is illegal. Pregnant people in these states, unless able to travel elsewhere like Cox, have no other option than to continue their pregnancies knowing their child will die. But none of the states where abortion is illegal have done anything to expand access to PHPC, either pre- or post-

Dobbs. Post-*Dobbs*, aside from this Texas Right to Life statement, there's little to no antiabortion advocacy of PHPC in states where abortion is illegal (or in states where abortion is still legal). There's no push to expand access to this care, despite the clear need for it if abortion is illegal. This shows that PHPC was a tool to dissuade people from abortion. And that tool isn't needed anymore now that abortion is illegal.

PHPC, however, is not just an antiabortion weapon. PHPC and access to it is a reproductive-justice issue. This care should be an option for those in pregnancies diagnosed with fetal abnormalities—for those who choose it in states where abortion is legal, and for those who are forced to continue their pregnancies in states where abortion is illegal. Many issues about access exist. The American College of Obstetricians and Gynecologists specifically describes that issues exist relating to the "availability of programs, patient access issues, and physician education and training barriers."[20] Women, especially women in rural areas, would likely need to travel. Even if a facility is nearby, cost issues may also affect access.[21] It's not at all clear whether or how much of PHPC insurance would cover given its traditional use of a global fee or bundled payment for pregnancy.[22] Researchers also note that more research is needed to determine why fewer people of color seek this care compared to white pregnant persons.[23] PHPC may have developed into an antiabortion pawn, but it is really care that pregnant people have a reproductive-justice right to in pregnancies with a fatal fetal condition diagnosis.

(STILL)BIRTH JUSTICE

Reproductive-justice advocates have long focused on the mistreatment many women, especially marginalized women, experience during childbirth. Professor Elizabeth Kukura has vividly described these injustices, including forced episiotomies (a surgical cut between the vagina and anus), labor induction, use of forceps or vacuum in delivery, and C-section deliveries.[24] Hospitals have even taken women to court to try to override her lack of consent to a C-section.

The concept of "birth justice" focuses on rights within childbirth.[25] It is the "right to give birth with whom, where, when, and how a person chooses" and "without pressure or aggressive nonemergency interventions."[26]

Reproductive Justice and Stillbirth

The same birth justice rights should exist for stillbirth. Stillbirth is still birth. The process is "physiologically identical."[27] Any childbirth involves extreme vulnerability, possibly even more vulnerability with stillbirth than with live childbirth. There should similarly be rights regarding the "where, when, and how" of childbirth of a stillborn baby.

Starting with "when" and "how," it's very possible that medical emergencies will dictate some or all the details. Stillbirths can be more physically dangerous. A 2019 study of stillbirths and live births in California found that the chances of life-threatening complications are five times greater in stillbirth than live birth.[28] The study was unable to conclude whether the increased risk was due to the delivery itself or the same reasons why the stillbirth occurred in the first place. Regardless, the increased chance of life-threatening complications is dramatic.

But many stillbirths will not be emergency situations and the pregnant person should be able to make decisions regarding birth. Many will hear that dreaded, "I'm sorry, but there's no heartbeat," and labor hasn't started. In those circumstances, the "when" of childbirth doesn't have to be immediate. The birthing person could choose to delay delivery for a period, possibly providing some needed time to process. Doctors should educate birthing parents about the ability to wait on childbirth. A delay may also avoid the need for a labor induction.

Then, there's the question of rights related to the "how" of delivery—vaginal or a C-section. The birth justice "how" of childbirth right is usually focused on enabling women to choose vaginal birth—to avoid being pressured or forced into a C-section. The situation is flipped, however, in cases of stillbirth. Then, it's women wanting a C-section and the doctor instead pressuring or forcing vaginal birth.

Understandably, some women are daunted by the idea of vaginal delivery of their stillborn baby and instead want a C-section.[29] Studies explain the reasons for this. Sometimes women think incorrectly that a quick C-section would enable the baby to be resuscitated. Others fear that the baby will still feel pain and would be less traumatized by a C-section. Others desire a C-section as a means of obtaining some control over the situation. Others resent the idea they should give birth vaginally because then the next baby could also be birthed vaginally; they resent the idea of focusing on a next baby. And maybe some just worry "how exactly am I supposed to push my dead baby out of my vagina?" All of these are understandable, especially if you've been through it.

But, absent some type of emergency, a C-section isn't medically necessary and thus not recommended. It's major abdominal surgery. The risks to the birthing person from a C-section include infection, blood clots, blood loss, and increased risks in the next pregnancy. The consequences can be dramatic. The risk of maternal mortality is three times higher with C-sections than vaginal births.[30] Some believe that the US C-section rate, around 33%—double the World Health Organization's 15% maximum recommended rate—helps explain the alarmingly high US maternal mortality rate.[31] Other researchers dispute whether the increased mortality risk is due to the C-section or the medical condition that preceded it.[32] But other researchers found an increased risk of mortality even in planned (not emergency) C-sections.[33] Regardless, C-sections should be avoided if possible. The risks of a C-section fall on the pregnant person, and the benefits of a C-section fall on the baby. In stillbirth, the baby is already dead.

There's no doubt that the United States has a C-section epidemic. That said, I don't think the lack of medical necessity should be a reason to deny a birthing parent a C-section when the baby is stillborn. The goal of reducing the C-section rate should not have to go through deliveries of stillborn babies.

And birth justice rights means the birthing parent gets to choose how to give birth to their stillborn baby. Unfortunately, ACOG's guidelines do not recognize birth justice for stillbirth. According to ACOG, the method of delivery should depend on the timing of the pregnancy, the woman's medical history, and "maternal preference."[34] As far as maternal preference, the guidelines state that "shared decision making plays an important role in determining the optimal method for delivery in the setting of fetal demise." But the guidelines also say, "Health care providers should weigh the risks and benefits of each strategy in a given clinical scenario and consider available institutional expertise," and, "in general, cesarean delivery for fetal demise should be reserved for unusual circumstances because it is associated with potential maternal morbidity without any fetal benefit."[35] There's a definite level of deference to the doctor in the ACOG guidelines, and there's little sentiment of empowering the birthing parent.

Language more consistent with birth justice is found in the Royal College of Obstetricians and Gynaecologists (England's ACOG) guidelines. They state that the doctor should seek "to identify and understand [the] women's thoughts and wishes but without trying to shape them" and that "discussions should aim to support maternal/paternal choice."[36] The language focuses on educating the birthing parent—providing accurate information on "the risks and benefits of medical procedures, including cesarean delivery, and information about any misconceptions that might be motivating the woman to desire one type of delivery over the other (e.g., misconceptions regarding the baby's potential survival or ability to feel pain)."

Studies support RCOG's approach—that providing information regarding the benefits of vaginal birth and resolving misconceptions about a C-section lead to positive (as possible) birth experiences. "When supported and given good information about potential physiological, psychological and social benefits most women see the value in a vaginal birth, and many have positive and valuable experiences."[37] Experts caution that "it is manifestly important that women feel in control of the decision-making process and that the mode of delivery isn't imposed."

The "how' components of the reproductive-justice, birth-justice right for stillbirth also should include non-childbirth options. Such options are medically feasible for early stillbirths (and late miscarriages). They include surgical procedures like a dilation and extraction (D&X) or dilation and evacuation (D&E). These procedures are also, however, the surgical procedures used for abortion, including abortions/terminations due to fetal abnormalities, when the pregnant person learns that the baby will die either in the womb or after birth. And abortion bans have limited their availability.

Even before *Dobbs*, many state legislatures and Congress banned these procedures because of their controversial natures. In a D&X, the doctor removes the fetus whole, which enables the doctor to make fewer passes through a woman's cervix with instruments, reducing the risks of damaging the uterus.[38] To enable so, the D&X involves partially delivering the fetus in a breech (feet first) position, and emptying the contents of the skull, so that it can collapse and safely pass through the cervix. The fetus typically dies in the procedure if fetal demise isn't initiated beforehand. The D&X is politically known as the "partial-birth abortion" procedure.

Many states had banned D&Xs, and Congress did the same in 2003. The Supreme Court upheld Congress's ban in 2007 in *Carhart v. Gonzales*.[39] Justice Anthony Kennedy's opinion explained, without citing any evidence, that some women eventually regret their decision to abort and such regret will be even stronger when they learn the exact details of the D&X procedure.[40] Maya Manian powerfully criticized the *Carhart* opinion, identifying that the law does not interfere with the medical decisions of non-pregnant people based on possible regret. Yet, *Carhart* holds that "someone other than the [pregnant] patient knows better what life choices will lead to mentally healthy consequences."[41]

Justice Kennedy's opinion also ignores evidence that some women whose baby had a fetal anomaly specifically benefited psychologically from the D&X procedure.[42] These women specifically wanted the D&X procedure because the baby's body remained intact. The D&X enabled what's known in the stillbirth world as "memory making," providing time to hold the baby, look at the baby, and say goodbye. The D&X gave women the ability to hold their child without also having to induce labor. It was a cheaper, safer, and less invasive procedure that still allowed a face-to-face goodbye. But none of that mattered to Justice Kennedy.

The crusade against D&Es came later. The D&E procedure is controversial as it involves removing the fetus in body parts, which also requires the doctor making multiple passes into the uterus.[43] Before *Dobbs*, states banned the D&E just as they had banned the D&X. Everything in *Carhart* seemed to point to the constitutionality of potential D&E bans except that Justice Kennedy used the availability of D&Es to claim that the D&X ban did not pose an undue burden on a woman's right to abortion. But none of this matters anymore after *Dobbs*.

Even after *Carhart* and *Dobbs*, D&Xs and D&Es are still legal for late miscarriages and stillbirths, assuming the baby's heartbeat has already stopped. But abortion restrictions affect medical training, especially in antiabortion states, and doctors are less likely to even be trained to do D&Xs or D&Es anymore.[44] It doesn't matter if the procedure is legal if there's no doctor trained to do it. Then childbirth is the only option.

Birth justice, however, means a birthing parent should have the right to a D&E or a D&X. *Dobbs* and the resulting abortion bans in many states have reinforced that abortion is health care—and reinforced the need to stop silo-ing reproductive health care. A ban on D&E's and D&X's does not just affect those patients desiring abortions. It also affects those experiencing late mis-carriages or early stillbirths. These are standard of care medical procedures, but abortion bans mean decreased training and availability for patients.

Birth-justice rights also mean rights related to the "where" of the child-birth of your stillborn baby. "Delivery areas on obstetric units are designed to welcome new babies, not to mourn babies who have died."[45] In studies, parents report hearing noises of live births in surrounding rooms, and medi-cal staff not checking charts and making comments assuming live birth like "do you have your baby?" I'm not expecting hospitals to have separate units for pregnancy losses. But hospitals could do something as simple as a sticker on the door to represent that the baby was stillborn. This may not seem like a big deal, but it is.

After birth, all parents should also be given the opportunity to hold and be with their child, the memory-making mentioned earlier. Not long ago, standard of care after stillbirth was to take the baby as if nothing had hap-pened and instead encourage the woman to try to get pregnant again. Grass-roots efforts by stillbirth parents starting in the 1980s led to doctors chang-ing their practices. Researchers almost unanimously agree that parents benefit from being able to spend time with and hold the baby.

RCOG practice guidelines explain the value of giving parents time to hold the baby, name him, and obtain mementos.[46] They explain that carers should not persuade parents to hold the baby, but strongly support any expressed parental desires to do so. Carers should also support desires to make mementos. Specifically, "maternity units should have the facilities for producing photographs, palm and foot prints and locks of hair with presen-tation frames." If parents do not want mementos, carers should securely store the mementos in case parents later change their mind. The RCOG guidelines cite the many studies demonstrating the benefit to parents of spending time with and holding their stillborn baby, a study about why par-ents should not be forced to do so, and studies showing that parents value mementos.

The ACOG guidelines lack this amount of detail. Unfortunately, the ACOG guidelines on stillbirth mention holding the baby only twice. And neither mention is about the value of holding the baby for the parents. The first is a quick sentence in the section on fetal autopsy that "parents should be given the opportunity to hold the baby and perform cultural or religious activities before the autopsy."[47] The second is a mention that holding the baby is not possible if a D&E is performed.[48]

As the RCOG guidelines detail, no one should be forced to hold the baby obviously, but encouragement is proper. And this encouragement may be necessary for Black fathers; studies show that they are more likely than others to be hesitant.[49] It's important for health-care workers to encourage and offer "professional guidance about exactly how to see and hold" the baby, including for "how long," "how best to see and photograph," "what to expect if they want to bathe, dress or sleep next to their baby, and how the passing of time will alter the baby's temperature, appearance, and touch."[50]

Something that could help with that passing of time—and something to which parents should have a right—is a CuddleCot. A CuddleCot is a cooling bassinet designed to maintain the baby's body longer and thus enable the parents and family more time with their stillborn baby. The CuddleCot provides bereaved parents the one thing they most desperately want: more time. The CuddleCot was invented in England, and 92% of hospitals in Britain have at least one. A 2019 *New York Times* article estimated that 400–500 hospitals in the United States have one.[51] That would be less than 20% of the approximately 2,700 hospitals offering labor and delivery. We could also easily have geographic disparity access issues. It wouldn't be surprising if there's many more CuddleCots in urban areas versus rural areas, or more in the Northeast than in Southern states.

I don't think expense can explain the lack of a CuddleCot in every labor and delivery unit. They're not that expensive. My husband and I have now worked with a group called Ashlie's Embrace to donate three CuddleCots in Caleb's honor to three hospitals. It's about $2500 for each. That's not a lot for a hospital. One of my most prized Caleb possessions is a thank-you card from a grandma whose family was able to spend more time with their stillborn grandchild due to one of Caleb's CuddleCots.

Even when the baby is stillborn, there are still decisions to be made about "when," "how," and "where" to give birth (or not). There are also decisions and options regarding care after the baby is born—care that is so important for the overall experience. When medically feasible, the birthing parent has the right and should be empowered to make these decisions.

THE RIGHT TO MENTAL AND EMOTIONAL HEALTH CARE

Health-care reproductive-justice rights with respect to stillbirth do not end after the baby is born. Stillbirth can be life-altering. It can be one of the hardest experiences an adult can endure. Studies confirm that stillbirth parents report "high rates of depressive symptoms, anxiety, post-traumatic stress, suicide ideation, panic and phobias."[52] Stillbirth can also easily lead to breakdown of relationships, which can lead to "hardship, ill health, low income and poor satisfaction with life."[53] Stillbirth can affect parents' employment, and it can even have long-lasting and intergenerational effects for siblings.[54]

Stillbirth parents need "long-term therapy and treatment."[55] This mental and emotional health care also, however, needs to start with the medical providers with the pregnant person for birth. Research has shown what practices are helpful for parents emotionally and mentally after stillbirth, but the United States lacks any set standard of care on these practices. Despite this, most hospitals do something. A national survey of practices at randomly sampled hospitals was published in 2023.[56] Most responding hospitals provided tangible memorabilia like a memory box and handprints or footprints. But memorabilia were more extensive in larger hospitals than smaller ones and more likely to be offered, including memorabilia such as a card with the baby's information and photos. Similarly, "the largest volume hospitals were more likely than the smallest volume to offer education" about grief or about mental health risks. But overall, "a quarter of the hospitals reported not routinely offering grieving parents oral or written education about normal grief, giving a hospital contact for follow-up, or addressing grief of fathers or partners, despite these being fundamental components of bereavement care." Respondents identified financial limitations and lack of staff education as the main barriers to not doing more. In short, however, people who give birth in a larger volume hospital are more likely to start off with more helpful mental and emotional health care.

After the hospital, ACOG guidelines state, "referral to a bereavement counselor, peer support group, or mental health professional may be advisable for management of grief and depression."[57] No two people's experiences are the same, however. And ACOG guidelines recognize this. ACOG's regulations appropriately note that "bereavement care should be individualized to recognize bereaved parents' personal, cultural, or religious needs."[58]

Lower socioeconomic status can make things more difficult. Studies have found greater despair after stillbirth for persons with lower income and lesser education.[59] The surprising costs of stillbirth can add stress for these families.[60] People with lower incomes may also need to return to work after stillbirth sooner than they would desire. Paid leave from work for bereavement even for the death of a (living) child is far from standard and is likely unavailable in lower-paying jobs. Leave under the Federal Medical Leave Act (FMLA) may be available if a doctor certifies that recovering from childbirth is a "serious medical condition." FMLA leave is automatic after childbirth of a living child, but not stillbirth. Regardless, FMLA leave is unpaid, making it unhelpful for someone who needs an income.

Access to counseling and support also can be especially difficult for people with lower socioeconomic status. Medicaid covers therapy; the extent of the coverage will depend on the state. But if the birthing person had only been able to obtain Medicaid due to pregnancy, that insurance coverage can disappear soon after pregnancy. In some states, coverage can end as early as 60 days after birth. Many other states have extended that coverage to a year after birth, which is better. But still, mental health needs can persist after stillbirth. And even if insurance coverage exists, therapy is a bit of luxury. Appointments are usually during the day, and not everyone can take time away from work. Insurance coverage isn't needed for a support group, but the same problems with getting time off work can hamper access.

Lived experience based on race could also affect the mental and emotional health consequences of stillbirth. A study published in 2014 explained that "the grief experienced by bereaved African American parents may be of particular concern, given the unique aspects of their experience and culture."[61] The "realities of everyday life added to the burden African Americans faced after the loss of a child"—including "socioeconomic stressors, the prevalence of illness and death in families, a lack of support by others, and negative encounters with healthcare and other professionals."[62] Another study focusing on stillbirth and Black women explained that "compounded loss and trauma from the beginnings of slavery in this country 400 years ago, to racism and segregation, to present-day realities of high rates of poverty, single-parent families, incarceration, education disadvantage, and health disparities have been part of the experience of African Americans in the US and may play a significant role in how some cope with further loss and trauma."[63]

More concretely, studies create concern regarding whether support groups, the usual go-to solution for mental and emotional health care after stillbirth, are effective for African American women. The lessened effectiveness is due to the lack of diversity. In one study, "the participants indicated that groups they attended had few or no other African American women, which made their sharing somewhat constrained. They wanted the opportunity to talk with women of their culture in that setting."[64] Similarly, another study explains that some Black "parents may find it difficult to share their experiences and emotions in groups that often have few or no other parents from their own race or culture."[65] Support groups are theoretically helpful for Black women after stillbirth. But increased diversity is likely needed before support groups are practically helpful.

Other cultural differences may dissuade parents from attending a support group or counseling or therapy. In a study of Black women's experience, one woman explained that "cultural differences make our grieving that much harder. We are not expected to go to counseling and [are] brought up to make it on our own, to try to be strong, but can't."[66] Similarly, another study explained that "being 'strong in grief' is unique to the African American culture because of the enormous adversity that this population has historically faced. Strength is learned, modeled, and valued across generations."[67]

Geography can also create problems with accessing support groups. Support groups don't exist everywhere, and are possibly less likely to exist in rural areas. The internet provides additional opportunities, but not all have quality internet access.

Another factor that can affect a person's mental and emotional healthcare needs post-stillbirth is religion. Some have trouble maintaining their religious convictions after their child's stillbirth.[68] Others, however, find those beliefs "an important source of solace." Even if not religious before their child's stillbirth, people sometimes find comfort in religious ideas of an afterlife or of some master plan. Race may also play a role in whether a person is comforted by religion. In a study of Black women, many "spoke of having faith and putting their trust in God. Believing that God does everything for a reason, can fix anything, and is a protector was a source of strength for those who held these beliefs."[69] But again, every person is different. And some may not find religion comforting.

ACOG's guidelines recognize the importance of long-term mental and emotional health care. But there is no one-size-fits-all mental and emotional health care after stillbirth. Care needs to be tailored to the individual and family as much as possible. And the care must be accessible. Reproductive justice means that parents have a right to this care.

RAINBOW CLINIC CARE

Speaking of needing additional support, stillbirth parents also need access to special care in subsequent pregnancies. The decision whether to try again for another child is difficult, full of fear that the next baby could die too. And once one is pregnant, the experiences of prenatal care and childbirth can "stimulat[e] painful memories. Rather than being a time of joy, expectation, and a new beginning, the subsequent pregnancy can become a reactivation of the previous event, causing fear and anxiety that death can happen again."[70] Pregnant people are usually excited for ultrasounds; but for a stillbirth mom, the last time she had an ultrasound could have been the one that revealed her child's death in the womb. A new pregnancy can bring joy, but the joy coexists with the anxiety and fear.

Standard prenatal care is just not enough. Not only is a subsequent pregnancy difficult mentally and emotionally, but it also presents additional medical challenges given that a prior stillbirth increases the risk of another stillbirth.

A UK doctor, Dr. Alexander Heazell, created the concept of a rainbow clinic.[71] (I don't love the name given the reference to a "rainbow baby" but that's not the point of this.) Rainbow clinic care includes a focus on determining the cause of the prior stillbirth(s), flexible prenatal care appointments and testing, emotional support, and an express affirmation to do whatever the pregnant patient needs for reassurance. The results in the UK clinics are fantastic. These are high-risk patients due to their prior stillbirths, yet the stillbirth rate for those treating in the Rainbow Clinic is lower than the rate for the general population in the UK.

This care is far from available for all who desire or need it. The care has expanded to 20 clinics in the UK. As for the United States, we have about two. There's the Hope After Loss Clinic at the University of Wisconsin in Madison, Wisconsin, and the new Rainbow Clinic at Mount Sinai in New York City.[72] Consistent with reproductive justice, however, this care needs to expand and be available to any person pregnant after stillbirth.

* * * *

Reproductive justice rights are *human* rights. The right to have a child and parent him with dignity. This is a human right to which all persons are entitled. As part of that right, people have the right to health care that will help prevent stillbirth, rights concerning the birth of their stillborn baby, the right to mental and emotional health care after stillbirth, and proper care in any subsequent pregnancies.

SEVEN

That First Breath

I didn't expect to be able to claim Caleb as a dependent when I did our 2017 federal taxes. I knew he died before he was born. It was annoying, but it wasn't high on the list of things that bothered me about how stillbirth is treated.

I later learned, however, that had Caleb been born alive and died shortly after birth, I could have claimed him as a dependent on my 2017 taxes. If he had been born alive, he would have been issued a birth certificate and a Social Security number, and thus I could have claimed him on our federal taxes. But because he died just before birth, only a fetal death certificate is issued and that's not enough for a Social Security number.

That discovery is when I became officially bothered by my inability to claim Caleb as a dependent.

* * * *

Laws often have dividing lines. One of the most famous dividing lines came from *Roe v. Wade:* allowing states to ban abortion after viability but prohibiting the state from doing so before viability. That led to fiftyish years of arguing whether viability made any sense as a dividing line.

Live birth—defined by the Model Vital Statistics Act as a breath or "any other evidence of life such as a beating of the heart, pulsation of the umbilical cord, or definite movement of voluntary muscles" after expulsion from the mother—is a dividing line for many laws.[1] It's a dividing line that provides legal recourse or benefits for parents whose child is born alive and then dies but denies legal recourse or benefits for parents whose child is stillborn. It's also a dividing line that expresses a distinction—that there's something different enough between the two circumstances to justify the dividing line. It's a line that symbolizes that a child born alive and then dying is different enough from stillbirth to justify distinct legal treatment.

I'm not here to compete in the grief Olympics. I don't want to argue that infant death is not worse than stillbirth. It's all horrible. But I do want to ask a question about whether the two are different enough to justify live birth as a dividing line. Part of my job as law professor is teaching students critical thinking, including the ability to determine what the law is trying to accomplish and whether the law will help to accomplish that purpose. It's common for me to discuss a rule and then ask students "does this make sense?" This chapter is all about whether the live birth dividing line makes sense.

Not surprisingly, many in the stillbirth community argue that "the metaphor of taking that first breath in the world carries strong moral significance for many people even though, at the end of gestational development, such a cutoff makes little sense medically and is essentially arbitrary."[2] I would argue the same holds true for many laws.

This chapter details two laws that (at least originally) depended on live birth—wrongful death laws and tax benefits. Parents had no wrongful death claim if their child was killed by tortious conduct before the child was born. Similarly, parents lack any federal tax benefits for their stillborn child. I'm focusing on these two legal contexts because they provide tangible benefits to parents, mainly. I focus on both of these legal contexts from the perspectives of parents.

This chapter won't discuss another legal context that historically depended on live birth—murder statutes. Historically, murder was possible only of living people, not fetuses. Today though, the vast majority of states apply murder laws to fetuses. Often, state legislatures did so due to lobbying by bereaved parents wanting some criminal consequence for the fetal death. Other state legislatures were motivated by antiabortion sentiment. Regardless, I'm not going to discuss murder statutes because criminal law isn't really about the bereaved parents. The state chooses whether to bring criminal charges, and a conviction serves the state's interest. I assume that a criminal conviction provides an intangible feeling of justice for parents. But criminal law is about the state, not the parents, making the question of the arbitrariness of the dividing line very different. It is worth mentioning that states sometimes apply murder laws or abortion bans as of conception, yet only allow parents wrongful death relief after quickening or viability; examples include Mississippi, Indiana, Kentucky, Arizona, and Idaho. I'm at a loss as to how a state's interest in the unborn can be greater than the parents' interest. Regardless, criminal law is different and not discussed here.

Similarly, please let me also set aside the implications of this discussion for abortion jurisprudence. Antiabortion advocates have long advocated for laws treating "unborn" still in the womb as children/persons the same as living children/persons. This was explicitly part of antiabortion strategy and is the subject of chapter 8.

This chapter focuses on two laws that provide tangible legal benefits to parents, and asks whether it makes sense to condition those benefits on live birth. I hope to convince you that it doesn't.

WRONGFUL DEATH

I already discussed wrongful death law and the damages available for wrongful death claims in chapter 4. But I'd like to review some of that history here. Wrongful death law is the law that enables a tort claim for the death of a family member. It didn't exist at common law. There was no way at common law for a parent to sue the tortfeasor who killed the parent's child.[3] State legislatures changed that starting in the 1850s, creating wrongful death statutes.[4] As discussed, the lawsuit is technically under the statute, but still requires the plaintiff to show that the tortfeasor committed a tort (still defined by the common law). As an example, Missouri's wrongful death statute creates a lawsuit for "the death of a person" due to tortious conduct for the "spouse or children or the surviving lineal descendants of any deceased children, natural or adopted, legitimate or illegitimate, or by the father or mother of the deceased, natural or adoptive."[5] So the spouse of the deceased can sue the tortfeasor who killed the deceased. Or the parents of the deceased can sue the tortfeasor who killed the deceased child.

Wrongful death statutes create a lawsuit for the death of a *person*. Originally, this meant someone born alive and living when tortiously killed. Live birth was the dividing line.

Live birth as the dividing line means that parents whose baby is tortiously killed right after birth have a wrongful death claim. Parents also have a wrongful death claim if their baby is tortiously injured during pregnancy but the baby is born alive and then dies due to that tortious conduct. Parents do not have a wrongful death claim, however, if their baby is tortiously killed during pregnancy or even during birth. That first breath defined the availability of a wrongful death claim.

As early as 1916, courts were wondering whether the birth dividing line made any sense and whether wrongful death law should apply to tortious deaths before birth.[6] The Wisconsin Supreme Court noted that "very cogent reasons may be urged for a contrary rule" and classified the live birth rule as "merely practical."

Despite the questions, most courts remained firm that live birth before death was a necessary precondition to the availability of wrongful death claims. Some of this is because of the court's position interpreting a statute. Many courts believed that "person" in the wrongful death statute assumed only live birth before tortiously caused death, and that if the legislature had meant to include the unborn, it would have used language to clearly do so. As late as 1995, the Arkansas Supreme Court refused to find that "person" in the wrongful death statute included the unborn even though the Arkansas Constitution had recently been amended to declare the public policy of Arkansas to "protect the life of every unborn child."[7] (The legislature shortly after did amend the wrongful death statute with that clear language.)

Other courts also defended the supposed logic of birth as a dividing line. In a 1969 case, New York's highest court insisted that proof of injury and causation were "immeasurably more vague" in suits where the child dies before birth.[8] The court noted that the line was a bit arbitrary, especially when comparing cases where the child dies just before versus just after birth, but also maintained that any dividing line would likely be arbitrary to some extent. In 1977, the California Supreme Court defended the live birth dividing line, explaining that lost relationship damages for stillbirth are lesser than for death of a baby after birth:

> Without in any way denying the reality of that loss, we are compelled to observe that the class of parents who suffer the greater deprivation of this nature are those whose child has been born alive. The parents of a stillborn

fetus have never known more than a mysterious presence dimly sensed by random movements in the womb; but the mother and father of a child born alive have seen, touched, and heard their baby, have witnessed his developing personality, and have started the lifelong process of communicating and interacting with him. These are the rich experiences upon which a meaningful parent-child relationship is built, and they do not begin until the moment of birth.[9]

This was 1977. Think of how much has changed in pregnancy since then. Now, the parents would have seen the unborn baby on ultrasound at least twice before twenty weeks of pregnancy (the time where stillbirth is possible). As Justice Samuel Alito recently explained, "when prospective parents who want to have a child view a sonogram, they typically have no doubt that what they see is their daughter or son."[10] The parents may have even put the ultrasound picture up on their refrigerator. There are no "random movements in the womb" (if there even were in 1977); today, there is the baby kicking and bringing the parents joy when he does so. Today, there are weekly emails documenting the baby's growth. All of that happens in a pregnancy that ends in stillbirth too.

Additionally, medical care for stillbirth has changed since 1977. At the time, standard of care was to take the stillborn baby away, so it is unlikely that the parents would have ever seen or touched their baby. Now, best practices are to encourage parents to spend time with their baby.[11] Thus, even when the baby is stillborn, parents now have seen and touched their baby. There's a body, a body to hold and kiss and to count fingers and toes. A baby stillborn at 28 weeks will look just like a baby who dies right after birth at 28 weeks. Similarly, a baby stillborn at 40 weeks will look like just a sleeping newborn. Especially in term stillbirth, the fact that the baby was fully developed means the experience will be more like death after birth despite the lack of that first breath. Not surprisingly, stillbirth parents explain that stillbirth is more like the experience of newborn death than it is similar to a miscarriage, especially early miscarriage.

The California Supreme Court's description also overstates the meaning of live birth. It states that "the class of parents who suffer the greater deprivation . . . are those whose child has been born alive." But remember that live birth includes the baby whose umbilical cord pulsates once after birth or has one voluntary muscle movement, maybe even a random yet voluntary movement. Death shortly after birth means very limited interaction and built parent–child relationship, yet still a wrongful death claim exists if the child's death is tortious. California Supreme Court Justice M. Stanley Mosk's description, on the other hand, assumes a "lifelong" parent–child process and relationship, which also won't be present if the child dies shortly after birth. I agree that one could argue that the lost parent–child relationship in stillbirth is more of just an expectation of a relationship, but the same is true in the death of any young baby.

Despite the problems with the analysis affirming live birth as a dividing line, some states still restrict wrongful death law to deaths post-birth. Those states include California, New York, Florida, and Texas (no wrongful death claim if due to medmal), all of which are very populous states. Making this denial of wrongful death applicability easier is that relief for negligence still exists, but that recovery is based on the pregnant person's injured body part, not a lost parent–child relationship.

Most states, however, have eliminated the live birth requirement for wrongful death law, often due to its arbitrariness. As examples, the Iowa Supreme Court noted that lost relationship damages "do not necessarily relate to the child's birth. And the parents' loss certainly does not vanish because the deprivation occurred prior to birth. To the deprived parent the loss is real either way."[12] Similarly, an Arizona court described that "a parent's loss of a child's expected love and companionship does not vanish simply because the child is lost before birth."[13]

But even if I've convinced you that birth makes little sense as the dividing line, the next question is what should be the dividing line? (Note that abortion-rights advocates opposed any dividing line besides live birth, but more on that in chapter 8.) Most states set that line at viability. Some state courts did so long before *Roe*. The historical logic seems to rely on the idea that a viable fetus is close enough to a separate "person." The Wisconsin Supreme Court suggested a viability line in 1916.[14] In 1949, the Minnesota Supreme Court explained, "It seems too plain for argument that where independent existence is possible and life is destroyed through a wrongful act a cause of action arises under the statutes cited."[15] More analysis in the opinion centers on how the fetus isn't a mere part of the mother anymore once it has developed enough to survive on its own, not dependent on the mother for its existence anymore. Viability does seem like a logical dividing line if one is focused on possible separate existence, which would be consistent with interpreting the word "person" in wrongful death statutes.

Then the Supreme Court decided *Roe,* and viability seemed like an obvious dividing line for wrongful death claims. *Roe* mentions that some states had allowed a wrongful death claim for stillbirth, but only to also mention that commentators oppose these claims, and that this claim does not create any rights for the fetus as it is the parents' claim.[16] Note that the Court said wrongful death claim for "a stillborn child." That's not accurate. The few states that had recognized a wrongful death claim pre-*Roe* had limited the claim to viable stillbirths—so only stillbirths after at least 28 weeks, which was viability at the time of *Roe*.[17] Note also though that *Roe* did not rely on nor mention wrongful death claims depending on viability in determining viability as the point at which states could ban abortion.

In a 2012 Alabama Supreme Court opinion, noted antiabortion jurist Justice Tom Parker criticized *Roe,* its viability standard, and its application to wrongful death claims. He states that the viability standard was created in 1946 in a case called *Bonbretz v. Kotz* allowing recovery for prenatal injury incurred after viability but before birth if the baby survived birth.[18] In shorthand, this is called the born-alive rule: the baby has a claim for injuries incurred after viability but before birth, but only if born alive. As already mentioned, just a few years later, relying on *Bonbretz,* the Minnesota Supreme Court adopted the viability line for the parents' wrongful death claims based on stillbirth.[19] Back to 2012, Justice Parker claims that the viability standard was "waning by 1961."[20] He was right with respect the baby's legal claim for injuries incurred after viability but before (live) birth. Courts realized that if the baby was born alive, it really shouldn't have made a difference if the injury incurred pre- or post-viability. But the viability line was not at all waning for parents' wrongful death claims. More states adopted it, and it remains today the majority rule for wrongful death recovery, allowing parents to recover for their unborn child's wrongful death only if the stillbirth occurred after viability.

A minority of states, including Alabama, do apply wrongful death law to all pregnancy losses pre- and post-viability. No state did so, however, until long after *Roe*, suggesting that those state legislatures and courts were motivated by efforts to undermine abortion rights. It was and is long-term antiabortion strategy to establish that fetuses are "persons" under the Fourteenth Amendment. One tactic was to try to get courts or legislatures to treat fetuses the same as a living "person" in as many contexts as possible, including wrongful death statutes.[21] As discussed more in chapter 8, antiabortion advocates weaponized grief after pregnancy loss and tried to use wrongful death law to "place proper value on an unborn child."[22]

In February 2024, the Alabama Supreme Court went a step even further, interpreting "minor child" in the Alabama wrongful death act to include not only all unborn children in the womb but also unborn children outside the womb—in a freezer, waiting to possibly be transferred to a uterus in IVF.[23] It's a remarkable decision, but also not surprising from the Alabama Supreme Court. Almost all states' application of wrongful death law to all pregnancy losses (pre- and post-viability) was through the legislature amending the statute. Even the Arkansas Supreme Court refused the application, stating it could only be done legislatively, as previously discussed. But the Alabama Supreme Court had no issues extending wrongful death law to pre-viability pregnancy losses via court decision, just as it had no issue with the extension to frozen embryos via court decision. The decision is also logical. Why would the location—womb or freezer—dictate if it's a child?[24] At the same time, the decision is comical, claiming that of course the *1872* Alabama legislature— long before IVF was a scientific possibility—meant child to include frozen embryos, and claiming the case was instead an attempt to create an exception for "extrauterine children." The decision sparked outcry for its potential dramatic effects on the practices of IVF in the United States, where common practice is to retrieve and fertilize as many eggs as possible and often later destroy any unused ones. And numerous Alabama IVF clinics did pause, and some have even stopped providing IVF services. Not long after the Alabama Supreme Court decision, the Alabama legislature passed a law making those who provide IVF services immune from civil suit (or criminal prosecution) for damage to or the death of an embryo.

But most states that apply wrongful death claims to pregnancy do so only for pregnancy losses after viability. And viability is a relatively easy dividing line for wrongful death. But that doesn't mean it makes sense.

Again, courts used viability because of the theoretically possible separate existence. But why would possible separate existence define whether the lost relationship is the kind that the wrongful death statute is meant to compensate? Separateness is seemingly necessary for a relationship. But also not. Surely if one of conjoined twins was killed tortiously, the law would recognize a lost sibling relationship even though separation was not possible.

The viability line may also originally have had something to do with causation. Especially early miscarriages are often related to abnormalities, creating an idea that many pregnancy losses are inevitable and could thus not be due to tort. Concerns about causation, however, wouldn't really translate to a viability standard. Causation concerns would better translate to a 20-week dividing line between miscarriage and stillbirth. But really, if the miscarriage is due to abnormalities, it's probably going to happen before 12 weeks. So maybe 12 weeks should be the dividing line. Note that causation would not be similarly difficult in frozen embryo cases where there's little dispute that negligent conduct enabled destruction of the embryos.[25] Regardless, if causation is the concern, the law could just as easily allow the claim and give the plaintiff a chance at proving causation. Mere difficulty of proving elements really shouldn't be a reason to deny the claim. Allow the claim; the plaintiff won't win if unable to show that the tortious conduct caused the miscarriage.

I've also thought the viability line may have something to do with reasonable expectations. Arguably, it is reasonable to develop and expect a parent-child relationship only after the point at which live childbirth is very, very likely to occur. I've never seen any court describe the viability standard as based on reasonable expectations of live childbirth, but it makes some sense. If the baby could survive on its own outside of the womb, it's extremely likely that the baby will be born alive. When courts started basing wrongful death recovery on viability, viability was around 28 weeks, also the start of the third trimester of pregnancy. Now, viability is closer to 24 weeks.

A problem with expectations though is a distinction between reasonable and subjective expectations. Most people today expect that their pregnancy will end with live childbirth long before they hit 24-ish weeks of pregnancy. That is their subjective expectation, but it is also reasonable given the medicalization of prenatal care and childbirth and the erasure of pregnancy loss in the abortion debate. Today, most people think every pregnancy ends with live childbirth. That's not true, but people (reasonably) think it. What is true is that the chances of live childbirth dramatically increase after 12 weeks of pregnancy. The vast majority of miscarriages happen before 12 weeks, in the first trimester, even though the possibility of miscarriage remains until 20 weeks. This is also behind the traditional thought of not sharing pregnancy news until 12 weeks. And thus it does seem reasonable to expect live childbirth if the pregnancy gets past 12 weeks, and thus maybe the dividing line for the availability of wrongful death recovery should be 12 weeks.

A line based on reasonable expectations would have stark effects on early miscarriages and also destruction of frozen embryos. Society overestimates the success rates of IVF.[26] Generally speaking, IVF leads to successful pregnancy for a woman under 35 and using her own eggs about 50–60% of the time. The percentage dwindles to 30–40% for women over 35. Yet, we all think IVF is amazing and always works. Tort law would say otherwise. It uses a preponderance of the evidence burden of proof. In tort terms, any IVF chance of success under 51% means that frozen embryo will *not* turn into a living child. Yet the Alabama Supreme Court believes plaintiffs whose frozen embryos are negligently destroyed should be able to sue for the death of their extrauterine children no different than the death of their living children.

Drawing lines is difficult. But if the birth line makes no sense, convenience alone can't justify it. Nor should we allow the line to be drawn for political reasons (i.e., abortion) that have nothing to do with pregnancy loss. Either a 12- or 20-week line likely makes the most sense and is the least arbitrary.

TAXES

Federal tax law has long allowed tax benefits for parents in the form of a tax credit and/or allowing a deduction for having dependents. A tax credit is money directly back to parents; a $2000 tax credit equals $2000 off what you owe in taxes (and can include a payment to parents if the parents owe less than $2000 in taxes when the credit is refundable as opposed to nonrefundable). A deduction reduces the amount of the parents' taxable income, and how much of a benefit it will be financially depends on the rate at which the parents' income is taxed.

The ability to claim a deduction for dependents existed until 2018. The Tax Cuts and Jobs Act, passed by Congress and signed by President Donald Trump, effective in 2018, suspended the deduction for dependents (while also increasing the amount of the standard deduction). The Act suspends the ability to claim this deduction for dependency exemptions until 2025.[27] Currently, you can and must still claim a dependent to obtain other tax benefits/credits, but no deduction exists.

One of those benefits a taxpayer can claim for a dependent is the child tax credit. The first child tax credit was created in the Taxpayer Relief Act of 1997. It was a $500 nonrefundable tax credit that phased out for higher levels of incomes. Congress increased the amount of the credit in later years and also adjusted the higher income phase-out and refundability. The amount was up to $1000 per child in 2010 (and the amount of refundability was more generous).[28] The Tax Cuts and Jobs Act suspended the deduction for the dependency exemptions, but also increased the amount of the child tax credit to $2000 (and again made refundability more generous).[29]

Then the pandemic hit and Congress passed the American Rescue Plan. Seeing the need to help families, the law increased the amount of credit to $3,600 for kids under 5 and $3,000 for kids 6–17 years old. The bill also made the credit fully refundable for taxpayers with low income and includes income threshold phase outs.[30] There was also a huge change in how the child tax credit was delivered. The pandemic increased interest in direct cash benefits to families to help. Thus, instead of just applying the child tax credit when taxes are paid, the credit was set up to be delivered to families in monthly payments throughout 2021. The effect was to dramatically reduce child poverty in this country.[31] More than 61 million children in the country benefited. July–December monthly payments kept 3.7 million children out of poverty. The first payment alone in July reduced the monthly child poverty rate by 26%. The six payments also cut food insufficiency among families by 26%. In short, it was amazing. Also, Congress didn't extend the monthly payments and child poverty rates are back up again.

Federal tax benefits, however, only exist for parents of *living* children. Any taxpayer claiming a dependent has to provide a taxpayer identification

That First Breath

number for the child. Usually, that's a Social Security number.[32] You can only get a Social Security number if you have a live birth certificate for the child.

But also remember what counts as live birth—a breath, a heartbeat, a pulsation of the umbilical cord, or a voluntary muscle movement. Any of those things means a live birth certificate and the tax credit. Even if the baby dies seconds later.

Does it make sense to base entitlement to a tax credit on an umbilical cord pulsation? That depends on the purpose of tax benefits for children. That main purpose of tax benefits is to help families raising children. Raising children in this country is very expensive. In 2022, the Brookings Institute estimated that the cost of raising a child in the United States is $310,000, and that doesn't include the cost of college.[33] Plainly speaking, the child tax credit "helps families manage the cost of raising children."[34] The benefit recognizes that even if their gross income is the same, a couple living off that income will be much better off than a couple with children will be. The benefit thus "treats the larger family more generously on ability-to-pay grounds and imposes a lower tax liability."[35]

Focus on a baby stillborn at term and a newborn infant who dies just after birth. Both sets of parents spent money preparing for the child. Both sets of parents prepared the nursery, bought the car seat, and have a closet full of diapers and baby clothes. The amount of expenses incurred in raising the child will be very similar. But only one set of parents will get the benefit of the child tax credit—the parent whose child died just after birth.

That makes no sense. There doesn't seem to be any argument that the parents with the deceased baby born alive incur expenses for "raising" a child and that parents of a stillborn baby do not. The parents whose baby dies shortly after birth doesn't buy any more diapers than the parents whose baby is stillborn at term.

The tax credit also applies to extreme premature births with no chance of survival for the baby. Note that the Model Vital Statistics Act's definition of live birth specifically says, "irrespective of the duration of pregnancy."[36] Even if the pregnant person's water breaks way too early and the baby is born at like 16 or 18 weeks, if that umbilical cord pulsates, a birth certificate is legally appropriate and the parents are eligible for the child tax credit. The duration of pregnancy is likely very relevant to how much in expenses the parents could have already incurred in preparing for the baby. There's likely a pretty significant difference in the amounts spent before 16 weeks versus the amounts spent when the baby is born alive at 40 weeks and dies shortly thereafter. But that doesn't matter. What matters is whether the umbilical cord pulsates.

The tax credit could also easily apply to a pregnant person who had a pre-viability labor induction abortion without fetal demise beforehand. As mentioned in chapter 6, this is where the line between abortion, birth, and pregnancy loss is extremely blurry. If abortion is via labor induction before viability and the baby is born alive, according to the definitions in the Model Vital Statistics Act, that is a live birth. Even though it's before viability and death is imminent, that is a live birth and issued a live birth certificate. I'm not at all implying that a tax credit necessarily shouldn't be available for abortion; although it's safe to say that Congress didn't intend so. I am, however, arguing that it doesn't make any sense for a child tax credit—meant to help parents with the costs of raising children—to be based on an umbilical cord pulsating.

There's another possible related purpose of the child tax credit—to help raise children out of poverty. This was an especially common refrain with the American Rescue Plan and the effects of monthly distributions of the child tax credit.

The problem of child poverty, however, also cannot explain the live birth dividing line. Child poverty can't (technically) apply to unborn children. But it also can't justify application of the child tax credit to parents with children no longer living (i.e., dead children). Dead children can't be living under the poverty line and in need of credit payments such that they could live above the poverty line.

Thus, neither of the purposes of tax benefits for children—helping parents with the costs of raising children and alleviating child poverty—justify a birth dividing line. Live birth is an easy dividing line. It's also a traditional line. But the ease and tradition can't overcome the illogic.

Some states have recognized that illogic in federal tax law. Prompted by advocacy from stillbirth parents, states have created state tax benefits, whether dependent exemptions or credits, for stillbirth. Arizona allows a $2300 deduction, North Dakota allows a $4150 deduction, and Michigan

That First Breath

similarly allows parents a $3700 deduction.[37] As for credits, which would benefit lower-income taxpayers more than deductions, Minnesota allows a fully refundable $2000 tax credit for the year the child was stillborn, Arkansas allows a nonrefundable $500 tax credit, and Connecticut's largest in the nation $2500 tax credit for stillbirth was effective in 2022.[38]

These tax benefits can really help parents after stillbirth. And it makes sense; if parents whose child dies right after birth get a tax benefit, then so should parents whose child dies right before birth. Those parents likely have very similar expenses incurred in expectation of raising their child.

It's important to note that a tax benefit is also symbolic for some parents. The inability to claim your child on your taxes, a child that you gave birth to, can be jarring. It's a legal denial of parenthood. The symbolism is difficult though because it varies for parents. The symbolism wasn't that big of a deal for me; I knew that he wasn't born alive, and I wasn't really affected by tax law's denial of my parenthood of Caleb. My later annoyance was based on illogic—why would I be eligible for a tax credit if Caleb had died right after birth, but not before.

Even if I've convinced you that the live birth dividing line is arbitrary, really any line will be arbitrary to some extent, including the 20-week dividing line that states use for stillbirth tax benefits. There's no significant distinction in the expenses incurred to prepare for the child as of 19 weeks versus 20 weeks, but there is likely a difference between expenses incurred in the 5th week of pregnancy versus 20 weeks. And there's also a significant difference between expenses incurred at 20 weeks of pregnancy versus 40 weeks. Excluding early stillbirths between 20 and 24 weeks would align with viability, but it would also problematically affect Black women specifically who have triple the rate of stillbirth between 20 and 24 weeks.

Some state legislatures have been talking about tax credits for parents of "unborn children" even earlier in pregnancy. Starting in 2022, Georgia allowed a $3000 deduction/exemption for all "unborn children with a detectable human heart."[39] Later guidance from the state explained that a detectable human heart "may occur as early as 6 weeks." Missouri legislators introduced in 2022 a bill allowing a $1200 deduction for an unborn child if "pregnancy is confirmed by physician" and if the taxpayer will be "entitled to a dependency exemption for federal income tax purposes once the unborn child is born."⁴⁰

While I support tax credits for stillbirth, I don't think tax benefits for earlier pregnancy losses make a lot of sense. There's just really nothing comparable to spending money to raise (living) children with an early pregnancy loss. There certainly can be some medical expenses, but not a lot. There's a first appointment at 6 or 8 weeks and then another at 12 weeks, all of which are legally required to be covered by insurance now (although delays can exist with Medicaid). Out-of-pocket costs can exist if the miscarriage does not clear on its own.⁴¹ Either abortion medication (if doctors are unafraid to prescribe it) or a D&C cost money. But those are more about expenses for the "child's" death than about the costs of raising the child; raising the child stops at the child's death.

The earlier and earlier in pregnancy that we allow people to claim their unborn children, the more it seems like we're just paying them for getting pregnant. This is ironic given that many of the same politicians pushing these measures also still believe in racist and classist stereotypes about women of color and poor women as breeders and "Welfare Queens." Regardless, if these laws are about helping with pregnancy expenses, can't we just call them that? The same goes for bills requiring "child support" during pregnancy. These could more easily be bipartisan initiatives if the focus was on support during pregnancy instead of the unborn child.

The state legislators advocating for tax benefits for early pregnancies don't seem to know much about pregnancy loss. The Missouri bill states that the taxpayer is entitled to an exemption if the pregnancy is confirmed by a doctor and the "taxpayer *will* be entitled to a dependency exemption for federal income tax purposes once the unborn child is born." *Will be entitled* presumes the baby will be born alive as federal dependency exemptions depend on live birth. If the pregnancy is confirmed in January but a miscarriage occurs a week later, the Missouri tax benefit seems inapplicable. The same is true if the baby is stillborn in June. What if pregnancy is confirmed in November or December of the tax year? If the pregnancy has ended before tax time, the taxpayer can't claim the exemption for the prior year's taxes. Or even more complicated, what if the pregnancy is confirmed in November, the person is still pregnant at tax time and claims the benefit, but then the pregnancy ends in stillbirth after taxes are filed and thus no federal dependency exemption will exist? I assume that's not tax fraud because there was no intent, but would the stillbirth parent have to amend their state taxes?

State legislators also don't seem to understand how many pregnancy losses occur each year. If you knew the number of pregnancy losses each year, you'd quickly realize how much money this could be. I once saw a draft of a bill providing a $2000 tax credit for every "spontaneous fetal death," as in every pregnancy loss. I'll stick with Missouri statistics here to demonstrate the potential fiscal effect. Missouri had 430 stillbirths and 69,285 live births in 2020. Doing some quick math based the number of live births and 1 in 4 pregnancies ending in miscarriage, that's about 23,000 miscarriages. Adding together the miscarriages and stillbirths, that's about 23,430 pregnancy losses in the state of Missouri in 2020. A $2000 tax credit for each would total about $46.8 million dollars of lost tax revenue just based on pregnancy losses. The fiscal effect of deductions is less predictable because their amount usually depends on amounts of income. Regardless, maybe state legislators will start caring about pregnancy losses if they start hurting their tax revenue.

It's also curious how state legislators think people would be able to provide documentation of pregnancy (and of pregnancy loss when there's not a baby nine months later). Again, Georgia's law provides a deduction for an unborn child with a detectable heartbeat. The Georgia guidance mentions providing "medical documentation."[42] What is that? Presumably, it's more than a picture of a positive pregnancy test. That's not doctor-issued. Plus, a pregnancy at four weeks doesn't yet have a detectable heartbeat. At the same time, detectable heartbeat is different than a heartbeat actually detected at a doctor's appointment. Often, that first doctor's appointment isn't even until eight weeks, in which case there'd be no medical documentation of a pregnancy that was detectable at six weeks, but miscarried before eight weeks. There's been reports that Louisiana providers are pushing that first prenatal appointment until 12 weeks due to fear of any overlap between abortion restrictions and miscarriage care, meaning there'd be no medical documentation for miscarriages between 6 and 12 weeks.[43] The need to apply for Medicaid for pregnancy can also easily delay that first prenatal appointment. And simply having less access to prenatal care can easily delay that first appointment after 8 weeks or even after 12 weeks. Requiring medical documentation will harm marginalized persons' ability to claim this exemption.

The Missouri bill explicitly requires doctor documentation, which could be a doctor-issued pregnancy test before a heartbeat is detectable. People receiving fertility treatment or using IVF would have doctor confirmation via blood tests as early as four weeks. But only people with relatively higher socioeconomic status are using IVF because of sparse insurance coverage, meaning women with means will be better able to take advantage of Missouri's version of this tax benefit. In one of the two times I was on clomid to try to get pregnant, my period was late, but I was negative on a home pregnancy test. A doctor-ordered blood test said I was pregnant. Two days later, I bled. According to some Missouri legislators, I deserve a $1200 exemption on my taxes for whatever you want to label that experience. (But don't call it the death of my child because it wasn't.)

Most reproductive rights scholars decry any idea of tax benefits for unborn children.[44] I'm a unique voice in this field because I believe that tax benefits should exist for stillbirth, especially late stillbirths, because those parents incur similar costs of raising their child as do parents whose newborn dies soon after birth. But these newly popular laws providing tax benefits don't really seem to be about helping people with the costs of raising children; they instead seem to be about further ingraining ideas of prenatal personhood.

This brings us back to the ultimate question of what the dividing line for tax benefits should be. If the child tax credit is about helping parents with the costs of raising children, I think the least arbitrary line would likely be stillbirths in the third trimester (after 28 weeks). That aligns best with the similar experience of babies dying shortly after birth. Another less arbitrary line would be to use the 20-week stillbirth dividing line, which is arguably more arbitrary than a 28-week line but still more defensible than the live birth dividing line.

EIGHT

Abortion and Stillbirth

I supported abortion rights before Caleb's death and do so even more after. His death accentuated to me how difficult everything is concerning pregnancy and children. No one should be forced to do any of it.

I couldn't handle antiabortion rhetoric after his death. It's common to see signs urging prayer to end abortion. I've never seen one urging prayer to end miscarriage or stillbirth. Are they not also "unborn human beings"? While holding Caleb, we scrambled to find a priest (we're Catholic) to come do some sort of blessing. Of course, the only one who we could find was my least favorite priest in the area—the one who always found a way to bring up abortion in his homilies. He loved to talk about life at conception. He very awkwardly told us that he couldn't baptize Caleb. Sacraments are only for the "living." (Disclaimer that I am still forever grateful that he came to the hospital.)

What does abortion have to do with stillbirth? Nothing. But also everything. Stillbirth advocacy groups sometimes try to remain neutral on abortion; neutrality on abortion, however, isn't possible. Plus, denying the elephant in the room is only counterproductive. Every day, I'm more and more convinced that our country's obsession with abortion is a significant reason why we don't have any useful stillbirth prevention measures—really why we can't even talk about stillbirth.

. . . .

In 1973, the Supreme Court decided *Roe v. Wade,* declaring that a federal constitutional right to abortion existed and states could not criminalize abortion before viability.[1] Viability is the point at which the fetus could likely survive on its own outside the womb. In 1973, viability was 28 weeks, coinciding with the beginning of the third trimester of pregnancy, and the World Health Organization's still current dividing line between miscarriage and stillbirth. Today, because of medical advancements, viability is generally at 24 weeks.

In 2022, the Supreme Court decided *Dobbs v. Jackson Women's Health Organization*, declaring that no federal constitutional right to abortion exists, overruling *Roe*, and leaving states to do whatever they want with abortion—keep it legal, make it illegal throughout pregnancy, and so on.[2]

Roe is gone, but the abortion debate is not over. As of February 2024, around thirty states still have legal abortion similar to what they had pre-*Dobbs*. *Dobbs* is a success in ending *Roe*, but it's not a success in ending the legality of abortion. There's two ways to ban abortion in all states: a federal law doing so, or a Supreme Court decision that "person" in the Fourteenth Amendment includes prenatal life. Such a Supreme Court holding would mean that prenatal life has due process rights, including to not be killed. That's not what *Dobbs* did; *Dobbs* is "not based on any view about if and when prenatal life is entitled to any of the rights enjoyed after birth."[3] But Justice Samuel Alito's opinion also left the door wide open for prenatal personhood arguments, mentioning supposed "ample evidence" that pre-1868 state legislatures banned abortion due to their "sincere belief that abortion kills a human being."[4] It's not surprising that mere months after *Dobbs*, a petition for certiorari was filed asking the Court to interpret "person" to include prenatal life.[5] The Court declined to hear the case. For now.

How does stillbirth fit in this picture? It doesn't. In fact, the abortion debate has and continues to essentially erase pregnancy loss. The abortion debate fuels our public consciousness of pregnancy. And according to the debate, the only thing that prevents live birth is abortion. More plainly, all pregnancies either end with abortion or with the birth of a living baby; pregnancy loss doesn't exist.

The erasure has one exception—the antiabortion side likes to revive pregnancy loss to weaponize it. They argue that the realities of grief after stillbirth, of stillbirth moms identifying their babies as their children, and of some even having funerals for their stillborn child all demonstrate fetal personhood. These are powerful weapons. Much about pregnancy loss aligns with antiabortion narratives and contradicts abortion-rights narratives. This is also why the abortion-rights movement tends to avoid pregnancy loss as much as possible.

But any supposed tension between pregnancy loss and abortion rights is just that, supposed. In 2022, Greer Donley—a wonderful friend and fellow law professor—and I published a paper introducing an idea called subjective fetal personhood into the abortion debate. Stillbirth parents may very well identify their stillborn child as their child. That is a subjective assignment of "personhood." It exists only because the pregnant person decided so; other pregnant people might not make such an assignment in their pregnancies. It depends on the pregnant person. Recognition of this subjectivity doesn't threaten abortion rights. Subjectivity is fundamentally inconsistent with the antiabortion idea that every fetus is a person at the moment of conception. Subjectivity is thus a way to properly recognize the loss some experience in pregnancy loss without also ceding ground on abortion rights.

Dobbs is a dramatic setback for abortion rights. But, as Donley and I framed it, it is also an opportunity for new coalitions between abortion-rights and pregnancy-loss communities. The realities of pregnancy loss create serious questions about the claimed state interest in protecting fetal life that underlies abortion bans. The realities of pregnancy loss can also help normalize that pregnancies often end with something other than live childbirth. In short, minimizing the fetus did not prevent *Dobbs*. The post-*Dobbs* future is an opportunity to recognize the breadth of reproductive experiences—infertility, pregnancy, abortion, pregnancy loss, and live childbirth.

THE ERASURE

If your main focus is stillbirth or pregnancy loss more generally, it's easy to feel lost in the abortion debate. That's because you don't really exist in the debate. The abortion debate has essentially erased pregnancy loss. Historian Lara Freidenfelds elegantly explains that before *Roe*, the opposite of pregnant was miscarriage. But after *Roe*, the opposite of pregnant became abortion.[6]

The abortion debate assumes a binary—pregnancies end in either abortion or with the birth of a living baby. Others have labeled this the "single-path narrative" of pregnancy. Anthropologist Linda Layne refers to this as the depicted linear progression of pregnancy and fetal development.[7] Both sides are responsible for this binary. The antiabortion side emphasizes that abortion ends a would-be life, that it kills a baby, presuming the baby would otherwise be born alive. The abortion-rights side emphasizes that the unavailability of abortion forces parenthood of a living baby.

The Supreme Court also assumes the binary. In *Roe*, Justice Harry Blackmun emphasized the burdens on women that assume pregnancy will result in a living baby—how childcare can tax mental and physical health, the distress associated with a child from an unwanted pregnancy, and the burdens associated with bringing a child into a family without the means to care for it.[8] All of this assumes live childbirth. The same assumption is apparent in *Dobbs*. Justice Alito's majority opinion mentions that abortion is not necessary anymore because of safe haven laws (allowing one to drop off a newborn at a fire station without consequence) and the numerous couples wanting to adopt.[9] Neither fire stations nor couples looking to adopt want a stillborn baby.

The binary, however, is simply false. Millions of pregnancies end in miscarriage in this country each year. And tens of thousands more end in stillbirth each year. But you'd never know it from the abortion debate, the same debate that controls so much of our discourse surrounding pregnancy. The abortion debate's binary essentially erases Caleb and all pregnancy losses.

The abortion debate is far from the only factor erasing pregnancy loss. Another factor is the medicalization of pregnancy. Amazing medical advancements like IVF and the increased survival odds for premature birth make us think medicine fixes all reproductive woes these days. Another factor is what I call pregnancy capitalism—the fact that marketers target pregnant people and call them "mom" at only five weeks pregnant.[10] But there's also no doubt that the abortion debate is contributing to the erasure. The abortion debate has been so prevalent and intense for so long; it has affected all public thought about pregnancy.

This erasure is increasing the stigma of pregnancy loss. The abortion-influenced cultural script of pregnancy does not include pregnancy loss. But then it happens. The real-life experience "clashe[s] . . . dramatically" with the learned understanding of pregnancy from the abortion debate.[11] This wasn't supposed to happen; this is not how pregnancies end. Pregnancy loss is "shocking" and alienating because of the lack of knowledge of the frequency of pregnancy loss.

Abortion-rights "choice" rhetoric also increases alienation and feelings of blame, both self-blame and external blame (more on this in chapter 9).[12] Women (particularly privileged women) of my generation and younger have been raised thinking they had choice—and control—over their reproductive lives. But nothing about pregnancy loss feels like choice. Plus, choice implies control, and control implies responsibility or, even worse, blame. Pregnancy loss often creates a double bind for women.[13] "Either they accept responsibility for the pregnancy loss and therefore blame themselves for the death of their 'baby,' or they must admit that this was a bodily event over which they had no control." And accepting lack of control is "hardly more palatable than self-blame."

This erasure has somehow even gotten worse post-*Dobbs* with abortion bans as of conception—implying that all conceptions will turn into living babies. At least medically, mere conception does not equal pregnancy. Conception is when the sperm fertilizes the egg. But pregnancy doesn't medically begin until that fertilized egg implants in the uterine lining, usually a week or two after conception. Implantation is also the first time at which pregnancy can be detected because tests detect human chorionic gonadotropin (hcG), and the body does not start producing hcG until implantation. There is no medical test right now that can detect conception.[14] If the fertilized egg doesn't implant, the person will have a normal period and never know that conception had occurred.

This implication that all conceptions turn into living babies erases the reality that many fertilized eggs do not successfully implant in the uterine wall. Scientists already knew that, but experience with in vitro fertilization has enabled them to better estimate how many fertilized eggs do not implant. In IVF, the embryo is created and then transferred into the uterus. But that embryo does not always successfully implant into the uterine lining; it implants successfully far less frequently than is assumed.[15] In one study, an IVF cycle ended with live birth (and thus successful implantation) only 30% of the time for women in the 18–34 age group.[16] The percentage decreased to 25% for patients 35–37, and less than 20% for patients 38–39.

From IVF data, scientists estimate that about 35% of fertilized eggs do not implant. Yet post-*Dobbs* abortion bans presume that every fertilized egg will now turn into a living baby because abortion is illegal.

And, if pregnancy begins at conception, pregnancy-loss rates increase dramatically. Every fertilized egg that doesn't implant is now a miscarriage. Between non-implantation miscarriages and other pregnancy losses, scientists estimate that as many as 70% of fertilized eggs *do not turn into living babies*.[17] Even if it's 60% or 50%, that's astounding given the abortion debate's assumption that every fertilized egg ends up as a living baby.

Again, as high as 70%. Yet in response to a proposed Senate bill protecting the right to interstate travel to obtain abortion care, Senator James Lankford, a Republican from Oklahoma, said: "Does that child in the womb have the right to travel in their future?"[18] Oklahoma's most recent abortion ban applied as of conception.[19] Only about 30% of those fertilized "children" will ever take a breath outside the womb. The other 70% of fertilized eggs will never travel outside of the womb.

THE WEAPONIZATION

There's one exception when antiabortion advocates are happy to mention pregnancy loss—when they can weaponize it. Early in the abortion debate, antiabortion advocates realized that they could use pregnancy loss as a weapon. The realities that some parents grieved their stillborn child and identified their stillborn child as their child help arguments for fetal personhood. Antiabortion advocates leaned into the "loss" in pregnancy loss as the loss of a child.

An important beginning point is that antiabortion narratives are one reason why a person may experience pregnancy loss as the loss of a child.[20] Emphasis that "life" begins at conception affects the experience of an eight-week miscarriage, affecting ideas about what was lost. Teaching us strategies to see a baby at an eight-week ultrasound affects the experience of a nine-week miscarriage, again affecting ideas of the loss. Antiabortion narratives help cause people to see pregnancy loss as the death of a child—and to grieve even early pregnancy loss as the death of the child.

In fairness, ultrasounds have had a similar effect, especially with technicians using language like "the baby's foot," "he has his father's nose," or "the baby is being shy and won't turn around for us." That language, however, is at the 20-week ultrasound, not the 8-week one. Antiabortion narratives thus likely have more influence on thoughts surrounding early pregnancy losses than do ultrasounds.

And then antiabortion advocates used that grief from pregnancy loss to further their agenda. These advocates realized that they could use "the emotional power of parents pleading for legal recognition of their unborn children" to "sway societal views and incite political action" about abortion.[21] That legal recognition included attempts to get wrongful death law applied to pregnancy loss (discussed in chapter 7), and attempts to pass laws creating memorial birth certificates after stillbirth (discussed in chapter 2). Antiabortion advocates quickly realized that these legal recognitions could aid their cause, consistent with part of "the longterm, end-game strategy of pro-life forces . . . to have fetuses declared 'children' or 'persons' in as many legal contexts as possible."[22] Antiabortion advocates hoped to create what lawyers call a "slippery slope." The more legal contexts in which a fetus was treated the same as a living child, the greater the likelihood that the Supreme Court would also interpret "person" in the Fourteenth Amendment to include prenatal life.

Antiabortion judges have been happy to participate in this weaponization. In 2011, the Alabama Supreme Court held that the wrongful death law applies to all tortiously caused pregnancy losses, departing from the rule limiting that recovery to losses post viability. In 2012, the Alabama Supreme Court determined that that holding also applied to a case that had been pending on appeal when it made the 2011 decision. The 2012 case was essentially only procedural, about retroactivity. Justice Tom Parker, however, a noted antiabortion jurist, used that 2012 (wrongful death pre-viability stillbirth) case to criticize *Roe*'s viability standard as not persuasive, dictum, and incoherent.[23]

That same 2012 wrongful death pre-viability stillbirth case was again before the Alabama Supreme Court in 2018.[24] The parents had lost their wrongful death claim and appealed because the trial court refused to use the child's name, Tristian, in the jury instructions. The Alabama Supreme Court found no error because the jury instructions included "unborn child" and "stillborn child" language, which "acknowledged the fact that Tristian was a human being, and those terms were not demeaning."[25] Plus, the trial court allowed the mom to use Tristian's name throughout the trial. Justice Parker agreed with the lack of error, but felt the need to write separately to "emphasize the well established principle in Alabama law that unborn children are human beings entitled to full and equal protection of the law."[26] Justice Parker explained that trial courts should not interpret the majority's ruling "as condoning or suggesting" that they should "omit[] the names of unborn children in jury instructions.[27] He also explained that Alabama law does not allow any "stifl[ing] [of] the recognition of an unborn child's humanity."[28] Judge Parker twice used a grieving mother's legal claim as a platform to argue against *Roe*.

THE HYPOCRISIES

Even though they're happy to weaponize stillbirth and pregnancy loss more generally in the abortion debate, do not be confused that the antiabortion movement has any interest in preventing stillbirth.

Many of the same states that are obsessed with protecting fetal lives from abortion have no problem with fetal lives dying within pregnancy loss. Three easy examples are Mississippi, Alabama, and Arkansas. These are some of the most antiabortion states in the nation, all of which ban all abortion post-*Dobbs*. They also have the worst stillbirth rates in the nation. The rate nationally in 2021 was 5.73 stillbirths per 1000 births.[29] Mississippi's rate was 10 stillbirths per 1000 births, Alabama's was 8.71 per 1000 births, and Arkansas's was 8.38 per live births. All three states also have dramatic disparities in the risk based on race: using 2020 stillbirth data, a Black woman is 2.35 times more likely to give birth to a stillborn baby in Mississippi than a white woman, 2.18 times more likely in Alabama, and 2.14 times more likely in Arkansas.[30] It's hard to take seriously these states' claims that they care so much about fetal life when they're literally letting their stillbirth rates—i.e., fetal death rates—run rampant.

In the fall of 2021, when *Roe* was still good law, Texas's SB8 went into effect and banned abortions after six weeks of pregnancy. To evade judicial review, Texas made the law enforceable via individual tort lawsuits (despite Texas's disgust with tort law). Texas went out of its way and developed this creative enforcement strategy to make it more difficult for a court to enjoin the law (enjoin meaning stop the law from being in effect). Texas did all this to protect embryos at six weeks. Yet Texas does little to prevent stillbirth. To the contrary, it refuses to expand Medicaid access, making people wait until after pregnancy to gain Medicaid access and unnecessarily delaying prenatal care (same for Mississippi and Alabama). Texas also specifically has a noneconomic damage cap (discussed in chapter 4) that protects doctors from lawsuits based on stillbirth, reducing the incentive to prevent stillbirth.

More concretely, the 2021 SHINE for Autumn Act in chapter 2, a measure that could dramatically improve data collection on stillbirths in this country, passed the House of Representatives with wide bipartisan support. The few votes against were Republicans, including noted antiabortion House members Lauren Boebert, Matt Gaetz, Louis Gohmert, and Marjorie Taylor Greene.[31] Why? Why oppose a bill to improve stillbirth data and data collection—a bill that could help protect fetal lives?

The hypocrisy is thick and hurtful. How can one care so much about six-week embryos, yet so little about stillborn babies? *Dobbs* specifically mentions a state's legitimate interest in protecting "fetal life at all stages of development." Antiabortion states, however, aren't doing anything to protect fetal life from anything except the "bad mothers" who would choose abortion.

There is some bioethics literature focused on these fetal life hypocrisies, including literature defending it.[32] A lot of the defenses of the hypocrisy rely on pregnancy loss as unpreventable versus abortion as preventable. The unpreventability idea assumes all pregnancy losses are due to chromosomal abnormalities. There's little to no acknowledgement of any later pregnancy losses. There's no acknowledgment that only about 10% of stillbirths globally are due to unpreventable abnormalities. Regardless, if one really cares about fetal life, why not still push for research? It wasn't that long ago in this country that we simply accepted the fact of infant mortality too.

The defense of the fetal life hypocrisies also focuses on the moral distinction between killing and failing to protect. But if we know that some stillbirths are preventable, and we choose not to do anything to prevent them, that's not just failing to protect anymore. How can it be morally sound to ignore that other countries are implementing measures to reduce stillbirth, measures like communicating the importance of monitoring fetal movement? Ignoring respected, successful measures that could prevent some stillbirths is a choice, and it's a choice much closer to killing than it is failing to protect. Last, this killing versus failing to protect distinction sloppily assumes that in terminated pregnancies, the baby would have been born alive. Most will, yes. But far from all. As we're about to learn post-*Dobbs*, more pregnancies mean more pregnancy losses.

Another fetal life hypocrisy that can be especially difficult for stillbirth moms is fetal pain. Justice Alito specifically mentioned preventing fetal pain as a legitimate state interest in *Dobbs*.[33] Fetal pain has long been a rallying cry for antiabortion advocates.

A recent example is using it to justify calls for a federal 15-week ban. In an August 2023 *Washington Post* op-ed, Kellyanne Conway and Marjorie Dannenfelser, president of Susan B. Anthony Pro-Life America, urged Republican politicians to be the "national defender of life" that this country needs.[34] They urged leaders to use "evidence that unborn children can feel pain by 15 weeks" offensively to advocate for a federal ban on abortion. They argued for a "popular and humane policy" banning abortion by at least 15 weeks because of this evidence of fetal pain.

What is this evidence of fetal pain? The Mississippi legislature has previously explained that a fetus has pain receptors in its body no later than 20 weeks, that the unborn child reacts to touch by 8 weeks, and recoils from stimuli that would be recognized as pain by adults no later than 20 weeks.[35] The legislature also cited to the fact that doctors use fetal anesthesia during fetal surgery. That's it. In the meantime, the actual experts on this issue— ACOG, the Society for Maternal-Fetal Medicine, the Royal College of Obstetricians and Gynaecologists, and the US Association for the Study of Pain— all agree that a fetus cannot experience pain before 24 weeks or viability.[36]

If you really want to prevent fetal pain, I have a suggestion. Reallocate your efforts to stillbirth prevention. The number of stillbirths is quadruple the number of abortions after 20 weeks. And after 24 weeks, the experts agree that the fetus is at least theoretically capable of feeling pain. This includes over 10,000 stillbirths after 28 weeks. That number includes almost 3,500 stillbirths at term, almost 50% of which are preventable. Numerous causes of stillbirth could seemingly cause fetal pain—if a baby is abruptly deprived of oxygen due to placental abruption (separation of placenta from uterus) or severe umbilical cord blockage.

Studies support the possibility of fetal pain within stillbirth. Studies recount women's reports of having felt frantic or violent fetal movement shortly before their child's death.[37] In a study in Sweden, women reported a "period of abnormal or extremely vigorous activity" then "followed by no movement or only limited movement."[38] Some described their baby's last movement as "death-jerk" and intense.[39] Others described that "the fetus repeatedly kicked, felt as if he was trying to break out, or twitched a lot."[40] Specifically, one women said "he kicked an awful lot, felt like he was trying to get out through my stomach."[41] The study authors said that "vigorous fetal activity followed by no movements at all indicat[ed] that the baby died suddenly."[42]

Leading stillbirth researchers posit that the violent movement could be "fetal seizures induced by asphyxia or infection," or "an attempt to release cord entanglement or a change in fetal behaviour (including signs of distress) in response to a noxious stimulus."[43] The researchers admit that the violent movement could also be related to maternal anxiety, either that the woman imagined it or the baby reacted to that anxiety. Ultimately, they hypothesized that a "sudden episode of excessive fetal activity indicates fetal compromise relating to underlying disturbance of the in utero environment, which if it persists can lead to fetal death."

This is evidence of babies thrashing possibly in pain and then dying in the womb. Yet those concerned about preventing fetal pain are trying to ban abortion at 15 weeks.

I cannot move on from fetal pain without also mentioning how triggering it is for many stillbirth moms. Caleb died at 37 weeks. There's no doubt that he was capable of feeling pain. I will always be haunted by the idea that Caleb was in pain when he died in my womb—that he was in pain and I couldn't stop it or help him. My doctor and a specialist have assured me that he probably wasn't in pain, which I appreciate, but they also don't know. I wish antiabortion advocates would realize how traumatizing discussions of fetal pain can be for stillbirth parents.

That the antiabortion side cares very little about pregnancy loss is also evident in their lack of acknowledgment that abortion bans will only increase pregnancy losses. More pregnancies mean more pregnancy losses, especially miscarriages. But stillbirths will increase too, especially for marginalized populations. Pre-*Dobbs*, Black women and poor women disproportionately sought abortion care. In Justice Alito's words: "A highly disproportionate percentage of aborted fetuses are [B]lack."[44] Justice Alito implies that overruling *Roe* will mean those Black fetuses will be born alive—again erasing pregnancy loss and specifically erasing the dramatic racial and class disparities in pregnancy loss rates. Even with abortion unobtainable, so many pregnancies in marginalized populations will still not end with living babies.

More stillbirths will occur simply due to more pregnancies, but also due to the inability to terminate for life limiting fetal anomalies. When abortion is an option, stillbirths due to abnormalities "account for less than 10% [of] all stillbirths after 22 weeks of gestation, with a median of 7.4% and a median rate of 0.4 per 1000 births. . . . Conversely with good diagnostics and where termination of pregnancy is illegal, a higher proportion of congenital abnormalities is reported (eg, 21% in Ireland)."[45] Linda Layne similarly explains that the "'fetal death rate due to lethal abnormalities declined by almost half between the 1970's and 1980's because of abortion."[46] It's hard to know exactly what effect *Dobbs* will have on stillbirths due to abnormalities since abortion is still legal in many states, but a significant increase should be expected.

Additionally, more abortions will be registered as stillbirths due to pregnant people's use of mifepristone and misoprostol, otherwise known as abortion pills, to end their pregnancies.[47] Mifepristone and misoprostol are FDA-approved for abortions up to 10 weeks of pregnancy. But they work after that too, including even after 20 weeks of pregnancy. If pregnant people take those medicines, the baby can die in the womb. If the pregnant person goes to the hospital for birth, she will present at the hospital as stillbirth. And, if taken orally, there's currently no medical test that would be able to determine that she took abortion pills. Purvi Patel, an Indiana woman, did this. The police only figured out about the medication once they searched her text messages.[48] Similarly, a woman in South Carolina was arrested in early 2023 after she gave birth to a stillborn baby. She confessed that she had taken the medication when at the hospital.[49] Both of these instances were likely initially registered with fetal death certificates. And they definitely would have been issued FDCs absent the discovery of the abortion pills. This same thing was likely happening pre-*Dobbs*, with pregnant people traveling to a state where abortion was legal later in pregnancy, getting an injection for fetal demise, and then returning home to give birth at the hospital. It's going to happen more now that mifepristone and misoprostol are relatively easy to obtain over the internet.

State legislators rarely, if ever, acknowledge that banning abortions will increase stillbirths due to fetal abnormalities. Either antiabortion state legislators don't know, or they don't care.

One exception where the issue did arise was in debates in the Arkansas legislature on its post-*Roe* trigger law and the fact that the ban would prohibit abortions due to life-limiting fetal anomalies. One Arkansas legislator who supported a ban even for anomalies explained that the pregnancy should continue for organ donation.[50] Besides the horrific idea of forcing pregnant women to be organ factories, it's also uneducated. Again, abnormalities can easily mean stillbirth, and organ donation is far from a guaranteed possibility with stillbirth. It depends on the length of time between fetal death and birth. Even couples who know their child will be stillborn and plan to donate the child's organs often have their plans fall through because the timing didn't work out.[51] Caleb died sometime after 9:00 p.m. and was born the next morning at 6:00 a.m. No one ever brought up organ donation.

Antiabortion legislators similarly never acknowledge how abortion bans will affect care in pregnancy loss, which was immediately apparent post-*Dobbs*.[52] The most obvious effect is the unavailability of any treatment for inevitable miscarriages. Legally, doctors cannot do anything until the fetal heartbeat stops on its own. The same is true with stillbirths before viability. If the water breaks before 24 weeks and the doctors cannot stop the premature labor, doctors cannot legally do anything until the fetal heartbeat stops on its own—or wait until the medical situation becomes life-threatening, at which point doctors can legally perform an abortion to save the life of a pregnant person. But those standards are vague and ambiguous, not defining how *almost dead* one needs to be before doctors can terminate the pregnancy. In the meantime, the pregnant person just waits, undoubtedly increasing trauma. Antiabortion advocates either pretend that these situations won't happen, or they essentially accept increasing trauma as a necessary part of banning abortion.

The hypocrisy is thick. Do whatever possible—jail time, enforcement via tort claims—to protect fetal life and prevent fetal pain. But only from abortion. There's no concern for anything else that might kill a fetus or cause it pain.

THE ABORTION-RIGHTS MOVEMENT'S OPPOSITION AND AVOIDANCE

Hypocrisy aside, the antiabortion movement has weaponized pregnancy loss within the abortion debate. And, honestly, it's a strong weapon. So many people grieve after pregnancy loss. So many explain that they lost a "baby" or their "child." Obviously, I am one of those people. If Caleb is my child, how can I support abortion rights? How can we allow pregnant people to kill their unborn children?

It's such a strong argument that the abortion-rights movement felt the need to oppose any legal measures recognizing stillbirth. The biggest opposition to applying wrongful death law to stillbirth was from abortion-rights groups. They were afraid of any official laws treating unborn children the same as living children, and especially (and understandably) afraid of defining "person" in a statute to include fetus.[53] Specifically, abortion-rights advocates argued that wrongful death claims for parents bereaved after pregnancy loss would take away a woman's right to abortion and that it was a first step in overruling abortion. Advocates were also concerned that any recognition of fetal rights would spill over into abortion and eventually lead to the illegality of abortion (the slippery slope I mentioned earlier). To quote an abortion-rights advocate: "The fetal rights cases are very dangerous because the end goal of the other side is to have the fetus achieve equal status with the woman or with all of us having a constitutionally protected right to life before birth."[54]

Similarly, the biggest opposition to the memorial birth certificates for stillbirth came from abortion-rights groups. Again, they were afraid of these certificates somehow legitimizing unborn life or communicating that the death of a fetus is the death of a child.[55] "Pro-choice advocates have opposed the laws on the grounds that they could fuel the anti-abortion cause by acknowledging that an unborn fetus is a person."[56] Similarly, fear existed that these memorial birth certificates were just one more step within antiabortion efforts to "improve the legal status of embryos and fetuses" and would "push anti-choice groups one step further in their quest to make abortion tantamount to murder."[57] Planned Parenthood of New Mexico specifically opposed the attempts to create these birth certificates in New Mexico.[58] The bill passed unanimously in the legislature, but then Governor Bill Richardson vetoed it. He claimed the veto was due to administrative confusion in having both a birth certificate and a fetal death certificate for stillbirths. But numerous media reports suggested that the veto was related to his upcoming expected run for president and his desire to be seen as strictly pro-choice. In California, the first bill to create memorial birth certificates never made it out of legislative committee.[59] In the second try, the opposition from reproductive rights-minded groups was vast—including the National Organization for Women, Planned Parenthood Federation of America, the American Civil Liberties Union, the National Abortion Rights Action League, ACOG, and the California Medical Association. All were concerned about the (dreaded) slippery slope. But the bill passed and then Governor Arnold Schwarzenegger signed it into law in 2007.

The same opposition has surfaced within parents' efforts to get state legislatures to create tax credits for stillbirths. One noted abortion scholar decried the idea of tax benefits after stillbirth as showing how "prenatal life can take on a life of its own."[60]

The opposition is understandable, especially since these measures fell in line with long-term antiabortion strategy.

But the opposition is very reactionary, and likely over-reactionary. Are you really wanting to deny a parent wrongful death recourse for their child's stillbirth—after giving birth to her dead baby at 37 weeks? Are you okay with a law that allows parents a wrongful death claim if their baby dies three minutes after birth, but not three minutes before? Doesn't that seem a bit arbitrary? There's also a simple answer here: wrongful death claims do not give the fetus any rights. Wrongful death cases are *not* "fetal rights" cases. The fetus does not have a legal claim, the parents do. This emphasis on the parents also fits in well with the subjectivity of fetal personhood that Donley and I introduced and is discussed next. There were other ways for abortion-rights supporters to respond to the antiabortion push for wrongful death claims.

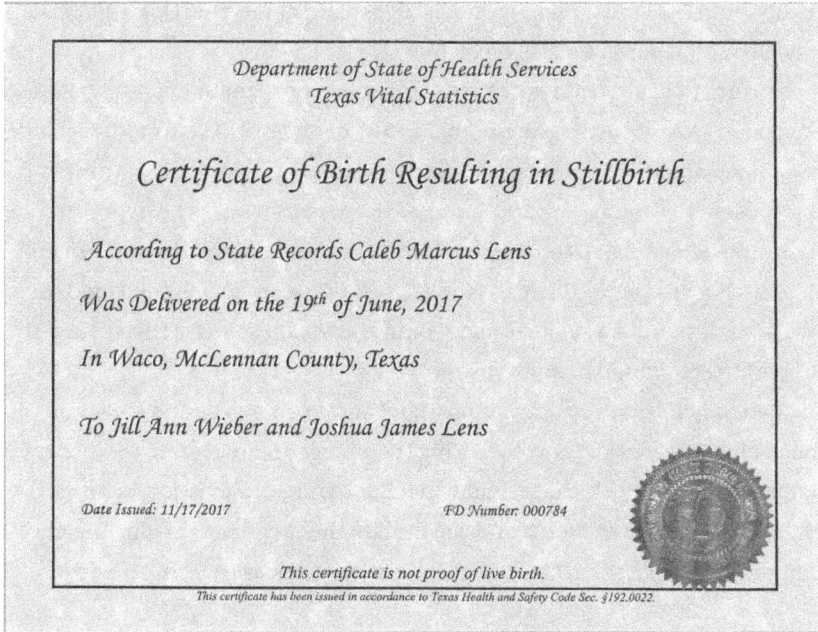

Figure 4. Certificate of Birth Resulting in Stillbirth for Caleb Lens.

Similarly, is it worth denying stillbirth moms a state-issued piece of paper with their child's name on it, showing that he was actually born? To be fair, not all abortion-rights supporters opposed these birth certificates; some noted that this type of rigidity wasn't necessary.[61] Also, even those who usually opposed these birth certificates eventually dropped that opposition if language was added to the laws clarifying that they would not be issued for abortions and could not be obtained by third parties.[62] Those are fine compromises. But they are also wholly unnecessary. The laws already said that the birth certificates could only be issued when an FDC was issued, and FDCs aren't issued for abortions. Plus, the laws already said that only parents could obtain the birth certificates, and only the parents would have the details about the FDC needed to obtain one.

Knowing of this controversy negates any possibility of Caleb's "Certificate of Birth Resulting in Stillbirth" (see figure 4) meaning much of anything to me. When I see it, I think of abortion-rights groups overreacting as opposed to anything sentimental. Also, it's very cheap looking. Hindsight is

20/20, but there were and are much bigger threats to abortion rights than this piece of paper in Caleb's box in my closet.

Fortunately, abortion-rights advocates do not seem to expressly oppose pregnancy-loss measures anymore. But avoidance is still common. As Linda Layne explained: "Because anti-abortion activists base their argument on the presence of fetal . . . and embryonic personhood," the reproductive rights movement has "studiously avoided anything that might imply or concede such a presence. The fear . . . is that if one were to acknowledge there was something of value lost, one would thereby automatically accede the inherent personhood of embryos/fetuses."[63]

Avoidance is better than opposition. But even avoidance feels out-of-touch and unrealistic. People wanting their pregnancies refer to their "baby" bump, to the "baby" kicking, and so on. But part of the abortion-rights strategy is to minimize the fetus and accentuate the pregnant person. The question though is whether that minimization is a *necessary* part of strategy.

SUBJECTIVE FETAL VALUE

From the beginning, I saw no inconsistency between Caleb as my child and abortion rights. The reason is because it was *my* thought of him as a child. He was and is my son. (And I may fight you if you call him a fetus.) My thoughts about my own child are not relevant to what others should be able to do or to abortion generally. My thoughts are my thoughts; how I value him is how *I* value him. That's what we call in the law "subjective."

Historically, nineteenth-century women "had a wide range of interpretations of pregnancy."[64] Some thought "it was a person in the making, and for others it was a more nebulous object, or an object that became a person only at birth."[65] Women knew that whatever was in their womb "moved and grew," but they didn't necessarily consider it to be "distinct body or person."[66] Even with the development of embryology (the realization of embryo and fetal development), many women still thought of the thing in their womb as similar to animals or insects.[67] A woman's circumstances affected her perception, no different than when a woman was relieved by a miscarriage in an undesired pregnancy.

The same is true in modern day; circumstances still affect how a pregnant person values and thinks of whatever it is in their womb.[68] Every person is different, but studies do show some common affecting factors. One factor is the length of the pregnancy; as the pregnancy progresses, we are more likely to think of it as a "baby" or "child" or even by a specific name. Another factor is what is now commonly called "social birth"—introducing the unborn baby to the family and greater community. And technology has obviously changed a pregnant person's ideas of the fetus. Justice Alito noted the role of ultrasounds in *Dobbs*—that they have created a "new appreciation of fetal life" and that parents have "no doubt" that they see their child on the monitor.[69] Similarly, as mentioned, antiabortion narratives—"life begins at conception"—have no doubt affected how people value their fetus and experience early pregnancy and early miscarriages.

Another intuitive but less-discussed factor is wantedness.[70] After *Roe*'s legalization of abortion, most pregnancy losses occur in desired pregnancies, and pregnancy-loss research pretty much assumes wantedness. But even wantedness doesn't equal more attachment. For instance, research in the surrogacy content shows surrogates certainly wanting to give birth to a baby, but not become attached to the pregnancy. And even in the pregnancy-loss context, studies show that women who have previously experienced pregnancy loss are less likely to get attached to a next pregnancy, specifically downplaying possible prenatal personhood in that next pregnancy.

The point though is that pregnant people vary in their thoughts about whatever it is that is growing in their uterus. Both historically and in modern day, it depends on the circumstances. Some people think of a miscarriage at five weeks as losing a baby; others have an emotionally uncomplicated abortion at eight weeks. The same person can have these different fetal valuations in different pregnancies. Donley and I call this "subjective fetal value."

Tort law already recognizes subjective fetal value.[71] As detailed in chapter 3, if a parent wins a lawsuit against a doctor for causing the stillborn child's wrongful death, the parent will be awarded damages. The jury will determine the amount of damages based on the parent's injury, and the damages must be specific to the parent's injury. The amount of damages will vary depending on whatever it was the parents believe they lost. A baby? Their child? The jury will have to determine that and then award damages specific to the injury that the parent suffered.

Importantly, the law doesn't presume any injury in that tort lawsuit. We don't presume that a child–parent relationship existed and was lost within the baby's stillbirth. To the contrary, the parent needs to demonstrate their injury.

Donley and I argued that recognizing this subjective valuation of a pregnancy does *not* threaten abortion-rights. In fact, subjective fetal value is fundamentally inconsistent with the antiabortion idea of personhood starting at conception in every pregnancy.[72] The antiabortion idea dictates that, in every pregnancy, the pregnancy is a person at the moment of conception (before the person can even know they're pregnant). This antiabortion idea erases the pregnant person. The subjective valuation, on the other hand, is dependent on the pregnant person; the pregnant person controls any assignment of fetal "personhood" to the fetus. This idea of subjective fetal value is thus consistent with abortion rights. The abortion-rights movement could recognize it without threatening abortion rights.

On a broader level, forcing objective definitions on pregnancy loss is a bit bewildering. As I mentioned, between my two daughters, I had a very early miscarriage, just days after I learned I was pregnant. I bled. I was really upset, especially because we had been struggling with infertility. But I never said, "we lost the baby." At most, I lost a pregnancy. But abortion bans dictate that that miscarriage was the death of a person, and many antiabortion states would make me sue for the wrongful death of a "person" had the miscarriage been due to tort. At the other extreme, Caleb was stillborn at 37 weeks. He was just under six pounds and I held him in my arms while deciding to have him cremated. Yet, if I had a tort claim for his death, some states would classify him as my body part. The state forces an objective definition onto my experience. The state, which has an abstract interest at best, defines and classifies my experience.

Subjectivity better reflects pregnant peoples' actual experiences. It is more nuanced and thus more difficult, but also more honest. Plus, it won't alienate the many of us who support abortion rights but also believe our pregnancy loss involved the death of a "child." Caleb was not a clump of cells; he was not a fetus. He was my child who should be in elementary school. And my love for him does not threaten my or anyone else's abortion rights (to the extent we still have any).

ALIGNING PREGNANCY-LOSS AND ABORTION-RIGHTS COMMUNITIES

Overruling *Roe* could theoretically open a space for a more honest discussion of stillbirth and pregnancy loss generally. Discussing stillbirth and pregnancy loss more generally can't threaten the right to abortion if there is no right to abortion.

That hasn't been the effect thus far. In the wake of *Dobbs*, more and more states freed from *Roe* took the opportunity and banned all abortion as of conception. This move doubles down on the idea that all pregnancies that can't end in abortion will now end in live childbirth.

And antiabortion advocates seem to still be weaponizing pregnancy loss against abortion rights. In January 2023, Arkansas Senator Tom Cotton introduced a bill in the United States Senate creating a federal tax credit for stillbirth and also extending leave under the Family & Medical Leave Act (unpaid) to miscarriages and stillbirths.[73] It was called the "Helping with Equal Access to Leave and Investing in Needs for Grieving Mothers and Fathers Act" or the "HEALING Mothers and Fathers Act." The bill dictates that miscarriage is the "loss" of an unborn child. Similarly, the bill dictates that people who experience miscarriage are parents, who are (and should be) grieving and need healing. These are antiabortion objective narratives and definitions. These objective labels of "unborn child," "mother," and "father" will reflect some people's experiences, but not others. Most problematically, Senator Cotton's bill included a mandate that no Title X funds could go to medical providers that provide abortion care or refer patients to abortion care. It has no place in a bill about pregnancy loss. But once again, stillbirth and pregnancy loss get abortion-politicized.

Abortion-rights advocates may be even more hesitant to discuss pregnancy loss post *Dobbs* because of its (supposed) link to fetal personhood—especially since fetal personhood, meaning a Supreme Court interpretation that "person" in the Fourteenth Amendment includes prenatal life, is the way forward to ban abortion in all states. That hesitance (turned overreaction) was apparent in early 2024 coverage of a Florida bill to apply wrongful death law to the tortious death of an "unborn child."[74] Some commentary labeled the bill "frightening," "dangerous," and "anti-choice." The bill is not perfect. It does not contain language clearly exempting legal abortions like wrongful death laws usually do, although proving a legal abortion is tortious would be difficult. It also veers from the majority rule and applies wrongful death law to pre- and post-viability pregnancy losses instead of just post-viability losses like most states do. But these imperfections do not necessarily make the bill dangerous or anti-choice. Arguably, the bill is very much consistent with the reproductive justice recognized right to have a child. Potential plaintiffs include people who wanted their child and a tortfeasor deprived them of their child.

But I would encourage the abortion-rights movement to think about this more. As Donley and I suggested, acknowledging pregnancy loss could do more good than harm for abortion rights. For fifty years, the movement minimized the fetus, necessarily undervaluing pregnancy loss. *Roe* was still overturned. Minimizing the fetus does not seem to be a necessary part of the fight for abortion rights. It's also unrealistic at this point. It's inconsistent with how many if not most experience pregnancy and pregnancy loss. And the minimization ultimately meant surrendering the discourse on pregnancy loss to the antiabortion side.[75] But far from everything about pregnancy loss fits only antiabortion narratives.

First, the reality of pregnancy loss raises questions about the state's interest in protecting fetal life. Again, as many as 70% of conceptions (fertilized eggs) *do not turn into living babies.* The tenuousness of fetal life is something we should be talking about within the abortion debate. It's always been the pregnant person's interest versus the fetus's interest. Now the pregnant person's interest is gone—we even more need to talk about the fetus. Court decisions talk about the state's interest in "fetal life" and "unborn human beings." But what is that really? For most prenatal life, that's a few days or weeks in the uterus. Can the state really justify forcing people to remain pregnant when only 30% of fertilized eggs turn into living babies?

Second, the antiabortion hypocrisy between protecting fetal life from abortion yet being content to have the highest stillbirth rates in the nation is thick. How can the state truly be interested in protecting "unborn human beings" when it shows strikingly little interest in preventing pregnancy loss? How can one claim a genuine interest in protecting fetal life, yet have such high stillbirth rates—when at least 25% percent of stillbirths are preventable?

The realities of pregnancy loss can also help normalize abortion. Pregnancy loss shows that it is normal for pregnancy to end in other than live childbirth. Freidenfelds notes that, historically, there was no way to know whether a miscarriage was because of "something the woman did, or *whether it would have happened anyway.*"[76] Put another way, the loss could easily have happened anyway, so what did it really matter how it happened. This is dramatically different from our view today that any not-aborted pregnancy will end with live childbirth. Breaking what Freidenfelds coins "the myth of the perfect pregnancy" may help to normalize abortion. We've never had these honest discussions about the tenuousness of fetal life within the abortion debate.

Instead of shrinking away when the antiabortion movement weaponizes pregnancy loss in its quest for fetal personhood, it's time to question the antiabortion movement's sincerity in supporting those suffering pregnancy loss. It's time to ask why antiabortion legislators haven't expanded access to PHPC, expanded Medicaid, or worked to increase the quality of prenatal care. It's time to ask why there's not more research about stillbirth and miscarriage prevention. It's time to stop letting those who do not care about "fetal life" in the pregnancy-loss context claim an interest in protecting "fetal life" in the abortion context.

Moreover, post-*Dobbs* abortion bans should make pregnancy-loss advocates very aware of the need to increase access to abortion care. These bans have dramatically illustrated the overlap between pregnancy loss and abortion. People experiencing pregnancy loss need abortion care. We're seeing people suffering inevitable miscarriages (baby has stopped developing, but heart is still beating) having to just wait for the heartbeat to stop. We're seeing people having to just wait to almost die when their water breaks before viability but the fetal heart is still beating. We're seeing people being forced to continue pregnancies in cases of fetal abnormalities and just wait until they no longer feel their baby move. The common ground between the two communities is clear.

Moreover, a blatant alliance between pregnancy-loss and abortion-rights communities promotes the rights delineated by the broader reproductive justice framework discussed in chapter 6. There's much more to reproductive life than abortion. The right to abortion is important, but the right to have a child is equally important. And pregnancy loss must be a part of discussions about the right to have a child.

It would also be helpful for pregnancy-loss advocacy groups to be blatant with any abortion-rights views. The public assumes that pregnancy-loss advocates are antiabortion. It's the same reason Republican presidential nominee hopefuls Florida Governor Ron DeSantis and Vivek Ramaswamy shared their stories of their wives' miscarriages—of how they lost their first babies, with Ramaswamy describing the miscarriage as a loss of life.[77] But far from all who experience grief after pregnancy loss believe abortion should be illegal.

And again, any tension between abortion rights and pregnancy loss is not inherent; it is artificial. Recent laws in Connecticut reaffirm this. After *Dobbs,* Connecticut was the first state in the nation to provide extra protections for doctors providing abortions to out-of-state residents, called a provider shield law. The very first state. The legislature wanted to protect abortion rights and moved swiftly and creatively to do so.

At the same time, Connecticut legislators were also working to do something remarkable for stillbirth parents. Brittney Crystal, yet another amazing stillbirth mom, worked with her state legislator, Aimee Berger-Girvalo, to get a tax credit passed for stillbirth.[78] Their efforts were successful, and Connecticut passed the largest state income tax credit, $2500, in the country.

The provider shield law and the stillbirth tax credit became effective the exact same day. No one balked at the tax credit as somehow creating fetal personhood, threatening the law it passed just weeks before protecting abortion rights. Partially why no one balked is because Representative Berger-Girvalo is a known supporter of abortion rights. Also, Berger-Girvalo met with relevant abortion-rights groups ahead of time to confirm their lack of opposition. Connecticut shows that laws to protect abortion rights and to recognize stillbirth can (and should) coexist.

Similarly, other countries show the possible coexistence of abortion-rights and pregnancy-loss advocacy. Abortion is legal until 24 weeks of pregnancy in England and has been so since 1967. As discussed in chapter 4, England has also launched numerous initiatives to reduce its stillbirth rate, and was very successful in doing so. The slogan of Tommy's, a pregnancy and infant-loss advocacy charity, was "Together, for every baby."[79] Tommy's has since joined with Sands, a stillbirth and infant-loss advocacy charity, and now has a joint "Saving babies' lives" slogan.[80] And no one asks how these slogans might conflict with the legality of abortion. Part of that is because it's not just about the baby. Tommy's had a recent, successful campaign called "We See a Mum," which centers pregnancy loss on the person who experienced the pregnancy loss (instead of on the baby).[81]

Most of the United States has a long way to go. But *Dobbs* does create an opportunity for a society that recognizes the many nuances that affirm the consistency of abortion-rights and pregnancy-loss advocacy.

NINE

Stillbirth as a Crime

The nurses reassured me over and over that Caleb's death wasn't my fault. Really, at the time, I hadn't even thought to blame myself (and fortunately still don't—not to blame, but I will forever feel guilt that I didn't protect him even though I know that I couldn't have). Regardless, I appreciated the reassurance.

One of those reassurances stood out to me. One nurse said, "it's not like you did cocaine or anything." Even in my foggy, extended period of shock, confusion, and disbelief, I heard her and immediately thought—how do you know I didn't do cocaine, and how would you be treating me right now if you thought I had done cocaine?

I'm white and they knew I was a local law professor (I learned later that the spouse of one of my students was one of my nurses). Like I said, I appreciated the nurse's reassurance that I wasn't at fault. But I also wonder about the assumptions she would have made if I wasn't white and if I didn't have money. And I wonder how that might have affected my medical care, my grief, and my overall stability. I'm privileged in many ways, which is why I only wonder about these possible scenarios.

* * * *

Others experience their child's stillbirth completely differently. More specifically, marginalized persons are at an increased risk of being treated not with compassion, but with suspicion and blame. They might not be encouraged to spend time with their baby—or worse, denied time with their baby. They might not be offered keepsakes like footprints or pictures. Doctors may test them and their babies for drugs without their consent. Medical professionals may be more focused on calling the police than on the pregnant person's well-being.

A call to the police can lead to a state-paid-for fetal autopsy, performed by someone having no business performing it, concluding that the birthing parent's drug use caused the baby's stillbirth even though the umbilical cord was wrapped around the baby's neck. The birthing parent could be arrested. She could sit in jail while her milk comes in and she lacks any baby to feed. She is prosecuted despite the little to no evidence connecting drug use and stillbirth. Maybe she's convicted and she remains in jail. Or maybe the charges are eventually dismissed, but still she spent time in jail. Either way, the prosecutor pats himself on the back for a job well done.

This isn't hypothetical. These are details of real lived experiences of stillbirth. And there will be more of these stories now that abortion is illegal in many states—turning every pregnancy loss in those states into a potential crime scene. Pre-*Dobbs* prosecutions targeted women of color and poor women, women who already face an increased risk of stillbirth. This will only continue post-*Dobbs* as racist and classist stereotypes about bad mothers persist.

Arrests and prosecutions are very curious from a causation standpoint. In almost every other context, stillbirth is seen as inevitable and unpreventable. But there's one exception—when the bad mom caused her child's stillbirth. Then, many are convinced that drug use causes stillbirth and that criminal consequences will deter such drug use and prevent stillbirth.

Criminalization of pregnancy loss, however, is a very poor stillbirth prevention strategy—which is probably why countries actually devoted to reducing their stillbirth rates don't use it. Arresting pregnant people will traumatize stillbirth moms, cruelly reinforcing the self-blame that is already rampant after stillbirth. But it won't prevent stillbirths. It will likely only lead to *more* stillbirths as the possibility of arrest deters pregnant people from seeking prenatal care.

Prosecutions of birthing parents must be legally prevented. But more work is also necessary to undermine the many reasons why so many are quick to conclude that drug use causes stillbirth. That includes increasing public awareness of stillbirth and increasing research on the causes of stillbirth, especially on possible systemic causes.

THE PROSECUTIONS THAT HAVE ALREADY HAPPENED

Regina McKnight, a poor Black farmworker in South Carolina, gave birth to her near-term stillborn baby girl in 1999.[1] McKnight had already named her daughter—Mercedes. The baby's autopsy showed a byproduct of cocaine in the placenta and umbilical cord. McKnight had used cocaine recently, seeking to self-medicate her depression and anxiety due to her mother's death in a hit-and-run the year before. McKnight also had a history of syphilis—which we do know, medically, causes stillbirth.

The doctors gave McKnight's medical records to the police and she was later charged with "homicide by child abuse." A jury convicted McKnight and she was sentenced to 20 years in prison. McKnight spent 8 years in prison before the South Carolina Supreme Court unanimously overturned her conviction due to ineffective assistance of counsel.[2]

In 2006, Rennie Gibbs, a Black teenager in Mississippi, gave birth to her stillborn daughter at 36 weeks.[3] Gibbs had already named her Samiya. The umbilical cord was wrapped around Samiya's neck. The typical medical reaction to cord accidents is the "this happens" shrug. But the police decided they needed to investigate. Mississippi's de facto medical examiner did an autopsy and found traces of cocaine byproduct in the baby's blood, but not traces of actual cocaine. Gibbs had tested positive for marijuana and/or cocaine three times during her pregnancy and missed several prenatal care appointments.

Gibbs was arrested for "deprived heart murder" of her stillborn child and prosecutors argued that the stillbirth was due to cocaine use. Gibbs faced life in prison if convicted. In 2014, after eight years of legal wrangling, a Mississippi judge later dismissed the murder charge against Gibbs.[4]

In September 2019, Chelsea Becker, a (white) California woman, was preparing for the birth of her fourth child.[5] It was a boy named Zachariah. Becker grew up and lived in an area 200 miles outside of Los Angeles where unemployment is twice the average rate of California and 15% of residents live in poverty. The area is also known for having a lot of meth. Becker had struggled with addiction to meth and battled homelessness. She was eight months pregnant when rushed by ambulance to the hospital due to uncontrollable bleeding. Two hours after arriving at the hospital, Becker's son died and she gave birth to him.

The hospital staff believed the child's stillbirth to be suspicious. Without her consent, they tested Becker for drugs and the test was positive for meth. Two months later, Becker was arrested for "murder of a human fetus," allegedly acting with malice based on her drug addiction and the meth in her system. Becker spent 16 months in prison before a judge dismissed the charges against her due to insufficient evidence of knowledge and intent.

Adora Perez gave birth to her term stillbirth baby named Hades in 2017—notably at the same hospital as Becker gave birth years later.[6] A nurse wrote in Perez's medical records that Perez and her boyfriend were extremely upset, "emotional," and "tearful." Perez had a medical history of gestational diabetes and hypertension, both risk factors for stillbirth.[7] She also had a history of drug use in pregnancies—and the nurses knew it as she had given birth previously in this same hospital. While Perez spent time with Hades, hospital staff were talking to police and Child Protective Services.

While still at the hospital, Perez was arrested and charged with murder. Her milk came in while she sat in jail. Perez was charged with murder based on her methamphetamine use during pregnancy. Her court-appointed counsel encouraged her to plead guilty to manslaughter of a fetus (a crime that doesn't exist), which she did. She was sentenced to 11 years in prison. Perez's case received little media attention until Becker was also arrested. Once Becker's case got attention, reporters also discovered Perez and efforts began to reopen her case. In June 2022, a judge vacated her conviction because no fetal manslaughter crime exists in California law. Perez was free after having spent four years in prison.

These are just a few of the many, many people who have been prosecuted for conduct while pregnant. Pregnancy Justice (formerly National Advocates for Pregnant Women) documented more than 413 instances between 1973 (the year *Roe* was decided) to 2005 of people being "arrested for reasons related to their pregnancy."[8] It found another 1,396 criminal arrests between 2005 and June 23, 2022 (the day before *Dobbs* was released). That's a total of 1,809 arrests from 1973 forward. And the numbers are no doubt an undercount.

Focusing on the 2005-2023 data, 90% of the documented cases were based on substance abuse, most commonly methamphetamine, marijuana, and cocaine use. Twenty-five percent of the cases involve legal substances like prescription opiates, nicotine, and alcohol.

The cases were based on substance abuse, but the charges were not drug charges. Instead, over 80% of the charged crimes were "criminal child neglect, abuse, and/or endangerment."[9] These are laws that were not intended to apply to conduct to unborn children. But some state supreme courts, notably Alabama, South Carolina, and Oklahoma, have explicitly interpreted them to apply to unborn children. These court interpretations also explain why so many of the cases that Pregnancy Justice documented occurred in these states (46.5% in Alabama, 13% in South Carolina, and 8.1% in Oklahoma).[10] Note that neglect and endangerment charges do not require any harm to the child, but instead criminalize conduct that (supposedly) creates a risk of harm.[11]

McKnight, Gibbs, Becker, and Perez were arrested for drug use causing pregnancy loss. But they are not representative of this data; arrests aren't usually about pregnancy loss. In the overwhelming majority of prosecutions for drug use in Pregnancy Justice's recent data, the baby is born healthy. In 66% of the cases, the baby was born alive without any noted negative health issues. In just under 15%, the baby was born alive with some health problems at birth. Put together, that's 81% of the cases involving live birth. Only 7.2% of the cases documented by Pregnancy Justice involved stillbirth. And only 1.4% of the cases involved miscarriage. The other arrests were during pregnancy, so before any pregnancy outcome. These percentages show that outcomes of pregnancies that include drug use mirror the outcomes of pregnancies without drug use; the vast majority end with live birth, but some end in miscarriage or stillbirth.

It's perhaps surprising that the proportion of stillbirth cases was greater than miscarriage cases given that miscarriage is so much more common. But stillbirth is much more likely to involve medical care than miscarriage. And that's how most of these arrests start—with medical professionals or hospital social workers reporting drug use or suspected drug use of pregnant people to the police.[12]

Police and prosecutors have overwhelmingly targeted marginalized women.[13] In the thirty years after *Roe*, "pregnancy criminalization disproportionately targeted Black communities."[14] Drug use, including in pregnancy, is "equally common among racial and socioeconomic groups" in the United States, yet prosecutions for drug use during pregnancy were overwhelmingly of women of color.[15]

That racial disparity, however, has lessened if not disappeared. That is because the opioid epidemic has more significantly affected white populations. And thus it is overwhelmingly white women who are being arrested in the more recent waves of prosecutions for use of opioids during pregnancy. In its newer data, Pregnancy Justice found that now the majority of criminalizations are of white pregnant people.

What has remained constant with the different waves of prosecutions, however, is the class disparity. Almost 85% of Pregnancy Justice's more recent documented cases were of poor people; they qualified as indigent, meaning courts determined the person could not afford an attorney.[16] As Khiara Bridges explains, "It does not overstate things to describe criminal prosecutions for substance abuse during pregnancy as having been reserved for the poor."[17]

Prosecutions are only likely to increase now that the Supreme Court overruled *Roe*. In states where abortion is illegal, every pregnancy loss is a potential crime.[18] Was this a pregnancy loss or was it an illegal abortion? And it's often impossible to tell the difference. An abortion via mifepristone and misoprostol (oral medication) is indistinguishable from a miscarriage. As mentioned in chapter 8, Purvi Patel was arrested in 2013 after presenting as a pregnancy loss. It was only after police searched text messages that they realized she had obtained and taken medication abortion.

And we know who will most likely be suspected post-*Dobbs*—the same marginalized persons who fit "bad mother" stereotypes who were already suspected before *Dobbs*.

A NOTE ON FETAL AUTOPSIES

Chapter 1 discussed that fetal autopsies are the "gold standard" for determining the cause(s) of fetal death. They won't always be able to do so, but the fetal autopsy is the best tool we have for doing so. That's why I argue we need more fetal autopsies. But also remember that those fetal autopsies need to be performed by qualified perinatal pathologists. If not, fetal autopsies are *not* a gold standard.

Remember also from chapter 1 that the cause of death on a fetal death certificate is normally to be completed by the medical attendant but state law sometimes mandates referral to the medical examiner or coroner. For instance, state law may mandate medical-examiner involvement if there's a reasonable belief that the death was due to "homicide, suicide, or casualty"; "an accident involving lack of due care on the part of a person other than the deceased"; "violence by homicide, suicide, or accident"; "criminal abortions, including those self-induced"; or the death occurred "in any unusual or suspicious manner."[19]

It's interesting to think about how these listed crimes or circumstances could apply to stillbirth. For instance, a stillbirth should not be inherently unusual or suspicious; stillbirth is rare, but it is common enough to not be inherently unusual or suspicious. Also, the homicide question is interesting given that state law often expressly precludes arrest and charging of the pregnant woman with homicide; as will be discussed, most state laws have such exclusionary language. Can it be homicide for purposes of referral to the medical examiner if the woman cannot legally be charged with homicide? The same is true for state abortion prohibitions. The woman cannot be arrested for abortion under state law, yet the Missouri statute dictates a coroner's inquiry if the abortion is self-induced. Wrongful death statutes also generally preclude suit against the pregnant woman, stating she can't be sued for causing the unborn child's (tortious) wrongful death with failure to exercise due care. Yet Rhode Island law says inquest is proper if the fetal death is suspectedly due to a lack of due care. In short, there are numerous questions whether referral of stillbirth cases to the coroner or medical examiner is legally required. But it happens.

If referred, a fetal autopsy will likely happen. As discussed in chapter 1, fetal autopsies are generally not common, occurring in maybe 20% of stillbirths in the United States. But fetal autopsies are very common when the fetal death is referred to the coroner or medical examiner. And the state pays for it.

The quality of that fetal autopsy, however, is suspect. Generally, state laws require that medical examiners be certified by the American Board of Pathology. So the fetal autopsy should be performed by a certified pathologist. But the best assurance of quality is if the fetal autopsy is performed by someone with experience in perinatal pathology. And that's not legally required. So instead, at best, the fetal autopsy will be performed by a general pathologist, which is less than ideal.

And sometimes, the medical examiner isn't even certified by the American Board of Pathology. Rennie Gibbs's stillborn daughter's autopsy was performed by Steven Hayne, Mississippi's de facto medical examiner at the time. Remember that Gibbs's daughter was born with her umbilical cord wrapped around her neck. Yet the fetal autopsy concluded drug use caused the stillbirth. Mississippi lacked an official medical examiner, and somehow Hayne ended up performing autopsies for decades. He was *not*, however, certified by the American Board of Pathology as Mississippi law required. Despite this, he performed autopsies from the late 1980s to 2008, eventually performing 80–90% of autopsies annually.[20] He estimated that he performed as many as 1,800 autopsies a year even though the National Association of Medical Examiners recommends a doctor conduct no more than 250 annually. Between 2007 and 2014, at least four murder convictions based on Hayne's evidence had been overturned. Hayne wasn't qualified to do any autopsies, much less a fetal autopsy.

To include one other example, in 2017, Alabama woman Brooke Shoemaker gave birth to her stillborn baby around 25 weeks.[21] She had done meth the day before. The pathologist found a tear in the fetus's liver that he believed was due to attempts to resuscitate the baby. He also found a small hemorrhage on the placenta. In the autopsy report, the pathologist ruled the cause of death "undetermined" and noted the presence of drugs in the baby's system. Yet the coroner, who, unlike the pathologist, has no medical training, listed "chemical endangerment and methamphetamine toxicity" as the cause of death on the FDC. Supposedly, he came to that conclusion after talking with a pathologist unconnected to the case. A jury later convicted Shoemaker and she was sentenced to 18 years in prison.

In short, there's many reasons to question the conclusions on fetal autopsies performed within criminal investigations. And it's important to remember that fetal autopsies are only the "gold standard" if performed by a perinatal pathologist.

SURPRISING CONFIDENCE ON CAUSATION

The confidence behind these precise conclusions that drug use causes stillbirth is surprising. Stillbirth is normally thought of as inevitable, as unpreventable. The all-too-common response to stillbirth is a "this happens" shrug. This is the normal response to a cord accident, like how Gibbs's daughter was born. There's little curiosity about whether some stillbirths are preventable; there's little initiative to explore whether some stillbirths are preventable.

All of that changes, however, if drug use is involved. Then, there's a medical examiner's conclusion that drug use caused the stillbirth, creating probable cause to arrest a person for causing their child's stillbirth. Then, there's a prosecutor who thinks he can prove to a jury—beyond a reasonable doubt, the highest burden of proof that exists in the law—that a person's drug use caused their child's stillbirth. Then, there's a jury that has no reasonable doubt that drug use caused stillbirth. And all of this occurs despite the known fact that the vast majority of babies are born alive and healthy even with drug use in pregnancy.

There will never be a randomized, controlled study of whether drug use causes stillbirth. It won't happen.

But this discussion is not about whether drug use causes stillbirth. This discussion is about how the usual response to stillbirth is so lackadaisical, yet many prosecutors are convinced drug use causes stillbirth. Essentially, stillbirth is inevitable except when it's the pregnant person's fault—or really, when it's the marginalized pregnant person's fault.

The enthusiasm for the conclusion that drug use causes stillbirth is especially striking given the "beyond a reasonable doubt" burden of proof in a criminal prosecution. The jury should convict only if it has no reasonable doubts about whether the elements are met—no reasonable doubt that the drug use caused the stillbirth.

And juries have found so. There are many reasons why a jury might be inclined to determine that drug use caused stillbirth. The War on Drugs is, of course, a large factor. The War on Drugs has programmed Americans to believe the worst possible consequences of drug use. And pregnant drug users have long been a casualty of the War on Drugs. "Pregnant drug users in the 1980s and 1990s endured a particularly intense and unique attack, not only as intensified targets of the drug war but also as 'bad mothers.'"[22] The targets were overwhelmingly Black women, who were supposedly going to overwhelm the United States with "crack babies, who develop into uneducable, disabled, and malformed children."[23] It wasn't true. Even years before Rennie Gibbs's arrest, leading medical journals were publishing studies debunking the idea of "crack babies." Exposure to crack cocaine in the womb was no more dangerous than exposure to alcohol and cigarettes. Poverty was much more likely to explain any differences in child development. As a 2009 *New York Times* article described: "crack babies: the epidemic that wasn't."

Quick note that even though the media coverage was sensational, the worry never seemed to be that crack cocaine use would cause stillbirth. Dorothy Roberts argued that these prosecutions were part of broader efforts to devalue Black motherhood. They were punishment "in essence, for having babies," biologically inferior babies that the United States would then have to figure out how to raise.[24] That burden wouldn't exist if the baby died (although villainization of the bad mother would have likely still occurred). Similarly, Khiara Bridges describes that the media portrayed Black women as needing punishment for "'ruining' their fetuses, and for burdening society with their costly babies"—not for killing their fetuses.[25] Relatedly, Tennessee's 2014 law that specifically criminalized drug use during pregnancy, even though use while not pregnant was legal, was not because of worries about stillbirth. It was due to a dramatic increase in babies being born with neonatal abstinence syndrome, essentially going through withdrawal. But the babies were born alive. Tennessee lawmakers were not worried about pregnancy loss when they criminalized drug use during pregnancy.

The original War on Drugs focused on pregnant people—but the concern does not seem to have ever been about drug use causing stillbirth or pregnancy loss generally. Arguably, the same is true today given that only a small proportion of arrests for drug use involve pregnancy loss. But the influence of the War of Drugs means society is still quick to believe that drug use causes pregnancy loss.

Regardless, more than just the War on Drugs influences jurors to conclude, beyond a reasonable doubt, that drug use caused stillbirth. Stillbirth is tragic and blame is a natural reaction when something bad happens to someone else.[26] Jurors want to believe that that same bad thing couldn't happen to them or their loved ones. Consciously or subconsciously, they believe that the person the bad thing happened to must have done something to cause it. It's a natural impulse. More specific to pregnancy, people want to believe that if they do everything right in pregnancy, the baby will be born alive. That also implies that, if the baby dies, it must have been something the pregnant person did. Studies confirm that women feel blamed after their child's stillbirth—that others suggest to them that their child's death is their fault.[27] A conviction is merely that blame in very tangible form.

The low public awareness of stillbirth also contributes. ACOG recognizes that stillbirth is "one of the most common adverse pregnancy outcomes." But public awareness of this commonality and really of anything about stillbirth is very low. That stillbirth seemingly doesn't happen anymore implies that the pregnant person must have done something to cause it.

The many forces erasing pregnancy loss from public consciousness also contribute to the causation discussion. One of those forces is the abortion debate. As discussed in chapter 8, the abortion debate assumes all babies are either aborted or born healthy. That binary has been part of public consciousness for more than fifty years. Again, all pregnancies end in either abortion or live childbirth. Stillbirth doesn't and shouldn't happen. So when it does happen, it must have been something that the pregnant woman did.

Another of those forces is the extreme medicalization of pregnancy and childbirth. Medical advancements now mean that even a baby born severely premature, at 21 or 22 weeks, can survive. If this is true, "then assuredly medicine has also developed to the point where stillbirth, especially at term, must not occur anymore."[28] Beliefs about medicalization are consistent with common beliefs that stillbirth is a thing of the past in the United States and only currently happens in lower-income countries lacking quality medical care. If stillbirth were to still occur in the United States nowadays, "surely it was not due to medicine's failure."[29] The extreme medicalization also suggests that if stillbirth were to still occur, it couldn't be unexplained. All of this implies that when stillbirth does occur, it was something the pregnant woman did.

The erasure of pregnancy loss was front and center in the prosecution of Regina McKnight. As Michelle Goodwin explained, the "prosecution advanced a seriously distressing proposition related to perfection in pregnancy" that assumed "all pregnancies produce healthy babies and that absent so-called depraved conduct on the part of pregnant women, stillbirths do not occur."[30] This is not true. But it taps effectively into the natural desire to blame, a lack of awareness of stillbirth, and the erasure of pregnancy loss.

The focus on "choice" in the abortion debate also affirms causation. Choice implies individual control. Control implies that one can control whether pregnancy ends in pregnancy loss. Linda Layne long ago explained that "an unintended and unexamined consequence" of choice and the resulting implication of control is that "women may be assumed to be responsible for their pregnancy losses."[31] Choice and control "contribute[] to maternal blame . . . when pregnancies are not perfect." As the reproductive justice movement emphasizes, choice is a farce. It's a farce with respect to abortion because of inadequate access, and it's a farce with respect to reproductive life generally as not everyone has the ability to choose—and because little about reproduction involves choice. But the abortion-rights movement relied heavily on choice language for decades, creating unintended consequences like implying blame when pregnancy ends in other than live childbirth.

These factors help explain why the jury might be inclined to determine that drug use causes stillbirth—but the evidence should still be insufficient to conclude *beyond a reasonable doubt* that drug use caused stillbirth. Again, this is the highest burden of proof in law. The jury can only convict if it has zero reasonable doubts that drug use caused stillbirth. That the overwhelming majority of babies are born healthy after drug use alone should create that reasonable doubt.

Similarly, even if population-based studies indicate an increased risk to the baby from drug use during pregnancy, increased risks don't always mean the baby will be harmed—far from it. Smoking during pregnancy increases the risk of stillbirth. But that doesn't mean any particular stillbirth is due to smoking. This is the disconnect between population-based studies versus causation in a specific individual case. Population-based studies showing increased risk are relevant to the question of whether a specific woman's drug use caused her child's stillbirth, but they're not proof of causation in an individual case, especially not beyond any reasonable doubt.

This discussion about the difficulty of proving that drug use causes stillbirth may seem contradictory. In one context, mainly prenatal care, I emphasize the preventability of some stillbirths and how US doctors could do more medically to prevent at least one quarter of stillbirths in our country. Yet, in this chapter, I question the findings that McKnight's, Gibbs's, Becker's, or Perez's stillbirths could have been prevented had they not used drugs. But it's not inconsistent given the criminal beyond a reasonable doubt burden of proof, a burden of proof that exists to protect people from imprisonment. Numerous reasons exist to doubt that drug use causes stillbirth.

The burden of proof for showing that medical malpractice caused stillbirth, on the other hand, is only a preponderance of the evidence (more likely than not) because it's a civil case where the consequence is payment of damages (and not imprisonment). This is a much easier burden of proof. These burdens mean it should be much easier to show that medical conduct caused stillbirth than it is to show that drug use caused stillbirth. But the opposite is true.

To me, the more problematic inconsistency is the immediate assumption of unpreventability of stillbirth when the topic is medical care versus our immediate assumption of preventability of stillbirth when the topic is drug use. Again, think of Rennie Gibbs. The cord was wrapped around the baby's neck. We don't stop and wonder whether the doctor could have prevented that. Instead, we shrug and say it happens. But not so when the mom is a Black teenager. Then we're convinced her cocaine use caused the baby's stillbirth and she's put in jail. Similarly, Becker was arrested for murder. But Becker's baby was very much alive when she arrived at the hospital. According to news reports, Zachariah didn't die until two hours after Becker arrived at the hospital. Yet no one ever seems to inquire whether the doctor could have prevented the child's stillbirth. (And two hours is plenty of time for an emergency C-section.)

COUNTERPRODUCTIVE

Many proponents of criminalization would likely claim criminalization is about stillbirth prevention. Proponents would claim that these laws deter women from "engaging in risky behavior" that would (supposedly) endanger fetal or infant life.

Numerous problems exist with this idea of deterrence. Plainly, it doesn't make any sense. The vast majority of arrests and prosecutions do not involve stillbirth (just like the vast majority of births are live births). Plus, there's little to no evidence connecting drug use and stillbirth. I feel confident concluding that Gibbs's arrest hasn't prevented any other umbilical cord accidents in Mississippi, or any other stillbirths given Mississippi's consistently high stillbirth rate.

Plus, public health advocates and empirical evidence demonstrates that criminalization is, to put it mildly, a poor prevention strategy. It is more likely to *increase* stillbirths than decrease them. That is because criminalization will deter pregnant people from seeking prenatal care. Would you go to the doctor for prenatal care if it also means the possibility of being reported to the police? Probably not. Even if you really wanted help with your addiction, just seeking help creates a risk of being reported to the police or to child welfare systems. Numerous studies confirm that women have chosen to forego or delay prenatal care, or withhold information about their addiction from their doctors, due to fears of child welfare involvement or criminal consequences.[32]

In chapter 6, I briefly mentioned an important empirical study by law professors Meghan Boone and Ben McMichael—a study that confirms that criminalization will increase stillbirths.[33] The study examined birth and fetal death data from Tennessee from 2014 to 2016, the years it had laws specifically criminalizing drug use during pregnancy. Boone and McMichael concluded that the laws "reduced the probability of" a pregnant person "receiving prenatal care by approximately 6.2 percentage points." Pregnant people were deterred from seeking prenatal care even after the law lapsed.

Boone and McMichael found an increase in stillbirths and infant deaths in Tennessee. Specifically, it concluded that Tennessee's law increased "fetal deaths by 0.225 for every 1,000 births."[34] Translated to the number of babies born in 2015 in Tennessee, this means that "Tennessee sponsored the deaths of approximately twenty fetuses in 2015."[35] For infant deaths, Boone and McMichael found that the laws "increased the death rate of infants per 1,000 births by approximately 0.711," translating to 60 additional infant deaths (within the first 28 days after birth).[36] That's 80 additional babies dying after 20 weeks of pregnancy and within 28 days after birth.

Boone and McMichael's finding of an increase in stillbirths due to decreased prenatal care is not surprising. Numerous studies conclude that the risk of stillbirth increases if prenatal care is limited.[37] More specifically, as discussed in chapter 6, a 2012 study concluded that women who attended less than 50% of the recommended prenatal visits had an almost threefold increased risk of late stillbirth, defined as after 28 weeks.[38]

In sum, criminalization will not decrease stillbirths. To quote Boone and McMichael, arresting pregnant people for drug use has "a *perverse* effect" on the stated goals of protecting unborn children; criminalization "increase[s] the exact outcome [the laws] are intended to protect against."[39] Criminalization likely will only increase stillbirths—and thus is a very poor stillbirth prevention strategy.

COMPOUNDING THE TRAUMA

I shudder at the thought of all the additional traumas that criminalization causes.

There's the initial trauma of your child dying in your womb and having to give birth to him still.

Then there's the additional trauma of how medical professionals treat you during that birth. "Critically, the provision of care for families when a child is stillborn is vitally important to prevent short and long-term negative outcomes."[40] The treatment received in the hospital is "believed to have a significant effect on how" parents are eventually able to resolve their grief.[41] Another study stated that the care and "support received by the mother following the death of her child was the single most important factor in predicting the nature of the grief process that she would experience."[42] Health-care worker "behaviours and actions" and "verbal and non-verbal communications with and around parents can have a memorable impact."[43] And negative treatment can make the experience even more difficult. Unfortunately, in studies, many African American parents report "negative treatment by healthcare providers," and additional stress due to that treatment.[44]

Chelsea Becker was eight months pregnant and bleeding uncontrollably when she got to the hospital.[45] Her son died two hours after she got to the hospital (again, begging the question of why the doctors didn't do an emergency C-section). Becker briefly held her baby. The hospital staff left her baby boy "on a table at the other end of the room." It had a memorable impact. To quote her: "That image of me lying in the hospital bed with my deceased son left on a table, seemingly abandoned, is an image I will never forget."[46]

Adora Perez gave birth to Hades around midnight.[47] At first, Perez remembers the nurses being supportive and kind, encouraging her to spend time with Hades. But at some point in the night "hospital staff sedated her and took Hades away to test his body for meth." When she woke up, he was gone. Again, it had a memorable impact. Perez was distraught and blamed herself for sleeping. Perez doesn't even have a picture of Hades.

This depraved and dehumanizing care will have a memorable impact on Becker and Perez and anyone else subjected to it. As discussed in chapter 6, there are evidence-informed recommended practices for care during still-birth. Parents should be supported, given multiple opportunities to spend time with their child. Both Becker and Perez were denied this care, and that denial of proper medical care will likely have long-lasting effects on them.

Criminalization also involves the additional trauma of state reinforcement of self-blame. Self-blame is common after stillbirth. Blame and guilt "can be overwhelming, as the mother goes meticulously over the events of her pregnancy."[48] Another study confirms that stillbirth moms "agonized over both the decisions they made and the decisions they did not make" and frequently use words like "*guilt, kill, regret, wish,* and *should have.*"[49] The same study explains that some women expressed "unrealistic expectations that they should have had a prescient experience forewarning them of the impending death. Many mothers blamed themselves for the baby's death, citing their 'body's failure' such as 'I have moments when I apologize for killing our daughter even though there was nothing I could do to stop it.'"[50] Self-blame is prevalent even when illogical and irrational.

The women who have been investigated for their child's stillbirth know they did do something—they took drugs. Although little to no scientific evidence shows that the drugs caused their child's death, the state believes in that causation and is trying to put them in jail because of it. Perez blamed herself for her son's death. She eventually determined that she "deserved to be" in jail because "my son is gone."[51]

This is societal reinforcement of self-blame. This is traumatic and cruel. It's "a shockingly callous and inhuman response to personal tragedy."[52]

And the pregnant person has already suffered a natural punishment. Her child is dead. In late summer 2022, ABC News ran a news story on Chelsea Becker.[53] At the end of the interview, the reporter asked Becker: what do you say to those who think there has to be some "accountability for Zachariah." Becker responded: "At the end of the day, I'm the one who lives with the loss. I'm the one that has to deal with the fact that he's never going to have a birthday."

Even if we were able to convince Becker that she didn't cause her son's death, she'll always live with it. She'll always live with questions about what would have happened had she acted differently. She has suffered the ultimate natural punishment, a punishment surely disproportionate to anything that she did or failed to do.

These compounding traumas are most likely to be experienced by marginalized persons—the Black women and/or poor women most likely to be arrested for their child's stillbirth. These are people who are also likely to lack access to needed to mental and emotional health care. Access to mental health care already isn't great in this country, and marginalized persons are least likely to have that access. Notably, Chelsea Becker forewent any counseling in prison because she was afraid what she said might be used against her.[54]

THE WRONG AND RIGHT WAYS TO LOSE A PREGNANCY

Some may argue that these additional traumas are appropriate. Underlying criminalization is the sense that any grief or trauma the pregnant person feels is not enough. Becker may say that she has to live with her son's death every day, but it's not enough; she should have to suffer more because she used drugs during her pregnancy.

There's an assumption that these are bad moms who don't care about their baby, and don't care when their baby is stillborn. Importantly, studies show this is not true. Wendy Bach explains in her book about prosecutions under the Tennessee drug-use-during-pregnancy law that "women who become pregnant do make substantial efforts to curtail their drug use and obtain prenatal care."[55] They seek prenatal care because they know how important it is for their baby and they do so despite the risks due to their drug use. Yet the perception is that these are bad moms who don't deserve any compassion within medical care or otherwise. We assume that the bad mom isn't grieving properly; that she didn't care about the baby in the first place and doesn't care that he died.

Stillbirth researchers and advocates attempted to dispel this perception in the Indiana prosecution of Bei Bei Shuai, who was charged with murder and attempted feticide after she ingested rat poison at 33 weeks pregnant. The attempted suicide was due to a break up with the (married to another person) father of the baby. Shuai and the baby were in stable condition at the hospital, but doctors later had to deliver the baby via emergency C-section due to unusual fetal heart rate. Shuai's baby girl died after some time in the NICU. Eventually, Shuai pled guilty to a misdemeanor for recklessly causing her daughter's death and was not sentenced to any jail time.

Initially, Shuai was arrested, detained, and denied bail. In the appeal for that denial of bail, a group of perinatal-loss academic experts, advocates, and organizations filed an amicus brief urging the court to grant bail and ultimately dismiss the prosecution. The brief begins by arguing that "the death of a baby to stillbirth or neonatal death is a life-altering, often traumatic, event" and that "it is inordinately cruel to prosecute and hold without bail a woman who became so depressed that she tried to commit suicide, and then experienced the death of her newborn baby."[56] The brief zeroes in on the perception that a woman who ingested rat poison is not properly grieving her child's death:

> Grief after perinatal loss is suffered differently from person to person, and is influenced by the individual's culture and religious beliefs. But while the manifestations of grief may vary, the feelings of grief are not unique to any particular group or class of women. A woman who has been targeted for prosecution after a perinatal loss shares these same feelings of despair. Although the voices of women in these circumstances are often obscured by societal reprobation, anecdotal reports confirm what is obvious: a woman, regardless of circumstances, also and just as poignantly grieves her loss.[57]

Similar perceptions about sufficient or proper grief also arise in abuse of corpse cases. Two percent of the cases that included charge information in Pregnancy Justice's September 2023 report included a charge for abuse of a corpse.[58] Numerous women have been arrested for miscarrying or giving birth to their stillborn babies in the toilet. In late 2023, a Black woman, Brittany Watts, was charged with felony abuse of a corpse in Ohio after she gave birth to her 22-week-old stillborn baby on the toilet. (Reports inaccurately called the pregnancy loss at 22 weeks a miscarriage.) Reports said she used the plunger to try to flush the baby.

Ohio's law prohibits treating a human corpse in a way that "would outrage reasonable family" or "reasonable community" sensibilities.[59] The Legislative Service Commission notes that accompany the law explain that its purpose was to arrest people for grave robbing, dissecting a dead body, or having sex with a corpse. And prosecutors were trying to use it to prosecute a woman for her stillbirth. Notably, the law does not define corpse or human corpse—which likely explains why a grand jury fortunately ultimately chose to not indict Watts.

As the stillbirth advocates argued in the Shuai case, studies confirm that parent reactions to stillbirth vary. "Parent reactions to the diagnosis of stillbirth are unique. Parents describe a diverse range of emotions from sorrow to anger and denial. Parents commonly found it difficult to comprehend what had happened. Health-care professionals need to be aware of this normal range of responses, allow parents to express their feelings, and support them through this time."[60]

But the variance hasn't prevented cultural ideas about the wrong way and the right way to react to a child's stillbirth. Ohio prosecutors think that this woman's possible shock, panic, confusion, and just general not knowing what to do was the wrong way to react to her child's stillbirth.

Yet parents are frequently criticized for reacting the seemingly right way—by treating stillbirth as the death of their child. Parents encounter "awkwardness and discomfort" from others when "parents of a stillborn try to discuss their experience, or when they try to normalize it by mentioning their stillborn child alongside their live children as part of their family.[61] In studies, stillbirth parents report feeling unable to "grieve openly." One very public example was the criticism Chrissy Teigen received when she shared pictures of her experience with her unborn son Jack's death; she was criticized for publicizing such a personal matter.[62] Wanting to share grief openly, however, and wanting to "openly celebrate or remember their baby's birth and death, long after the experience" is something stillbirth parents often want to do.[63] But their attempts are rebuffed. Apparently, grieving your decreased child is also the wrong thing to do. In studies, stillbirth parents explain they wish society would understand is that they're "not mentally unstable because we like to honor/celebrate/remember our stillborn child," and that there's nothing abnormal about a funeral for a stillborn child.[64]

This discomfort with grief for a stillborn child is consistent with the common cultural platitudes that tell people to "move on," "have another child," and "'forget the loss' by becoming busy with another child."[65]

So, grieve, maybe even grieve the loss as the death of your child. But not too much; it's not really the same as the death of your child. And then get over it. But apparently not too over it.

Reactions to stillbirth and to pregnancy loss more generally will become even more complicated now that abortion is illegal in many states. Historically, relief and even celebration were common responses to miscarriage in cases of undesired pregnancy. Relief and celebration are not, however, socially acceptable today. Relief and celebration today will instead be reason for suspicion of self-inducement.[66]

Compounded even greater post-*Dobbs*, people experiencing pregnancy loss are in a lose-lose situation, especially marginalized pregnant people. They must treat even a six-week miscarriage tantamount to the death of a living child to avoid suspicion of self-inducement and possible arrest. (And avoidance of suspicion may be impossible for marginalized persons regardless of their reaction.) Yet they'll also be seen as mentally unstable if they don't just quickly get over it and move on from that same six-week miscarriage.

GOING FORWARD

Prosecutions of the formerly pregnant person for supposed causation of stillbirth are problematic for numerous, numerous reasons. State laws must be reinforced to affirm that the birthing parent cannot be charged with the death of their unborn child. According to Pregnancy Justice, 28 of the 38 states that authorize homicide charges for causing pregnancy loss have explicit language precluding charging and prosecuting the pregnant person as of 2022.[67] California has also since passed an explicit prohibition.[68] As an example, Illinois law specifically states its homicide of an unborn child law does not apply to "the pregnant woman whose unborn child is killed."[69]

Post-*Dobbs*, bills were introduced in both Arkansas and Oklahoma to delete this explicit language.[70] Another was introduced in Missouri a bit later.[71] Fortunately, those bills went nowhere, but more such attempts are expected.

When California passed its explicit prohibition, it also created a civil cause of action against the state actor who arrested or prosecuted a pregnant person.[72] This mechanism could further deter a prosecutor from attempting to stretch the law and prosecute the pregnant person. The mechanism is unfortunate in that it puts the onus on the formerly pregnant person to remedy the violation. A structural solution would be preferable, but it's a start.

Notably, Pregnancy Justice advocates not just for express preclusionary language, but also the repeal of all "fetal personhood legislation." I disagree. Repealing all of these statutes would include repealing wrongful death statutes that allow a stillbirth parent to sue for the death of their child, affirming the parent's subjective view of their child's personhood. This is the idea of subjective fetal value discussed in chapter 8. Far from all fetal personhood legislation is limited to subjective value, however. That includes the inclusion of a fetus as a person in murder statutes. That is an objective valuation that all fetuses should be treated as persons no matter the parent's valuation. And the state prosecutes that murder charge no matter the parent's valuation. At the same time, some expansion of murder statutes to fetuses was driven by bereaved parents; they believed their unborn child was their child and wanted "justice" in the sense of the wrongdoer being held criminally responsible. It's true that antiabortion advocates have capitalized on the expansion of murder statutes. But repealing the application of murder to fetuses also denies some bereaved parents of their desired justice.

The better compromise is to immunize the pregnant person from civil liability and criminal consequences. But it's not enough to ban the prosecutions of the pregnant person. We also need to brainstorm solutions to undermine the reasons so many think prosecution is appropriate.

One potential solution is to increase awareness of stillbirth and pregnancy loss. This means education to reintroduce pregnancy loss to the public narrative, including education that stillbirth is still a thing that happens in high-income countries like the United States even in twenty-first century. It's public education that medicine and science have not evolved yet to the point that doctors can explain why a full-term baby can and does die in the womb. (And general public education that medicine and science on pregnancy are not nearly as evolved as would seem; even still in 2024, doctors have no idea why childbirth starts.) Greater awareness of stillbirth would reaffirm that stillbirth happens—and can be unexplained, even still today. That stillbirth happens and is sometimes still unexplained minimizes the urge to immediately assume drug use is the cause.

More research regarding the causes of stillbirth would also undermine the assumption that drug use causes stillbirth.[73] The lack of research perpetuates blame. If we know more about what causes stillbirth, it's less likely that a jury would be so quick to blame drug use. It's often assumed that any additional awareness and research will increase blame. But the opposite could also be true. In May 2022, a study was released that found a biochemical marker making a baby more likely to die from SIDS. The doctor who wrote the study, also a parent of a child who died from SIDS, explained that the research would help alleviate the inclination to blame parents and for parents to self-blame.

Research on systemic causes would be especially helpful to take the attention away from the individual pregnant person. Fuller incorporation of stillbirth prevention into the reproductive justice framework would help with this emphasis on possible systemic causes. Reproductive justice specifically rejects the type of individualization and choice narratives that lead many to believe the pregnant person is at fault when something goes wrong. Pregnancy loss similarly needs to be evaluated on a systemic level.

There's also room for a coalition of stillbirth prevention and anti-criminalization communities. A major focus in the stillbirth community is to improve and standardize bereavement care during stillbirth. Everyone giving birth to their stillborn child deserves compassionate care. Again, Adora Perez does not even have a picture of her son. Stillbirth advocacy groups should prioritize not only the improvement and standardization of care, but also measures to ensure that *all* birthing parents receive that care. This potential coalition is between stillbirth and anti-criminalization communities is tenuous because of anti-criminalization efforts to repeal fetal personhood legislation. But there is common ground between these communities: ensuring that everyone experiencing pregnancy loss receives proper medical care.

Related closely to this suggestion is Pregnancy Justice's advocated reforms to expand Health Insurance Portability and Accountability Act protections to prevent health professionals from reporting drug use of pregnant patients and/or to end mandated reporting of child abuse or neglect based on drug use during pregnancy. The focus of health professionals should be on the birthing parent. Again, the care received "is vitally important to prevent short and long-term negative outcomes." Medical professionals are medical professionals, not police.

Ultimately, prosecution is lazy. It's easier to blame the pregnant person than to investigate why stillbirth happens. It's easier to blame cocaine use than to actually investigate why umbilical cords can wrap around the baby's neck. It's easier to blame methamphetamine use than it is to ask why the baby was still alive for two hours after getting to the hospital.

Dorothy Roberts explained long ago that "prosecution" of pregnant people "blinds the public to the possibility of nonpunitive solutions and to the inadequacy of the nonpunitive solutions that are currently available."[74] It also "does nothing to address perinatal loss" and "diverts both attention and resources from research and education that could prevent perinatal loss."[75]

The many other high-income countries that have reduced their stillbirth rates didn't threaten jail time or put stillbirth parents in jail. They've altered their medical practices to help pregnant people have a healthy baby. Further traumatizing the birthing parent by putting her in jail will not reduce stillbirths.

Conclusion

Genuine (and Forced) Optimism for the Future

This book has not been optimistic. There are many reasons to be pessimistic about the possibility of effective stillbirth prevention in the United States despite our clear need for it. But there are numerous reasons to be optimistic.

Effective journalism has helped increase awareness. Duaa Eldeib wrote a series of articles about stillbirth for ProPublica in 2022 and 2023, and her work was a finalist for a Pulitzer Prize. In her February 2023 piece, Eldeib got multiple politicians on record pledging to fight for comprehensive action on stillbirths.[1] Senator Jeff Merkley of Oregon said that "we should be doing everything we can to prevent Americans from experiencing stillbirth." Senator Tammy Duckworth of Illinois said that both the numbers of moms who die and babies who are stillborn in our country are "unconscionable" and "shocking." Representative Lauren Underwood and Representative Alma Adams, who co-chair the Black Maternal Health Caucus, told Eldeib that stillbirth would be a "priority" for the caucus. Senator Elizabeth Warren expressed that the failure to listen to women, especially women of color, is contributing both to maternal mortality and stillbirth. Hearing these leaders whom I admire pledge support for stillbirth prevention was very powerful for me.

Even more encouraging is the creation of the Eunice Kennedy Shriver National Institute of Child Health and Human Development Stillbirth Working Group of Council. Rewind to 2022, in conjunction with attempts to pass the SHINE for Autumn Act (discussed in chapters 1 and 2), lawmakers included a provision in the fiscal year 2022 Consolidated Appropriations Act mandating that the Department of Health and Human Services (HHS) establish a task force on stillbirth.[2] HHS asked the National Institute of Child Health and Human Development (NICHD, one of the National Institutes of Health) to do so, and it formed the Stillbirth Working Group of Council. The Group was to focus on four topics: (1) current barriers to data collection, (2) communities at higher risk, (3) the psychological impact of stillbirth for parents, and (4) known risk factors.[3]

The Working Group held numerous meetings in late 2022. I was invited to present my work on fetal death certificates at one meeting. In March 2023, the Working Group released a very powerful report entitled "Working to Address the Tragedy of Stillbirth." The report explained that the US stillbirth rate was "unacceptably high."[4] The findings included that the current FDC system "needs substantial improvement."[5] The Working Group also affirmed the racial disparities and the need to "significantly reduce[]" stillbirth rates for marginalized populations.[6] It also noted the need to improve medical care after stillbirths "to ensure that families receive the support they need."[7] Last, the Group emphasized the need for research on the risk factors for stillbirth.

The Group made twelve recommendations, some more specific than others.[8] To mention just a few, the Group recommended development of procedures to improve data collection, including the creation of surveillance registries; anything we can possibly do to improve the number and quality of fetal autopsies; research specifically devoted to the racial disparities in our stillbirth rate; research to develop "culturally sensitive programs to support families after stillbirth"; and further research of risk factors and causes. The report was also clear on the need to involve stillbirth families in the implementation of these recommendations.

Congress appropriated funding again and the Working Group reconvened in the fall of 2023, this time with additional members including myself. The Working Group has three subgroups, one focused on stillbirth prevention, one focused on improvement of data collection, and the last on improving resources for those families whose child is stillborn (of which I was privileged to serve as co-lead).

The Working Group released its next report in summer 2024. All of the subgroups had numerous recommendations, and there is also a list of overlapping recommendations. They include standardizing data reporting and collection; exploring population-based surveillance; creating tools to educate doctors and patients on stillbirth risk factors; standardization of testing after stillbirth; creating a system for audits after stillbirth; and additional research on how obstetrical racism may be affecting stillbirth prevention and care after stillbirth.[9]

In the meantime, the National Institute of Health has also implemented measures to improve and encourage additional research.[10] For instance, it launched a "Rapid Acceleration of Diagnostics Technology (RADx Tech) Fetal Monitoring Challenge," a prize competition for inventions and innovations in methods of diagnosing and monitoring the fetus. The NICHD has also reported increased emphasis on stillbirth data within its Maternal-Fetal Medicine Units and Neonatal Research Networks. And the NICHD has announced it expects to issue new funding opportunities for stillbirth research specifically as part of a possible "Road to Stillbirth Prevention" initiative.

As discussed in chapter 3, reform is easier in countries with government provided and run health care. The governmental medical officers can require changes to medical care. The United States doesn't have that. But we do have the National Institutes of Health, a federal agency that conducts and supports medical research. The NIH's interest in stillbirth prevention means something. Interest from the NIH may be what's necessary to spark additional interest at ACOG.

I'm also optimistic that, with the fall of *Roe* and the emerging strength of the reproductive justice framework, there is a place for stillbirth and pregnancy loss generally within future discussions of reproductive rights and reproductive justice. I'm not applauding the fall of *Roe*. But this is where we are. And where we are can also be an opportunity for the abortion-rights movement to more blatantly acknowledge the breadth of reproductive experiences—and embrace that many people will experience infertility, abortion, pregnancy loss, and live childbirth all in their lives. It's an opportunity to normalize pregnancy loss and abortion.

That said, I'm realistic that stillbirth prevention measures likely must come from known supporters of abortion rights—to make clear from the start that this is not just another antiabortion weaponization. Support for those experiencing pregnancy loss immediately hits differently when introduced by Republican Senator Tom Cotton versus Democratic Senator Tammy Duckworth. Or, at a minimum, the lack of opposition from abortion-rights groups and supporters must be clear from the start. Too often, the strategy on these measures is just to try to avoid the abortion issue. That's not realistic or practical in 2024 (or really for the last several decades).

And we need any and all stillbirth prevention measures. Again, the US stillbirth rate is much higher than other high-income countries. And it's not decreasing like in some of those other countries (with already lower stillbirth rates). To the contrary, the illegality of abortion in many states will likely worsen stillbirth rates in those states.

It doesn't have to be like this. I do what I can to advocate because I don't want anyone else to have to give birth to their stillborn baby. And if they do, I want them to have the best possible experience like we did. I want them to be as empowered as possible.

This book describes numerous legal reforms that could help. Some legal reforms could specifically help with prevention. We could reduce our stillbirth rate like other countries have. Things like state-paid-for autopsies, data registries, changes to tort law standards of care and damage measurements, and prenatal education for pregnant people about fetal movement and the risk of stillbirth could help.

We could also enact legal reforms to help those experiencing stillbirth. These include reforms like relying on informed consent law to mandate disclosure of the risk beforehand, which would help prevent stillbirth and alleviate the shock and confusion that accompanies it; and ensuring reproductive justice-based rights, empowering the birthing parent with supportive care during birth and after.

We also need legal reforms to help change societal and cultural conceptions of stillbirth. These possible legal reforms should emphasize the parents' perspective, including the subjectivity of that perspective—a subjectivity that is consistent with abortion rights. Legal reforms must also include further affirmation and strengthening of immunity of pregnant people from criminal prosecution for stillbirth—and further thought on how to undermine ideas motivating the criminalization of stillbirth.

* * * *

After Caleb died, I finished sewing his baby blanket and his little stuffed turtle. I cut off a corner of the blanket and put it in his columbarium niche, where his cremains are. His nursery was turtle themed. I decorate our kiddos' nurseries around an animal; my kids call them their "birth animals." Caleb's birth animal is a turtle, which also happens to be my favorite animal (long before Caleb). I sleep with Caleb's turtle every night. I also got a tattoo of a sea turtle mama and baby on my wrist.

It later dawned on me that mama sea turtles don't raise their babies. They bury the eggs on the beach and then it's up to the baby turtles to make it to the ocean. That realization made me sad. But it also somehow seems even more appropriate. I also don't get to raise Caleb; he and I are swimming separately, but we're still connected. I'm still his mama and he's still my son.

INTRODUCTION: CALEB

1. Centers for Disease Control and Prevention, "About Stillbirth."

2. Gregory et al., "Trends from 2014 to 2019 and Changes Between 2018–2019 and 2019–2020," 5.

3. Gregory et al., "Fetal Mortality: United States, 2021," 1; Gregory et al., "Trends from 2014 to 2019 and Changes between 2018–2019 and 2019–2020," 5.

4. Cacciatore, "Effects of Support Groups," 72.

5. Cacciatore et al., "When a Baby Dies," 443.

6. Page et al., "Potentially Preventable Stillbirth," 337.

7. Heazell et al., "Information About Fetal Movements," 1.

8. Willinger et al., "Racial Disparities in Stillbirth Risk," 469.e6.

9. Stephansson et al., "Stillbirth Risk in Sweden," 1299.

10. Centers for Disease Control and Prevention, National Vital Statistics System "CDC WONDER Online Database."

11. Gregory et al., "Fetal Mortality: United States, 2021," 4.

12. Page et al., "Potentially Preventable Stillbirth," 342.

13. Senate, Commonwealth of Australia, Select Comm. on Stillbirth," § 7.29, at 113.

14. "Number of Stillbirths in the UK Falls," Tommy's.

15. Flenady et al., "Stillbirths: Recall to Action," 693.

16. UN Inter-agency Group for Child Mortality Estimation, *A Neglected Tragedy*, 74–80.

17. Page et al., "Potentially Preventable Stillbirth," 336.

ONE. MISSING OUT ON CAUSE-OF-DEATH DATA

1. US Standard Report of Fetal Death (November 2003).

2. Centers for Disease Control and Prevention (CDC), National Center for Health Statistics, "Facility Worksheet for the Report of Fetal Death."

3. CDC. National Center for Health Statistics, "Facility Worksheet for the Report of Fetal Death," 5.

4. CDC. National Center for Health Statistics, "Facility Worksheet for the Report of Fetal Death," 5.

5. CDC, National Center for Health Statistics, "Guide to Completing the Facility Worksheets."

6. CDC, National Center for Health Statistics, "Guide to Completing the Facility Worksheets," 32.

7. CDC, National Center for Health Statistics, "Guide to Completing the Facility Worksheets," 42.

8. CDC, National Vital Statistics System, "Applying Best Practices for Reporting Medical and Health Information on Birth Certificates."

9. R.I. STAT. § 23-3-17 (West 2023).

10. CDC, "Coroner and Medical Examiner Laws."

11. R.I. STAT. § 23-4-4 (West 2023).

12. MO. STAT. § 58.451 (West 2023).

13. CDC, National Center for Health Statistics, *Medical Examiners' and Coroners' Handbook*.

14. CDC, National Center for Health Statistics, *Medical Examiners' and Coroners' Handbook*, 74.

15. CDC, National Center for Health Statistics, *Medical Examiners' and Coroners' Handbook*, 74.

16. CDC, National Center for Health Statistics, *Medical Examiners' and Coroners' Handbook*, 76.

17. CDC, National Center for Health Statistics, *Medical Examiners' and Coroners' Handbook*, 74.

18. CDC, National Center for Health Statistics, *Medical Examiners' and Coroners' Handbook*, 81.

19. CDC, National Center for Health Statistics, *Medical Examiners' and Coroners' Handbook*, 40.

20. CDC, National Center for Health Statistics, *Medical Examiners' and Coroners' Handbook*, 75.

21. CDC, National Center for Health Statistics, *Medical Examiners' and Coroners' Handbook*, 75.

22. State of Iowa Department of Health and Human Services, Fetal Death Evaluation Form.

23. Miller et al., "Stillbirth Evaluation," 115.e3.

24. "ACOG Obstetric Care Consensus No. 10," e118.

25. Miller et al., "Stillbirth Evaluation," 115.e3.

26. Eldeib, "Autopsy can Provide Answers."

27. Eldeib, "Autopsy can Provide Answers."

28. Oliver et al., "Stillbirth and Fetal Autopsy Rates," 166S.

29. Lens, "Reproductive Justice," 1113.

30. Meaney et al., "Parental Decision Making," 3164.

31. Heazell et al., "A Difficult Conversation?" 995.

32. Schirmann et al., "Understanding Mothers' Decision-Making," 259.

33. Kirkley-Best and Kellner, "The Forgotten Grief," 426.

34. Horey et al., "Decision Influences and Aftermath," 538–39.

35. Horey et al., "Decision Influences and Aftermath," 538; Schirmann et al., "Understanding Mothers' Decision-Making," 259.

36. Lens, "Counting Stillbirths," 546–57.

37. Horey et al., "Decision Influences and Aftermath," 538–39.

38. Horey et al., "Decision Influences and Aftermath," 538.

39. Lens, "Counting Stillbirths," 548.

40. Lens, "Counting Stillbirths," 548.

41. Lens, "Counting Stillbirths," 548.

42. Lens, "Miscarriage, Stillbirth, and Reproductive Justice," 1113.

43. "ACOG Obstetric Care Consensus No. 10," e119.

44. Law, "Shortage of Forensic Pathologists."

45. SHINE for Autumn Act, H.R. 5487, 117th Cong.

46. R.I. STAT. § 23-4-5 (West 2023); MO. STAT. § 58.725 (West 2023).

47. MO. STAT. § 58.452 (West 2023).

48. CAL. GOV. CODE. § 27491.41(b) (West 2017).

49. Lens, "Counting Stillbirths," 551n193.

50. Walsh and Mortimer, "Unexplained Stillbirths," 73.

51. LA. STAT. ANN. § 40:2019(A)(1)(a)-(b) (2022).

52. Lens, "Counting Stillbirths," 569.

53. Webster et al., "Child Death Review," 58.

54. Webster et al., "Child Death Review," 58.

55. Quinton, "Child Death Review," 529.

56. Committee on Child Abuse and Neglect, Committee on Injury, Violence, and Poison Prevention, Council on Community Pediatrics, "Policy Statement-Child Fatality Review," 592.

57. Lens, "Counting Stillbirths," 571–72.

58. National Center for Fatality Review and Prevention, "FIMR Map."

59. Cummins, "In a Post Dobbs World."

60. S.B. 298, 220th Leg. (NJ 2022).

61. Kirkley-Best and Kellner, "The Forgotten Grief," 426.

TWO. PRIMITIVE DATA COLLECTION

1. Pepper and Lewis, *Pepper and Lewis Digest*, 2870.

2. Lens, "Counting Stillbirths,"555–56.

3. Lunde, *Organization of the Civil Registration System*, 1.

4. Wilbur, "Federal Registration Service of the United States," Appendix 4: Sec. 6.

5. Brumberg et al., "History of the Birth Certificate," 407, 408.

6. Hetzel, "History and Organization of the Vital Statistics System," 6–7.

7. Hetzel, "History and Organization of the Vital Statistics System," 6–7.

8. Hetzel, "History and Organization of the Vital Statistics System," 7.

9. Lens, "Counting Stillbirths,"555–56.

10. Kukura, "Giving Birth Under the ACA," 812.

11. Kirkley-Best and Kellner, "The Forgotten Grief," 425 ("Mothers were almost never allowed to see their infants for fear they would be unduly upset, as if they were not already."); Murphy and Cacciatore, "Impact of Stillbirth on Families," 130 ("Until the 1970s, mothers were not allowed to see or hold a baby who died.").

12. Lens, "Tort Law's Devaluation," 965–66.

13. 42 U.S.C.A. § 242k(b)(1), (h)(1) (1998); 42 U.S.C.A. § 242m(c) (1998).

14. Hamilton et al., "Births: Provisional Data."

15. ARIZ. REV. STAT. ANN. § 36–329 (West 2021); DEL. CODE ANN. tit. 16 § 3124 (West 2018); MONT. CODE ANN. § 50-15-405 (West 2001); OR. REV. STAT. ANN. § 432.143 (West 2013); S.C. CODE ANN. REGS 61-19 (West 2022); TENN. CODE ANN. § 68-3-504 (West 2012); TEX. HEALTH AND SAFETY CODE ANN. § 674.001 (West 2007).

16. Centers for Disease Control (CDC), National Center for Health Statistics, *Model State Vital Statistics Act and Regulations*, 8.

17. 35 PA. STAT. and CONS. STAT. ANN. § 450.105 (West 2012); ARK. CODE ANN. § 20–18–603 (West 2019).

18. Salomon et al., "Estimation of Fetal Weight," 552.

19. TENN. CODE ANN. § 68-3-504(a)(1) (West 2011); N.M. STAT. ANN. § 24-14-22 (West 2014).

20. Gregory et al., "Fetal Mortality: United States, 2020," 16n3.

21. S.D. CODIFIED LAWS § 34-25-32.1 (West 2007).

22. Martin and Hoyert, "National Fetal Death File," 3.

23. Duke and Gilboa, "Using an Existing Birth Defects Surveillance Program," 17–18.

24. Kowaleski, *State Definitions and Reporting Requirements,* 3–5.

25. CDC, National Center for Health Statistics *Reporting of Induced Termination,* 2.

26. US Standard Report of Fetal Death.

27. Christiansen-Lindquist et al., "Fetal Death Certificate Quality," 466.

28. Duke et al., "Using Active Birth Defects Surveillance Programs," 801.

29. Christiansen-Lindquist, "Fetal Death Certificate Quality," 467.

30. Christiansen-Lindquist, "Fetal Death Certificate Quality," 467.

31. Christiansen-Lindquist, "Fetal Death Certificate Quality," 467.

32. Christiansen-Lindquist, "Fetal Death Certificate Quality," 467.

33. Christiansen-Lindquist, "Fetal Death Certificate Quality," 467.

34. Christiansen-Lindquist, "Fetal Death Certificate Quality," 468.

35. Greb et al., "Accuracy of Fetal Death Reports," 1206.

36. Gaudino et al., "Quality Assessment of Fetal Death Records in Georgia," 1323–27.

37. Iowa Code Ann. § 144.29 (West 2022) (requiring filing of FDC within three days after delivery); Or. Rev. Stat. Ann. § 432.143 (West 2013) (requiring filing of FDC within five days after delivery); W.Va. Code Ann. § 16-5-21 (West 2022) (same).

38. US Standard Certificate of Death.

39. Irene Hwang, Sophie Chou, and Duaa Eldeib, "The Failure to Track Data on Stillbirths Undermines Efforts to Prevent Them."

40. Mo. Code Regs. Ann. tit. 19 § 10-10.110(4)(B)(2) (1992) (allowing amendment of the information of the cause of death on an FDC by a "medical certifier, coroner, or medical examiner"); 25 Tex. Admin. Code § 181.30 (2022); 28 Pa. Code § 1.37 (2022) (same).

41. King, "Doctors Investigate Several Stillbirths."

42. Shammas, "Stillbirths Have Doubled."

43. Edwards, "Hard-hit States."

44. Eldeib, "God No, Not Another One."

45. DeSisto et al., "Risk for Stillbirth," 1640.

46. Schwartz et al., "Placental Tissue Destruction," 671; Schwartz and Han, *Covid Infection Can Attack Placenta.*

47. Pediatrics, COVID Data Tracker, CDC, "Data on COVID-19 During Pregnancy."

48. Woodworth et al., "Birth and Infant Outcomes," 1635; CDC, "Emerging Threats."

49. Martin et al., "Maternal and Infant Characteristics," 1.

50. CDC, National Center for Health Statistics, "Recommendations for Wording and Placement."

51. CDC, "Deletion of Data Items."

52. CDC, "Facility Worksheet for the Report of Fetal Death."

53. "Births in England and Wales: 2021," Office for National Statistics.

54. Moss, "Stillbirths Increased Last Year."

55. "Births and Deaths in England and Wales: 2022," Office for National Statistics.

56. Gregory et al., "Fetal Mortality, United States: 2021."

57. Duke and Gilboa, "Using an Existing Birth Defects Surveillance Program," 18.

58. ARK. CODE ANN. § 20-16-201 (West 2015).

59. N.J. STAT. ANN. § 26:8-40.27 (West 2015).

60. Lens, "Counting Stillbirths," 569.

61. SHINE for Autumn Act, H.R. 5487, 117th Cong.

62. CAL. HEALTH AND SAFETY CODE § 103005 (West 2023).

63. Lewin, "Out of Grief."

64. ABC News, "New Pennsylvania Law."

65. Snyder, "The Missing Angels Act," 544.

66. Snyder, "The Missing Angels Act," 544.

67. Lewin, "Out of Grief."

THREE. STANDARDS OF CARE AND MALPRACTICE

1. Scott and Bevan, *Saving Babies' Lives Report.*

2. Healthcare Improvement Scotland, "Every Move I Make."

3. Healthcare Improvement Scotland, "Scottish Patient Safety Programme"; Scottish Government, "The Best Start."

4. O'Connor, *Saving Babies Lives: Care Bundle for Reducing Stillbirth.*

5. National Health Service England, *Saving Babies' Lives Version Two.*

6. National Health Service England, *Saving Babies' Lives Version Three.*

7. National Health Service England, *Saving Babies' Lives Version Three,* 4.

8. Centre for Research Excellence, Stillbirth: *Safer Baby Bundle,* 11.

9. "ACOG Committee Opinion 828," e177.

10. "ACOG Committee Opinion 828," e180-81.

11. "SMFM Consult Series No. 60."

12. "ACOG Committee Opinion 828," e181.

13. "ACOG Obstetric Care Consensus 11," 355-56.

14. "ACOG Committee Opinion 828."

15. National Health Service England, *Saving Babies' Lives Version Three,* 39.

16. Centre for Research Excellence, *Safer Baby Bundle,* 27.

17. "ACOG Committee Opinion 828," e183.

18. "ACOG Obstetric Care Consensus No. 10," e125.

19. "ACOG Practice Bulletin 229," e117, e122.
20. Centre for Research Excellence, *Safer Baby Bundle*, 29.
21. Centre for Research Excellence, *Safer Baby Bundle*, 30.
22. Centre for Research Excellence, *Safer Baby Bundle*, 30.
23. National Health Service England, *Saving Babies' Lives Version Three*, 39.
24. Isburg, "Iowa Lowers Stillbirth Rate."
25. Gregory et al., "Fetal Mortality: United States, 2020," 6.
26. Heazell et al., "Information About Fetal Movements," 2.
27. Heazell et al., "Information About Fetal Movements," 4.
28. Heazell et al., "Information About Fetal Movements," 8.
29. Tveit et al., "Reduction of Late Stillbirth," 4.
30. Centre for Research Excellence, *Safer Baby Bundle*, 73.
31. Tommy's, "Leaflet and banner."
32. Tommy's, "Leaflet and banner."
33. "ACOG Practice Bulleting 229," e122.
34. "Special Tests for Monitoring."
35. Williams, "What My Life-Threatening Experience Taught."
36. Munz, "U.S. Rep. Cori Bush."
37. Munz, "U.S. Rep. Cori Bush."
38. Thompson et al., "Racism Runs Through It," 195.
39. Thompson et al., "Racism Runs Through It," 197.
40. Thompson et al., "Racism Runs Through It," 200.
41. Isburg, "Iowa Lowers Stillbirth Rate by 32 Percent in 10 Years."
42. "ACOG Practice Bulletin 229," e117, e121.
43. "ACOG Committee Opinion 828," e183.
44. Centre for Excellence, *Safer Baby Bundle*, 74.
45. National Health Service England, *Saving Babies' Lives Version Two*, 33.
46. National Health Service England, *Saving Babies' Lives Version Three*, 38.
47. Centre for Excellence, *Safer Baby Bundle*, 33.
48. National Health Service England, *Saving Babies' Lives Version Three*, 71-72.
49. ACOG, "Can I sleep on my back?"
50. Centre for Excellence, *Safer Baby Bundle*, 34.
51. National Health Service England, *Saving Babies' Lives Version Three*, 27.
52. Centre for Excellence, *Safer Baby Bundle*, 16.
53. National Health Service England, *Saving Babies' Lives Version Two*, 24.
54. National Health Service England, *Saving Babies' Lives Version Three*, 25.
55. Centre for Excellence, *Safer Baby Bundle*, 40.
56. "ACOG Committee Opinion No. 807, e221."
57. "ACOG Committee Opinion 828," e186.
58. "ACOG Committee Opinion No. 807, e223-26."

59. Centre for Excellence, *Safer Baby Bundle,* 37.

60. "ACOG Committee Opinion 828," e186.

61. National Health Service England, *Saving Babies' Lives Version Three,* 34.

62. National Health Service England, *Saving Babies' Lives Version Three,* 74.

63. National Health Service, *Saving Babies' Lives,* 17.

64. National Health Service England, *Saving Babies' Lives Version Three,* 78–79.

65. National Health Service England, *Saving Babies' Lives Version Three,* 28.

66. National Health Service England, *Saving Babies' Lives Version Three,* 34.

67. Centre for Excellence, *Safer Baby Bundle,* 22.

68. Centre for Excellence, *Safer Baby Bundle,* 72.

69. Centre for Excellence, *Safer Baby Bundle,* 26.

70. "ACOG Practice Bulletin 227," e18.

71. "ACOG Practice Bulletin 227," e18-e19.

72. "ACOG Practice Bulletin 227," e19-e20.

73. Geiger et al., "Association of Prenatal Care Services," 5, 7.

74. Geiger et al., "Association of Prenatal Care Services," 8.

75. Center for Research Excellence, *Safer Baby Bundle,* 37.

76. Center for Research Excellence, *Safer Baby Bundle,* 36–38.

77. Center for Research Excellence, *Safer Baby Bundle,* 40–41.

78. National Health Service England, *Saving Babies' Lives Version Three,* 35–36.

79. National Health Service England, *Saving Babies' Lives Version Three,* 40–41.

80. Roth, *Business of Birth,* 102, 106.

81. Roth, *Business of Birth,* 102-3.

82. Roth, *Business of Birth,* 28–29.

83. Roth, *Business of Birth,* 103.

84. Morris, *Cut it Out,* 93.

85. Brody, "A Campaign."

86. Brody, "A Campaign."

87. "ACOG Practice Bulletin No. 107."

88. "ACOG Committee Opinion No. 579," 1139.

89. "ACOG Committee Opinion 561," 913-14.

90. "ACOG Committee Opinion 765," e160.

91. Little et al., "A Multi-State Analysis," 1139-40.

92. MacDorman et al., "Trends in Stillbirth," 1147-48.

93. National Quality Forum Maternity Action Team, "Playbook," 6-7; Specifications Manual for Joint Commission National Quality Measures, *Measure Information Form.*

94. Dahlen et al., "Texas Medicaid Payment Reform," 461.

95. Allen and Grossman, "The Impact of Voluntary and Nonpayment Policies," 64.

96. "ACOG Committee Opinion No. 831."

97. "ACOG Committee Opinion No. 831," e38.

98. "ACOG Practice Bulletin 229," e121.

99. "ACOG Committee Opinion No. 831," e35.

100. "ACOG Obstetric Care Consensus 11," 356–57.

101. Thompson et al., "Placental Pathology Findings."

102. Author interview with Ann O'Neill, February 5, 2023.

103. Reproductive and Placental Research Unit, Obstetrics, Gynecology and Reproductive Sciences, "Estimated Placental Volume."

104. Lai et al., "Using Ultrasound and Angiogenic Markers"; Dahdouh et al., "In Vivo Placental MRI shape."

105. Yale School of Medicine, "Estimated Placental Volume."

106. "Measure the Placenta."

107. Murdaugh and Florescue, "Small Estimated Placental Volume."

108. Kirkup, *Report of the Morecambe*, 5, 15.

109. Titcombe and Kirkup, "Saving Babies' Lives."

110. Roth, *Business of Birth*, 63.

111. T..J. Hooper v. Northern Barge Corp., 60 F.2d 737 (2d Cir. 1932).

112. Helling v. Carey, 519 P.2d 981, at 982 (Wash. 1974).

113. Furrow et al., *Health Law*, 78.

114. Nowatske v. Osterloh, 543 N.W.2d 265, 271 (Wis. 1996).

115. Sawicki, "Choosing Medical Malpractice," 891.

116. *Morrison*, 407 A.2d at 567.

117. Sawicki, "Choosing Medical Malpractice," 893.

118. Sawicki, "Choosing Medical Malpractice," 925–26.

119. "ACOG Obstetric Care Consensus No. 10," e125–26.

120. Kukura, "Obstetric Violence," 740.

121. "ACOG Committee Opinion No. 439," 6.

FOUR. VALUING STILLBORN BABIES

1. Justus v. Atchison, 565 P.2d 122, at 136 (Cal. 1977).

2. Lens, "Tort Law's Devaluation of Stillbirth," 969–70.

3. Lens, "Tort Law's Devaluation," 971.

4. Lens, "Tort Law's Devaluation," 971–72.

5. Freidenfelds, *The Myth of the Perfect Pregnancy*, 28–29.

6. Chamallas and Kerber, "Women, Mothers, and the Law of Fright," 819.

7. Chamallas and Kerber, "Women, Mothers, and the Law of Fright," 821.

8. Dillon v. Legg, 441 P.2d 912, at 920 (Cal. 1968).

9. Justus, 565 P.2d at 122.

10. Justus, 565 P.2d at 135.

11. Justus, 565 P.2d at 136.

12. Austin v. Regents of the University of California, 152 Cal. Rptr. 420, at 422 (Cal. Ct. App. 1979).

13. Broadnax v. Gonzalez, 809 N.E.2d 645, at 648 (N.Y. 2004).

14. Lens, "Tort Law's Devaluation," 976.

15. Krishnan v. Ramirez, 42 S.W.3d 205, at 215 (Tex. App. 2001).

16. Lens, "Children, Wrongful Death, and Punitive Damages," 445.

17. Lens, "Children, Wrongful Death," 445–46.

18. Lens, "Children, Wrongful Death," 446–47.

19. Lens, "Children, Wrongful Death," 446–47.

20. Lens, "Children, Wrongful Death," 461–62.

21. Lens, "Children, Wrongful Death," 451–53.

22. Pollock, *Forgotten Children*, 51.

23. Lens, "Children, Wrongful Death," 456–57.

24. Zelizer, *Pricing the Priceless Child*, 22–55, 56–112.

25. Lens, "Children, Wrongful Death," 471–72.

26. Lens, "Children, Wrongful Death," 471–72.

27. Lens, "Children, Wrongful Death," 464.

28. Lind, "Valuing Relationships," 305.

29. Lind, "Valuing Relationships," 305.

30. Lind, "Valuing Relationships," 306.

31. Lens, "Children, Wrongful Death," 472–73.

32. Krishnan v. Sepulveda, 916 S.W.2d 478, at 489 (Tex. 1995) (Gonzalez, J., dissenting) ("The Court is asking the trier of fact to do the impossible: ascertain damages for mental anguish to the mother 'as a result of the occurrence in question' yet unrelated to the unborn baby's death").

33. Danos v. St. Pierre,, 383 So. 2d 1019 (La. Ct. App. 1980), 1030–31, n.15, aff'd, 402 So. 2d 633 (La.1981).

34. Arsenault and Dombeck, "Maternal Assignment of Fetal Personhood," 651.

35. Arsenault and Dombeck, "Maternal Assignment of Fetal Personhood," 660.

36. Arsenault and Dombeck, "Maternal Assignment of Fetal Personhood," 653.

37. Fox and Lens, "Valuing Reproductive Loss," 82–83.

38. *Robinson*, 140 F.Supp. 2d 488, at 490–91 (D. Md. 2001).

39. Meaney et al., "Parents' Concerns," 558 (discussing the unhelpful responses received by parents of stillborn babies, including being "told that they

were young and that they would [have] plenty of opportunities to have more children"); Kelley and Trinidad, "Silent Loss," 8 ("For [the] parents in these focus groups, the most common and most hurtful comments were reassurances that they would have another baby"); Kirkley-Best and Kellner, "The Forgotten Grief," 425 (explaining that "society expected that a young mother would not grieve for a stillbirth," a thought validated by the immediate response of telling the mother to not worry because she could have another child).

40. Willets, "What It Really Feels Like to Have a 'Rainbow Baby.'"

41. Carey v. Lovett, 622 A.2d 1279, at 1290 (N.J. 1993).

42. Modaber v. Kelley, 348 S.E.2d 233, at 238 (Va. 1986).

43. Randles v. Ind. Patient's Comp. Fund, 860 N.E.2d 1212, at 1232 (Ind. Ct. App. 2007) ("Indiana has long held that evidence of remarriage is not admissible to mitigate damages in a wrongful death action"); *Stuart*, 496 P.2d at 529–30 (discussing that evidence of remarriage is inadmissible in a wrongful death claim).

44. Landry v. Clement, 711 So. 2d 829, at 836 (La. Ct. App. 1998).

45. Fox and Lens, "Valuing Reproductive Loss," 100–1.

46. Karoline Gundersen Sarmon et al., "Assisted Reproductive Technologies," 786.

47. Solinger, "Incompatibility," 39-40 ("Pursuing fertility treatments is a class privilege").

48. Fox and Lens, "Valuing Reproductive Loss," 73-74.

49. Fox and Lens, "Valuing Reproductive Loss," 76.

50. Lens, "Children, Wrongful Death," 471.

51. Jager, "There Was No Jewish Way."

52. Fox and Lens, "Valuing Reproductive Loss," 74-75.

53. Ranji et al., "Expanding Postpartum."

54. Kukura, "Giving Birth under the ACA," 825.

55. National Federation of Independent Business v. Sebelius, 567 U.S at 552 (2012).

56. Martin and Belluz, "Extraordinary Danger."

57. Fox and Lens, "Valuing Reproductive Loss," 74-75.

58. Donley and Lens, "Abortion, Pregnancy Loss, and Subjective Fetal Personhood," 1678-79.

59. Finley, "Female Trouble," 847-79, 850-51.

60. Lens, "Children, Wrongful Death," 447.

61. Finley, "Female Trouble," 855.

62. Finley, "Female Trouble," 861-62.

63. Fox and Lens, "Valuing Reproductive Loss," 70-71; Tex. Civ. Prac. and Rem. § 74.301 (West 2003).

64. N.H. Rev. Stat. Ann. § § 556:12 (West 2019).

65. TENN. CODE ANN. § 29-39-102(a)(2) (West 2019).

66. TEX. CIV. PRAC. AND REM. § 71.001 (West 2003).

67. TEX. CIV. PRAC. AND REM. § 71.003 (West 2003).

68. TEX. CIV. PRAC. AND REM. § 71.303 (West 2003).

69. DeVito and Jurs, "'Doubling-Down,'" 556–58.

70. Roth, *Business of Birth*, 64.

71. DeMillo, "Church's Group."

72. Fox and Lens, "Valuing Reproductive Loss," 83–102.

FIVE. BLINDSIDING PARENTS

1. Kelley and Trinidad, "Silent Loss and the Clinical Encounter," 13.

2. Kelley and Trinidad, "Silent Loss and the Clinical Encounter," 13.

3. Kelley and Trinidad, "Silent Loss and the Clinical Encounter," 3.

4. Layne, *Motherhood Lost*, 95.

5. Goldenbach, "Blindsided," 7–8.

6. Kirkley-Best and Kellner, "The Forgotten Grief," 421.

7. Kelley and Trinidad, "Silent Loss," 4.

8. Layne, *Motherhood Lost*, 86.

9. Kirkley-Best and Kellner, "The Forgotten Grief," 424.

10. "ACOG, Obstetric Care Consensus No. 10," e110.

11. Lens, "Medical Paternalism, Stillbirth, and Blindsided Mothers," 679.

12. Beauchamp and Childress, *Principles of Biomedical Ethics*, 13.

13. Beauchamp and Childress, *Biomedical Ethics*, 14.

14. Beauchamp and Childress, *Biomedical Ethics*, 104.

15. Beauchamp and Childress, *Biomedical Ethics*, 121.

16. Beauchamp and Childress, *Biomedical Ethics*, 125.

17. Beauchamp and Childress, *Biomedical Ethics*, 133.

18. Beauchamp and Childress, *Biomedical Ethics*, 134.

19. "ACOG Committee Opinion No. 439," 401.

20. "ACOG Committee Opinion No. 439," 402.

21. "ACOG Committee Opinion No. 439," 405.

22. "ACOG Committee Opinion No. 819," e35.

23. "ACOG Committee Opinion No. 819," e39.

24. Planned Parenthood Ass'n of Kansas City, Missouri, Inc. v. Ashcroft, 655 F.2d 847, at 866 (8th Cir. 1981); Leigh v. Olson, 497 F. Supp. 1340, at 1344 (D.N.D. 1980).

25. Lens, "Medical Paternalism, Stillbirth," 681–85.

26. Sawicki, "A Malpractice-Based Duty," 665.

27. Pearce v. United Bristol Healthcare NHS Trust [1999] AC 167-168, at 168 (appeal taken from Eng.).

28. Munz, "U.S. Rep. Cori Bush."

29. Lens, "Medical Paternalism, Stillbirth," 696–97.

30. Oberman, "Mothers and Doctors' Orders," 454.

31. "Listeriosis During Pregnancy," The Bump.

32. Lens, "Medical Paternalism, Stillbirth," 673–74.

33. Cacciatore, "Effects of Support Groups," 72.

34. Smith, "Bonfire," 1307 (reviewing Catherine Y. Spong ed., *Stillbirth: Prediction, Prevention, and Management* [Wiley-Blackwell, 2011]).

35. DeSisto et al., "Risk for Stillbirth," 1641.

36. Lens, "Medical Paternalism, Stillbirth," 692–93.

37. Abrams, "Distorted and Diminished," 1994.

38. Donley and Lens, "Second-Trimester Abortion Dangertalk," 2176–77.

39. *Pearce* [1999] AC 167, at 170.

40. Pollock et al., "Breaking through the Silence," 82.

41. Pollock et al., "Knowing Your Audience," 394.

42. Canterbury v. Spence,, 464 F.2d 772, at 789 (D.C. Cir. 1972).

43. "ACOG Committee Opinion No. 819," e38.

44. Lens, "Medical Paternalism, Stillbirth," 705–7.

45. Lens, "Medical Paternalism, Stillbirth," 705–7.

46. Lens, "Medical Paternalism, Stillbirth," 698–99.

47. Kukura, "Obstetric Violence," 768.

48. Tveit et al., "Reduction of Late Stillbirth," 4.

49. Lens, "Medical Paternalism, Stillbirth," 690.

50. Clark, "Centering Black Pregnancy," 98.

51. "ACOG Committee Opinion No. 819," e35.

52. "ACOG Committee Opinion No. 819," e38.

53. "ACOG Committee Opinion No. 439," 404–5.

54. Pollock et al., "Voices of the Unheard," 5; Pollock et al., "Understanding Stillbirth Stigma," 215.

55. Lens, "Medical Paternalism, Stillbirth," 715.

56. Montgomery v. Lanarkshire Health Board [2015] UKSC 11 (appeal taken from Scot.), 2015 WL 997495.

57. Kukura, "Obstetric Violence," 752.

58. Block, *Pushed: The Painful Truth*, 91–92.

59. Kukura, "Obstetric Violence," 752.

60. Lens, "Medical Paternalism, Stillbirth," 702.

SIX. REPRODUCTIVE JUSTICE AND STILLBIRTH

1. Ross and Solinger, *Reproductive Justice*, 19, 27–28.

2. Ross and Solinger, *Reproductive Justice*, 10.

3. Sistersong, "What is Reproductive Justice"; Solinger, "Conditions of Reproductive Justice," 4.

4. Lens, "Miscarriage, Stillbirth, and Reproductive Justice," 1084.

5. Wiley, "Health Law."

6. Tomasina et al., "Antenatal Care," 244.

7. Tomasina et al., "Antenatal Care," 244.

8. Boone and McMichael, "State-Created Fetal Harm," 507.

9. Stephansson et al., "Influence of Socioeconomic Status," 1300.

10. Lens, "Miscarriage, Stillbirth, and Reproductive Justice," 1085.

11. Denney-Koelsch et al., "Introduction to Perinatal Palliative Care," 4.

12. Denney-Koelsch et al., "Introduction to Perinatal Palliative Care," 5.

13. Wool et al., "Provision of Services in Perinatal Palliative Care," 279.

14. Paquette, "Perinatal Hospice Care."

15. Americans United for Life, *Perinatal Hospice Information Act;* Americans United for Life, "Defending Life."

16. Donley and Lens, "Second-Trimester Abortion Dangertalk," 2167–68.

17. Donley and Lens, "Second-Trimester Abortion Dangertalk," 2181.

18. ARK. CODE ANN. § 20-16-2302(a)(4)-(5) (West 2021).

19. Klibanoff and Bohra, "Judge Says Texas Woman."

20. "ACOG Committee Opinion No. 786," e87.

21. Perinatal Hospice Palliative Care, "Frequently Asked Questions," https://www.perinatalhospice.org/faqs.

22. Hollenbach et al., "Obstetric Management in Life-Limiting Fetal Conditions," 82.

23. Henner et al., "Considerations in Unique Populations," 359–80, 363.

24. Kukura, "Obstetric Violence," 732–33.

25. Solinger, "Conditions of Reproductive Justice," 42.

26. Ross and Solinger, *Reproductive Justice,* 262.

27. Cacciatore, "Unique Experiences," 135.

28. Wall-Wieler et al., "Severe Maternal Morbidity," 310 (explaining that the chances of life-threatening complications for the woman are five times greater in a stillbirth than a live birth).

29. Lens, "Miscarriage, Stillbirth, and Reproductive Justice," 1093–94.

30. Morris, *Cut it Out,* 17.

31. Morris, *Cut it Out,* 17.

32. Bridges, "Racial Disparities," 1245–46.

33. Morris, *Cut it Out,* 15.

34. "ACOG Obstetric Care Consensus No. 10," e122.

35. "ACOG Obstetric Care Consensus No. 10," e123.

36. Siassakos et al., *Late Intrauterine Fetal Death and Stillbirth*, 4.

37. Cassidy, "Care Quality Following," 9.

38. Donley and Lens, "Second-Trimester Abortion Dangertalk," 2157–58.

39. Carhart v. Gonzales, 550 U.S. 124, at 161 (2007).

40. *Carhart*, 550 U.S. at 159.

41. Manian, "The Irrational Woman," 259.

42. Donley and Lens, "Second-Trimester Abortion Dangertalk," 2177–78.

43. Donley and Lens, "Second-Trimester Abortion Dangertalk," 2160.

44. Rabkin Peachman, "*Dobbs* Decision," 1668–70.

45. Kelley and Trinidad, "Silent Loss," 6.

46. Siassakos et al., *Late Intrauterine Fetal Death and Stillbirth*, 19–20.

47. ACOG Obstetric Care Consensus No. 10," e118.

48. ACOG Obstetric Care Consensus No. 10," e122.

49. Kavanaugh and Hershberger, "Perinatal Loss," 603–4.

50. Carol Kingdon et al., "Role of Healthcare," 17.

51. Brody, "A Device That Gives Parents of Stillborn Babies Time to Say Goodbye."

52. Heazell et al., "Economic and Psychosocial Consequences," 604, 606.

53. Ogwulu et al., "Intangible Economic Costs," 8.

54. Heazell et al., "Stillbirths: Economic and Psychosocial Consequences," 605.

55. Ogwulu, "Exploring the Intangible Economic Costs of Stillbirth," 7.

56. Katherine J. Gold, Martha E. Boggs, and Melissa A. Plegue, "Gaps in Stillbirth Bereavement Care," 887–94.

57. "ACOG Obstetric Care Consensus No. 10," e124.

58. "ACOG Obstetric Care Consensus No. 10," e123.

59. Boyden et al., "Experiences of African American Parents," 376.

60. Boyden et al., "Experiences of African American Parents," 376.

61. Boyden et al., "Experiences of African American Parents," 376.

62. Boyden et al., "Experiences of African American Parents," 376.

63. Willinger et al., "Racial Disparities," 375.

64. Van and Meleis, "Coping with Grief," 32.

65. Boyden et al., "Experiences of African American Parents," 378.

66. Van and Meleis, "Coping with Grief," 32.

67. Boyden et al., "Experiences of African American Parents," 378.

68. Linda Layne, "I Remember the Day I Shopped for Your Layette," 256

69. Van and Meleis, "Coping with Grief," 35.

70. O'Leary, "Trauma of Ultrasound," 183, 185.

71. Tommy's, "The Rainbow Clinic,"

72. "The Rainbow Clinic: Pregnancy after Loss," Push.

SEVEN. THAT FIRST BREATH

1. Centers for Disease Control and Prevention, National Center for Health Statistics, *Model State Vital Statistics*, 2.

2. Kelley and Trinidad, "Silent Loss," 13.

3. Lens, "Children, Wrongful Death, and Punitive Damages," 445.

4. Lens, "Children, Wrongful Death, and Punitive Damages," 445-46.

5. Mo. Stat. § 537.080 (West 2023).

6. Lipps v. Milwaukee Elec. Ry. and Light Co., 159 N.W. 916, at 916 (Wis. 1916).

7. Chatelain v. Kelley, 910 S.W.2d 215, at 219 (Ark. 1995).

8. Endresz v. Friedberg, 248 N.E. 901, at 903 (Ct. App. N.Y. 1969).

9. Justus v. Atchison, 565 P.2d 122, at 133 (Cal. 1977).

10. Dobbs v. Jackson Women's Health Org., 597 U.S. 215, 259 (2022).

11. Kelley and Trinidad, "Silent Loss," 13.

12. Dunn v. Rose Way, Inc., 333 N.W.2d 830, at 833 (Iowa 1983).

13. Burnham v. Miller, 972 P.2d 645, at 647 (Ariz. Ct. App. 1998).

14. *Lipps*, 159 N.W. at 917.

15. Verkennes v. Corniea, 38 N.W.2d 838, at 841 (Minn. 1949).

16. Roe v. Wade, 410 U.S. 113, at 162 (1973).

17. *Verkennes*, 38 N.W.2d at 841; White v. Yup, 458 P.2d 617, at 624 (Nev. 1969); Williams v. Marion Rapid Transit, 87 N.E.2d 334, at 339 (Ohio. 1949); Kwaterski v. State Farm Mut. Auto. Ins. Co., 148 N.W.2d 107, at 112 (Wis. 1967); Baldwin v. Butcher, 184 S.E.2d 428, at 435 (W.Va. 1971); Worgan v. Greggo & Ferrara, Inc., 128 A.2d 557, 557 (Del. Super. Ct. 1956).

18. Hamilton v. Scott, 97 So.3d 728, 743 (Ala. 2012).

19. *Verkennes*, 38 N.W.2d at 841.

20. *Hamilton*, 97 So.3d at 744.

21. De Ville and Kopelman, "Fetal Protection in Wisconsin," 335.

22. Klasing, "Death of an Unborn Child," 978-79.

23. LePage v. Center for Reproductive Medicine, __So.3d__ (Ala. 2024).

24. Fox and Lens, "Valuing Reproductive Loss," 105.

25. Fox and Lens, "Valuing Reproductive Loss," 75 n101.

26. Fox and Lens, "Valuing Reproductive Loss," 94-95.

27. Internal Revenue Service, *Personal Exemptions*, 5-1.

28. Congressional Research Service, *The Child Tax Credit*, 6.

29. Congressional Research Service, *The Child Tax Credit*, 9.

30. Congressional Research Service, *The Child Tax Credit*, 10.

31. Turner, "Expanded Child Tax Credit."

32. Congressional Research Service, *The Child Tax Credit*, 4-5.

33. Sawhill et al., "It's Getting More Expensive to Raise Children."

34. Slemrod and Bakija, *Taxing Ourselves*, 92.

35. Slemrod and Bakija, *Taxing Ourselves*, 92.

36. Centers for Disease Control and Prevention, *Model State Vital Statistics*, 2.

37. ARIZ. REV. STAT. ANN. § 43-1023 (West 2020); N.D. CENT. CODE § 57-38-30.3 (2020); MICH. COMP. LAWS § 206.30 (West 2020).

38. MINN. STAT. ANN. § 290.0685 (West 2020).

39. ARK. CODE ANN. § 26-51-516 (West 2022); CT. GEN. STAT. ANN. § 22-118, 412 (2022); GA. CODE ANN. § 48-7-26 (West 2020).

40. H.B. 457, 2023 Leg. (Mo. 2023); S.B. 133, 2023 Leg. (Mo. 2023).

41. Lens, "Miscarriage, Stillbirth, and Reproductive Justice," 1095.

42. Department of Revenue, "Guidance Related to House Bill 481."

43. Westwood, "Bleeding and in Pain."

44. Sanger, "Lopsided Harms," 46.

EIGHT. ABORTION AND STILLBIRTH

1. Roe v. Wade, 410 U.S. 113 (1973).

2. Dobbs v. Jackson Women's Health Org., 597 U.S. 215 (2022).

3. *Dobbs*, 597 U.S. at 263.

4. *Dobbs*, 597 U.S. at 254.

5. Petition for Writ of Certiorari, Benson v. McKee, 273 A.3d 121 (No. 22-201) at 2-3 (2022), WL 4096782.

6. Freidenfelds, *Myth of the Perfect Pregnancy*, 144.

7. Layne, *Motherhood Lost*, 59-74.

8. *Roe*, 410 U.S. at 153.

9. *Dobbs*, 597 U.S. at 358-59.

10. Freidenfelds, *Myth of the Perfect Pregnancy*, 208.

11. Freidenfelds, *Myth of the Perfect Pregnancy*, 143-44.

12. Lens, "Miscarriage, Stillbirth, and Reproductive Justice," 1081-82.

13. Layne, "True Gifts from God," 174.

14. Donley and Lens, "Abortion, Pregnancy Loss, and Subjective Fetal Personhood," 1699-1700

15. Donley and Lens, "Abortion, Pregnancy Loss, and Subjective Fetal Personhood," 1700-1.

16. Bhattacharya et al., "Factors Associated with Failed Treatment," e82249.

17. Freidenfelds, *Myth of the Perfect Pregnancy,* 137.

18. Sullivan, "GOP Senator Blocks Bill."

19. OKLA. STAT. ANN. tit. 63 § 1-745.51 (West 2022).

20. Freidenfelds, *Myth of the Perfect Pregnancy*, 147-48.

21. Klasing, "Death of an Unborn Child," 978-79.

22. De Ville and Kopelman, "Fetal Protection in Wisconsin," 335.

23. Hamilton v. Scott, 97 So.3d 728, at 742-747 (Ala. 2012) (J. Parker, concurring).

24. Hamilton v. Scott, 278 So.3d 1180 (Ala. 2018).

25. *Hamilton*, 278 So.3d at 1185.

26. *Hamilton*, 278 So.3d at 1189.

27. *Hamilton*, 278 So.3d at 1192.

28. *Hamilton*, 278 So.3d at 1192.

29. Gregory et al., "Fetal Mortality: United States, 2021," 17.

30. Centers for Disease Control and Prevention, National Vital Statistics System "About Fetal Deaths 2005-2022," CDC WONDER Online Database.

31. SHINE for Autumn Act, H.R. 5487, 117th Cong. (2021).

32. Ord, "The Scourge," 12; Blackshaw and Rodger, "Problem of Spontaneous Abortion," 103-20.

33. *Dobbs*, 597 U.S. at 301.

34. Conway and Dannenfelser, "If They Want to Win."

35. MISS. CODE ANN. § 41-41-131 (2014).

36. Brief of Society for Maternal-Fetal Medicine, Royal College of Obstetricians and Gynaecologists, U.S. Association for the Study of Pain, and 27 Scientific and Medical Experts as Amici Curiae, Dobbs v. Jackson Women's Health Org., 597 U.S. 215 (2022) (No. 19-1392). 2021 WL 4441335.

37. Heazell et al., "Excessive Fetal Movements," 20.

38. Linde et al., "Women's Experiences," 191.

39. Linde et al., "Women's Experiences," 191.

40. Linde et al., "Women's Experiences," 191.

41. Linde et al., "Women's Experiences," 191.

42. Linde et al., "Women's Experiences," 192.

43. Heazell et. al., "Excessive fetal movements," 20.

44. Dobbs, 597 U.S. at 255, n. 41.

45. Lawn et al., "Stillbirths: Rates, Risk Factors, and Acceleration Towards 2030," 597.

46. Layne, *Motherhood Lost*, 12.

47. Donley and Lens, "Abortion, Pregnancy Loss, and Subjective Fetal Personhood," 1708-90.

48. Donley and Lens, "Abortion, Pregnancy Loss, and Subjective Fetal Personhood," 1710-11.

49. Noor, "South Carolina Woman."

50. Herzog, "House OKs Abortion Ban."

51. "Doomed Baby Stillborn," *Associated Press*.

52. Donley and Lens, "Abortion, Pregnancy Loss, and Subjective Fetal Personhood," 1712.

53. Siano, "A Woman's Right to Choose," 288.

54. Lehigh, "Common Sense," D1.

55. Stevens, "The Politics of Stillbirth."

56. Lelchuk, "Wrenching Politics."

57. Stevens, "The Politics of Stillbirth."

58. Cacciatore and Bushfield, "Stillbirth: A Sociopolitical Issue," 382.

59. Cacciatore and Bushfield, "Stillbirth: A Sociopolitical Issue," 382–83.

60. Sanger, "Lopsided Harms," 46.

61. Cacciatore and Bushfield, "A Sociopolitical Issue," 383.

62. Stevens, "The Politics of Stillbirth."

63. Layne, *Motherhood Lost*, 240.

64. Withycombe, *Lost: Miscarriage in Nineteenth-Century America*, 34.

65. Withycombe, *Lost*, 39.

66. Withycombe, *Lost*, 36.

67. Withycombe, *Lost*, 39.

68. Donley and Lens, "Abortion, Pregnancy Loss, and Subjective Fetal Personhood," 1697–98.

69. *Dobbs*, 597 U.S. at 259.

70. Donley and Lens, "Abortion, Pregnancy Loss, and Subjective Fetal Personhood," 1681–82.

71. Donley and Lens, "Abortion, Pregnancy Loss, and Subjective Fetal Personhood," 1684–90.

72. Donley and Lens, "Abortion, Pregnancy Loss, and Subjective Fetal Personhood," 1691–94.

73. S. 166, 118th Cong. (2023).

74. Vagianos, "Florida Republicans."

75. Layne, *Motherhood Lost*, 240.

76. Freidenfelds, *Myth of the Perfect Pregnancy*, 38.

77. Stracqualursi and Maher, "DeSantis and Ramaswamy."

78. Brittney Crystal, interview with author, March 3, 2023.

79. Tommy's, "Together, for Every Baby." https://www.welbournehealth-centre.co.uk/help-and-support/tommys-advice/.

80. Sands, "Saving Babies' Lives."

81. Tommy's, "We See a Mum."

NINE. STILLBIRTH AS A CRIME

1. Goodwin, *Policing the Womb*, 16.

2. McKnight v. State, 661 S.E.2d 354, at 361 (S.C. 2008).

3. Martin, "A Stillborn Child."

4. Martin, "Judge Throws Out Murder Charge."

5. Levin, "She Was Jailed for Losing a Pregnancy."

6. Pishko, "California Prosecutions."

7. Nowell, "She Used Drugs While Pregnant."

8. Kavattur et al., "The Rise of Pregnancy Criminalization," 4.

9. Kavattur et al., "The Rise of Pregnancy Criminalization," 28.

10. Kavattur et al., "The Rise of Pregnancy Criminalization," 4.

11. Kavattur et al., "The Rise of Pregnancy Criminalization," 28.

12. Goodwin, *Policing the Womb*, 80.

13. Boone and McMichael, "State-Created Fetal Harm," 489.

14. Kavattur et al., "The Rise of Pregnancy Criminalization,"4.

15. Boone and McMichael, "State-Created Fetal Harm," 489.

16. Kavattur et al., "The Rise of Pregnancy Criminalization,"23.

17. Bridges, "Race, Pregnancy and the Opioid Epidemic," 815.

18. Donley and Lens, "Abortion, Pregnancy Loss & Subjective Fetal Personhood," 1707-8.

19. R.I. STAT. § 23-4-4 (West 2023); MO. STAT. § 58.451 (West 2023).

20. Martin, "A Stillborn Child."

21. Yurkanin, "She Lost her Baby."

22. Goodwin, *Policing the Womb*, 88.

23. Goodwin, *Policing the Womb*, 89.

24. Roberts, "Punishing Drug Addicts," 1445.

25. Bridges, "Race, Pregnancy, and the Opioid Epidemic," 817.

26. Devine, *It's OK That You're Not OK*, 40-41.

27. Pollock et al., "Voices of the Unheard," 5.

28. Lens, "Counting Stillbirths," 577.

29. Lens, "Counting Stillbirths," 577.

30. Goodwin, "How the Criminalization of Pregnancy," S21.

31. Layne, "Unhappy Endings," 1889.

32. Bach, *Prosecuting Poverty*, 170-71.

33. Boone and McMichael, "State-Created Fetal Harm," 488.

34. Boone and McMichael, "State-Created Fetal Harm," 505.

35. Boone and McMichael, "State-Created Fetal Harm," 505.

36. Boone and McMichael, "State-Created Fetal Harm," 505.

37. Lens, "Counting Stillbirths," 574.

38. Tomasina et al., "Antenatal Care," 244.

39. Boone and McMichael, "State-Created Fetal Harm," 518.

40. Ellis et al., "Systematic review," 2.

41. Kirkley-Best and Kellner, "The Forgotten Grief," 424.

42. Ellis et al., "Systematic review," 2.

43. Ellis et al., "Systematic review," 10.

44. Willinger et al., "Racial Disparities," 377.

45. Levin, "She Was Jailed for Losing a Pregnancy."

46. Levin, "She Was Jailed for Losing a Pregnancy."

47. Nowell, "She Used Drugs While Pregnant."

48. Kirkley-Best and Kellner, "The Forgotten Grief," 422.

49. Cacciatore, "Unique Experiences of Women," 140.

50. Cacciatore, "Unique Experiences of Women," 140.

51. Nowell, "She Used Drugs While Pregnant."

52. Brief of Amicus Curiae of Legal Voice and Perinatal Loss Support Organizations and Experts, Shuai v. State of Indiana, 966 N.E.2d 619 (Ind. Ct. App. 2011). 2011 WL 3892889, 17.

53. Dwyer and See, "Prosecuting Pregnancy Loss."

54. Levin, "She Was Jailed for Losing a Pregnancy."

55. Bach, "Prosecuting Poverty," 33.

56. Brief of Amicus Curiae of Legal Voice, 7.

57. Brief of Amicus Curiae of Legal Voice, 15.

58. Kavattur et al., "The Rise of Pregnancy Criminalization," 33.

59. OH STAT. § 2927.01 (West 2023).

60. Ellis et al., "Systematic review," 11.

61. Kelley and Trinidad, "Silent Loss and the Clinical Encounter," 9.

62. Schweitzer, "Why is Chrissy Teigen."

63. Kelley and Trinidad, "Silent Loss and the Clinical Encounter," 10.

64. Kelley and Trinidad, "Silent Loss and the Clinical Encounter," 10.

65. Kirkley-Best and Kellner, "The Forgotten Grief,"423.

66. Donley and Lens, "Abortion, Pregnancy Loss & Subjective Fetal Personhood," 1709-10.

67. Shennan, Who Do Fetal Homicide Laws Protect? 1.

68. CAL. HEALTH & SAFETY CODE § 123467 (West 2023).

69. 38 ILL. COMP. STAT. ANN. 720 ILCS 5/9-1.2 (West 2019).

70. Vagianos, "2 States Introduce Radical Bills."

71. Bayless, "Missouri Republicans."

72. CAL. HEALTH & SAFETY CODE § 123469 (West 2023).

73. Lens, "Counting Stillbirths," 578-79.

74. Roberts, "Punishing Drug Addicts," 1422.

75. Brief of Amicus Curiae of Legal Voice, 17, 19.

CONCLUSION: GENUINE (AND FORCED) OPTIMISM FOR THE FUTURE

1. Eldeib, "Lawmakers Pledge to Fight."

2. Stillbirth Working Group, Working to Address the Tragedy of Stillbirth, 45.

3. Stillbirth Working Group, *Tragedy of Stillbirth*, 6.

4. Stillbirth Working Group, *Tragedy of Stillbirth*, 1.

5. Stillbirth Working Group, *Tragedy of Stillbirth*, 1–2.

6. Stillbirth Working Group, *Tragedy of Stillbirth*, 2.

7. Stillbirth Working Group, *Tragedy of Stillbirth*, 2.

8. Stillbirth Working Group, *Tragedy of Stillbirth*, 3–5.

9. Stillbirth Working Group, *Working to Address the Tragedy of Stillbirth: Implementation Recommendations*, NIH (July 2024), https://www.nichd.nih.gov/sites/default/files/inline-files/NICHD_Stillbirth_WG_Report_July_2024_508.pdf.

10. Eunice Kennedy Shriver, "Addressing the Tragedy."

ABC News. "New Pennsylvania Law Allows Birth Certificates for Stillborns." July 13, 2011. https://abcnews.go.com/Health/w_ParentingResource/pennsylvania-law-birth-certificates-stillborns/story?id=14064338.

Abrams, Jamie R. "Distorted and Diminished Tort Claims for Women." *Cardozo Law Review* 34, no. 4 (2013): 1955–97.

"ACOG Committee Opinion No. 439: Informed Consent." *American College of Obstetricians and Gynecologists* 114, no. 2 (2009): 401–8. https://doi.org/10.1097/AOG.0b013e3181b48f7f.

"ACOG Committee Opinion No. 561: Nonmedically Indicated Early-Term Deliveries." *Obstetrics and Gynecology* 121, no. 4 (April 2013): 911–15.

"ACOG Committee Opinion No. 579: Definition of Term Pregnancy." *Obstetrics and Gynecology* 122 no. 5 (November 2013): 1139–40. https://doi.org/10.1097/01.AOG.0000437385.88715.4a.

"ACOG Committee Opinion No. 765: Avoidance of Nonmedically Indicated Early-Term Deliveries and Associated Neonatal Morbidities." *Obstetrics and Gynecology* 133, no. 2 (February 2019): e156–63.

"ACOG Committee Opinion No. 786: Perinatal Palliative Care." *American College of Obstetricians and Gynecologists* 145, no. 3 (September 2019): e84–89. https://doi.org/10.1097/AOG.0000000000003425.

"ACOG Committee Opinion No. 807, Tobacco and Nicotine Cessation During Pregnancy." *Obstetrics and Gynecology* 135, no. 5 (May 2020): e221–29.

"ACOG Committee Opinion No. 819: Informed Consent and Shared Decision Making in Obstetrics and Gynecology." *American College of Obstetricians and Gynecologists* 137, no. 2 (February 2021): e34–e41. https://doi.org/10.1097/AOG.000000000000424.

"ACOG Committee Opinion No. 828: Indications for Outpatient Antenatal Fetal Surveillance." *Obstetrics and Gynecology* 137, no. 6 (June 2021): e 177–97.

"ACOG Committee Opinion No. 831 Medically Indicated Late-Preterm and Early-Term Deliveries." *Obstetrics and Gynecology* 138 no. 1 (July 2021): e35–39. https://doi.org/10.1097/AOG.0000000000004447.

"ACOG Obstetric Care Consensus No. 10: Management of Stillbirth." *Obstetrics and Gynecology* 135, no. 3 (March 2020): e110–32. https://doi.org/10.1097/AOG.0000000000003719.

"ACOG Obstetric Care Consensus No. 11: Pregnancy at Age 35 Years or Older." *Obstetrics and Gynecology* 140, no. 2 (August 2022): 348–66.

"ACOG Practice Bulletin No. 107: Induction of Labor." *Obstetrics and Gynecology* 114 no. 2 (August 2009): 386–97. https://doi.org/10.1097/AOG.0b013e3181b48ef5.

"ACOG Practice Bulletin No. 227: Fetal Growth Restriction." *Obstetrics and Gynecology* 137, no. 2 (February 2021): e16–28.

"ACOG Practice Bulletin No. 229: Antepartum Fetal Surveillance." *Obstetrics and Gynecology* 137, no. 6 (June 2021): e116–27.

Allen, Lindsey, and Daniel Grossman. "The Impact of Voluntary and Nonpayment Policies in Reducing Early-Term Elective Deliveries among Privately Insured and Medicaid Enrollees." *Health Services Research* 55, no. 1 (2020): 63–70. https://doi.org/10.1111/1475-6773.13214.

American College of Obstetricians and Gynecologists. "Can I Sleep on My Back When I'm Pregnant?" ACOG, January 2001. https://www.acog.org/womens-health/experts-and-stories/ask-acog/can-i-sleep-on-my-back-when-im-pregnant#:~:text = In%20the%20second%20and%20third,third%20 trimesters%20may%20be%20best.

Americans United for Life. "State Spotlight." https://aul.org/law-and-policy/state-spotlight/.

Americans United for Life. *Perinatal Hospice Information Act: Model Legislation and Policy Guide*. 2018.

Associated Press. "A New Arkansas Law Allows an Anti-Abortion Monument at the State Capitol." March 19, 2023. https://www.npr.org/2023/03/19/1164614996/arkansas-abortion-monument-sanders.

Bach, Wendy A. *Prosecuting Poverty, Criminalizing Care*. Cambridge University Press, 2022.

Bayless, Kacen. "Missouri Republicans Propose Bills to Allow Murder Charges for Women Who Get Abortions." *St. Louis Post Dispatch*. December 10, 2023. https://www.stltoday.com/news/local/government-politics/missouri-republicans-propose-bills-to-allow-murder-charges-for-women-who-get-abortions/article_53b406c0-95c4-11ee-a67d-9339832ec1a0.html.

Beauchamp, Tom L., and James F. Childress. *Principles of Biomedical Ethics*, 7th ed. Oxford University Press, 2009.

Brief for Petitioner, Benson v. McKee, 273 A.3d 121 (R.I. 2022) (No. 22-201.) 2022 WL 4096782.

Brief of Amicus Curiae of Legal Voice and Perinatal Loss Support Organizations and Experts, Shuai v. State of Indiana, 966 N.E.2d 619 (Ind. Ct. App. 2011). 2011 WL 389288.

Brief of Society for Maternal-Fetal Medicine, Royal College of Obstetricians and Gynaecologists, U.S. Association for the Study of Pain, and 27 Scientific and Medical Experts as Amici Curiae, Dobbs v. Jackson Women's Health Org., 597 U.S. 215 (2022) (No. 19-1392). 2021 WL 4441335.

Bhattacharya, Siladitya, Abha Maheshwari, and Jill Mollison. "Factors Associated with Failed Treatment: An Analysis of 121,744 Women Embarking on Their First IVF Cycles." *PLos ONE* 8, no. 12 (December 2013): e82249. https://doi.org/10.1371/journal.pone.0082249.

"Births in England and Wales: 2021." Office for National Statistics, Census 2021. August 9, 2022. https://www.ons.gov.uk/peoplepopulationandcommunity/birthsdeathsandmarriages/livebirths/bulletins/birthsummarytablesengla ndandwales/2021#:~:text = 4.-,Stillbirths,2021%2C%20from%203.8%20 in%202020.

"Births in England and Wales: 2022." Office for National Statistics, Census 2021. August 17, 2023. https://www.ons.gov.uk/peoplepopulationandcommunity/birthsdeathsandmarriages/livebirths/bulletins/birthsummarytableseng landandwales/2022.

Blackshaw, Bruce P., and Daniel Rodger. "The Problem of Spontaneous Abortion: Is the Pro-Life Position Morally Monstrous?" *New Bioethics* 25, no 2 (2019): 103–20. https://doi.org/10.1080/20502877.2019.1602376.

Blakeslee, Sandra. "Baby without Brain Is Stillborn; Organs Are Unfit for Transplants." *New York Times*, December 22, 1987: B12.

Block, Jennifer. *Pushed: The Painful Truth about Childbirth and Modern Maternity Care*. De Capo Press, 2008.

Bridges, Khiara. "Race, Pregnancy, and the Opioid Epidemic: White Privilege and the Criminalization of Opioid Use During Pregnancy, *Harvard Law Review* 133, no. 3 (January 2020): 770–851.

———. "Racial Disparities in Maternal Mortality." *New York University Law Review*, 95, no. 5 (November 2020): 1229–1318.

Boone, Meghan, and Benjamin McMichael. "State-Created Fetal Harm." *Georgetown Law Journal* 109, no. 3 (March 16, 2021): 475–522.

Boyden, Jackelyn Y., Karen Kavanaugh, L. Michele Issel, Kamal Eldeirawi, and Kathleen L. Meert. "Experiences of African American Parents Following

Perinatal or Pediatric Death: A Literature Review." *Death Studies* 38, no. 6 (2014): 374–80. https://doi.org/10.1080/07481187.2013.766656.

Brody, Jane E. "A Campaign to Carry Pregnancies to Term." *New York Times*, August 8, 2011. https://www.nytimes.com/2011/08/09/health/09brody.html.

———. "A Device That Gives Parents of Stillborn Babies Time to Say Goodbye." *New York Times*, January 14, 2019. https://www.nytimes.com/2019/01/14/well/family/a-device-that-gives-parents-of-stillborn-babies-time-to-say-goodbye.html.

Brumberg, H. L., D. Dozor, and S. G. Golombek. "History of the Birth Certificate: From Inception to the Future of Electronic Data." *Journal of Perinatology* 32, no. 6 (February 2, 2012): 407–11. https://doi.org/10.1038/jp.2012.3.

Cacciatore, Joanne. "Effects of Support Groups on Post Traumatic Stress Responses in Women Experiencing Stillbirth." *Omega* 55, no. 1 (2007): 71–90. https://doi.org/10.2190/M447-1X11-6566-8042.

———. "The Unique Experiences of Women and Their Families after the Death of a Baby." *Social Work Health Care* 49, no. 2 (2010): 134–48. https://doi.org/10.1080/00981380903158078.

Cacciatore, Joanne, and Suzanne Bushfield. "Stillbirth: A Sociopolitical Issue." *Journal of Women and Social Work* 23, no. 4 (2008): 378–87.

Cacciatore, Joanne, John DeFrain, and Kara L. C. Jones. "When a Baby Dies: Ambiguity and Stillbirth." *Marriage and Family Review* 44, no. 4 (December 12, 2008): 439–54. https://doi.org/10.1080/01494920802454017.

"CalMatters: Stillbirth and the Law—Bill Would End Coroner Investigations of Lost Pregnancies." *SFGate*, April 22, 2022. https://www.sfgate.com/news/bayarea/article/Calmatters-Stillbirths-And-The-Law-Bill-17118787.php.

Cassidy, Paul Richard. "Care Quality Following Intrauterine Death in Spanish Hospitals: Results from an Online Survey." *BMC Pregnancy and Childbirth* 18, no. 22 (January 10, 2018). https://doi.org/10.1186/s12884-017-1630-z.

Centers for Disease Control and Prevention. "Coroner and Medical Examiner Laws." https://www.cdc.gov/phlp/publications/coroner/death.html.

———. "Emerging Threats to Mothers and Babies, SET-NET: How it Works." Last reviewed August 10, 2022. https://www.cdc.gov/set-net/about/how-set-net-works.html.

———. "About Stillbirth." https://www.cdc.gov/ncbddd/stillbirth/facts.html.

Centers for Disease Control and Prevention. "Applying Best Practices for Reporting Medical and Health Information on Birth Certificates." Last reviewed June 25, 2021. https://www.cdc.gov/nchs/training/BirthCertificateElearning/course.htm#print.

———. National Center for Health Statistics, National Vital Statistics System, National Center for Health Statistics. "Birth Data." Last reviewed May 24, 2022. https://www.cdc.gov/nchs/nvss/births.htm.

———. National Center for Health Statistics. "Facility Worksheet for the Report of Fetal Death." February 2004. https://www.cdc.gov/nchs/data/dvs/fetal-death-facility-worksheet-2019-508.pdf.

———. National Center for Health Statistics, National Vital Statistics System. "Fetal Deaths." Last reviewed April 15, 2020. https://www.cdc.gov/nchs/nvss/fetal_death.htm.

———. National Center for Health Statistics. "About Fetal Deaths, 2005–2022." CDC WONDER Online Database. Last accessed Oct. 14, 2022. http://wonder.cdc.gov/fetal-deaths-current.html.

———. National Center for Health Statistics. "Guide to Completing the Facility Worksheets for the Certificate of Live Birth and Report of Fetal Death." Updated September 2022. https://www.cdc.gov/nchs/data/dvs/GuidetoCompleteFacilityWks.pdf.

———. National Center for Health Statistics. *Handbook on the Reporting of Induced Termination of Pregnancy.* Hyattsville, MD, April 1988.

———. National Center for Health Statistics. *Medical Examiners' and Coroners' Handbook on Death Registration and Fetal Death Reporting* Hyattsville, MD: 2003 revision. https://www.cdc.gov/nchs/data/misc/hb_me.pdf.

———. National Center for Health Statistics. *Model State Vital Statistics Act and Regulations.* 1992 revision. https://www.cdc.gov/nchs/data/misc/mvsact92b.pdf.

———. National Center for Health Statistics, National Vital Statistics System. "Deletion of Data Items from the Birth and Fetal Death National Files." September 25, 2015. https://www.cdc.gov/nchs/nvss/deleted_items_from_birth_fetal_death_files.htm.

———. National Center for Health Statistics. "Recommendations for Wording and Placement of COVID-19 Items on the Birth Certificate." https://www.cdc.gov/nchs/covid19/COVID-question-mock-up_4_22.pdf.

Centre for Research Excellence: Stillbirth, *Safer Baby Bundle Handbook and Resource Guide: Working Together to Reduce Stillbirth.* (2019). https://stillbirthcre.org.au/wp-content/uploads/2021/03/SBB-Handbook_Final-1.pdf.

Chamallas, Martha, and Linda K. Kerber. "Women, Mothers, and the Law of Fright: A History." *Michigan Law Review* 88, no. 4 (1990) 814–64.

Chasnoff, Ira, William Burns, Sidney Schnoll, and Kayreen Burns. "Cocaine Use in Pregnancy." *New England Journal of Medicine* 313, no. 11 (1985): 666–69. https://doi.org/10.1056/NEJM198509123131105.

Christiansen-Lindquist, Lauren, Robert M. Silver, Corette B. Parker, Donald J. Dudley, Matthew A. Koch, Uma M. Reddy, George R. Saade et al. "Fetal Death Certificate Quality: A Tale of Two U.S. Counties." *Annals of Epidemiology* 27, no. 8 (2017): 466–71. https://doi.org/10.1016/j.annepidem.2017.07.001.

Clark, Brietta R. "Centering Black Pregnancy: A Response to *Medical Paternalism, Stillbirth & Blindsided Mothers*." *Iowa Law Review Online* 106 (2021): 85.

Committee on Child Abuse and Neglect, Committee on Injury, Violence, and Poison Prevention, Council on Community Pediatrics. "American Academy of Pediatrics. Policy Statement Child Fatality Review." *Pediatrics* 126, no. 3 (September 2010): 592–96. https://doi.org/10.1542/peds.2010-2006.

"Confronting Pregnancy Criminalization: A Practical Guide for Healthcare Providers, Lawyers, Medical Examiners, Child Welfare Workers, and Policymakers." *Pregnancy Justice*, June 23, 2022. https://www.pregnancyjusticeus.org/confronting-pregnancy-criminalization//.

Congressional Research Service. *The Child Tax Credit: Legislative History.* https://sgp.fas.org/crs/misc/R45124.pdf.

Conway, Kellyanne, and Marjorie Dannenfelser. "If They Want to Win, Republicans Need to Go on Offense on Abortion." *Washington Post,* August 24, 2023. https://www.washingtonpost.com/opinions/2023/08/24/abortion-politics-2024-campaign-republican-message/.

Copeland, Libby. "Oxytots." *Slate,* December 7, 2014. https://slate.com/human-interest/2014/12/oxytots-and-meth-babies-are-the-new-crack-babies-bad-science-and-the-rush-to-demonize-the-most-vulnerable-pregnant-women.html.

Côté-Arsenault, Denise, and Mary T. B. Dombeck. "Maternal Assignment of Fetal Personhood to a Previous Pregnancy Loss: Relationship to Anxiety in the Current Pregnancy." *Health Care for Women International* 22, no. 7 (2001): 649–65. https://doi.org/10.1080/07399330127171.

Cummins, Eleanor. "In a Post Dobbs World, Pathologists Who Study Pregnancy Loss Walk a Thin Line between Medicine and the Law." *Stat,* January 19, 2023. https://www.statnews.com/2023/01/19/miscarriage-abortion-pregnancy-loss-pathology/.

Dahdouh, Sonia, Nickie Andescavage, Sayali Yewale, Alex Yarish, Diane Lanham, Dorothy Bulas, Adre J du Plessis, and Catherine Limperopouos. "In Vivo Placental MRI Shape and Textural Features Predict Fetal Growth Restriction and Postnatal Outcome." *Journal of Magnetic Resonance Imaging* 47, no 2 (2018) 449–58. https://doi.org/10.1002/jmri.25806.

Dahlen, Heather M., J. Mac McCullough, Angela R. Fertig, Bryan E. Dowd, and William J. Riley. "Texas Medicaid Payment Reform: Fewer Early Elective

Deliveries and Increased Gestational Age and Birthweight." *Health Affairs* 36, no 3 (2017): 460–67. https://doi.org/10.1377/hlthaff.2016.0910.

DeMillo, Andrew. "Church Group's Opposition Surprises Advocates of Arkansas 'Tort Reform.'" *Claims Journal,* August 20, 2018. https://www.claimsjournal.com/news/southcentral/2018/08/20/286328.htm.

Denney-Koelsch, Erin M., and Denise Côté-Arsenault. "Introduction to Perinatal Palliative Care." In *Perinatal Palliative Care: A Clinical Guide,* edited by Erin M. Denney-Koelsch and Denise Côté-Arsenault. Springer, 2020.

Department of Revenue. "Guidance Related to House Bill 481, Living Infants and Fairness Equality (LIFE) Act." August 1, 2022. https://dor.georgia.gov/press-releases/2022-08-01/guidance-related-house-bill-481-living-infants-and-fairness-equality-life.

DeSisto, Carla L., Bailey Wallace, Regina M. Simeone, Kara Polen, Jean Y. Ko, Dana Meaney-Delman, and Sascha R. Ellington. "Risk for Stillbirth Among Women With and Without Covid-19 at Delivery Hospitalization—United States, March 2020-September 2021." *Morbidity and Mortality Weekly Report* 70, no. 47 (November 26, 2021): 1640–45. http://dx.doi.org/10.15585/mmwr.mm7047e1.

De Ville, Kenneth A., and Loretta M. Kopelman. "Fetal Protection in Wisconsin's Revised Child Abuse Law: Right Goal, Wrong Remedy." *Journal of Law, Medicine, and Ethics* 27, no. 4 (December 1, 1999): 332–42. https://doi.org/10.1111/j.1748-720X.1999.tb01468.x.

Devine, Megan, *It's OK That You're Not OK: Meeting Grief and Loss in a Culture That Doesn't Understand.* Sounds True, 2017.

DeVito, Scott, and Andrew Jurs. "'Doubling-Down' for Defendants: The Pernicious Effects of Tort Reform." *Penn State Law Review* 118, no. 3 (2014): 543–99.

Donley, Greer, and Jill Wieber Lens. "Abortion, Pregnancy Loss, and Subjective Fetal Personhood." *Vanderbilt Law Review* 75, no. 6 (November 2022): 1649–1727.

———. "Second-Trimester Abortion Dangertalk." *Boston College Law Review* 62, no. 7 (2021): 2145–2208.

Duke, Wes, and Suzanne M. Gilboa. "Using an Existing Birth Defects Surveillance Program to Enhance Surveillance on Stillbirths." *Journal of Registry Management* 41, no. 1 (Spring 2014): 13–18.

Duke, Wes, Laura Williams, and Adolfo Correa. "Using Active Birth Defects Surveillance Programs to Supplement Data on Fetal Death Reports: Improving Surveillance Data on Stillbirths." *Birth Defects Research Clinical and Molecular Teratology* 82, no. 11 (November 4, 2008): 799–804. https://doi.org/10.1002/bdra.20526.

Dwyer, Devin, and Patty See. "Prosecuting Pregnancy Loss: Why Advocates Fear a Post-Roe Surge of Charges." ABC News, September 28, 2022. https://abcnews.go.com/Politics/prosecuting-pregnancy-loss-advocates-fear-post-roe-surge/story?id=89812204.

Edwards, Erika. "Hard-Hit States Add Another Concern: Stillbirths in Unvaccinated Women." NBC News. September 10, 2021. https://www.nbcnews.com/health/health-news/hard-hit-states-add-another-concern-stillbirths-unvaccinated-women-rcna1952.

Eldeib, Duaa. "After a Stillbirth, an Autopsy Can Provide Answers. Too Few of Them Are Being Performed." ProPublica, November 29, 2022. https://www.propublica.org/article/stillbirths-autopsy-placenta-exams-pregnancy.

———. "Lawmakers Pledge to Fight for Comprehensive Action on Stillbirths." ProPublica, February 2, 2023. https://www.propublica.org/article/lawmakers-pledge-to-fight-for-comprehensive-action-stillbirths.

———. "'Oh God, Not Another Case.' Covid-Related Stillbirths Didn't Have to Happen." ProPublica, August 4, 2022. https://www.propublica.org/article/covid-maternity-stillbirth-vaccines-pregnancy#:~:text = A%20CDC%20study%20looking%20at,rare%20overall%2C%20babies%20were%20dying.

Ellis, Allison, Caroline Chebsey, Claire Storey, Stephanie Bradley, Sue Jackson, Vicky Flenady et al. "Systematic Review to Understand and Improve Care after Stillbirth: A Review of Parents' and Healthcare Professionals' Experiences." *BMC Pregnancy and Childbirth* 16, no. 16 (January 25, 2016): 1–19. https://doi.org/10.1186/s12884-016-0806-2.

Eunice Kennedy Shriver National Institute of Child Health and Human Development. "Addressing the Tragedy of Stillbirth." September 29, 2023. https://www.nichd.nih.gov/about/org/od/directors_corner/prev_updates/addressing-tragedy-stillbirth-october2023.

Finley, Lucinda. "Female Trouble: The Implications of Tort Reform for Women." *Tennessee Law Review* 64, no. 3 (1997): 847–80.

Flenady, Vicki, Aleena M. Wojcieszek, Philippa Middleton, David Ellwood, Jan Jaap Erwich, Michael Coory, T. Yee Khong et al. "Stillbirths: Recall to Action in High-Income Countries." *Lancet* 387, no. 10019 (February 13, 2016): 691–702. https://doi.org/10.1016/S0140-6736(15)01020-X.

Fox, Dov, and Jill Lens. "Valuing Reproductive Loss." *Georgetown Law Journal* 112, no. 1 (2023): 61–110.

Freidenfelds, Lara. *The Myth of the Perfect Pregnancy: A History of Miscarriage in America.* Oxford University Press, 2020.

Furrow, Barry R., Thomas L. Greaney, Sandra H. Johnson, Timothy Stoltzfus Jost, and Robert L. Schwartz. *Health Law: Cases, Materials, and Problems,* 3rd ed. West Academic, 2015.

Gaudino, J. A. Jr., C. Blackmore-Prince, R. Yip, and R. W. Rochat. "Quality Assessment of Fetal Death Records in Georgia: A Method for Improvement." *American Journal of Public Health* 87, no. 8 (August 1997): 1323-27. https://doi.org/10.2105/ajph.87.8.1323.

Geiger, Caroline K., Mark A. Clapp, Jessica L. Cohen. "Association of Prenatal Care Services, Maternal Morbidity, and Perinatal Mortality with the Advanced Maternal Age Cutoff of 35 Years." *JAMA Health Forum* 2, no. 12 (2021): 2. https://jamanetwork.com/journals/jama-health-forum/fullarticle/2786896.

Gold, Katherine J., Martha E. Boggs, and Melissa A. Plegue. "Gaps in Stillbirth Bereavement Care: A Cross-Sectional Survey of U.S. Hospitals by Birth Volume." *Maternal Child Health* 28 (2024): 887-94.

Gold, Katherine J., Ananda Sen, and Xiao Xu. "Hospital Costs Associated with Stillbirth Delivery." *Maternal Child Health* 17, no. 10 (December 2013): 1835-41. https://doi.org/10.1007/s10995-012-1203-8.

Goldenbach, Alan. "Blindsided." In *They Were Still Born: Personal Stories About Stillbirth*, edited by Janel C. Atlas. Rowman and Littlefield, 2010.

Goodwin, Michele. "How the Criminalization of Pregnancy Robs Women of Reproductive Autonomy." *Hastings Center Report* 47 no. 6 (December 2017): S19-S27. https://doi.org/10.1002/hast.791.

———. *Policing the Womb: Invisible Women and the Criminalization of Motherhood.* Cambridge University Press, 2020.

Greb, A. E., R. M. Pauli, and R. S. Kirby "Accuracy of Fetal Death Reports: Comparison with Data from an Independent Stillbirth Assessment Program." *American Journal of Public Health* 77, no. 9 (September 1987): 1202-6. https://doi.org/10.2105/ajph.77.9.1202.

Gregory, Elizabeth C. W., Claudia P. Valenzuela, and Donna L. Hoyert. "Fetal Mortality: United States, 2019." *National Vital Statistics Reports* 70, no. 11 (October 2021): 1-20. https://www.cdc.gov/nchs/data/nvsr/nvsr70/nvsr70-11.pdf.

———. "Fetal Mortality: United States, 2020." *National Vital Statistics Reports* 71, no. 4 (August 2022): 1-20. https://www.cdc.gov/nchs/data/nvsr/nvsr71/nvsr71-04.pdf.

Gregory, Elizabeth C. W., Claudia P. Valenzuela, and Joyce A. Martin. "Fetal Mortality in the United States: Trends from 2014 to 2019 and Changes Between 2018-2019 and 2019-2020." *Vital Statistics Rapid Release* 18 (January 2022): 5. https://www.cdc.gov/nchs/data/vsrr/vsrr018.pdf.

———. "Fetal Mortality: United States, 2021." *National Vital Statistics Reports* 72, no. 8 (July 26, 2023): 1-21. https://www.cdc.gov/nchs/data/nvsr/nvsr72/nvsr72-08.pdf.

Hamilton, Brady E., Joyce A. Martin, Michelle J. K. Osterman. "Births: Provisional Data for 2021." *National Vital Statistics Rapid Release* 20 (May 2002): 1–11.

Healthcare Improvement Scotland, "Scottish Patient Safety Programme MCQIC Maternity Care. Core Measurement Plan. November 2018. https://ihub.scot/media/6396/2018-19-core-measurement-plan-mat-final-v10.pdf.

Health Improvement Scotland. "Every Move I Make: Contributing to the Reduction in Stillbirth in Scotland." https://nhsscotlandevents.com/sites/default/files/S-12-1555503608.pdf.

Heazell, Alexander E. P., Fiona Holland, and Jack Wilkinson. "Information about Fetal Movements and Stillbirth Trends: Analysis of Time Series Data." *BJOG: An International Journal of Obstetrics and Gynaecology* (February 17, 2023): 1–10. https://doi.org/10.1111/1471-0528.17426.

Heazell, Alexander E. P., M-J McLaughlin, E. B. Schmidt, P. Cox, V. Flenady, T. Y. Khong, and S. Downe. "A Difficult Conversation? The Views and Experiences of Parents and Professionals on the Consent Process for Perinatal Postmortem after Stillbirth." *BJOG: An International Journal of Obstetrics and Gynaecology* 119, no. 8 (July 2012): 987–97. https://doi.org/10.1111/j.1471-0528.2012.03357.x.

Heazell, Alexander E. P., Dimitrios Siassakos, Hannah Blencowe, Christy Burden, Zulfiqar A. Bhutta, Joanne Cacciatore, and Nghia Dang. "Stillbirths: Economic and Psychosocial Consequences." *Lancet* 387, no. 10018 (January 19, 2016): 604–16. https://doi.org/10.1016/S0140-6736(15)00836-3.

Heazell, Alexander E. P., Stacey Tomasina, Louise M. O'Brien, Edwin A. Michell, and Jane Warland. "Excessive Fetal Movements Are a Sign of Fetal Compromise Which Merits Further Examination." *Medical Hypotheses*, 111 (2018): 19–23. https://doi.org/10.1016/j.mehy.2017.12.024.

Henner, Natalia, Danuta M. Wojnar, and Erin M. Denney-Koelsch. "Considerations in Unique Populations in Perinatal Palliative Care: From Culture, Race, Infertility, and Beyond." In *Perinatal Palliative Care: A Clinical Guide*, edited by Erin M. Denney-Koelsch and Denise Côté-Arsenault. Springer, 2020.

Herzog, Rachel. "House OKs Abortion Ban." *Arkansas Democrat Gazette*. March. 6, 2021. https://www.eldoradonews.com/news/2021/mar/06/house-oks-abortion-ban/.

Hetzel, A. M. "History and Organization of the Vital Statistics System." National Center for Health Statistics, 1997.

Hollenbach, Stefanie J., Elizabeth A. Westen, and Loralei L. Thornburg. "Obstetric Management in Life-Limiting Fetal Conditions." In *Perinatal Palliative Care: A Clinical Guide*, edited by Erin M. Denney-Koelsch and Denise Côté-Arsenault. Springer, 2020.

Horey, Dell, Vicki Flenady, Liz Conway, Emma McLeod, and Teck Yee Khong. "Decision Influences and Aftermath: Parents, Stillbirth and Autopsy." *Health*

Expectations 17, no. 4 (August 2014): 534-44. https://doi.org/10.1111/j.1369
-7625.2012.00782.x.

Hwang, Irene, Sophie Chou, and Duaa Eldeib. "The Failure to Track Data on Stillbirths Undermines Efforts to Prevent Them." *ProPublica*, July 2, 2024. https://
www.propublica.org/article/
stillbirths-prevention-data-pregnancy-parents.

Internal Revenue Service. "Personal Exemptions." Publication 4491. Revised October 2021. https://apps.irs.gov/app/vita/content/globalmedia/4491_personal_
exemptions.pdf.

Isburg, Kimberly. "Iowa Lowers Stillbirth Rate by 32 Percent in 10 Years." *Count
the Kicks*. October 31, 2019. https://countthekicks.org/2019/10/iowas-
stillbirth-rate-all-time-low/.

Jager, Rae Hoffman. "There Was No Jewish Way to Mourn Stillbirth—So We Created Our Own." Kveller, May 16, 2022. https://www.kveller.com/there-was-
no-jewish-way-to-mourn-stillbirth-so-we-created-our-own/.

Kavanaugh, Karen, and Patricia Hershberger. "Perinatal Loss in Low-Income
African American Parents: The Lived Experience." *Journal of Obstetric Gynecologic and Neonatal Nursing* 34, no. 5 (2005): 595-605. https://doi.org/10.1177
/0884217505280000.

Kavattur, Purvaja S., Somjen Frzer, Abby El-Shafel, Kayt Tiskus, Laura Laderman,
Lindsey Hull et al. "The Rise of Pregnancy Criminalization: A Pregnancy Justice
Report." Pregnancy Justice, September 2023. https://www.pregnancy
justiceus.org/wp-content/uploads/2023/09/9-2023-Criminalization-report
.pdf.

Kelley, Maureen C., and Susan B. Trinidad. "Silent Loss and the Clinical Encounter: Parents' and Physicians' Experiences of Stillbirth-A Qualitative Analysis." *BMC Pregnancy Childbirth* 12, no. 137 (2012). https://doi.org/10.1186/1471-
2393-12-137.

King, Anthony. "Doctors Investigate Several Stillbirths Among Moms with
Covid-19." *The Scientist*, April 23, 2021. https://www.the-scientist.com
/news-opinion/doctors-investigate-several-stillbirths-among-moms-with
-covid-19-68703.

Kingdon, Carol, Emer O'Donnell, Jennifer Givens, and Mark Turner. "The Role of
Healthcare Professionals in Encouraging Parents to See and Hold Their Stillborn Baby: A Meta-Synthesis of Qualitative Studies." *PLoS ONE* 10, no. 7 (July
8, 2015). https://doi.org/10.1371/journal.pone.0130059.

Kirkley-Best, Elizabeth, and Kenneth R. Kellner. "The Forgotten Grief: A
Review of the Psychology of Stillbirth." *American Journal of Orthopsychiatry*
52, no.3 (July 1982): 420-29. https://doi.org/10.1111/j.1939-0025.1982
.tb01428.x.

Kirkup, Bill. *The Report of the Morecambe Bay Investigation*. United Kingdom: The Stationery Office, 2015. https://assets.publishing.service.gov.uk/government/uploads/system/uploads/attachment_data/file/408480/47487_MBI_Accessible_v0.1.pdf.

Klasing, Murphy S. "The Death of an Unborn Child: Jurisprudential Inconsistencies in Wrongful Death, Criminal Homicide, and Abortion Cases." *Pepperdine Law Review* 22, no. 3 (1995): 933–79.

Klibanoff, Eleanor, and Neelam Bohra. "Judge Says Texas Woman May Abort Fetus with Lethal Abnormality." *Texas Tribune*, December 7, 2023. https://www.texastribune.org/2023/12/07/texas-emergency-abortion-lawsuit/.

Kowaleski, J. *State Definitions and Reporting Requirements for Live Births, Fetal Deaths, and Induced Terminations of Pregnancy*. Centers for Disease Control/National Center for Health Statistics. 1997 revision. https://www.cdc.gov/nchs/data/misc/itop97.pdf.

Kukura, Elizabeth. "Giving Birth under the ACA: Analyzing the Use of Law as a Tool to Improve Health Care." *Nebraska Law Review* 94, no. 4 (2016): 799–861.

———. "Obstetric Violence." *Georgetown Law Journal* 106, no. 3 (2018): 721–801.

Lai, Jonathan, Argyro Syngelaki, Kypros H. Nicolaides, Peter von Dadelszen, and Laura A. Magee. "Using Ultrasound and Angiogenic Markers from a 19- to 23-Week Assessment to Inform the Subsequent Diagnosis of Preeclampsia." *American Journal of Obstetrics and Gynecology* 227, no. 2 (2016): e1–11. https://doi.org/10.1016/j.ajog.2022.03.007.

Law, Tara. "Experts Fear a Shortage of Forensic Pathologists Will Leave Deaths Unexplained." *Time*, November 16, 2022. https://time.com/6234125/forensic-pathologist-shortage/.

Lawn, Joy E., Hannah Blencowe, Peter Waiswa, Agbessi Amouzou, Colin Mathers, Dan Hogan, Vicki Flenady et al. "Stillbirths: Rates, Risk Factors, and Acceleration Towards 2030." *Lancet* 387, no. 10018 (February 2016): 587–603. https://doi.org/10.1016/S0140-6736(15)00837-5.

Layne, Linda. "I Remember the Day I Shopped for Your Layette: Consumer Goods, Fetuses, and Feminism in the Context of Pregnancy Loss," in *Fetal Subjects, Feminist Positions*, edited by Lynn M. Morgan and Meredith W. Michaels (251–78). University of Pennsylvania Press, 1999.

———. *Motherhood Lost: A Feminist Account of Pregnancy Loss in America*. Routledge, 2002.

———. "'True Gifts from God': Motherhood, Sacrifice, and Enrichment in the Case of Pregnancy Loss." In *Transformative Motherhood: On Giving and Getting in a Consumer Culture*, edited by Linda Layne, 167–214. NYU Press, 1999.

———. "Unhappy Endings: A Feminist Reappraisal of the Women's Health Movement from the Vantage of Pregnancy Loss." *Social Science and Medicine* 56, no. 9 (May 2003): 1881–91. https://doi.org/10.1016/S0277-9536(02)00211-3.

Lehigh, Scot. "Common Sense, Or a New Way to Ban Abortion?" *Boston Globe*, September 15, 1996, D1.

Lelchuk, Ilene. "Wrenching Politics Surround Stillborns / Bereft Moms Want Birth Papers, but Abortion Complicates Issue." *SFGATE*. April 10, 2007. https://www.sfgate.com/news/article/Wrenching-politics-surround-stillborns-Bereft-2565630.php.

Lens, Jill Wieber. "Children, Wrongful Death, and Punitive Damages." *Boston University Law Review* 100 no. 2 (March 2020): 437–500.

———. "Counting Stillbirths." *University of California, Davis Law Review* 56, no. 2 (December 2022): 525–90.

———. "Medical Paternalism, Stillbirth, and Blindsided Mothers." *Iowa Law Review* 106, no. 2 (January 2021): 665–720.

———. "Miscarriage, Stillbirth, and Reproductive Justice." *Washington University Law Review* 98, no. 4 (2021): 1059–1115.

———. "Tort Law's Devaluation of Stillbirth." *Nevada Law Journal* 18, no. 3 (2019): 955–1014.

Levin, Sam. "She Was Jailed for Losing a Pregnancy. Her Nightmare Could Become More Common." *The Guardian*, June 4, 2022. https://www.theguardian.com/us-news/2022/jun/03/california-stillborn-prosecution-roe-v-wade.

Lewin, Tamar. "Out of Grief Grows Desire for Birth Certificates for Stillborn Babies." *New York Times*, May 22, 2007.

Lind, Joellen. "Valuing Relationships: The Role of Damages for Loss of Society." *New Mexico Law Review* 35, no. 2 (2005): 301–36.

Linde, Anders, Karen Pettersson, and Ingela Radestad. "Women's Experiences of Fetal Movements before the Confirmation of Fetal Death-Contractions Misinterpreted as Fetal Movement." *Birth* 42, no. 2 (2015): 189–94. https://doi.org/10.1111/birt.12151.

"Listeriosis During Pregnancy." The Bump, updated June 7, 2017. https://www.thebump.com/a/listeriosis-during-pregnancy.

Little, Sarah, Chloe Zera, Mark Clapp, Louise Wilkins-Haug, and Julian Robinson. "A Multi-State Analysis of Early-Term Delivery Trends with the Association with Term Stillbirth." *Obstetrics and Gynecology* 126, no. 6 (December 2015): 1138–45.

Lunde, Anders S. *The Organization of the Civil Registration System of the United States*. Bethesda, MD: International Institute for Vital Registration and Statistics, Technical Paper, No. 8, May 1980. https://unstats.un.org/unsd/demographic-social/crvs/documents/IIVRS_papers/IIVRS_paper8.pdf.

MacDorman, Marian, Uma Reddy, and Robert Silver. "Trends in Stillbirth by Gestational Age in the United States, 2006–2012." *Obstetrics and Gynecology* 126, no. 6 (December 2015): 1146–50.

Maloni, Judith A., Ching-Yu Cheng, Cary P. Liebl, and Jeanmarie Sharp Maier. "Transforming Prenatal Care: Reflections on the Past and Present With Implications for the Future." *JOGNN* 25 (January 1996): 17–23. https://www.jognn.org/article/S0884-2175(15)33326-8/pdf.

Manian, Maya. "The Irrational Woman: Informed Consent and Abortion Decision-Making." *Duke Journal of Gender Law and Policy* 16, no. _ (April 20, 2009): 223–92.

Martin, Joyce A., and Donna L. Hoyert. "The National Fetal Death File." *Seminars in Perinatology* 26, no. 1 (February 2002): 3–11. https://doi.org/10.1053/sper:2002.29834.

Martin, Joyce A., Michelle J. K. Osterman, and Claudia P. Valenzuela. "Maternal and Infant Characteristics and Outcomes Among Women with Confirmed or Presumed Covid-19 During Pregnancy: 14 States and the District of Columbia." *National Vital Statistics Rapid Release* no. 17 (December 2021): 1–10. https://www.cdc.gov/nchs/data/vsrr/vsrr-17.pdf.

Martin, Nina. "Judge Throws Out Murder Charge in Mississippi Fetal Harm Case." ProPublica, April 4, 2014. https://www.propublica.org/article/judge-throws-out-murder-charge-in-mississippi-fetal-harm-case.

———. "A Stillborn Child, a Charge of Murder, and the Disputed Case Law on 'Fetal Harm.'" ProPublica, March 18, 2014. https://www.propublica.org/article/stillborn-child-charge-of-murder-and-disputed-case-law-on-fetal-harm.

Martin, Nina, and Julia Belluz. "The Extraordinary Danger of Being Pregnant and Uninsured in Texas." ProPublica, December 6, 2019. https://www.propublica.org/article/the-extraordinary-danger-of-being-pregnant-and-uninsured-in-texas.

Meaney, Sarah, Claire M. Everard, Stephen Gallagher, and Keelin O'Donoghue. "Parents' Concerns about Future Pregnancy after Stillbirth: A Qualitative Study." *Health Expectations* 20, no. 4 (2017): 555–62. https://doi.org/10.1111/hex.12480.

Meaney, Sarah, Stephen Gallagher, Jennifer E. Lutomski, and Keelin O'Donoghue. "Parental Decision Making around Perinatal Autopsy: A Qualitative Investigation." *Health Expectations* 18, no. 1 (December 2015): 3160–71. https://doi.org/10.1111/hex.12305.

Measure the Placenta. https://www.measuretheplacenta.org/.

Miller, Emily S., Lucy Minturn, Rebecca Linn, Debra E. Weese-Mayer, and Linda M. Ernst. "Stillbirth Evaluation: A Stepwise Assessment of Placental

Pathology and Autopsy." *American Journal of Obstetrics and Gynecology* 214, no. 1 (January 2016): 115.e1–6. https://doi.org/10.1016/j.ajog.2015.08.049.

Morris, Theresa. *Cut it Out: The C-Section Epidemic in America.* NYU Press, 2013.

Moss, Rachel. "Stillbirths Increased Last Year. Why Is Nobody Talking About It?" *HuffPost*, October 8, 2022. https://www.huffingtonpost.co.uk/entry/stillbirths-increased-in-2021-here-is-why_uk_62f3c027e4b001e175d997c9.

Munz, Michele. "U.S. Rep. Cori Bush Reveals How She Nearly Lost Her Two Babies." *St. Louis Post-Dispatch*, May 6, 2021. https://www.stltoday.com/lifestyles/health-med-fit/health/u-s-rep-cori-bush-reveals-how-she-nearly-lost-her-two-babies/article_2925e2b3-6720-595c-ad22-edfa2103e69c.html.

Murdaugh, Kimberly, and Heather Florescue. "Small Estimated Placental Volume (EPV) in the Setting of Decreased Fetal Movement." *Clinical Imaging* 104 (2023). https://doi.org/10.1016/j.clinimag.2023.110027.

Murphy, Samantha, and Joanne Cacciatore. "The Psychological, Social, and Economic Impact of Stillbirth on Families." *Seminars Fetal Neonatal Medicine* 22, no. 3 (February 14, 2017): 129–34. https://doi.org/10.1016/j.siny.2017.02.002.

National Center for Fatality Review and Prevention. "FIMR Map." Last accessed December 23, 2021. https://ncfrp.org/fimr-map/.

National Health Service England. *Saving Babies' Lives: A Care Bundle for Reducing Stillbirth.* March 21, 2016. https://www.england.nhs.uk/wp-content/uploads/2016/03/saving-babies-lives-car-bundl.pdf.

——— *Saving Babies' Lives Version Two: A Care Bundle for Reducing Perinatal Mortality.* March 23, 2019. https://www.england.nhs.uk/wp-content/uploads/2019/07/saving-babies-lives-care-bundle-version-two-v5.pdf.

———. *Savings Babies' Lives Version Three: A Care Bundle for Reducing Perinatal Mortality.* July 2023. https://www.england.nhs.uk/wp-content/uploads/2023/05/PRN00614-Saving-babies-lives-version-three-a-care-bundle-for-reducing-perinatal-mortality.pdf.

National Quality Forum Maternity Action Team 2015. *Playbook for the Successful Elimination of Early Elective Deliveries.* 2014. https://www.leapfroggroup.org/sites/default/files/Files/mat_eed-playbook.pdf.

Nicholson, James M. "The 39-Week Rule and Term Stillbirth: Beneficence, Autonomy, and the Ethics of the Current Restrictions on Early-Term Labor Induction in the US." *BMC Pregnancy and Childbirth* 15, no. 1 (April 15, 2015). https://doi.org/10.1186/1471-2393-15-S1-A9.

Nicholson, James M., Lisa C. Kellar, Shahla Ahmad, Ayesha Abid, Jason Woloski, Nadine Hewamudalige, George F. Henning et al. "US Term Stillbirth Rates and the 39-Week Rule: A Cause for Concern?" *American Journal of Obstetrics and Gynecology* 214, no. 5 (May 2016): 621.e1–9. https://doi.org/10.1016/j.ajog.2016.02.019.

Noor, Poppy. "South Carolina Woman Arrested for Allegedly Using Pills to End Pregnancy." *The Guardian*, March 3, 2023. https://www.theguardian.com/us-news/2023/mar/03/south-carolina-woman-arrested-abortion-pills.

Nowell, Cecilia. "She Used Drugs While Pregnant. Should She Be in Prison?" The Cut, September 20, 2021. https://www.thecut.com/2021/09/feature-adora-perez-stillbirth-prison.html.

"Number of Stillbirths in the UK Falls to Record Low." Tommy's, July 19, 2018. https://www.tommys.org/our-organisation/about-us/charity-news/number-stillbirths-uk-falls-record-low.

Oberman, Michelle. "Mothers and Doctors' Orders: Unmasking the Doctor's Fiduciary Role in Maternal-Fetal Conflicts." *Northwestern University Law Review* 94, no. 2 (2000): 451–501.

O'Connor, Dan. *Saving Babies' Lives: A Care Bundle for Reducing Stillbirth.* National Health Service England, March 21, 2016. https://www.england.nhs.uk/wp-content/uploads/2016/03/saving-babies-lives-car-bundl.pdf.

Ogwulu, Chidubem B., Louise J. Jackson, Alexander E. P. Heazell, and Tracy E. Roberts. "Exploring the Intangible Economic Costs of Stillbirth." *BMC Pregnancy and Childbirth* 15, no. 188 (September 1, 2015). https://doi.org/10.1186/s12884-015-0617-x.

Okie, Susan. "Crack Babies: The Epidemic That Wasn't." *New York Times*, January 27, 2009. https://www.nytimes.com/2009/01/27/health/27coca.html.

O'Leary, Joann. "The Trauma of Ultrasound during a Pregnancy following Perinatal Loss." *Journal of Loss and Trauma* 10, no. 2 (September 1, 2006): 183–204. https://doi.org/10.1080/15325020590908876.

Oliver, Emily A., Kara M. Rood, Marwan Ma'ayeh, Vincenzo Berghella, and Robert R. Silver. "Stillbirth and Fetal Autopsy Rates in the United States: Analysis of Fetal Death Certificates." *Obstetrics and Gynecology* 135 (May 2020): 166S. https://doi.org/10.1097/01.AOG.0000664004.95365.1c.

Ord, Toby. "The Scourge: Moral Implications of Natural Embryo Loss." *American Journal of Bioethics* 8, no. 7 (2008): 12–19. https://doi.org/10.1080/15265160802248146.

Osterman, M. J. K., C. P. Valenzuela, and J. A. Martin. "Maternal and Infant Characteristics Among Women with Confirmed or Presumed Cases for Coronavirus Disease (Covid-19) During Pregnancy." National Center for Health Statistics, National Vital Statistics System, Centers for Disease Control and Prevention. Last reviewed May 14, 2022. https://www.cdc.gov/nchs/covid19/technical-linkage.htm.

Page, Jessica M., Vanessa Thorsten, Uma M. Reddy, Donald J. Dudley, Carol J. Rowland Hogue, George R. Saade, Halit Pinar et al. "Potentially Preventable

Stillbirth in a Diverse U.S. Cohort." *Obstetrics and Gynecology* 131, no. 2 (February 2018): 337. https://doi.org/10.1097/AOG.0000000000002421.

Paquette, Danielle. "Perinatal Hospice Care Prepares Parents for the End, at Life's Beginning." *Washington Post*, April 16, 2016. https://www.washingtonpost.com/news/wonk/wp/2016/04/16/perinatal-hospice-care-prepares-parents-for-the-end-at-lifes-beginning/.

Peachman, Rachel Rabkin. "*Dobbs* Decision Threatens Full Breadth of Ob-Gyn Training." *JAMA* 328, no. 17 (2022):1668-70. https://doi.org/10.1001/jama.2022.13662.

Peahl, Alex, and Steve Bernstein. "New Prenatal Care Guidelines Emerge from COVID." Institute for Healthcare Policy and Innovation, University of Michigan, August 6, 2021. https://ihpi.umich.edu/news/new-prenatal-care-guidelines-emerge-covid.

Pediatrics, COVID Data Tracker, Centers for Disease Control and Prevention. "Data on COVID-19 during Pregnancy: Birth and Infant Outcomes." CDC, October 11, 2022. https://stacks.cdc.gov/view/cdc/122064.

Pepper, George W., and William D. Lewis. *Pepper and Lewis's Digest of the Laws of Pennsylvania, 1700 to 1907, the Constitution of the United States and the Constitution of Pennsylvania, with Notes and References to the Decisions Bearing Thereon and a Chronological Table of Acts, 1683 to 1907*, 2d ed. T. and J. W. Johnson Co., 1910.

Perinatal Hospice Palliative Care. "Frequently Asked Questions." https://www.perinatalhospice.org/faqs.

Pilliod, Rachel A., Mekhala Dissanayake, and Yvonne W. Cheng. "Association of Widespread Adoption of the 39-Week Rule with Overall Mortality Due to Stillbirth and Infant Death." *JAMA Pediatrics* 173, no. 12 (2019): 1180-85.

Pishko, Jessica. "California Prosecutions for Pregnancy Loss Spark Outrage, and a Bill to Stop Future Investigations." Bolts, June 6, 2022. https://boltsmag.org/california-pregnancy-prosecutions-kings-county/.

Pollock, Danielle, Elissa Pearson, Megan Cooper, Tahereh Ziaian, Claire Foord, and Jane Warland. "Voices of the Unheard: A Qualitative Survey Exploring Bereaved Parents Experiences of Stillbirth Stigma." *Women Birth* 33, no. 2 (2019): 5. https://doi.org/10.1016/j.wombi.2019.03.002.

Pollock, Danielle, C. C. J. Shepard, A. A. Adane, C. Foord, B. M. Farrant, and J. Warland. "Knowing Your Audience: Investigating Stillbirth Knowledge and Perceptions in the General Population to Inform Future Public Health Campaigns." *Women and Birth* 35, no. 4 (July 2022): e389-96. https://doi.org/10.1016/j.wombi.2021.06.008.

Pollock, Danielle, Tahereh Ziaian, Elissa Pearson, Megan Cooper, and Jane Warland. "Breaking through the Silence in Antenatal Care: Fetal Movement and

Stillbirth Education." *Women and Birth* 33, no. 1 (February 2020): 77–85. https://doi.org/10.1016/j.wombi.2019.02.004.

———. "Understanding Stillbirth Stigma: A Scoping Literature Review." *Women and Birth* 33, no. 3 (2020): 165–74. https://doi.org/10.1016/j.wombi.2019.05 .004

Pollock, Linda A. *Forgotten Children: Parent-Child Relations From 1500–1900*. Cambridge University Press, 1983.

Quinton, Reade A. "Child Death Review: Past, Present, and Future." *Academic Forensic Pathology* 7, no. 4 (December 2017): 527–35. https://doi.org/10 .23907/2017.045.

"The Rainbow Clinic: Pregnancy after Loss." Push. https://www .pushpregnancy.org/rainbow-clinic.

Ranji, Usha, Ivette Gomez, and Alina Salganicoff. "Expanding Postpartum Medicaid Coverage." Kaiser Family Foundation, March 9, 2021. https://www.kff .org/womens-health-policy/issue-brief/expanding-postpartum-medicaid-coverage/.

Reproductive and Placental Research Unit, Obstetrics, Gynecology and Reproductive Sciences, Yale School of Medicine. "Estimated Placental Volume: Information for Providers." https://medicine.yale.edu/obgyn/kliman /placenta/epv/?tab = For%20Providers.

Roberts, Dorothy. "Punishing Drug Addicts Who Have Babies: Women of Color, Equality, and the Right of Privacy." *Harvard Law Review* 104, no. 7 (1991): 1419–82.

Ross, Loretta, and Rickie Solinger. *Reproductive Justice*. University of California Press, 2017.

Roth, Louise Marie. *The Business of Birth: Malpractice and Maternity Care in the United States*. NYU Press, 2021.

Saemon, Karoline Gundersen, Troels Eliasen, Ulla Breth Knudson, and Bjorn Bay. "Assisted Reproductive Technologies and the Risk of Stillbirth in Singleton Pregnancies: A Systematic Review and Meta-Analysis. *Fertility and Sterility* 116, no. 3 (September 2021): 784–92. https://doi.org/10.1016/j.fertnstert .2021.04.007.

Salomon, L. J., J. P. Bernard, and Y. Ville. "Estimation of Fetal Weight: Reference Range at 20-36 Weeks' Gestation and Comparison with Actual Birth-Weight Reference Range." *Ultrasound in Obstetrics and Gynecology* 29, no. 5 (May 2007): 550–55. https://doi.org/10.1002/uog.4019.

Sands. Saving Babies' Lives, Supporting Bereaved Families. https://www.sands .org.uk/about-sands.

Sanger, Carol. "The Lopsided Harms of Reproductive Negligence." *Columbia Law Review Online* 118, no. 1 (December 11, 2017): 29–47.

Sawhill, Isabel V., Morgan Welch, and Chris Miller. "It's Getting More Expensive to Raise Children. And Government Isn't Doing Much to Help." *Brookings*, August 30, 2022. https://www.brookings.edu/blog/up-front/2022/08/30/its-getting-more-expensive-to-raise-children-and-government-isnt-doing-much-to-help/.

Sawicki, Nadia. "Choosing Medical Malpractice." *Washington Law Review* 93, no. 2 (2018): 891–966.

Sawicki, Nadia N. "A Malpractice-Based Duty to Disclose the Risk of Stillbirth: A Response to Lens." *Iowa Law Review Online* 106 (2021): 665.

Schirmann, Anne, Frances M. Boyle, Dell Horey, Dimitrios Siassakos, David Ellwood, Ingrid Rowlands, and Vicki Flenady. "Understanding Mothers' Decision-Making Needs for Autopsy Consent after Stillbirth: Framework Analysis of a Large Survey." *Birth* 45, no. 3 (September 2018): 255–62. https://doi.org/10.1111/birt.12344.

Schwartz, David A., Elyzabeth Avvad-Portari, Pavel Babál, Marcella Baldewijns, Marie Blomberg, Amine Bouachba, and Jessica Camacho. "Placental Tissue Destruction and Insufficiency from Covid-19 Causes Stillbirth and Neonatal Death from Hypoxic-Ischemic Injury." *Archives of Pathology and Laboratory Medicine* 146, no. 6 (February 10, 2022): 660–76. https://doi.org/10.5858/arpa.2022-0029-SA.

Schwartz, David A., and Christina Han. "Covid Infection Can Attack Placenta, Triggering Stillbirth." *U.S. News,* February 10, 2022. https://www.usnews.com/news/health-news/articles/2022-02-10/covid-infection-can-attack-placenta-triggering-stillbirth.

Schweitzer, Kate. "Why Is Chrissy Teigen Not Allowed to Grieve Her Pregnancy Loss in Public?" Popsugar, October 6, 2020. https://www.popsugar.com/family/chrissy-teigen-shouldnt-be-judged-for-grieving-in-public-47849138.

Scott, Janet, and Charlotte Bevan. *Saving Babies' Lives Report 2009.* Sands, 2009. https://www.sands.org.uk/sites/default/files/SANDS-SAVING-BABIES-LIVES-REPORT-FINAL.pdf.

Scottish Government, "The Best Start: A Five-Year Forward Plan for Maternity and Neonatal Care in Scotland." (2017). https://www.gov.scot/binaries/content/documents/govscot/publications/strategy-plan/2017/01/best-start-five-year-forward-plan-maternity-neonatal-care-scotland/documents/00513175-pdf/00513175-pdf/govscot%3Adocument/00513175.pdf.

Senate, Commonwealth of Australia 2018. Select Committee on Stillbirth Research and Education, 1–168. December 4, 2018. PDF 1984KB.

Shammas, Brittany. "Stillbirths Have Doubled During Covid in Mississippi. Officials are Sounding the Alarm." *Washington Post,* September 9, 2021. https://www.washingtonpost.com/health/2021/09/09/pregnant-covid-mississippi/.

Shennan, Claire. *Who Do Fetal Homicide Laws Protect? An Analysis for a Post-Roe America*. Pregnancy Justice, August 18, 202. https://www.pregnancyjusticeus.org/resources/who-do-fetal-homicide-laws-protect-an-analysis-for-a-post-roe-america/.

Siano, Julienne Rut. "A Woman's Right to Choose: Wrongful Death Statutes and Abortion Rights—Consistent at Last." *Women's Rights Law Reporter* 19 (1998): 279–92.

Siassakos, D., R. Fox, T. Draycott, and C. Winter. *Late Intrauterine Fetal Death and Stillbirth: Green-Top Guideline No. 55*. Royal College of Obstetricians and Gynaecologists, October 2010. https://www.rcog.org.uk/media/0fefdrk4/gtg_55.pdf.

Sistersong. "What is Reproductive Justice?" https://www.sistersong.net/reproductive-justice.

Slemrod, Joel, and Jon Bakija. *Taxing Ourselves: A Citizen's Guide to the Debate Over Taxes*, 4th ed. MIT Press, 2008.

Smith, Gordon C. S. "A Bonfire of the Tape Measures." *Lancet* 377, no. 9774 (April 6, 2011): 1289–1378. https://doi.org/10.1016/S0140-6736(11)60525-4.

Snyder, Colleen. "The Missing Angels Act: Recognizing the Birth of Stillborn Babies." *McGeorge Law Review* 39, no. 2 (2008): 544–50.

"Society for Maternal-Fetal Medicine Consult Series No. 60: Management of Pregnancies Resulting from In Vitro Fertilization." *SMFM Consult Series* (March 2002): B2–B12. https://doi.org/10.1016/j.ajog.2021.11.001,

Solinger, Rickie. "Conditions of Reproductive Justice." In *Reproductive Justice Briefing Book: A Primer on Reproductive Justice and Social Change*, 2007. https://www.law.berkeley.edu/php-programs/courses/fileDL.php?fID=4051

———. "The Incompatibility of Neo-Liberal 'Choice' and Reproductive Justice." In *Reproductive Justice Briefing Book: A Primer On Reproductive Justice and Social Change*, 2007.

"Special Tests for Monitoring Fetal Well-Being." ACOG, May 2019. https://www.acog.org/womens-health/faqs/special-tests-for-monitoring-fetal-well-being.

Specifications Manual for Joint Commission National Quality Measures. *Measure Information Form PC-01*. October 5, 2021. https://manual.jointcommission.org/releases/TJC2022A1/MIF0166.html.

State of California Department of Justice Office of the Attorney General. "Attorney General Bonta: California Law Does Not Criminalize Pregnancy Loss." January 6, 2022. https://oag.ca.gov/news/press-releases/attorney-general-bonta-california-law-does-not-criminalize-pregnancy-loss.

State of Iowa Department of Health and Human Services, Surveillance Fetal Death Evaluation Form. https://hhs.iowa.gov/media/368/download?inline=.

Stephansson, Olof, Paul W. Dickman, Anna L. V. Johansson, and Sven Cnattingius. "The Influence of Socioeconomic Status on Stillbirth Risk in Sweden." *International Journal of Epidemiology* 30, no. 6 (December 2001): 1296–1301. https://doi.org/10.1093/ije/30.6.1296.

Stevens, Allison. "The Politics of Stillbirth." *American Prospect,* July 13, 2007. http://prospect.org/article/politics-stillbirth.

Stillbirth Working Group of the Eunice Kennedy Shriver National Institute of Child Health and Human Development Council. *Working to Address the Tragedy of Stillbirth.* March 15, 2023. https://www.nichd.nih.gov/sites/default /files/inline-files/STILLBIRTH_WG_REPORT_03152023.pdf.

Stracqualursi, Veronica, and Kit Maher. "DeSantis and Ramaswamy Share Personal Stories on Campaign Trail of Their Wives' Miscarriages." CNN, November 18, 2023. https://www.cnn.com/2023/11/17/politics/desantis-ramaswamy-miscarriage/index.html.

Sullivan, Peter. "GOP Senator Blocks Bill to Protect Interstate Travel for Abortion." *The Hill,* July 7, 2022. https://thehill.com/homenews/senate/3559360-gop-senator-blocks-bill-to-protect-interstate-travel-for-abortion/.

Tangalakis-Lippert, Katherine. "The California District Attorney Who Prosecuted Women after Stillbirths Has Been Ousted from Office." Insider, June 10, 2022. https://www.businessinsider.com/california-da-who-prosecuted-women-after-stillbirths-ousted-in-primary-2022-6.

Thompson, Beatrix Parker Holzer, and Harvey J. Kliman. "Placental Pathology Findings in Unexplained Pregnancy Losses." *Reproductive Sciences,* 31 (2004): 488–504. https://doi.org/10.1007/s43032-023-01344-3.

Thompson, Terri-ann Monique, Yves-Yvette Young, and Tanya M. Bass. "Racism Runs Through It: Examining the Sexual and Reproductive Health Experience of Black Women in the South." *Health Affairs* 41, no. 2 (February 2022): 195–202. https://doi.org/10.1377/hlthaff.2021.01422.

Titcombe, James, and Bill Kirkup. "Saving Babies' Lives." *Health Services Journal,* February 11, 2019. https://www.hsj.co.uk/comment/saving-babies-lives/7024392.article.

Tomasina, Stacey, John M. D. Thompson, Edwin A. Mitchell, Jane M. Zuccullo, Alec J. Ekeroma, and Lesley, M. E. McCowan. "Antenatal Care, Identification of Suboptimal Fetal Growth and the Risk of Late Stillbirth: Findings from the Auckland Stillbirth Study." *Australian and New Zealand Journal of Obstetrics and Gynaecology* 52, no. 3 (June 2012): 242–47. https://doi.org/10.1111/j.1479-828X.2011.01406.x.

Tommy's. "Leaflet and Banner: Feeling Your baby Move Is a Sign That They Are Well." https://www.tommys.org/pregnancy-information/health-professionals/free-pregnancy-resources/leaflet-and-banner-feeling-your-baby-move-sign-they-are-well.

——— "The Rainbow Clinic." https://www.tommys.org/research/research-centres/rainbow-clinic.

———. Together, for Every Baby. https://www.welbournehealthcentre.co.uk/help-and-support/tommys-advice/.

———. "#We See a Mum." Mother's Day Campaign 2023. https://www.tommys.org/WeSeeAMum.

Turner, Cory. "The Expanded Child Tax Credit Briefly Slashed Child Poverty. Here's What Else It Did." NPR, January 27, 2022. https://www.npr.org/2022/01/27/1075299510/the-expanded-child-tax-credit-briefly-slashed-child-poverty-heres-what-else-itd#:~:text = The%20first%20Child%20Tax%20Credit,26%20percent.%22.

Tveit, Julie Victoria Holm, Eli Staad, Babill Stray-Pedersen, Per E. Børdahl, Vicki Flenady, Ruth Fretts, and J. Frederik Frøen. "Reduction of Late Stillbirth with the Introduction of Fetal Movement Information and Guidelines—A Clinical Quality Improvement." *BMC Pregnancy and Childbirth* 9, no. 32 (July 22, 2009). https://doi.org/10.1186/1471-2393-9-32.

UN Inter-Agency Group for Child Mortality Estimation. *A Neglected Tragedy: The Global Burden of Stillbirths.* 2020. https://www.unicef.org/media/84851/file/UN-IGME-the-global-burden-of-stillbirths-2020.pdf.

US Standard Certificate of Death. Revised November 2003. https://www.cdc.gov/nchs/data/dvs/death11-03final-acc.pdf.

US Standard Report of Fetal Death. 2003. https://www.cdc.gov/nchs/data/dvs/FDEATH11-03finalACC.pdf.

Vagianos, Alanna. "Florida Republicans Introduce 'Frightening; Bill that Could Threaten IVF." *Huffington Post*, January 30, 2024. https://www.huffpost.com/entry/florida-republicans-bill-ivf_n_65b927ade4b05c8779f643af/amp.

———. "2 States Introduce Radical Bills to Prosecute Pregnant People for Abortions." *Huffington Post*, January 20, 2023. https://www.huffpost.com/entry/states-introduce-radical-bills-to-prosecute-pregnant-people-for-abortions_n_63cad58be4b0c2b49ad52898.

Van, Paulina, and Afaf I. Meleis. "Coping with Grief After Involuntary Pregnancy Loss: Perspectives of African American Women." *Journal of Obstetric, Gynecologic and Neonatal Nursing* 32, no. 1 (January 2003): 28–39. https://doi.org/10.1177/0884217502239798.

Vital Statistics: Summary of a Workshop. The U.S. Vital Statistics System: A National Perspective. National Research Council Committee on National Statistics, National Academies Press, 2009. https://www.ncbi.nlm.nih.gov/books/NBK219884/.

Wall-Wieler, Elizabeth, Suzan L. Carmichael, Ronald S. Gibbs, Deirdre J. Lyell, Anna I. Girsen, Yasser Y. El-Sayed, and Alexander J. Butwick. "Severe Maternal Morbidity Among Stillbirth and Live Birth Deliveries in California." *Obstetrics and Gynecology* 134, no. 2 (August 2019): 310-17. https://doi .org/10.1097/AOG.0000000000003370.

Walsh, S., and G. Mortimer. "Unexplained Stillbirths and Sudden Infant Death Syndrome." *Medical Hypotheses* 45, no. 1 (July 1995): 73-75. https://doi.org/10 .1016/0306-9877(95)90206-6.

Webster, Romi A., Patricia G. Schnitzer, Carole Jenny, Bernard G. Ewigman, and Anthony J. Alario. "Child Death Review: The State of the Nation." *American Journal of Preventive Medicine* 25, no. 1 (July 2003): 58-64. https://doi.org /10.1016/s0749-3797(03)00091-6.

Westwood, Rosemary. "Bleeding and in Pain, She Couldn't Get 2 Louisiana ERs to Answer: Is It a Miscarriage?" NPR, December 29, 2022. https://www .npr.org/sections/healthshots/2022/12/29/1143823727/bleeding-and-in-pain-she-couldnt-get-2-louisiana-ers-to-answer-is-it-a-miscarria.

Wilbur, Cressy L. "The Federal Registration Service of the United States: Its Development, Problems, and Defects." Appendix 4: Sec. 6. Paper presented at the Second Pan American Scientific Congress, Washington, DC. December 27, 1915-January 8, 1916.

Wiley, Lindsay F. "Health Law as Social Justice." *Cornell Journal Law and Public Policy* 24, no. 1 (2014): 47-105.

Willets, Melissa. "What It Really Feels Like to Have a 'Rainbow Baby'—and Why They Are So Beautiful." *Parents*, June 19, 2022. https://www.parents.com /baby/what-it-means-to-be-a-rainbow-baby-and-why-rainbow-babies-are-beautiful/.

Williams, Serena. "What My Life-Threatening Experience Taught Me about Giving Birth." CNN, February 20, 2018. https://www.cnn.com/2018/02/20 /opinions/protect-mother-pregnancy-williams-opinion.

Willinger, Marian, Chia-Wen Ko, and Uma M. Reddy. "Racial Disparities in Stillbirth Risk across Gestation in the United States." *American Journal of Obstetrics and Gynecology* 201, no. 5 (2008): 469.e1-8. https://doi.org/10.1016/j.ajog .2009.06.057.

Withycombe, Shannon. *Lost: Miscarriage in Nineteenth-Century America.* Rutgers University Press, 2018.

Woodworth, Kate R., Emily O'Malley Olsen, Varsha Neelam, Elizabeth L. Lewis, Romeo R. Galang, Titilope Oduyebo, Kathryn Aveni et al. "Birth and Infant Outcomes Following Laboratory-Confirmed SARS-CoV-2 Infection in Pregnancy—SET-NET, 16 Jurisdictions, March 29-October 14, 2020." *Morbidity and Mortality Weekly Report* 69 no. 44 (November 6, 2020): 1635–40. http://dx.doi.org/10.15585/mmwr.mm6944e2.

Wool, Charlotte, Denise Cote-Arsenault, Beth Perry Black, Erin Denney-Koelsch, Sujeong Kim, and Karen Kavanaugh. "Provision of Services in Perinatal Palliative Care: A Multicenter Survey in the United States." *Journal of Palliative Medicine* 19, no. 3 (2016): 279–85. https://doi.org/10.1089/jpm.2015.0266.

Yale School of Medicine, Reproductive and Placental Research Unit. "Estimated Placental Volume." https://medicine.yale.edu/obgyn/kliman/placenta/epv/.

Yurkanin, Amy. "She Lost her Baby, Then Her Freedom." The Marshall Project, September 1, 2022. https://www.themarshallproject.org/2022/09/01/she-lost-her-baby-then-her-freedom.

Zelizer, Viviana A. *Pricing the Priceless Child: The Changing Social Value of Children.* Princeton University Press, 1994.

Page numbers in *italics* denote illustrations.

abortion medication *(continued)*
(undetectable) use of, 167, 185; as
treatment for miscarriage complications, 153; use later in pregnancy,
167; use of, and registration as
stillbirths, 167–168
abortion procedures: D&C (dilation &
curettage), 153; D&E (dilation &
evacuation), 130, 131–132, 133;
induction abortion, 35–36, 151. *See
also* abortion medication (mifepristone and misoprostol); D&X (dilation
and extraction) procedure
abortion-rights and pregnancy-loss
communities, coalitions of:
overview, 11, 158, 175, 178–179;
abortion-rights advocates' support
for stillbirth prevention measures,
need for, 205–206; antiabortion fetal
life hypocrisies, demanding
explanations for lack of interest in
preventing stillbirth, 176, 177;
antiabortion weaponization of
pregnancy loss in quest for fetal
personhood, questioning of, 177;
blatant support by pregnancy-loss
advocacy groups for abortion-rights,
need for, 178; common ground of
post-*Dobbs* abortion bans illustrating
the need to increase access to
abortion care, 177; Connecticut
lawmakers demonstrating, 178;
England demonstrating, 178–179;
normalcy of pregnancies ending in
other than live childbirth, assertion
of, 177; as promoting reproductive-
justice-based rights for pregnancy
loss, 177–178, 205; supposed tension
between the communities as
manufactured by antiabortion
groups, 11, 158, 178; the tenuousness
of fetal life (70% of fertilized eggs do
not turn into live babies), honest
discussions about, 176, 177. *See also*
subjective fetal value
abortion-rights laws: provider shield laws
for out-of-state residents, 178; the

right to interstate travel to obtain
abortion care (proposed), 161
abortion-rights movement: avoidance of
pregnancy loss (minimization of the
fetus), 123, 158, 176; "choice" rhetoric
of, blame of pregnant person after
stillbirth produced by, 123, 160, 191,
201; and the false binary that all
pregnancies end in either abortion or
live birth, as erasure of pregnancy
loss, 10–11, 158–159, 177; subjective
fetal value as no threat to abortion
rights, 158, 170, 174; supposed
tension between pregnancy-loss
communities and, as manufactured
by antiabortion groups, 11, 158, 178.
See also abortion-rights and
pregnancy-loss communities,
coalitions of
—FELT NEED TO OPPOSE LEGAL MEASURES
RECOGNIZING STILLBIRTH: general-
ized fear of the slippery slope to fetal
personhood, 169–172, 175–176;
memorial birth certificates for
stillborn children, 169–170, 171, 172;
tax benefits for unborn children, 155,
170; wrongful death for stillbirth,
169, 170, 175–176
ACOG. *See* American College of Obstetricians and Gynecologists
Adams, Alma, 203
adoption, 159
advocacy for pregnancy loss. *See*
pregnancy-loss advocacy by
stillbirth parents
Affordable Care Act, 95
age. *See* gestational age; maternal age
Alabama: abortion ban in, 163; Covid-19
and increased risk of stillbirth, 40;
criminal child neglect, abuse, and/or
endangerment applied to unborn
children, 184; Medicaid expansion
refused by, and delay in prenatal
care, 164; prosecution of birthing
parent for stillbirth, 187; prosecutions for conduct while pregnant,
184; racial disparity in stillbirth

rates, 163; stillbirth rates among highest in US, 163; wrongful death law does not apply to IVF services, 146

Alabama Supreme Court: criticism of *Roe* viability standard and wrongful death claims, 145, 162; wrongful death act interpreted to include IVF frozen embryos, 146; wrongful death pre-viability stillbirth, 145–146, 162–163

alcohol, crack cocaine as no more dangerous to fetus than, 189

Alito, Samuel, 143, 157, 159, 165, 167, 173

American Academy of Pediatrics, 26

American Board of Pathology, 186, 187

American Civil Liberties Union, 170

American College of Obstetricians and Gynecologists (ACOG): birth justice rights not recognized for stillbirth, 129; fetal autopsy and placental pathology recommended after stillbirth, 18; on fetal pain, 165; informed consent as ethical mandate, 108, 109, 114, 118; memorial birth certificates opposed by, 170; on perinatal hospice and palliative care access issues, 127; perinatal pathologists recommended to conduct fetal autopsies, 23; racism admitted to heighten stillbirth risk, 51; standards of care for pregnancy and childbirth set by, and the SMFM, 47–48, 50, 77–78; on stillbirth as one of the most common adverse pregnancy outcomes, 106, 110, 190; time spent with stillborn baby, mentions of, 132–133. *See also* standards of care for pregnancy and childbirth (US); standards of care for surveillance for known heightened risk of stillbirth (US); timing of birth, US 39-week rule (standard of care)

American Rescue Plan, 149, 151

Americans United for Life (UAL), 125–126

amniotic fluid volume: decreased (oligohydramnios), standard of care

for induction by 42 weeks (US), 68; standard of care of surveillance for (US), 50; testing methods, 51

analogous products liability law, 115

antiabortion groups: the binary narrative that all pregnancies end in abortion or live birth, as erasure of pregnancy loss, 10–11, 96, 157, 158–159, 177, 190–191; as manufacturing tension between abortion rights and pregnancy loss, 11, 158, 178; narratives of, and jury deliberations in negligence damages in stillbirth, 90; narratives of, as influence on thoughts about early losses, 161–162, 173; narratives of, in proposed bill offering parental leave for stillbirth, 175; opposition to expansion of damage caps, 101; perinatal hospice and palliative care used as political tool, 125–127; as weaponizing pregnancy loss, 145–146, 157–158, 161–163, 169, 175, 177. *See also* abortion bans; antiabortion laws; fetal life hypocrisies of antiabortion movement (lack of interest in preventing stillbirth); fetal personhood (prenatal personhood)

antiabortion laws: homicide laws applied to fetuses, 140, 141, 200; medically inaccurate claim in mandatory perinatal hospice and palliative care disclosure, 126; medically inaccurate claim of increased risk of stillbirth in "informed consent," 109; removal of language precluding charging the birthing parent with death of unborn child (proposed), 200; wrongful death law extended to all pregnancy losses from conception, 145–146. *See also* abortion bans

anxiety of pregnant person: Australian study on disclosure of stillbirth risk and myth of, 113–114; fetal autopsy as allaying self-blame, 19; going-to-sleep position and, 60; informed consent for early induction in

biases; medical paternalism; racial biases and racism

bioethics: defense of fetal life hypocrisies, 164–165. *See also* informed consent as bioethics principle

birth certificates: CDC recommendation to add Covid-19 tracking to, 41–42; data incompleteness rate on, 36; for extreme premature births with no chance of survival for the baby, 150; federal recommendation to switch to "stillbirth certificates" (1939), 32; historical issuance for both live and stillbirths, 31–32, *31*, 45; historical issuance of both birth and death certificates for stillbirths, 31, 32; induction abortion resulting in issuance of, 35–36, 151; NCHS materials to assist completion of, 15–16; Neonatal Intensive Care Unit admission, 15; required to obtain proof of dependents for tax purposes (Social Security number), 149–150. *See also* death certificates; fetal death certificates (FDCs)

birth justice rights: definition of, 127; established due to obstetric violence (coercion and mistreatment in pregnancy and childbirth), 119, 127; focus on enabling women to choose vaginal birth, 128. *See also* reproductive-justice movement

—AND STILLBIRTH: overview of applicability of birth justice rights to, 128, 133–134; ACOG lack of recognition, 129; choice of woman for C-section vs. vaginal birth, 128–130; choice of woman for non-childbirth options, 130–132; communication of doctors to educate birthing parent about, 128, 130; delay of delivery possible in, 128; delivery area of hospital, modifications for, 132; medical emergencies and, 128; time spent with stillborn child (memory making), 132–134

Black fathers, time with their stillborn baby, 133

Black Maternal Health Caucus, 203

Blackmun, Harry, 159

Black women: "crack baby" myth as effort to devalue Black motherhood, 188–189; higher rates of investigation and removal of children through the child welfare system, 122; historical removal of children from, 122; involuntary sterilization of, and dismissal of harm, 92; loss of parental rights, 122; mental and emotional health care access for stillbirth parents, 135–137; racism experienced from health care providers, 57–58, 92, 110, 194; religion as factor in stillbirth recovery, 137; as subject to medical care undermining bodily autonomy rights of, 118. *See also* "bad mom" stereotypes (class and race biases); Black women—and stillbirth; class biases and classism; racial biases and racism; racial disparities in stillbirth rates; reproductive-justice movement

—AND STILLBIRTH: 2019–2021 rates, 6; 2024 rate of (1 in 85 births), 6, 111–112; dismissal of concerns by doctors, 57–58; disparities of stillbirth rates persist even in countries with government-run health care, 117, 124; equity element in England's safer baby bundle, 49, 59; fetal autopsy rates, 19; and fetal death certificates, incomplete, 36, 37; health care inadequacies and, 124; the inevitability myth of stillbirth and, 117–118; prenatal care inadequacies and, 118, 124–125; racism as cause of disparities experienced by, 51, 52, 58, 102; risk of early stillbirth as tripled, 36, 51, 152; risk of late miscarriage as doubled, 123; risk of stillbirth as doubled, 6, 51, 102, 111–112, 123, 163; subsequent pregnancies and replaceability sentiment, 58, 92, 110 blame of birthing parent for stillbirth: "choice" rhetoric of abortion-rights movement as producing, 123, 160, 191, 201; convictions as reinforcement of self-blame, 181, 195; and the double bind in search for data, 28; fetal death certificates and appearance of, 28–29; jury convictions for drug use as cause in stillbirth, 189–191; studies show women experiencing, 190. *See also* criminalization of stillbirth

blame of self after stillbirth: "choice" rhetoric of abortion-rights movement and double bind of, 160; as common, even when illogical and irrational, 195; of criminalized stillbirth parents, as natural punishment, 181, 195–196; data as prevention of, 13; disclosure of stillbirth risk as mild discomfort compared to, 116, 120; fetal autopsy as alleviating, 20, 26–27; going-to-sleep position as alleviating, 60; lack of data as feeding, 28; maternal monitoring of fetal movement as alleviating, 55–56

blaming doctors for stillbirth: disclosure of stillbirth risk and reduction of, 119–120; fetal autopsies discouraged in light of potential for, 21; worries of doctors about, 21, 119. *See also* tort medical malpractice law—fear of liability

Block, Jennifer, 119

Blue Cross Blue Shield, 71

Boebert, Lauren, 164

Bonbretz v. Kotz, 145

Boone, Meghan, 124, 193–194

Bridges, Khiara, 185, 189

Bush, Cori, 58, 92, 110

Cacciatore, Joanne, as stillbirth parent, 45

Caleb. *See* Lens, Jill Wieber, as stillbirth parent of Caleb Marcus Lens

California: civil cause of action against state actors who arrest or prosecute a pregnant person, 200; damages measurements for stillbirth, 83–84; data privacy legislated to avoid prosecutions of stillbirth parents, 45; homicide law, explicit prohibition of charging a birthing person with the death of their unborn child, 199–200; memorial birth certificates, 170; noneconomic damage caps, increases of, 101; prosecutions of birthing parent for stillbirth (Becker, Perez), 182–183, 184, 192, 194–195, 196, 201; risk of life-threatening complications in stillbirth, 128; SIDS as public health emergency, 25; wrongful death restricted to live births, 144

California Medical Association, 170

California Supreme Court: *Dillon v. Legg*, 83–84, 85–86, 88–89; *Justus v. Atchison*, 86; on the live birth dividing line for wrongful deaths, 142–144

Canterbury v. Spence, 114

Carhart v. Gonzalez, 113, 131

cause of death. *See* fetal autopsies; fetal death certificates (FDCs)—cause-of-death information; placental pathologies; risk factors of stillbirth

Centers for Disease Control (CDC): birth certificates, recommendation to track Covid-19 on, 41–42; inaccurate state law stillbirth information and, 34; increased risk of stillbirth from Covid-19, 40–42; National Vital Statistics System, 33; Premier Healthcare Database Special Covid-Release, 40–41; Surveillance for Emerging Threats to Mothers and Babies Network ("SET-NET"), 41. *See also* National Center for Health Statistics (NCHS within the CDC)

cervical cerclage, 58

childbirth of stillborn child: ACOG recommendation of vaginal birth, 129; author as stillbirth parent and, 3, 30; choice of birthing parent for delivery by C-section, as reproductive-justice-based right, 128–130; England's medical standards and choice of birthing parents in (RCOG), 130; fatal fetal condition diagnosis, and perinatal hospice and palliative care, 125–127; lack of birth certificate, 30, 45; life-threatening complications as five times greater than live birth, 128; necessity of, as shock to birthing parent, 20, 104–105, 106; necessity of, in disclosure of stillbirth risk, 115; non-childbirth options foreclosed by abortion bans, 126–127, 130–132; as trauma, proposed damages for, 102. *See also* birth justice rights—and stillbirth; mental and emotional health care for stillbirth parents; trauma of stillbirth

child poverty: the American Rescue Plan and reduction of, 149, 151; reduction of, as purpose of the federal child tax credit, 151

children: cost of raising, 150; personal injury claims for prenatal injuries ("born-alive rule"), 145; removal by the state from women of color, 122. *See also* stillborn child; tax benefits for parents

—PREVIOUS: in damages considerations for wrongful death stillbirth, 92; rate disparities in fetal autopsies and, 19

—SUBSEQUENT: as cultural platitude for pregnancy loss, 92, 110, 218–219n39; in damages considerations for wrongful death stillbirth, and replaceability sentiment, 92–93, 219n43; fetal autopsy as protective for, 20; "rainbow baby" phenomenon, 92. *See also* pregnancy—subsequent to stillbirth; stillbirth, prior

child welfare systems: current investigations and removals of children from women of color, 122; health providers calling for suspected maternal drug use, 183, 193; historic removal of children from women of color, 122

Clark, Brie, 117–118

class biases and classism: in access to adequate prenatal care, 94–95, 102, 118, 124–125; in access to care requiring informed consent, 81–82, 118; in access to health care, 124; in access to IVF, 51, 94, 122, 155; in access to mental and emotional health care for stillbirth parents, 135; in access to specialist reviews, 23; criminal prosecutions of birthing parent for drug use causing pregnancy loss, as disproportionately distributed, 27, 180, 181, 182–183, 184–185, 188–189, 192, 196, 199; in damages considerations for wrongful death stillbirth, 91–95, 96, 97, 102; in damages measurements, tort reforms proposed to address, 102; fetal autopsy rates, 19, 20, 23; fetal autopsy, reforms proposed for access, 23; gender-based tables to predict lost wages, 102; the inevitability myth and, 117–118; informed consent undermined by doctor bias, 118; persistence in disparity of stillbirth rates in government-run health care countries, 124; post-*Dobbs* abortion bans and erasure of, 167; poverty as source of elevated stillbirth rates, 6, 22, 117, 123; prior stillbirth as factor in damages considerations, 92, 102; within stillbirth advocacy, need for awareness of, 28. *See also* "bad mom" stereotypes (class and race biases); poverty, people in; racial biases and racism

common law: negligence tort claims and, 84, 87; wrongful death claims must prove tort committed, 87, 141

communication between doctors and patients: on birth justice rights, 128, 130; cause-of-death information, parent dissatisfaction with, 28–29; disclosure of stillbirth risk and improvement of trust in, 119–120; dismissal of women based on

reactions to pregnancy loss must conform to social expectations of grief or cause suspicion, 199; state mandates for medical examiner/coroner involvement, 16, 186. *See also* criminalization of conduct while pregnant; criminalization of stillbirth

criminalization of stillbirth: overview, 11; "abuse of corpse" arrests and charges, 197–198; "bad mom" stereotype and, 181, 185, 188–189, 196–197; believed falsely to deter drug use and prevent stillbirth, 181, 192–194, 202; countries devoted to stillbirth prevention do not use, 181, 202; criticism of "bad mom" as insufficiently expressing grief, 196–198; as diversion of attention and resources from actual prevention, 202; state-paid fetal autopsies as magically available under, 27, 186. *See also* criminalization of conduct while pregnant; criminal prosecutions of birthing parent for drug use causing pregnancy loss; data privacy, criminalization of stillbirth and urgency of legislative protection for; homicide laws

criminal prosecutions of birthing parent for drug use causing pregnancy loss: overview, 180–181; as deterrent to obtaining prenatal care, increasing stillbirths, 124, 181, 193–194; as disproportionately distributed on poor women and women of color, 27, 180, 181, 182–183, 184–185, 188–189, 192, 196, 199; as exception to the usual assumption of stillbirth as unpreventable, 181, 187–188, 191–192; fetal autopsy quality is suspect, 181, 185–187; health providers calling the police, 27, 180–181, 182, 183, 184, 193, 202; health providers giving inhumane care to birthing parents, 180–181, 194–198, 201–202; health providers testing the pregnant person and/or baby for drugs without consent, 180, 182, 183, 195; homicide charges, 182–183, 197; homicide charges despite state law expressly precluding charging pregnant woman, 186; self-blame for loss reinforced by, 181, 195–196; time with stillborn baby denied, 180, 194–195; traumas compounded in, 181, 194–196

—DRUG LIST: overview of legal and illegal drugs, 183–184; cocaine, 180, 182, 192, 202; "crack baby" myth debunked, 188–189; marijuana, 182; methamphetamine, 182–183, 187, 195, 202; opiates and the opioid epidemic, 184, 185

—DRUG USE CLAIMED AS CAUSE OF DEATH: overview, 180–181; autopsy performed by unqualified medical examiner, 187; autopsy results overruled by coroner with no medical training, 187; burden of proof (beyond a reasonable doubt) not shown for, 188–192; class and race biases in, 188–189, 192; despite the fact that the overwhelming majority of babies are born healthy even with drug use, 184, 188, 191; despite syphilis, diabetes, hypertension, and other known risk factors present, 182, 183; despite the occurrence of fetal death two hours after arrival at hospital and no C-section given, 182, 192, 194, 202; despite the umbilical cord wrapped around neck, 181, 182, 187, 192, 202

—LEGAL AND SOCIAL PREVENTION OF: overview, 181, 202; anti-criminalization community advocating repeal of all "fetal personhood legislation," author's disagreement with, 200; civil cause of action against state actors who arrest or prosecute a pregnant person, 200; coalition of stillbirth-prevention and anti-criminalization communities, 201; compassionate bereavement care,

criminal prosecutions *(continued)*
reforms to ensure, 201–202; explicit language precluding arrests of birthing person for death of unborn child, and need to strengthen, 186, 199–200; general public education affirming that stillbirth happens and can be unexplainable even today, 200–201; HIPAA reform to prevent health providers reporting drug use of pregnant patients, 202; incorporating stillbirth prevention into reproductive-justice movement, 201; research into causes of stillbirth, especially systemic, 181, 201

Crystal, Brittney, stillbirth parent, 178

C-sections: Black women involuntarily sterilized during, 92; choice of stillbirth parent for delivery by, as reproductive-justice-based right, 128–130; economic incentives for doctor choice of, 116; as epidemic, 68, 116, 129; maternal monitoring of fetal movement claimed to increase, 54; maternal mortality risks in, 129; as obstetric violence (coercion into), 81, 113, 119–120, 127, 128; woman's preference for vaginal birth after (VBAC), court cases, 81, 113; World Health Organization maximum recommended rate for (15%), vs. US rate (33%), 129

—EMERGENCY: author's experience with fourth child, 12; disclosure of stillbirth risk as building trust in event of, 120; genuine need for, and communication of stillbirth risk, 120; not performed in the two hours after Becker's arrival at hospital (drug use case), 182, 192, 194, 202

CuddleCots, 133

cultural biases, in damages considerations for wrongful death stillbirth, 94

D&C (dilation and curettage), as standard of care for miscarriage complications, 153

D&E (dilation and evacuation) procedure, 130, 131–132, 133

D&X (dilation and extraction) procedure: banned for abortion on basis of regret, 113, 131; bans as decreasing medical training and access for standard of care medical procedures, 131–132; legality for late miscarriages and stillbirths, 131–132; as preferred by some women whose baby has a fetal anomaly, 113, 131; sexist categorization of women in debates about, 113

Dannenfelser, Marjorie, 165

data on stillbirths, as necessity: overview, 12–13, 30; the double bind of, 28; individual parents and, 13; state Fetal & Infant Mortality Review teams, 26; state Fetal Infant Death Review committees, 27–28. *See also* data privacy, criminalization of stillbirth and urgency of legislative protection for; fetal autopsies; placental pathologies

data collection: overview, 30–31; antiabortion Congress members voting against improvements in, 164; federal publishing lag time for, 33; fetal death certificates as the sole data source, 33, 37; historical issuance of birth certificates for both live and stillbirths, 31–32, *31*, 45; historical issuance of both birth and death certificates, 31, 32; issuance of vital statistics as power reserved to states, 31–32; Stillbirth Health Improvement and Education for Autumn Act ("Shine for Autumn Act," 2021 proposal), 24, 44, 164; the Stillbirth Working Group reports identifying need to improve, 204–205. *See also* data privacy, criminalization of stillbirth and urgency of legislative protection for; fetal death certificates (FDC); surveillance registries for stillbirths

data privacy, criminalization of stillbirth and urgency of legislative protection

for: advocates for stillbirth community must always recognize the need
for, 28; California law for coroners,
45; existing privacy laws as insufficient to protect stillbirth parents,
28; fetal autopsies and, 13, 27–28;
specific language needed in
legislation, 28; surveillance registries
and, 44–45

data quality, of fetal autopsies, perinatal
pathologist required to ensure, 18–19,
185, 187

death certificates: abortion resulting in
issuance of birth certificate and,
35–36; additional findings, and
importance of amending, 38; federal
recommendation for replacement
with "stillbirth certificates," 32;
historical registration of stillborn
children with both birth and death
certificates, 31, 32. See also fetal death
certificates (FDCs)

decreased fetal movement (DFM):
checklists for clinicians, 59; clinical
response (US), 58–59, 80; England
and Australia's instructions to
clinicians, 59, 64; risk of stillbirth
and, 53; timing of birth and, 67, 80

decreased fetal movement (DFM),
maternal monitoring for: acknowledged limited efficacy of, 56;
Australia's initiative for, 49, 53–54,
56–57, 59, 64; claim it causes excess
prenatal care visits, 55, 116–117; claim
it causes unnecessary anxiety, 55,
113–114; claim of preterm labor
increases due to, 54; as empowering
the pregnant person to express
concerns, 56–58; England's initiative
for, 49, 53–54, 56, 59, 67; fetal growth
restriction, detection of, 54, 64, 74;
Iowa study supporting efficacy of,
54–55; kick counts, 55, 57, 58;
self-blame for stillbirth as allayed by,
55–56; US standard of care does not
include, 51, 53–54, 55–56, 57, 58–59,
77–78

DeSantis, Ron, 178
DFM. See decreased fetal movement
(DFM)
diabetes, gestational: author as stillbirth
parent and, 1, 28, 29; failure to inform
pregnant person of risk, 28, 29; as
risk factor, 28, 29, 69, 183; standard of
care (US) allowing early-term
induction, 71
diabetes, preexisting: as fetal death
certificate "risk factor," 15; increase
of stillbirth risk, 69; standard of care
(US) allowing early-term induction,
71
Dillon v. Legg, 83–84, 85–86, 88–89
disclosure of stillbirth risk: overview of
benefits of, 10, 105, 118–120; anxiety
myth, studies of, 55, 113–114;
compared to customary disclosures
for even rarer outcomes, 111–112; in
genuine emergencies, 120; obligation
for (legal and ethical informed
consent), 108–109, 110; obstetric
violence (coerced procedures) and,
119; the shock and stigma of stillbirth
as reduced by, 118–119; temporary
discomfort of, compared to the
long-term devastation of self-blame,
116, 120; trust in doctor and
reduction of blame fostered by, 108,
119–120; warning language must
sufficiently convey the risk, 115–116,
120. See also informed consent as
bioethics principle; informed consent
law
—NONDISCLOSURE AS STATUS QUO:
overview, 9–10, 104–105, 109; the
anxiety myth as reason for, 112–116;
author as stillbirth parent, 105, 157;
economic disincentives, 116–117; the
inevitability myth as reason for,
117–118; parents do not know about
the potential for stillbirth, 104–106;
pregnancy books do not mention,
105–106; rarity of stillbirth cited as
reason for, 110–112; the shock and
trauma of stillbirth made worse by

birthing parent for drug use causing pregnancy loss

Duckworth, Tammy, 203, 206

early induction. *See* timing of birth to prevent stillbirth; timing of birth, US 39-week rule (standard of care)

early stillbirths (20-24 weeks): Black women's risk as nearly triple compared to white women, 36, 51, 152; data incompleteness in fetal death certificates, 36; non-childbirth options foreclosed due to abortion bans, 130-132; tax-benefit dividing line and, racial disparities in, 152. *See also* stillbirths

e-cigarettes, 62. *See also* smoking in pregnancy

economically advantaged people: author acknowledging privilege in stillbirth experience, 12, 180; "choice" and "control" rhetoric as double bind, 160; "deserving parent" classist ideas in damages considerations for wrongful death stillbirth, 92, 94, 96; fetal autopsy access for, 19, 20, 23; IVF access, 51, 94, 155; specialist reviews and, 23. *See also* class biases and classism; poverty, people in; racial biases and racism

ectopic pregnancy, 61

Edber, Sari, as stillbirth parent, 45

education level of pregnant person, and disparities in fetal autopsy access, 19

Eldeib, Duaa, 203

England: abortion as legal since 1967, 178; AFFIRM trial of maternal fetal movement monitoring, 53-54; alliance of abortion-rights and pregnancy-loss communities demonstrated in, 178-179; Covid-19 and increase of stillbirths during, 43; CuddleCot for expanding time with stillborn baby, 133; government-run health care as giving greater flexibility, 76; initiative to lower stillbirth rate, 7; midwives as primary care providers for pregnancy

and childbirth, 49, 56, 57; RCOG guidelines for choice of vaginal vs. C-section stillborn birth, 130; RCOG guidelines for time spent with stillborn baby after birth, 132, 133; RCOG on fetal pain, 165; Sands report ("Saving Babies' Lives"), 48, 178-179. *See also* England, Saving Babies' Lives Care Bundle (safer baby bundle)

England, Saving Babies' Lives Care Bundle (safer baby bundle): overview, 49; for all pregnancies, 52; auditing of FGR cases not detected pre-birth, 63; checklists for health care providers, 59; choices offered to patients and respect for autonomy, 49; continuity of carer, 49; education on healthy pregnancies, 49; encouragement of patients to contact their health provider with any concerns, 57; equity for inequalities of ethnicity and deprivation, 49, 59; establishment and frequent updating of, 49; fetal growth restriction risk assessment and surveillance, 49, 62-63, 66-67; fetal monitoring during labor, 49; gestational diabetes, 49; malpractice liability as a motivation for, 76; maternal fetal movement monitoring, 49, 53-54, 56, 59, 67; reduction of stillbirths, 7, 49; sleep position in later pregnancy, 60; smoking cessation, 49, 61; timing of birth, considerations for early induction, 66-67, 72-73

epidemiology, importance of fetal autopsies to, 17-19

estimated placental volume (EPV) testing, 73-76, 79-80

ethics. *See* bioethics

ethnicity: in Australia's stillbirth risk factors, 66, 72; equity in England's safer baby bundle, 49, 59; standard of care for early induction (US) does not consider, 72. *See also* racial biases and racism; racial disparities in stillbirth rates

Eunice Kennedy Shriver Stillbirth
Working Group of Council, 203–205
expectations. *See* parental expectation of
live birth

fatalism myth. *See* inevitability myth of
stillbirth
Federal and Medical Leave Act (FMLA),
135; proposed extension to stillbirth
leave, 175
federal government: medical standards in
the US not set by, 47, 50. *See also*
Centers for Disease Control; federal
laws; federal-state partnership,
statistics collection as; National
Institutes of Health; tax benefits for
parents; U.S. Supreme Court
federal laws: Affordable Care Act, 95;
American Rescue Plan, 149, 151;
Consolidated Appropriations Act
(2022), 203–204; Federal and Medical
Leave Act (FMLA), 135; Federal and
Medical Leave Act expanded for
stillbirth leave (proposed), 175;
Health Insurance Portability and
Accountability Act (HIPAA), 202; the
right to interstate travel to obtain
abortion care (proposed), 161;
Stillbirth Health Improvement and
Education for Autumn Act ("Shine for
Autumn Act," 2021 proposal), 24, 44,
164; Tax Cuts and Jobs Act (2018), 149;
Taxpayer Relief Act (1997), 149; Title
X family planning funds restriction
if abortion services offered (proposed), 175; vital statistics, collection
from the states and publication of,
31–32, 33
federal-state partnership, statistics
collection as, 31–33; historical
registration of stillbirths with both
birth and death certificates, 32; laws
for collection of data from states and
publication of, 31–32, 33; model birth
and death certificates, 32; Model
Vital Statistics Act, 32, 33, 34, 35,
139, 150, 151; publishing lag time for

stillbirth data, 33. *See also* data
collection
fetal abnormalities: abortion care for, and
reduction of stillbirths due to, 167;
abortion for, issued fetal death
certificate (FDC), 35; early miscarriage as often related to, 147;
wrongful birth (informed consent
claim), 109
fetal abnormalities as cause of stillbirth:
abortion bans and increase of
stillbirths due to, 7, 167–168; abortion
bans forcing continued pregnancies
for, 168, 177; abortion bans foreclos-
ing non-childbirth options for,
126–127, 130–132; author as stillbirth
parent and, 7, 12, 47; as fetal growth
restriction risk factor, 64; organ
donation cited as justification for
requiring continued pregnancies for,
168; as percentage of stillbirths
(10%), 7, 164; perinatal hospice and
palliative care for continued
pregnancies, 125–127; "trophoblast
inclusions" in placenta, 12; as
unpreventable, 7, 47, 125; women
preferring the D&X procedure for,
113, 131
fetal autopsies: overview, 8, 13, 18–20;
2020 studies of rate of (20%), 19;
checkboxes on fetal death certificate,
38; conflict of interest, and separate
institution sought to perform, 21, 22;
criminalization of stillbirth, and
urgent need for legislative protection
of data privacy, 13, 27–28; criminalization of stillbirth mandating, and
suspect quality of, 181, 185–187; data
currently available is not representative, 19; disparities in who receives,
generally, 19; disparities in who
receives, race and class biases in, 19,
20, 23; expressive value of state
mandates for, 26; future pregnancies
benefiting from information, 20, 23,
27; as "gold standard" for determining cause of death only if performed

by perinatal pathologist, 18–19, 185, 187; parenting of stillbirth child enabled by, 19–20, 27; placental pathology combined with, percentage of causes of death identified with (65%), 18; regrets of parents who decide against, 20; as reproductive-justice-based right, 123; self-blame and guilt alleviated by, 20, 26–27; SIDS autopsies as a blueprint for, 24–26; state mandates proposed, 26; time required for, and amendment of FDCs, 38–39; time spent with stillborn child after birth, 133

—COMMUNICATION WITH PARENTS TO FACILITATE: overview, 22; expressive value of state mandates in, 26; informed that autopsy might not reveal the cause of death, 21, 22; informed that autopsy requires their child will be cut into, 21; preventable stillbirth research, importance of, 22, 26

—COST OF: overview, 13, 22–23; criminalization of stillbirth and state-payment as magically available for, 27, 186; the hospital may or may not pay for, 13, 22; Medicaid does not cover, 13, 22–23; parents paying for, and class disparities in who receives, 23; private insurance may or may not cover, 13, 22, 23; reforms proposed for access to all, 23; SIDS autopsies as model of state-paid autopsies, 24–26

—DISCOURAGEMENT FROM OBTAINING: overview, 20–21; author as stillbirth parent and, 12; body of child will be cut into, 21; cause of death may not be revealed by, 21, 23; criminal consequences as deterrent to parents, 27; doctor discomfort with discussing, 21; doctor's overconfident diagnosis, 21; doctors unaware of importance of, 21; liability concerns of doctor, 21; medical paternalism, 21; parents report experiencing, 21; possibility is never brought up, 20;

the shock of stillbirth and decision for, 20; the "this happens" shrug (unpreventability), 21–22

—PERINATAL PATHOLOGISTS NEEDED FOR: ACOG recommendation, 23; coroner or medical examiners performing vs., 24, 185–187; criminal consequences and finding fault, pressure on pathologists to find, 27; as "gold standard" for cause of death, 18–19, 185, 187; shortage of, and attempts to alleviate, 23–24, 26; state mandates for nonspecialist pathologists, 24; state mandates recommended for, 26

fetal death certificates (FDCs): overview, 8–9, 30–31; best-practice recommendations from CDC, state resistance should not preclude, 42; "fetal death record" as official name for, 32–33; filing required within days of stillbirth (state law), 13, 38; health care providers taking importance less seriously, 36–38; historical shift from birth certificates to, 31–33, 45; information requested on, 36; medical professional present, 15; medication abortions registered as stillbirths, 167–168; memorial birth certificates as dependent on, 171; method of disposition (question 13), 15; other infections present or treated, removal of question from, 42–43; removal of items of data from, 42–43; risk factors, 15, 28; as sole source of data on stillbirths, 33, 36–37, 38; the Stillbirth Working Group reports identifying need to improve, 204; vs. birth certificate, as jarring for stillbirth moms, 30, 45

—CAUSE-OF-DEATH INFORMATION: amendment to be filed when further test results arrive, 17, 38–39; attending medical professional must complete (state laws), 15; attending medical professional must file amendment to correct, 38–39; autopsy checkboxes, 38; coroner

fetal death certificates (continued)
overruling pathologist to claim drug use as cause, 187; coroners or medical examiners required to complete (state laws), 16–17; fault of birthing parent implied by, 28, 29; importance of specific and precise information for medical and epidemiological research, 17–19; NCHS materials for doctors, limited utility of, 15–16, 38; NCHS resources for medical examiners and coroners, 17–18, 38; obstetricians as not trained or prepared to determine, 15–16, 18, 38, 104; standard form, 13–15, 14
—DATA QUALITY PROBLEMS: overview, 8–9; amendment of FDC as extremely difficult and rarely found, 38–39; Covid-19 infections not tracked on, 41–43; data inaccuracies, 37–39; date incompleteness, 36–37; non-still-births counted as stillbirths, 35–36; nonuniformity of standards for issuance of FDCs, 8, 33–35, 36; origins of, in state-by-state vital statistics system, 31–33; surveillance registries as improving data, 44; undercounting stillbirths, 8, 33–35, 36. See also surveillance registries for stillbirths
fetal growth restriction (FGR): assess-ment of low and high risk, 62–63; audits of cases where not detected pre-birth, 63; Australia's initiative, 49, 62, 63–64; communication with women about, 64; definitions of, 63, 64; England's initiative, 49, 62–63, 66–67; fundal height measurement charting, 63, 64; maternal monitor-ing of fetal movement and identifica-tion of, 54, 64, 74; risk factors for, 64; as risk for stillbirth, 63; Scotland's initiative, 48; smoking increases risk of, 61, 62; standard of care (US) surveillance for, 62, 64–65; timing of birth and, 62, 63, 66–67, 71, 72; ultrasound scan increases, 63–64;

"weight first" definition of stillbirth as undercounting, 34
fetal heartbeat: abortion bans prohibiting medical treatment if present, 168, 177; states discussing tax benefits for all pregnancy losses with detectable, 152–153, 154, 155
fetal life hypocrisies of antiabortion movement (lack of interest in preventing stillbirth): overview, 11, 163–164; alliance between preg-nancy-loss and abortion-rights communities and demand for explanation of, 176, 177; bioethics literature defending, 164–165; Congress members voting against data collection law, 164; fetal pain prevention, 165–166; lack of acknowledgment that abortion bans will increase pregnancy losses, 166–168; moral distinction of killing vs. failing to protect, as fallacy, 164–165; the most-obsessed antiabortion states have the highest rates of stillbirth, 163–164; organ donation as justification for continu-ing pregnancy with fetal abnormal-ity, 168; refusal to expand Medicaid access, 164; thickness of the hypocrisy, 164, 169; trauma of lack of medical care for pregnancy loss, disregard for, 168; unpreventability of pregnancy loss vs. preventability of abortion, as fallacy, 164
fetal monitoring: NIH prize competition for inventions and methods to improve, 2–05; Scotland's initiative and, 48
fetal movement. See decreased fetal movement (DFM)
fetal pain: discussions of, as triggering and traumatizing for stillbirth moms, 166; medically inaccurate claims to justify federal 15-week abortion ban, 165; stillbirth prevention as best strategy to prevent, 165–166

grief and grieving *(continued)*
bereaved parents, 140–141, 200; criminalization of pregnancy and suspicion of expressions of relief at pregnancy loss, 199; criminalization of stillbirth and criticism of birthing parent's expression as insufficient, 196–198; criticism of parents as excessive for treating stillbirth as the death of their child, 198–199; gestational age may (or may not) be a factor, 91; as hardest bereavement for adults, 106, 134; historical expression of relief and celebration in cases of undesired pregnancy, 199; hospital care received as crucial to healing from, 134, 194–195; studies show variance in parent reactions to pregnancy loss, 197, 198; weaponized by antiabortion narratives as demonstrating fetal personhood, 145–146, 157–158, 161–163, 169, 175, 177. *See also* mental and emotional health care for stillbirth parents; stillborn child; time spent with stillborn child ("memory making")

guilt feelings of stillbirth parent: of author as stillbirth parent, 180; of criminalized stillbirth parents, 195; fetal autopsies as alleviating, 20, 26–27. *See also* blame of self after stillbirth

Hand, Judge Learned, 79
Hayne, Steven, 187
health care providers: calling child protective services for suspected maternal drug use, 183, 193; calling police about patients' possible drug use, 27, 180–181, 182, 183, 184, 193; calling police, HIPAA reform to prevent, 202; criminalization of stillbirth and dehumanizing treatment of women, 180–181, 194–198; criminalization treatment, reforms of, 201–202; federal Title X family planning funds restriction if

abortion services offered (proposed), 175; fetal death certificate's importance taken less seriously by, 36–38; racism experienced by Black parents from, 57–58, 194. *See also* doctors; hospitals; mental and emotional health care for stillbirth parents

health care, structural obstacles to, and racial and class disparities in stillbirth risk, 117

health insurance: Affordable Care Act, 95; Medicare reimbursement, and hospitals prohibiting induction before 39 weeks, 70–71. *See also* Medicaid

Health Insurance Portability and Accountability Act (HIPAA), reform proposed, 202

health insurance, private: coverage mandates (federal or state), 22; fetal autopsies may or may not be covered by, 13, 22, 23; "nonmedically needed" deliveries before 39 weeks not reimbursed by, 71; prenatal care, mandates for providing, 153

Healthy Birth Day, Inc., Count the Kicks program, 55

Heazell, Alexander, 137–138
Helling v. Carey, 79–80

Hispanic women and stillbirth: fetal autopsy rates, 19; prosecution of, 183, 184, 192, 195, 201

HIV, standard of care (US) allowing early-term induction, 71

homicide laws: civil cause of action against state actors who arrest or prosecute a pregnant person, 200; conception/viability differentials in, 141; explicit language precluding arrests of birthing person for death of unborn child, and need to strengthen, 186, 199–200; for fetuses, and feeling of justice for bereaved parents, 140–141, 200; for fetuses, anti-criminalization movement to repeal, 200; for fetuses, in antiabortion "fetal personhood" movement,

infant and child deaths *(continued)*
  SIDS deaths, autopsy mandates, 13,
  25, 26; smoking during pregnancy as
  increased risk, 61; unexpected,
  autopsies mandated by states for all,
  25. *See also* negligence tort claims;
  Sudden Infant Death Syndrome
  (SIDS); wrongful death claims
informed consent as bioethics principle:
  ACOG adoption of as ethical mandate,
  108, 109, 114, 118; beneficence
  principle, 107, 114, 116; justice
  principle, 107, 108; materiality
  standard, 108; as more demanding
  than the legal version, 107, 109;
  nonmaleficence principle, 107, 108;
  obligation of doctors to disclose the
  risk of stillbirth, 108, 109; patient
  capacity to understand, race and class
  bias and, 118; as strengthening
  relationship with doctor, 108, 120;
  therapeutic exception, rejection of,
  114. *See also* disclosure of stillbirth risk
  —BODILY AUTONOMY AND SELF-DETER-
  MINATION: Black women as subject to
  undermining of, 118; definition of,
  107; as "first among equals" of the
  four bioethics principles, 108, 114;
  free consent as requirement of, 107,
  108; the inevitability myth does not
  alter, 117–118; as right of the patient,
  105, 108; understanding (freedom
  from ignorance) as requirement of,
  107, 108, 109, 116; warning language
  in disclosure of stillbirth risk, 116
informed consent law: bodily autonomy
  and self-determination, patient's
  right to, 105, 107, 108; defined as tort
  medical malpractice lawsuit,
  106–107; disclosure of unvaccinated
  Covid-19 infection as stillbirth risk,
  112; expansion outside the confines of
  a specific procedure, 109; failure to
  disclose as medical malpractice claim
  (not workable), 109; lack of U.S. case
  law on stillbirth, 108–109; limits of,
  and tort law near-presumption of

patient incapacity to understand,
  81–82; materiality standard, 107, 108,
  109, 110, 114, 119; obligation of
  doctors to disclose the risk of
  stillbirth, 108–109; shift from
  paternalistic accepted practice
  standard to materiality, 107, 108, 114,
  119; therapeutic exception, 114; UK
  case (*Pearce*), 110, 113; wrongful birth
  claims, 109
Iowa: continued racial disparity in
  stillbirth rates, 58; Healthy Birth Day,
  Inc., Count the Kicks program, 55,
  58; maternal monitoring of fetal
  movement and reduction of
  stillbirths, 54–55, 58; surveillance
  registry for stillbirths, 18, 44
Iowa Supreme Court, wrongful death for
  stillbirth, 144
Ireland: Covid-19 and increased risk of
  stillbirth, 40; fetal autopsy study, 19;
  stillbirths due to fetal abnormalities,
  167
IVF and other reproductive technologies:
  author as stillbirth parent, 1, 155; cost
  of, and the reproductive-justice right
  to have a child, 94, 122; in damages
  considerations for wrongful death
  stillbirth, and class and race biases,
  93–94; frozen embryo destruction as
  common practice in, 146, 148; frozen
  embryos, interpretation as "minor
  child" in wrongful death, 146, 148;
  frozen embryos, negligent destruction
  of, 147; frozen embryos, state law
  protecting IVF services from
  wrongful death and criminal claims,
  146; as risk factor for stillbirth, 15,
  50–51, 66, 155; standard of care for
  surveillance of (US), 50–51; state tax
  benefits for pregnancy loss, 155;
  success rates of, as overestimated,
  148, 160–161; white, wealthier couples
  as primary users of, 51, 94, 155

Jager, Rae Hoffman, 94
Jewish customs, 94

situations mandated to complete the cause of death information on fetal death certificates, 16–18, 186; unqualified to do autopsies (Louisiana), 187

medicalization of pregnancy and childbirth: in assumption stillbirth doesn't happen anymore (erasure of pregnancy loss), 105, 115, 119–120, 159; denial of efficacy of maternal monitoring of fetal movement, 56; denial of informed consent for stillbirth prevention measures, 81–82; expert status of doctors as incompatible with the "this happens" shrug, 82; historical shift from birth certificates to fetal death records and, 32–33; and lack of public awareness of likelihood of pregnancy loss, 96, 190; midwives ousted in, 56. *See also* medical advancements and assumption stillbirth doesn't happen anymore; obstetric violence (coercion and mistreatment in pregnancy and childbirth)

medical malpractice. *See* tort medical malpractice law ("medmal law")

medical paternalism: directing focus to subsequent pregnancy, 32–33, 58, 92, 110; fetal autopsy discouraged, 21; historical removal of stillborn child from contact with mother, 21, 32–33, 132, 143; and informed consent, shift from accepted practice to materiality standard, 107, 108, 114, 119; mandatory perinatal hospice and palliative care disclosure, claims of psychological benefits, 126; maternal monitoring of fetal movement claimed to increase anxiety, 55; nondisclosure of stillbirth risk for fear of excess anxiety, 112–114; patient cannot assume the risks of medical malpractice, 80; stereotype of pregnant women as overly emotional and possibly hysterical, 55, 113. *See also* doctors

medical standards (US). *See* prevention of stillbirth; standards of care for pregnancy and childbirth (US)

Medicare reimbursement, and hospitals prohibiting induction before 39 weeks, 70–71

medmal law. *See* tort medical malpractice law ("medmal law")

memorial birth certificates, 45–46, 169–170, 171–172, *171*

mental and emotional health care for stillbirth parents: bereavement of adults after stillbirth is difficult, 106, 134; class disparities in access to support, 135; counseling and support, 135, 136; criminal prosecution of stillbirth and inhumane denial of care to birthing parent, 180–181, 194–197; criminal prosecution of stillbirth, and reforms to ensure health care, 201–202; culturally appropriate care, importance of, 135–137; geography as factor in access to, 136; in the hospital, importance of, 134, 194–195, 202; intergenerational effects of stillbirth, 134, 135–136; long-term therapy and treatment often needed, 134, 135, 137; racial disparities in access to support, 135–137; religion and, 136–137; standard of care for (US), 134–135, 137, 195; the Stillbirth Working Group reports identifying need to improve, 204; support groups, 135, 136. *See also* parental leave from work after pregnancy loss; time spent with stillborn child ("memory making"); trauma of stillbirth

Merkley, Jeff, 203

Michigan, state tax benefits for stillbirth, 151–152

midwives: medicalization of prenatal care and childbirth and ousting of, 56; as primary care providers for pregnancy and childbirth (England and Australia), 49, 56, 57 mifepristone. *See* abortion medication (mifepristone and misoprostol)

Minnesota: historical birth certificates applicable to both live and stillbirths, *31, 32*; state tax benefits for stillbirth, 152; wrongful death stillbirths, viability requirement, 144–145

miscarriages: Black women's doubled risk of late-, 123; cause-of-death determinations not legally required for, 16; defined as loss before 20 weeks, 6, 148; defined by the World Health Organization (28 weeks), 157; early, and fetal abnormalities, 147; expenses for complications with, 153; as generally known risk, 106; late, non-childbirth options foreclosed due to abortion bans, 130–132; leave from work (unpaid), mandated by FMLA, 175; medical documentation demand for state tax benefits, 154–155; as much more common than stillbirth, 110; number of losses per year, 199; percentage of pregnancies affected by, 6; percentage of pregnancies affected by, if conception defined as beginning, 161; prior, in damages considerations for wrongful death stillbirth, 91–92, 95; race and class disparities in rates of, 92; reasonable expectation of live birth (12 weeks), 148; stillbirth as more like death after birth than similar to, 143. *See also* pregnancy loss; stillbirths

misoprostol. *See* abortion medication (mifepristone and misoprostol)

Mississippi: abortion ban in, 163; conception/viability differentials in laws, 141; Covid-19 and increased risk of stillbirth, 40; fetal pain claims not substantiated by experts, 165; Medicaid expansion refused by, and delays in prenatal care, 164; medical examiner unqualified to do autopsies (Hayne), 187; prosecution of birthing parent for stillbirth (Gibbs), 182, 184, 187, 188, 189, 192, 193; racial disparity in stillbirth rates, 163; stillbirth rates among highest in US, 163, 193

Missouri: child death autopsies require specialist pathologists, 24; coroner involvement in stillbirth deaths, 16, 186; "Fetal & Infant Mortality Review" teams, 26; homicide law, removal of language precluding charging the birthing parent with death of unborn child (proposed), 200; "informed consent" abortion statute, 109; state tax benefits for stillbirth, 152–154, 155; wrongful death statute, 141

Model Vital Statistics Act, 32, 33, 34, 35, 139, 150, 151

Morris, Theresa, 68

Mosk, M. Stanley, 144

multiple gestations: as risk factor for fetal growth restriction, 64; standard of care for early induction (US), 71

National Abortion Rights Action League (NARAL), 170

National Association of Medical Examiners, 187

National Center for Health Statistics (NCHS within the CDC), Handbook on the Reporting of Induced Terminations, 35

National Center for Health Statistics (NCHS within the CDC), and fetal death certificates (FDCs): cause of death (Question 18), 13–15, *14*; "Facility Worksheet for the Report of Fetal Death" ("Worksheet"), 15, 16, 18, 42; "Guide to Completing the Facility Worksheets of Live Birth and Report of Fetal Death" ("Guide"), 15, 16, 18, 38; "Medical Examiners' and Coroners' Handbook on Death Registration and Fetal Death Reporting" ("Handbook"), 17–18, 38; standard form, 13; video training ("Applying Best Certificates for Reporting Medical and Health

Information on Birth Certificates"), 16

National Institute of Child Health and Human Development (NICHD): Maternal-Fetal Medicine Units, 205; Neonatal Research Networks, 205; "Road to Stillbirth Prevention," 205; Stillbirth Working Group of Council, 203–205

National Institutes of Health (NIH): interest in stillbirth prevention, 205; "Rapid Acceleration of Diagnostics Technology (RADx Tech) Fetal Monitoring Challenge," 205

National Organization for Women, 170

National Vital Statistics System (National Cooperative Health Statistics System at the CDC), 33

Native American women: higher rates of investigation and removal of children through the child welfare system, 122; historical removal of children from, 122; loss of parental rights, 122. *See also* reproductive-justice movement

NCHS. *See* National Center for Health Statistics (NCHS within the CDC)

negligence tort claims: overview, 84; involuntary sterilization of women of color, dismissal of harm, 92; perverse incentive to kill instead of injuring, 83, 87, 99–100, 103; recovery for mother's emotional distress of observing her child killed by negligent driver (*Dillon v. Legg*), 83–84, 85–86, 88–89. *See also* tort law; wrongful death claims

—AND STILLBIRTH: overview, 84; as common law claim, 84, 87; compensation limited to emotional distress (noneconomic damages), 84–87, 90, 96, 218n32; damage caps limiting recovery in medical malpractice claims, 83, 84, 96–99, 101; damages as unlimited in non-medical malpractice claims (e.g. negligent driving), 98; difficulties for non-

birthing parent to claim, 86; jury deliberations and award of damages, 90, 218n32; loss of fetus treated as bodily injury to the mother, 86–87, 98; medical malpractice damages as inexpensive compared to damages for an injured baby, 9, 84, 99–100

neonatal abstinence syndrome, 189

Neonatal Intensive Care Unit: birth certificate question regarding admission to, 15; early induction and risk of admission to, 67, 68

neonatology advancements, 105, 157. *See also* medical advancements

Netherlands, initiative to lower stillbirth rate, 7

New Hampshire, damage caps on wrongful deaths, 97

New Jersey: data privacy requirements for Fetal Infant Death Review committee, 27–28; surveillance registry for stillbirths, 44

New Jersey Supreme Court, damages for stillbirth, 93

New Mexico: memorial birth certificates, proposed, 170; standard for issuance of FDCs, 34

Newsom, Gavin, 101

New York: tort claims for stillbirth, 86; wrongful death restricted to live births, 142, 144

New York City: Rainbow Clinic care, 137–138; as vital statistic registration area, 33

nondisclosure of stillbirth risk. *See* disclosure of stillbirth risk—nondisclosure as status quo

North Dakota: "informed consent" abortion statute, 109; state tax benefits for stillbirth, 151–152

Norway, maternal monitoring of fetal movement, 55, 116–117

Oberman, Michelle, 110–111

obstetricians. *See* doctors

obstetric racism. *See* doctor biases and prejudices; racial biases and racism obstetric violence (coercion and mistreatment in pregnancy and childbirth): C-sections as, 81, 113, 119–120, 127, 128; involuntary sterilization as, 92, 122. *See also* birth justice rights

Ohio: charging birthing parent for "abuse of corpse" in stillbirth (Watts), 197–198; Covid-19 and increased risk of stillbirth, 40

Oklahoma: abortion ban as of conception, 161; criminal child neglect, abuse, and/or endangerment applied to unborn children, 184; homicide law, removal of language precluding charging the birthing parent with death of unborn child (proposed), 200; prosecutions for conduct while pregnant, 184

O'Neill, Ann, as stillbirth parent, 73–74

organ donation, stillbirth and, 168

orofacial clefts, 61

parental expectation of live birth: erasure of pregnancy loss as raising, 96, 147–148; extensive misinformation in society regarding, 96; as factor in damages considerations for wrongful death stillbirth, 91, 95–96, 102; as hardest bereavement in adult life, 106; IVF and overestimation of, 148; miscarriage risk waning (12 weeks), 148; nondisclosure of stillbirth risk and, 105–106; subjective vs. reasonable, 95–96, 102, 147–148; viability as dividing line in wrongful death stillbirth and, 147–148

parental leave from work after pregnancy loss: difficulty of obtaining, paid or unpaid, 135; as reproductive-justice-based right, 122, 135; unpaid leave by FMLA extension (proposed), 175

parental preparation for forthcoming child: the child tax credit and illogic of the live-birth dividing line, 150–151, 152; in damages considera-

tion, and racial, class, and cultural biases in, 94, 95–96

parenting of stillborn child: author as stillbirth parent and, 8; fetal autopsy as enabling, 19–20, 27

Parker, Tom, 145, 162, 163

Patel, Purvi, 167, 185

pathologists, shortage of, 23–24. *See also* fetal autopsies, perinatal pathologists needed for

Paxton, Ken, 126

Pennsylvania: historical registration of stillborn children with both birth and death certificates, 31, 32; standard for issuance of FDCs (16 weeks), 34

Perez, Adora, 183, 184, 192, 195, 201

perinatal hospice and palliative care (PHPC), 125–127, 177

Perinatal Hospice Information Act Model Legislation and Policy Guide, 125–126

perinatal pathologists. *See* fetal autopsies—perinatal pathologists needed for

phone text messages, prosecution for medication abortion based on evidence in, 167, 185

placental abruption: author as stillbirth parent and, 3, 12, 28, 47, 68, 104; fetal pain as possible in, 165–166; smoking as risk factor, 61; in standard of care for extra surveillance (US), 50

placental conditions: insufficiency, and standard of care for induction by 42 weeks (US), 68, 73–74; insufficiency, maternal monitoring of fetal movement and detection of, 53, 54; small, EPV (estimated placental volume) testing for, 73–76, 79–80; smoking as risk factor, 61; in standard of care for surveillance (US), 50. *See also* amniotic fluid volume; placental abruption

placental pathologies: 2020 rate of occurrence following stillbirth (65%), 19; author as stillbirth parent and, 12; Covid-19 and deterioration of, 40, 41,

43; fetal autopsies combined with, percentage of causes of death identified with (65%), 18; time required for, and amendment of FDCs, 38–39; "trophoblast inclusions" in, 12

placenta previa, 50, 61

Planned Parenthood, 170

police: health care providers calling for suspected drug use by pregnant patients, 27, 180–181, 182, 183, 184, 193, 202; searching text messages and arresting woman who took abortion medication, 167, 185

poverty, people in: access issues in mental and emotional health for stillbirth parents, 135; access to fetal autopsy, moral and economic arguments for, 23; access to prenatal care, proposals for, 124–125; in Australia's early induction consideration, 66, 72; developmental disparities in children explained by, 189; disparities in stillbirth rates even in countries with government-run health care, 124; equity in England's safer baby bundle, 49, 59; post-*Dobbs* abortion bans and increase of stillbirth numbers among, 167; risk of stillbirth doubled for, 6, 22, 117, 123; standard of care for early induction (US) does not consider, 72. *See also* child poverty; class biases and classism; criminalization of conduct while pregnant; criminalization of stillbirth; Medicaid; racial biases and racism; tax benefits for parents

pregnancy: changes in parents' experiences today, 101–102, 143, 172–173; conception does not equal, 160, 176; implantation as defining, 160; implantation, percentage of fertilized eggs that fail (70%), 160–161, 176; prior, fundal height measurements less accurate in cases of, 64; "term" redefined as early, full, and late, 68; tests for, implantation as basis of, 160. *See also* subjective fetal value

—SUBSEQUENT TO STILLBIRTH: anxiety in, 137; fetal autopsies as providing information for, 20, 23; increased unplanned prenatal visits as need in, 117; medical paternalism directing pregnant person's attention to, 32–33, 58, 92, 110; the need for special health care in, 117, 137–138; rainbow clinic care, 137–138; subjective fetal value and, 173. *See also* children—subsequent; stillbirth, prior

pregnancy capitalism, 159

Pregnancy Justice, advocacy by: for explicit language precluding charging pregnant person for death of unborn child, 199–200; reforms to expand the HIPAA protections to prevent reporting of drug use of pregnant patients, 202; for repeal of all "fetal personhood legislation," 200, 201; research into prosecutions of pregnant person for stillbirth, 183–185, 197–198

pregnancy loss: abortion bans and increases in, 7, 166–168; abortion-rights movement avoiding topic of, 123, 158, 176; antiabortion narratives' influence on thoughts about early losses, 161–162; antiabortion narratives weaponizing, 145–146, 157–158, 161–163, 169, 175, 177; historical public knowledge of frequency and realities of, 85, 177; lack of modern public awareness regarding likelihood of, 96, 101–102, 190–191; lack of state legislators' knowledge of, 153–155, 165, 168; laws do not reflect plaintiff's experience today, 101–102; objective valuations forced by the state, as inconsistent with lived experience, 174, 175, 200; week 20 of pregnancy as dividing line between miscarriage and stillbirth, 6, 34, 148. *See also* miscarriages; stillbirths; subjective fetal value

—ERASURE OF: by the abortion debate's false binary—all pregnancies end either in abortion or live birth, 10–11, 96, 157, 158–159, 177, 190–191; "choice" rhetoric of abortion-rights movement as, and blame of pregnant person, 123, 160, 191, 201; expectation of live birth raised by, 96, 147–148; as factor in jury convictions for drug use as cause of stillbirth, 189–191; the medicalization of pregnancy and, 105, 115, 119–120, 159; the perfect pregnancy myth, 177, 190–191; post-*Dobbs* abortion bans and false assumption that all conceptions become living babies, 160–161, 167, 175; pregnancy capitalism as factor in, 159; of racial and class disparities in pregnancy loss rates, 167; the stigma and shock of pregnancy loss as increased by, 159–160

pregnancy-loss advocacy by stillbirth parents: changing the practice of removing the stillborn baby after birth, 32–33, 132; Count the Kicks program, 55, 58; CuddleCot access, 133; legal data privacy protection must be high priority for, 28; Measure the Placenta (EPV awareness), 74; memorial birth certificates resulting from, 45–46; public assumption of antiabortion stance of, 178; racial and class differentials within, need for awareness of, 28; state tax benefits for stillbirth, 151, 178; supposed tension between abortion-rights and, as manufactured by antiabortion groups, 11, 158, 178. *See also* abortion-rights and pregnancy-loss communities, coalitions of

pregnant women, stereotype as overly emotional and possibly hysterical, 55, 112–113

premature birth: disclosed as possible complication, 115; the federal tax credit applies even with no chance of survival for the baby, 150–151; general awareness of risk of, 105; March of Dimes campaign against early inductions to prevent, 68; medical advances for, 159, 190; smoking as risk factor, 61

prenatal care: criminalization of stillbirth as deterrent to obtaining, 124, 181, 193–194; data inaccuracies on FDCs, 37; delayed by medical providers to avoid early-miscarriage window, 154; disclosure of stillbirth risk claimed to increase number of appointments, 55, 116–117; early stillbirths and incompleteness of data on FDCs, 36; as factor in damages considerations for wrongful death, and class biases, 94–95, 102; "global billing" for, 55, 116, 127; insurance mandates for providing, 153; lack of access to, and racial and class disparities in state tax benefits for stillbirth, 155; lack of access to, and racial and class disparities in stillbirth rates, 118, 124–125; maternal monitoring of fetal movement claimed to increase number of appointments, 55, 116–117; Medicaid eligibility issues and delay of access to, 95, 153, 154–155, 164; pregnancies subsequent to stillbirth, the need for special care in, 117, 137–138; proposal to increase access to, 124–125; underutilization of, and increased risk of stillbirth, 124, 193–194. *See also* Australia, Safer Baby Bundle; England, Saving Babies' Lives Care Bundle (safer baby bundle); standards of care for pregnancy and childbirth (US)

prenatal injury claims, "born-alive rule" for prenatal injuries, 145

prenatal personhood. *See* fetal personhood (prenatal personhood)

prevention of stillbirth: criminalization of maternal drug use does not work, 181, 192–194, 202; Ireland, 19, 40, 167;

the moral incentive for, 9, 78; National Institutes of Health and Congressional funding of the Stillbirth Working Group as reasons for optimism in, 203–205; Netherlands, 7; Norway, 55, 116–117; other high-income countries and lower rates of, 6, 7; other high-income countries and reduction of rate of, 7, 48, 49, 50; percentage of preventable stillbirths (25%), 7; percentage of preventable stillbirths at term (46%), 7, 165; potential Congressional interest in, 203–204, 205–206; rainbow clinic care for subsequent pregnancies and risk reduction, 137–138; Scotland, 7, 48; Sweden, 124, 166; Wales, 43. *See also* Australia, Safer Baby Bundle; data privacy, criminalization of stillbirth and urgency of legislative protection for; England, Saving Babies' Lives Care Bundle (safer baby bundle); fetal autopsies; placental pathologies; pregnancy-loss advocacy by stillbirth parents; reproductive-justice movement—stillbirth and pregnancy-loss prevention and care; state laws—reforms proposed; timing of birth to prevent stillbirth; tort law reforms proposed

—UNPREVENTABILITY AS ASSUMPTION IN THE US: overview, 7; bioethics defenses of fetal life hypocrisies, 164–165; with the exception of drug use by the mother, 181, 187–188, 191–192; the "this happens" shrug, 21–22, 82, 187–188, 192; unpreventable fetal abnormalities, statistics on, 7, 164; US medical malpractice law and, 192; US medical malpractice law as disincentivizing prevention measures, 9, 77–78, 83, 87, 99–100, 103, 164. *See also* fetal life hypocrisies of antiabortion movement (lack of interest in preventing stillbirth); inevitability myth of stillbirth

privacy of data. *See* data privacy, criminalization of stillbirth and urgency of legislative protection for

ProPublica, 19, 39, 40, 95, 203

public awareness: advocacy for general education affirming that stillbirth happens and can be unexplainable, 200–201; current lack of awareness about likelihood of pregnancy loss, 96, 190; disclosure of stillbirth as benefit to, 105, 114, 118–120; effective journalism as increasing, 203; historical public knowledge of frequency and realities of pregnancy loss, 85, 177; lack of, as factor in jury convictions for drug use as cause of stillbirth, 190–191; pregnancy-loss advocates are assumed to be antiabortion, 178; state legislators' lack of knowledge about pregnancy loss, 153–155, 165, 168. *See also* pregnancy loss—erasure of

public health: formalized state infant and child fatality review teams, 25–26, 27; state mandates for fetal autopsies as expressive value of, 26; Sudden Infant Death Syndrome (SIDS) recognized as emergency, 13, 24–26

racial biases and racism: ACOG admitting heightened risk of stillbirth due to, 51; "breeder" and "Welfare Queen" stereotypes, 92, 94, 153; checklists for clinicians as alleviating influences of, 59; countries with government-run health care and persistence of disparities in stillbirth rates, 117, 124; criminal prosecutions of birthing parent for drug use causing pregnancy loss, as disproportionately distributed, 27, 180, 181, 182–183, 184–185, 188–189, 192, 196, 199; in damages considerations for wrongful death stillbirth, 91–95, 96, 102; in damages measurements, tort reforms proposed to address, 102; dismissal of women's concerns,

racial biases and racism *(continued)*
57–58; equity in England's safer baby bundle, 49, 59; the inevitability myth of stillbirth and, 117–118; informed consent, doctor bias in assessment of patient capacity, 81–82, 118; intergenerational trauma of, 135–136; involuntary sterilization and dismissal of harm, 92; in mental and emotional health care access for stillbirth parents, 135–137; number of living children, 92; in perinatal hospice and palliative care access, 127; in prenatal care access, 118; race-based tables to predict future lost wages, 102; as risk factor in elevated stillbirth rates, 51, 52, 58, 102; standard of care (US) denying surveillance due to risks of, 51, 52; subsequent pregnancies and replaceability sentiment, 58, 92, 110; within stillbirth advocacy, need for awareness of, 28. *See also* "bad mom" stereotypes (class and race biases); Black women; class biases and classism; poverty, people in; racial disparities in stillbirth rates

racial disparities in stillbirth rates: 2019–2021 rates, 6, 163; in Australia's stillbirth risk factors, 66, 72; early stillbirths, 36, 51, 152; fetal autopsy rates, 19, 20; fetal death certificate data incompleteness or inaccuracies, 36, 37; in Iowa, continued, 58; post-*Dobbs* abortion bans and erasure of, 167; prenatal care access, 118, 124; and prior stillbirth as factor in damages considerations for wrongful death stillbirth, 92, 102; racism as source of, 51, 52, 58, 102; standard of care for early induction (US) does not consider, 72; the Stillbirth Working Group reports identifying need to improve, 204, 205; tax benefits for stillbirth parents and, 153–155

"rainbow baby" phenomenon, 92

rainbow clinic care, 137–138

Ramaswamy, Vivek, 178

"Rapid Acceleration of Diagnostics Technology (RADx Tech) Fetal Monitoring Challenge," 205

reduced fetal movement. *See* decreased fetal movement (DFM)

religion: antiabortion narratives in homilies, 156; recovery from stillbirth and, 136–137; sacraments for the stillborn child, refusal, 156

renal disease, as stillbirth risk factor, 50

reproductive-justice movement: "choice" rhetoric rejected as farce by, 191; establishment due to the reproductive oppressions women of color have faced, 122; historical removal of children from Black and Native American women, 122; human rights approach ("what governments owe to the people they govern"), 122, 138; investigations by child welfare system and removals of children today, 122; involuntary sterilization, 92, 122; positive rights and negative rights, 10, 122; as recognizing the right not to have a child, 122; as recognizing the right to have a child and to parent him with dignity, 122, 123, 125, 138, 176; termination of parental rights, 122. *See also* birth justice rights

—AS FRAMEWORK OF RIGHTS AND ACCESS: abortion, 122; adequate wages to support family, 122; alternative birth options, 122; child care, 122; comprehensive sex education, 122; contraception, 122; domestic violence assistance, 122; IVF, 94, 122; parental leave from work after childbirth, 122, 135; prenatal and pregnancy care, 122; safe and secure homes, 122; STI prevention and care, 122

—STILLBIRTH AND PREGNANCY-LOSS PREVENTION AND CARE: overview, 10, 123; alliance of abortion-rights and pregnancy-loss communities and promotion of, 177–178, 205; "choice" rhetoric rejected as blaming the pregnant person for pregnancy loss, 123, 160, 191, 201; elevated stillbirth and late-miscarriage rates for Black women, 123; elevated stillbirth rates for poor women, 123; fetal autopsy, right to, 26, 123; financial assistance via tax credits or similar vehicles, 123; lack of interest in, as oppression falling hardest on marginalized persons, 123; research into systemic and institutional causes as focus of, 123, 201; right to culturally appropriate mental and emotional health care following, 134–137; the right to have a child as dependent on, 123, 125; right to perinatal hospice and palliative care, 125–127; right to preventative prenatal care, 123–125; silence about pregnancy loss, fetal personhood concerns and, 123; special care needed in subsequent pregnancies, 137–138. *See also* birth justice rights—and stillbirth

reproductive-rights movement: overview, 121–122; "choice" rhetoric and focus on the individual, 123, 201; "choice" rhetoric of, and blame of pregnant person after stillbirth, 123, 160, 191, 201; contraception, 121, 122. *See also* abortion-rights and pregnancy-loss communities, coalitions of; abortion-rights movement; reproductive-justice movement

Republicans, 97, 164, 178

research on causes, need for, 17–18, 22, 26, 123; the National Institutes of Health and the Stillbirth Working Group working for, 203–205; systemic and institutional causes, 123, 181, 201

Rhode Island, medical examiner involvement in stillbirth deaths, 16, 186

Richardson, Bill, 170

risk assessment, Scotland's initiative and, 7, 48

risk factors of stillbirth: causation in individual case distinguished from,

191; on fetal death certificate, as implying fault of mother, 28, 29; as fetal death certificate section, 15, 36; pregnant patients should be informed of, 28, 29; the Stillbirth Working Group reports identifying need to improve, 204, 205. *See also* standards of care for surveillance for known heightened risk of stillbirth (US)

—SPECIFIC FACTORS: drug use, 64, 66; hypertension, 15, 50, 71, 183; infections, 15; lupus, 50; maternal weight, 50, 66; poverty as, 6, 22, 117, 123; racism as, 51, 52, 58, 102; renal disease, 50; sickle cell disease, 50; sleep position in late pregnancy, 59–60; syphilis, 15, 29, 182; teratogen exposure, 64; thyroid problems, 50, 61. *See also* amniotic fluid volume; decreased fetal movement (DFM); diabetes; fetal abnormalities; IVF and other reproductive technologies; maternal age; placental conditions; pregnancy—subsequent to stillbirth; smoking in pregnancy

Roberts, Dorothy, 189, 202

Robinson v. Cutchin, 92

Roe v. Wade (1973): *Dobbs* overturning, 157; the false binary that all pregnancies end in either abortion or a live birth and, 159; as overturned despite 50 years of minimizing the fetus, 176; Texas's SB8 abortion ban as evading judicial review during, 163–164; viability as dividing line, 139, 156–157; viability standard, weaponization of grieving stillbirth parent to argue against, 145, 162. *See also Dobbs v. Jackson Women's Health Organization* (2022)

Roth, Louise Mari, 99–100

safe haven laws, 159

safer baby bundles. *See* Australia, Safer Baby Bundle; England, Saving Babies' Lives Care Bundle (safer baby bundle)

Sands report ("Saving Babies' Lives"), 48,
178–179
Sawicki, Nadia, 81
Schwarzenegger, Arnold, 170
Scotland, initiative to lower stillbirth
rate, 7, 48
self-blame. *See* blame of self after stillbirth
Shoemaker, Brooke, 187
Shuai, Bei Bei, 197, 198
sickle cell disease, as stillbirth risk factor,
50
SIDS. *See* Sudden Infant Death Syndrome
(SIDS)
sleep position in later pregnancy, as
stillbirth risk factor, 59–60
SMFM. *See* Society for Maternal-Fetal
Medicine
smoking in pregnancy: Australia's
initiative, 49, 61, 62; crack cocaine as
no more dangerous to fetus than, 189;
dangers other than stillbirth, 61;
England's initiative, 49, 61; as risk
factor for stillbirth, 61, 62, 66, 191;
Scotland's initiative, 48; standard of
care for (US), 61–62
—CESSATION OF: behavior-change
counseling, 49, 61, 62; carbon
monoxide testing, 49, 61; nicotine
replacement therapy, 61, 62
social birth, 173
social demographic factors. *See* class
biases and classism; ethnicity;
maternal age; poverty, people in;
racial biases and racism; racial
disparities in stillbirth rates
Social Security number, obtaining for
dependents, 149–150
Society for Maternal-Fetal Medicine
(SMFM): fetal autopsy and placental
pathology recommended after
stillbirth, 18; on fetal pain, 165;
Obstetric Care Consensus, 51, 72, 81;
standards of care set by, and ACOG,
47–48, 50, 77–78. *See also* standards
of care for pregnancy and childbirth
(US); timing of birth, US 39-week
rule (standard of care)

South Carolina: criminal child neglect,
abuse, and/or endangerment applied
to unborn children, 184; "nonmedically needed" deliveries before 39
weeks not reimbursed by insurance
in, 71; prosecution for (undetectable)
oral abortion medication, 167;
prosecution of birthing parent for
stillbirth (McKnight), 182, 184,
190–191, 192; prosecutions for
conduct while pregnant, 184
South Dakota, standard for issuance of
FDCs, 34
specialist reviews of stillbirth: amendment of fetal death certificates for
findings of, difficulty in, 38–39; class
disparities in ability to obtain, 23
standards of care for pregnancy and
childbirth (US): overview, 9;
decreased fetal movement, clinician
response, 58–59, 80; historical
removal of stillborn baby from
contact with parents, 21, 32–33, 132,
143; medical malpractice law
deferring to, even if other practices
would prevent stillbirth, 48, 75, 76,
77–78; mental and emotional health
care for stillbirth parents, 134–135,
137; prior stillbirth history, early
induction with informed consent, 81;
screening for fetal growth restriction
risk factors, 64; as set by medical
professionals (ACOG and SMFM),
47–48, 50, 77–78; smoking cessation,
61–62. *See also* standards of care for
surveillance for known heightened
risk of stillbirth (US); timing of birth,
US 39-week rule (standard of care)
standards of care for surveillance for
known heightened risk of stillbirth
(US): conditions allowable, generally,
50; early induction allowed if tests
indicate, 71; fetal growth restriction,
62, 64–65; IVF, 50–51; lack of clinical
trials to guide frequency of testing,
52; maternal age, 51, 65; maternal
monitoring of decreased fetal

movement excluded from, 51, 53–54, 55–56, 57, 58–59, 77–78; racism risks excluded from, 51, 52; smoking excluded from, 62; surveillance techniques, 51–52

state laws: abortion provider shield law for out-of-state residents, 178; abuse of corpse, 197–198; child death autopsies must be performed by pathologist, 24; conception/viability differentials in, 141; fetal death certificates (FDC), 13, 15, 16–17; formalized infant and child fatality review teams, 25–26; IVF services protected from wrongful death or criminal claims, 146; memorial birth certificates, 45–46, 169–170, 171–172, *171*; Sudden Infant Death Syndrome (SIDS), mandate for state-paid fetal autopsies, 13, 25, 26. *See also* abortion bans; birth certificates; death certificates; fetal death certificates (FDCs); homicide laws; Medicaid; medical examiners and coroners mandated for suspicious deaths; memorial birth certificates; tax benefits for parents—state tax benefits for stillbirth; tort law; tort medical malpractice law ("medmal law"); *specific states*

—REFORMS PROPOSED: overview, 206; change to 20-week standard for issuance of FDCs, 35; civil cause of action against state actors who arrest or prosecute a pregnant person, 200; explicit language precluding arrests of birthing person for death of unborn child, and need to strengthen, 186, 199–200; fetal autopsy mandates, 26; Medicaid to allow induction prior to 39 weeks, 78. *See also* data privacy, criminalization of stillbirth and urgency of legislative protection for; tort law reforms proposed

StatNews, 27

sterilization, involuntary: among oppressions leading to reproductive-

justice movement, 122; of Black women, and dismissal of harm, 92

stillbirth certificates, 32. *See also* fetal death certificates (FDCs)

Stillbirth Health Improvement and Education for Autumn Act ("Shine for Autumn Act," proposed 2021), 24, 44, 164

stillbirth, prior: in damages considerations for wrongful death stillbirth, 91–92, 95; as risk factor in subsequent pregnancies, 66, 137–138; standard of care allowing early induction with informed consent (US), 81. *See also* pregnancy—subsequent to stillbirth

stillbirths: abortion bans and increase in, 166–168; ACOG on, as one of the most common adverse pregnancy outcomes, 106, 110, 190; cost of, as surprising expensive, 23; defined as loss after 20 weeks (generally), 6, 34; defined by fetal weight, 33–34; defined by nonstandard gestational ages, 34; defined by the World Health Organization (28 weeks), 157; disclosure of stillbirth risk and better preparation for shock of, 118–119; medication abortions registered as, 167–168; organ donation and, 168; as shock, 20, 104–105, 106, 118–119, 159–160; stigma of, 118–119, 159–160; underestimation of the harms of, 110–111; as underreported due to nonuniformity of state reporting laws, 33–35, 36. *See also* childbirth of stillborn child; data; disclosure of stillbirth risk; early stillbirths (20–24 weeks); pregnancy—subsequent to stillbirth; pregnancy loss; pregnancy-loss advocacy by stillbirth parents; prevention of stillbirth; standards of care for pregnancy and childbirth (US); stillbirth, prior; stillbirth statistics; term stillbirths (after 37 weeks); trauma of stillbirth

stillbirth statistics: 2019–2021 rates per 1,000 births, 6, 163; compared to

stillbirth statistics *(continued)*
other high-income countries the US rate is much higher, 6, 7, 206; Covid-19 not producing significant change in, 43; criminalization of drug use during pregnancy and, 192–193; current national rate of one in 175 births, 6; increasing risk at term, 66; number as exceeding all infant deaths combined, 6; number per day, 6; number per year, 6, 159, 165; occurring ten times as often as sudden infant death (SIDS), 6, 111; poverty and disparities in rates of, 6, 22, 117, 123; preventable stillbirths (25%), 7; preventable stillbirths at term (46%), 7, 165; "prospective stillbirth rate," 70; as quadruple the number of abortions after 20 weeks, 165; underutilization of prenatal care and increased risk of, 124, 193–194. *See also* class biases and classism; racial biases and racism; racial disparities in stillbirth rates

stillborn child: burial or cremation, and funerals, 5, 199, 207; Catholic refusal to give sacraments, 156; and preference of some mothers for D&X procedure, 113, 131. *See also* childbirth of stillborn child; grief and grieving for stillborn child; subjective fetal value; time spent with stillborn child ("memory making")

subjective fetal value: overview, 158; abortion-rights minimization of the fetus as inconsistent with lived experience, 176; abortion rights not threatened by, 158, 170, 174; antiabortion idea of personhood starting at conception in every pregnancy as inconsistent with lived experience, 174, 200; author as stillbirth parent and, 172, 174; circumstances as affecting subjective fetal value, 172–173, 176; definition of "subjective," 172; definition of "subjective fetal value," 173; historical range of interpretations of pregnancy, 172, 173; the lived experience of pregnant people as better reflected by, 174; the pregnant person assigns "personhood" (or not), 158, 174; tort law recognizing subjective fetal value as demonstrated by the parent, 173–174, 200; wantedness as factor in, 173; wrongful death claims for stillbirth are claims by the parents, not "fetal rights," 170

substance use and abuse. *See* criminalization of conduct while pregnant; criminal prosecutions of birthing parent for drug use causing pregnancy loss; drug use

Sudden Infant Death Syndrome (SIDS): autopsies mandated and paid for by states, 13, 25, 26; disclosure of risk to parents, 111, 115; expressive value of state mandates for autopsies, 26; recognized as public health crisis, 13, 24–26; research showing biochemical marker for, as alleviating blame, 201; stillbirth occurring ten time more frequently than, 6, 111

surrogacy, 173

surveillance registries for stillbirths: adaptation from existing registries, 44; correction of fetal death certificates, 44; federal law proposed to fund (Shine for Autumn Act), 24, 44, 164; medical record access and retrieval of missing or inaccurate information, 44; states with, 18, 44

surveillance techniques: biophysical profile (BPP), 51; BPP score allowing early induction, 71; contraction stress test (CST), 51; fundal height measurement charting, 63, 64; modified biophysical profile, 51; nonstress test (NST), 51; NST false-negatives, and lack of triggers for further testing, 74–75; umbilical artery doppler velocimetry, 51–52, 63, 64; uterine artery doppler, 63–64. *See also* ultrasounds

done in nonmedical contexts (*T.J. Hooper* case), 78–79; emotional injury tests as obstacles to recovery, 85–86; gender-based tables to predict future lost wages as biased, 97, 102; gender bias in effects of damage caps, 97; preponderance of the evidence burden of proof used in, 148; race-based tables to predict future lost wages as biased, 102; sexual assault, 97; sexual harassment, 97; survivorship claims, 87, 89; Texas's abortion ban (SB8) enforced via individual lawsuits, 163–164; tort reform movement (damage caps and division of noneconomic damages), 96–99, 101. *See also* jury awards for damages in stillbirth; negligence tort claims; tort law reforms proposed; tort medical malpractice law ("medmal law"); wrongful death claims

tort law reforms proposed: overview, 48, 78, 103; addressing biases of race and class in jury awards, 96, 102; allowing the doctor a defense based on pregnant person's informed consent, 78, 80–82; damages measurements, proposed new formula covering all reproductive losses, 101–103; ending the separation between emotional distress and lost parent–child relationship, 101–102, 103; repealing noneconomic damage caps, 101; shift to reasonable doctor standard of care, 78–80

tort medical malpractice law ("medmal law"): burden of proof (preponderance of the evidence), 192; deference to accepted practice not done in nonmedical contexts (*T.J. Hooper* case), 78–79; deference to doctor-set standards of care, even if other practices would prevent stillbirth, 48, 75, 76, 77–78; as disincentivizing additional stillbirth prevention, 9, 77–78, 83, 87, 99–100, 103, 164;

immediate assumption of unpreventability in, 192; involuntary sterilization of Black women, dismissal of harm, 92; power of, to raise awareness and spark change, 83, 84, 99. *See also* informed consent law; tort law reforms proposed; tort medical malpractice stillbirth claims

—FEAR OF LIABILITY: adherence to standards of care removes liability, 77–78; amendment of fetal death certificates obstructed due to, 39; as deeply rooted in US medical profession, 77; earlier inductions due to, 68; fetal autopsies discouraged due to, 21; government-run health care practices as regulated by, unlike the US, 76; malpractice insurance, 97, 99–100; obstetricians/gynecologists as sued more often, 77; as theoretically motivating doctors to provide the best possible care, 76–77

tort medical malpractice stillbirth claims: as deferential to doctor-set standards of care, 77–78; definition of, 76; liability for deviation from standard of care, 77–78; non-liability for compliance with standard of care, 77–78

—DAMAGES MEASUREMENTS: overview, 9, 83–84; attempt to separate emotional distress and lost parent–child relationship, 86–87, 90, 101–102, 103, 218n32; attorneys difficult to find due to low-dollar damage caps, 83, 99; biases of race and class in jury considerations, 91–95, 96, 97, 102; court attitudes toward nature of the loss, 83–84, 92, 93; as disincentivizing additional stillbirth prevention, 9, 83, 87, 99–100, 103, 164; noneconomic damage caps as disproportionately biased against women, 97; noneconomic damage caps as limiting recoveries, 83, 84, 96–99, 101; noneconomic damages as (likely) only harm, 84–87, 88–89, 90, 96–97;

tort medical malpractice stillbirth claims (*continued*)

    stillbirth as inexpensive compared to damages for an injured baby, 9, 84, 99–100; subjective fetal value and, parent must demonstrate, 173–174, 200. *See also* jury awards for damages in stillbirth; negligence tort claims—and stillbirth; tort law reforms proposed; wrongful death claims—and stillbirth

trauma, of intergenerational experience of racism, 135–136

trauma of stillbirth: childbirth of stillborn child as, 102, 194; criminalization of stillbirth as compounding, 181, 194–196; denial of time with stillborn child, 195; fetal pain discussions as triggering, 166; lack of appropriate treatment due to abortion bans, 168; nondisclosure of stillbirth risk as worsening, 106; proposed damages for, 102

Trisomy 18, 126

Trump, Donald, 149

ultrasounds: anxiety in pregnancies subsequent to stillbirth and, 137; EPV (estimated placental volume) testing, 74–76, 79–80; fetal growth restriction and increase of, 63–64; maternal age and, 65; sonograms and changes in the experience of early pregnancy loss, 161–162, 173; sonograms and changes in the experience of pregnancy, 101–102, 143; stillbirth confirmed by, 106; umbilical artery doppler, 51–52, 63, 64; uterine artery doppler, 63–64. *See also* surveillance techniques

umbilical artery doppler, 51–52, 63, 64

umbilical cord accidents as cause of death: despite wrapped around neck, medical examiner ruling maternal drug use as cause of death, 181, 182, 187, 192, 202; discomfort of stillbirth parents with unpreventability implied by "accident," 39; specialist

diagnosing, 39; usually assumed to be unpreventable, 188

umbilical cord blockages, and fetal pain as possibility, 165–166

Underwood, Lauren, 203

UNICEF, 7

United Kingdom (UK): *Pearce v. United Bristol NHS Trust*, 110, 113; rainbow clinic care, 137–138; Sands report ("Saving Babies' Lives"), 48, 178–179; Scotland's initiative to lower stillbirth rate, 7, 48; Tommy's (pregnancy-loss charity), 43, 178–179; Wales, Covid-19 and increase of stillbirths during, 43. *See also* England; England, Saving Babies' Lives Care Bundle (safer baby bundle)

unpreventability of stillbirth. *See* prevention of stillbirth—unpreventability as assumption in the US

US Association for the Study of Pain, 165

U.S. Supreme Court: Affordable Care Act Medicaid expansion not mandatory, 95; ban on D&X procedure (*Carhart v. Gonzalez*), 113, 131; the false binary that all pregnancies end in either abortion or a live birth and, 159; fetal personhood advocates' goal of obtaining "personhood" interpretation under Fourteenth Amendment, 146, 157, 162, 175; fetal personhood petition for certiorari declined by, 157. *See also Dobbs v. Jackson Women's Health Organization; Roe v. Wade*

Utah, data incompleteness or inaccuracies in FDCs, 37

uterine artery doppler, 63–64

uterine fibroids, 64

viability: currently at 24 weeks, 157; as *Roe v. Wade* dividing line, 139, 156–157; as *Roe v. Wade* dividing line, weaponization of pregnancy loss grief to argue against, 145, 162. *See also* wrongful death claims—and stillbirth

Vick, Ana, and stillbirth advocacy, 38–39

violence. *See* obstetric violence (coercion and mistreatment in pregnancy and childbirth)

Virginia Supreme Court, damages for stillbirth, 93

vital statistics: as power reserved to the states, 31–32, 33; registration areas, 33. *See also* birth certificates; data collection; death certificates; fetal death certificates (FDCs)

Wales, Covid-19 and increase of still-births during, 43

War on Drugs: focus on Black pregnant women, 188–189; influence in suspicion that drug use causes stillbirth, 188–189

Warren, Elizabeth, 203

Washington, DC: patient cannot assume the risks of medical malpractice, 80; as vital statistic registration area, 33

Washington Supreme Court, *Helling v. Carey* and shift to "reasonable doctor standard of care," 79

Watts, Brittany, 198

weight. *See* fetal weight; maternal weight

white women and stillbirth: access to perinatal hospice and palliative care, 127; biases toward, in damage awards for wrongful death, 91, 92, 93–95, 96, 102; common characteristics of stillbirth prevention advocates, 28; criminal prosecutions for drug use causing pregnancy loss, 182–183, 185, 192, 194–195, 196; fetal autopsy rates, 19; IVF and, 51, 94, 155. *See also* class biases and classism; economically advantaged people; racial biases and racism; racial disparities in stillbirth rates; stillbirth statistics

Williams, Serena, 57–58

Wisconsin: data inaccuracies on FDCs, 37; Hope After Loss Clinic, 138

Wisconsin Supreme Court: shift to "reasonable doctor standard of care,"

79; wrongful death law applied to stillbirths, 89, 142, 144

women of color. *See* Black women; class biases and classism; ethnicity; poverty, people in; racial biases and racism

"Working to Address the Tragedy of Stillbirth" (Stillbirth Working Group of Council), 204

World Health Organization, 129, 157

wrongful death claims: child and infant death, for loss of parent–child relationship, 87, 88–90; child death, damages lower than for adults, 89–90, 97–98; child labor and, 88, 90; death of spouse, for loss of consortium damages, 88–90; death of spouse, for pecuniary (economic) damages, 87–88, 89–90; death of spouse, replaceability sentiment barred from evidence, 93; definition of, 141; *Dillon vs. Legg* and, 88–89; emotional distress damages not available in, 88–89; establishment by statute vs. common law, 87, 141; "person" as term in the law, 141, 142, 144–145, 146; tort (common law) must still be proved, 87, 141. *See also* negligence tort claims; tort law

—AND STILLBIRTH: overview, 84, 87, 89, 144; abortion-rights movement and opposition to, 169, 170, 175–176; causation as issue in, 147; compensation limited to loss of parent–child relationship (noneconomic damages), 84, 87, 88–89, 90, 96; damage caps limiting recovery in medical malpractice claims, 83, 84, 96–99, 101; damages as much lower for death of child than for adult, 89–90, 97–98; damages considerations, factors in, 91–96; damages considerations, race and class biases affecting, 91–95, 96, 97, 102; damages considerations, subjective fetal value applied in, 173–174, 200; expectations of live birth and, subjective vs. reasonable,

wrongful death claims *(continued)*
95–96, 102, 147–148; live birth as
original dividing line for, 10, 141–144;
live birth requirement eliminated in
most states, 144; medical malpractice
damages as inexpensive compared to
damages for injured baby, 9, 84,
99–100; pregnant woman generally
cannot be sued for causing, 186;
separate existence interpretation of
"person" in the law, 144–145, 147;
states laws applying to all pregnancy
losses from conception, 98–99,
145–146, 162–163, 175–176; states that
still exclude, 144; subjective fetal
value and, 170; viability requirement
(current), 87, 89, 141, 145; viability
requirement pre-*Roe*, 144–145;
viability requirement and *Roe*, 145;
viability requirement questioned and
proposal for change, 146–148

Zelizer, Vivian, 88
zone of danger test, 85

Founded in 1893,
UNIVERSITY OF CALIFORNIA PRESS
publishes bold, progressive books and journals
on topics in the arts, humanities, social sciences,
and natural sciences—with a focus on social
justice issues—that inspire thought and action
among readers worldwide.

The UC PRESS FOUNDATION
raises funds to uphold the press's vital role
as an independent, nonprofit publisher, and
receives philanthropic support from a wide
range of individuals and institutions—and from
committed readers like you. To learn more, visit
ucpress.edu/supportus.